MW00850980

PERJURY AND PARDON, VOLUME II

THE SEMINARS OF JACQUES DERRIDA

Edited by Geoffrey Bennington and Peggy Kamuf

Perjury and Pardon

VOLUME II

Jacques Derrida

Edited by Ginette Michaud, Nicholas Cotton, and Rodrigo Therezo

Translated by David Wills

The University of Chicago Press ‡ CHICAGO AND LONDON

The University of Chicago Press, Chicago 60637
The University of Chicago Press, Ltd., London
© 2023 by The University of Chicago
All rights reserved. No part of this book may be used or reproduced in any manner whatsoever without written permission, except in the case of brief quotations in critical articles and reviews. For more information, contact the University of Chicago Press, 1427 E. 60th St., Chicago, IL 60637.
Published 2023
Printed in the United States of America

32 31 30 29 28 27 26 25 24 23   1 2 3 4 5

ISBN-13: 978-0-226-82528-1 (cloth)
ISBN-13: 978-0-226-82529-8 (e-book)
DOI: https://doi.org/10.7208/chicago/9780226825298.001.0001

Originally published in French as *Le parjure et le pardon.*
Volume II. Séminaire (1998–1999) © Éditions du Seuil, 2020.

© Facsimiles: Courtesy of Princeton University

Library of Congress Cataloging-in-Publication Data

Names: Derrida, Jacques, author. | Michaud, Ginette, 1955–, editor. |
Cotton, Nicholas, editor. | Wills, David, 1953–, translator. |
Derrida, Jacques. Works. Selections. English. 2009.
Title: Perjury and pardon / Jacques Derrida ; edited by
Ginette Michaud and Nicholas Cotton ; translated by David Wills.
Other titles: Parjure et le pardon. English (Wills)
Description: Chicago ; London : The University of Chicago Press, 2022– |
Series: The seminars of Jacques Derrida |
Includes bibliographical references and index. |
Identifiers: LCCN 2022003727 | ISBN 9780226819174 (volume 1, cloth) |
ISBN 9780226819181 (volume 1, ebook) |
ISBN 9780226825281 (volume 2, cloth) |
ISBN 9780226825298 (volume 2, ebook)
Subjects: LCSH: Forgiveness—Philosophy. | Forgiveness in literature.
Classification: LCC BF637.F67 D4713 2022 | DDC 155.9/2—dc23/eng/20220207
LC record available at https://lccn.loc.gov/2022003727

♾ This paper meets the requirements of ANSI/NISO Z39.48-1992
(Permanence of Paper).

CONTENTS

When the decision was made to edit and publish Jacques Derrida's teaching lectures, there was little question that they would and should be translated into English. From early in his career, in 1968, and annually thereafter until 2003, Derrida regularly taught at US universities. It was his custom to repeat for his American audience the lectures delivered to his students in France the same year. Teaching first at Johns Hopkins and then at Yale, he read the lectures in French as they had been written. But from 1987, when he began teaching at the University of California, Irvine, Derrida undertook to lecture in English, improvising on-the-spot translations of his lectures. Recognizing that the greater part of his audience outside of France depended on translation proved easier, however, than providing a satisfying ad libitum English version of his own elegant, complex, and idiomatic writing. In the circumstance, to his evident joy in teaching was often added a measure of suffering and regret for all that remained behind in the French original. It is to the memory of Derrida the teacher as well as to all his students past and still to come that we offer these English translations of "The Seminars of Jacques Derrida."

The volumes in this series are translations of the original French editions published by Éditions du Seuil, Paris, in the collection "Bibliothèque Derrida" under the direction of Katie Chenoweth. In each case they will follow shortly after the publication of the corresponding French volume. The scope of the project, and the basic editorial principles followed in establishing the text, are outlined in the "General Introduction to the French Edition," translated here. Editorial issues and decisions relating more specifically to this volume are addressed in an "Editorial Note." Editors' footnotes and other editorial interventions are mostly translated without modification, but not in the case of footnoted citations of quoted material, which refer to extant English translations of the source as necessary. Additional translators' notes have been kept to a minimum. To facilitate scholarly reference, the page numbers of the French edition are printed in the margin on the line at which the new page begins.

Translating Derrida is a notoriously difficult enterprise, and while the translator of each volume assumes full responsibility for the integrity of the translation, as series editors we have also reviewed the translations and sought to ensure a standard of accuracy and consistency across the volumes. Toward this end, in the first phase of work on the series, we have called upon the advice of other experienced translators of Derrida's work into English and wish to thank them here: Pascale-Anne Brault, Michael Naas, Elizabeth Rottenberg, and David Wills, as well as all the other participants in the Derrida Seminars Translation Project workshops.

Geoffrey Bennington
Peggy Kamuf
MARCH 2019

GENERAL INTRODUCTION TO
THE FRENCH EDITION

Between 1960 and 2003, Jacques Derrida wrote some fourteen thousand printed pages for the courses and seminars he gave in Paris, first at the Sorbonne (1960–64), then at the École normale supérieure, rue d'Ulm (1964–84), and then, for the last twenty years of his life, at the École des hautes études en sciences sociales (EHESS, 1984–2003). The series "The Seminars of Jacques Derrida," in the collection "Bibliothèque Derrida," will make available the seminars that Derrida gave at EHESS, five of which have already appeared.[1] This corresponds to the period in Derrida's teaching

1. These five volumes were published by Éditions Galilée (Paris): *Séminaire La bête et le souverain. Volume I (2001–2002)*, edited by Michel Lisse, Marie-Louise Mallet, and Ginette Michaud (2008) [*The Beast and the Sovereign*, vol. 1 (2001–2), trans. Geoffrey Bennington (Chicago: University of Chicago Press, 2009)]; *Séminaire La bête et le souverain. Volume II (2002–2003)*, edited by M. Lisse, M.-L. Mallet, and G. Michaud (2010) [*The Beast and the Sovereign*, vol. 2 (2002–3), trans. Geoffrey Bennington (Chicago: University of Chicago Press, 2010)]; *Séminaire La peine de mort. Volume I (1999–2000)*, edited by Geoffrey Bennington, Marc Crépon, and Thomas Dutoit (2012) [*The Death Penalty*, vol. 1 (1999–2000), trans. Peggy Kamuf (Chicago: University of Chicago Press, 2014)]; *Séminaire La peine de mort. Volume II (2000–2001)*, edited by G. Bennington and M. Crépon (2015) [*The Death Penalty*, vol. 2 (2000–2001), trans. Elizabeth Rottenberg (Chicago: University of Chicago Press, 2017)]. In addition, two courses given prior to these seminars were also published by Éditions Galilée: *Heidegger: la question de l'Être et l'Histoire. Cours de l'ENS-Ulm 1964–1965*, edited by Thomas Dutoit, with the assistance of Marguerite Derrida (2013) [*Heidegger: The Question of Being and History* (1964–65), trans. Geoffrey Bennington (Chicago: University of Chicago Press, 2016)], and *Théorie et pratique. Cours de l'ENS-Ulm 1975–1976*, edited by Alexander García Düttmann (2017) [*Theory and Practice* (1976–77), trans. David Wills (Chicago: University of Chicago Press, 2019)]. *Le parjure et le pardon*, vol. II, is the third seminar volume to appear in the Éditions du Seuil "Bibliothèque Derrida" collection, following *La vie la mort (1975–1976)*, edited by Pascale-Anne Brault and Peggy Kamuf (Paris: Seuil, 2019) [*Life Death*, trans. Pascale-Anne Brault and Michael Naas (Chicago: University

career when he had the freedom to choose the topics he was going to treat, most often over two or even three years, in seminars that were themselves organized into the following thematic series: "Philosophical Nationality and Nationalism" (1984–88), "Politics of Friendship" (1988–91), followed by the long sequence of "Questions of Responsibility" (1991–2003), focusing successively on the secret (1991–92), testimony (1992–95), hostility and hospitality (1995–97), perjury and pardon (1997–99), the death penalty (1999–2001), and, finally, questions of sovereignty and animality under the title "The Beast and the Sovereign" (2001–3). We will here follow the logic previously established for the final seminars of Jacques Derrida, namely, publishing in reverse chronological order all the seminars given at EHESS, all the while respecting the internal chronology of each thematic series. *Perjury and Pardon*, vol. II, continues the return to that chronology begun with *Perjury and Pardon*, vol. I.

8

We have tried in our editorial work to remain as faithful as possible to the text as Jacques Derrida wrote it and we present it here with as few editorial interventions as possible. With very few exceptions (for example, improvised sessions), Derrida would prepare for each class session not notes but a continuous written text, sometimes punctuated by references to the texts he was quoting, didascalia (e.g., "comment") indicating a time for improvisation, and marginal or interlineal annotations. When we have been able to locate tape recordings of the seminars, we have also indicated in footnotes the oral comments that Derrida added to his text in the course of a seminar session. It is likely that if Derrida had himself published his seminars during his lifetime he would have reworked them. This practice of reworking was in fact rather common with Derrida, who frequently drew from the vast wealth of material of his courses for lectures and texts he intended for publication. This explains the fact that we sometimes find a partial reworking or adaptation of a seminar in an already published work, highlighting even further the dynamic and coherence that characterized Derrida's teaching, a laboratory where ideas were tested and then frequently developed elsewhere in a more or less modified form. That being said, most of the seminars that will be appear in the "Bibliothèque Derrida" have not been previously published in any form: their publication can only

---

of Chicago Press, 2020)] and *Le parjure et le pardon*, vol. I, edited by Ginette Michaud and Nicholas Cotton (Paris: Seuil, 2019) [*Perjury and Pardon*, vol. I, trans. David Wills (Chicago: University of Chicago Press, 2022)].

greatly enrich the corpus of Derrida's thought by making available one of its essential resources.

Katie Chenoweth, Head of the Editorial Committee
Geoffrey Bennington
Pascale-Anne Brault
Peggy Kamuf
Ginette Michaud
Michael Naas
Elizabeth Rottenberg
David Wills

The seminar entitled "Perjury and Pardon [*Le parjure et le pardon*]" was given by Jacques Derrida at the École des hautes études en sciences sociales (EHESS), in Paris, over a period of two academic years (1997–98 and 1998–99).[1] Presented first in French, the seminar was also the basis for classes given in the United States under the title "Justice, Perjury, and Forgiveness." In the biographical notes included in the *Cahier de L'Herne Derrida*, Derrida indicated that he taught in New York in fall 1998 (New York University, New School for Social Research, and Cardozo Law School), and at the University of California, Irvine, and Stanford University in spring 1999.[2] This volume contains the eight sessions presented at the EHESS in 1998–99.

1. As noted by the editors of the first volume of *Séminaire: La Peine de mort*, an error found its way into the *Annuaire de l'EHESS* [EHESS Annual Bulletin] for the following year (1999–2000): "We note that there is an error in the announcement for the seminar on the death penalty. . . . The title of the 1998–99 seminar is used again for 1999–2000, even though the subject and content had changed." See Jacques Derrida, *The Death Penalty*, vol. 1, trans. Peggy Kamuf (Chicago: University of Chicago Press, 2014), xiii–xiv n2 [*Séminaire: La peine de mort*, vol. 1 (1999–2000), ed. Geoffrey Bennington, Marc Crépon, and Thomas Dutoit (Paris: Galilée, 2012), 13–14n3]. The first year of the Death Penalty seminar does not in fact include a specific title, and appears under the same rubric as the previous year: "VII: Perjury and Pardon" (*Annuaire de l'EHESS 1999–2000* [Paris: Éditions de l'EHESS, 2000], 599).

2. See "Repères biographiques," in Marie-Louise Mallet and Ginette Michaud, eds., *Cahier de L'Herne Derrida* (Paris: Éditions de L'Herne, 2004), 605. Derrida's teaching at the University of California, Irvine, usually lasted five weeks (from the end of March to the beginning of May), and in New York, three weeks (from the end of September to mid-October). In his March 21, 1998, letter to Catherine Malabou, Derrida mentions "three seminars and two lectures in a week" given at Johns Hopkins University in Baltimore (see Jacques Derrida and Catherine Malabou, *Counterpath: Traveling with Jacques Derrida*, trans. David Wills [Stanford: Stanford University Press, 2004], 274; *La Contre-allée*

We should first note differences in the word order of the seminar's title from one year to the next. In 1997–98, Derrida's usual computer file name, and that used on the typescript, is "PAR J/D (Parjure/Pardon)," whereas for 1998–99 "Pardon/parjure" is the systematic title. In the typescript for the seminar given in 1997–98, Derrida himself comments on this matter on two occasions, in the First and Third Sessions;[3] he comes back to it also in the first session of the 1998–99 year, explicitly referring to the title "Parjure et pardon."[4] In the descriptions provided for the *Annuaire de l'EHESS*, the title for both years indeed reads "Parjure et pardon." Therefore, even though the note for the text *"Versöhnung, ubuntu,* pardon: quel genre?"—a published article corresponding to the first three sessions of the 1998–99 seminar—refers to "Le pardon et le parjure,"[5] we have chosen to use here

[Paris: La Quinzaine littéraire and Louis Vuitton, 1999], 269). In April 1998, Derrida gave three lectures at the University of California, Davis, corresponding to the first version of the text "Typewriter Ribbon: Limited Ink (2)" (published in Jacques Derrida, *Without Alibi,* ed. and trans. Peggy Kamuf [Stanford: Stanford University Press, 2002], 71–160; cf. "Le ruban de machine à écrire. *Limited Ink II,"* in *Papier Machine. Le ruban de machine à écrire et autres réponses* [Paris: Galilée, 2001], 33–147). See also Sessions 7–10 of *Perjury and Pardon,* vol. 1, trans. David Wills (Chicago: University of Chicago Press, 2021), 198–317 [*Le parjure et le pardon,* vol. 1 (Séminaire 1997–1998) (Paris: Seuil, 2019), 259–407]. Those sessions were presented in modified form at the conference "Culture and Materiality: A Post-millenarian Conference—à propos of Paul de Man's *Aesthetic Ideology,"* published as "Typewriter Ribbon: Limited Ink (2)" in Barbara Cohen, Tom Cohen, J. Hillis Miller, and Andrzej Warminksi, eds., *Material Events: Paul de Man and the Afterlife of Theory* (Minneapolis: University of Minnesota Press, 2001), 277–360 (slightly different version from Derrida, *Without Alibi).* The major lecture at Stanford, "The Future of the Profession or The University Without Condition," was given as part of the Presidential Lectures series on April 15, 1999, not in 1998 as indicated in the French version (Derrida, *L'Université sans condition* [Paris: Galilée, 2001]). See Kamuf's "Preface" in *Without Alibi,* xii; and "The University Without Condition," in *Without Alibi,* 202–37.

3. See *Perjury and Pardon,* vol. 1, 41–42, 67–68ff. [*Parjure et pardon,* vol. 1, 72–74, 116–17ff.].

4. See 25 below.

5. The article was revised by Derrida for the "Vérité, réconciliation, réparation" issue of *Le Genre humain* (43 [2004]: 111–56); it also appeared with the title "Le pardon, la vérité, la réconciliation: quel genre?" in Jacques Derrida and Evando Nascimento, *La Solidarité des vivants et le pardon. Conférence et entretiens, précédés du texte d'Evando Nascimento, "Derrida au Brésil"* (Paris: Hermann, 2016), especially 61–120. This lecture, delivered on August 16, 2004, in Rio de Janeiro, was Derrida's last international address.

the title as indicated in the *Annuaire de l'EHESS*, which Derrida himself provided, since that seems to us to take precedence for these two volumes.[6]

The most illuminating presentation of the "Perjury and Pardon" seminar is that given by Derrida himself in the *Annuaire de l'EHESS 1997–1998*, where he makes clear what is at stake in the reflection that he intends to develop over the course of the two-year class:

> We have continued the cycle of research initiated in past years concerning the current (philosophical, ethical, juridical or political) stakes of the concept of responsibility.
>
> Having privileged, as guiding thread, the themes of *secrecy*, *testimony* and *hospitality*, we shall attempt to develop a problematic of lying [*parjure*]. It concerns a certain experience of evil, of malignity, or bad faith in cases where that negativity takes the form of *renunciation*. With respect to the guarantee or performative commitment "before the law"[7] (the promise, oath-swearing, giving one's word, the word of honor, pledge, pact, contract, alliance, debt, etc.), we will study diverse forms of betrayal (lying, infidelity, denial, false testimony, perjury, unkept promise, desecration, sacrilege, blasphemy, etc.) in different fields (ethics, anthropology, law), and on the basis of various textual corpora (exegetical, philosophical or literary, for example).
>
> We have attempted to link these questions of "evil" to that of forgiveness. If forgiveness is neither excusing, forgetting, amnesty, prescription, nor the "political pardon," if the possibility of it is paradoxically measured against the unforgivable alone, how does one think the "possibility" of this "impossibility?"[8]

12

6. See "Editors' Note," *Perjury and Pardon*, vol. 1, xiv n4 [*Parjure et pardon*, vol. 1, 10n5].

7. Allusion to the Kafka text analyzed by Derrida in his *Before the Law: The Complete Text of Préjugés*, trans. Sandra van Reenen and Jacques de Ville (Minneapolis: University of Minnesota Press, 2018) ["Préjugés: Devant la loi," in *La Faculté de juger* (Paris: Minuit, 1985)]. We wish to recall that the "closed seminar" also given by Derrida at the EHESS was entitled "The Philosophical Institution Before the Law."

8. Jacques Derrida, "Questions de responsabilité (VI. Le parjure et le pardon)," in *Annuaire de l'EHESS 1997–1998* (Paris: Éditions de l'EHESS, 1998), 553–54. In the description of the seminar "Hostilité/hospitalité," given the previous year, Derrida announces the "Perjury and Pardon" seminar with this clarification: "The final sessions of the seminar began to deal with work projected for following year (1997–98) on perjury and pardon, by bringing them into relation with our current research (on responsibility and figures of hospitality)" ("Questions de responsabilité [V. Hostilité/hospitalité]," *Annuaire de l'EHESS 1996–1997* [Paris: Éditions de l'EHESS, 1997], 526).

In the description of his seminar for the 1998–99 year, Derrida repeats that outline, with the following modification of the fourth paragraph from 1997–98, which adds details concerning the readings to be discussed during the year:

> The trajectory sketched out this year works through readings and analysis of certain scenes of political "forgiveness" or "repentance" such as are today proliferating throughout the world, in France or in South Africa, but in fact on every continent (primary texts studied: Augustine, *City of God*, texts on forgiveness by Hegel — notably in "The Spirit of Christianity and its Fate" (*Early Theological Writings*), in *The Phenomenology of Spirit* — certain readings from Levinas, *Nine Talmudic Readings*, various writings by Nelson Mandela and Desmond Tutu concerning the South African Truth and Reconciliation Commission, press clippings dealing with different scenes of "repentance" in the U.S. — Clinton and slavery, Clinton and American foreign policy in Latin America, Clinton and "Monicagate," etc. — finally Henri Thomas's *Le Parjure*.[9]

13   In the "Lesson" that he presents at the Thirty-Seventh Colloquium of French-Speaking Jewish Intellectuals, dedicated to the question "How to Live Together?" and held in Paris on December 5–7, 1998, Derrida develops the stakes of the whole "Perjury and Pardon" seminar, which was then ongoing, in a detailed manner:

> If I have chosen the theme of confession, that is first of all because of what is occurring *today* in the world, a kind of general rehearsal, a scene, even a theatricalization of confession, of return, and of repentance, which seems to me to signify a mutation in process, a fragile one, to be sure, fleeting and difficult to interpret, but functioning as the moment of an undeniable rupture in the history of the political, of the juridical, of relations among communities, civil society, and the state, among sovereign states, international law, and NGOs, among the ethical, the juridical, and the political, between the public and the private, between national citizenship and an international citizenship, even a metacitizenship, in a word, concerning a social bond that crosses the borders of these ensembles called family, nation, or state. Sometimes accompanied by what one names rightly or wrongly repentance, sometimes preceded or accompanied by what one believes, rightly or wrongly, must condition them — namely confession, repentance, requests for forgiveness — scenes of confession are proliferating and have even been accelerating for a few years, months, weeks, every day in truth,

---

9. Jacques Derrida, "Questions de responsabilité (VII. Le parjure et le pardon)," in *Annuaire de l'EHESS 1997–1998* (Paris: Éditions de l'EHESS, 1999), 571–72.

in a public space transformed by tele-technologies and by media capital, by the speed and reach of communication, but also by the multiple effects of a technology, a techno-politics and a techno-genetics that unsettle at once all conditions: *both* the conditions of being together (the supposed proximity, in the same instant, in the same place and the same territory, as if the uniqueness of a place on earth, of a soil, were becoming more and more—as one says of a telephone and in the measure of the said telephone—*portable*) *and* the conditions of what lives in its technological relation to the nonliving, to hetero- or homografting, to prosthesis, artificial insemination, cloning, and so on. Largely exceeding the territory of the state or of the nation, all these scenes of confession and of reexamination of past crimes appeal to the testimony, even to the judgment of a community, and so of a modality of living-together, virtually universal but also virtually instituted as an infinite tribunal or worldwide confessional.[10]

14

Let us recall that beyond the movement of generalized repentance that was taking place at the end of the 1990s, Derrida broached, in this first year of the seminar, the matter of forgiveness from the perspective of questions of responsibility, beginning with this aporia: "One only ever asks forgiveness for what is unforgivable."[11] Whereas forgiveness is a notion inherited from *more than one* tradition—as he says, it concerns several *"quasi*-triangles"[12] among diverse heritages (Judaic, Christian, Koranic, Greek)—Derrida showed how the process of forgiveness also escapes those traditions and unsettles the categories of knowledge, meaning, history, and law that attempt to circumscribe it. Insisting therefore on the unconditionality of forgiveness, he concentrated on its complex temporality, which destabilizes every idea of presence and even of the subject, asking *"who* or *what* forgives?" *Pure* forgiveness, he proposes, is an event that breaks open

10. Jacques Derrida, "Avowing—The Impossible: Returns, Repentance, and Reconciliation: A Lesson," trans. Gil Anidjar, in Elisabeth Weber, ed., *Living Together: Jacques Derrida's Communities of Violence and Peace* (New York: Fordham University Press, 2013), 31, translation slightly modified. Derrida continues his address by enumerating different examples of those "acts of public repentance" (31–33); cf. Derrida, "Leçon," in Jean Halpérin and Nelly Hansson, eds., *Comment vivre ensemble? Actes du XXXVIIᵉ Colloque des intellectuels juifs de langue française* (Paris: Éditions Albin Michel, 2001), 200–201 and 201–4 (see also *Perjury and Pardon*, vol. 1, 8 [*Parjure et pardon*, vol. 1, 34]). The English version cited here was given as the opening keynote lecture of the conference "Irreconcilable Differences? Jacques Derrida and the Question of Religion," organized by Thomas A. Carlson and Elisabeth Weber at the University of California, Santa Barbara, in October 2003.

11. *Perjury and Pardon*, vol. 1, 91 [*Parjure et pardon*, vol. 1, 134].

12. *Perjury and Pardon*, vol. 1, 63–78 [*Parjure et pardon*, vol. 1, 101–17].

and exceeds the modalities of "comprehension," of memory or forgetting, of a certain work of mourning. It is neither manifest nor localizable, but instead remains heterogeneous to all phenomenality, all theatricalization, or even all verbal language. Interrupting at once history, right, and politics, unconditional forgiveness is thus tested against the impossible: it is and must remain exceptional, beyond either calculus or finality, outside all ex-
15 change and transaction, just like the gift whose logic it shares. Irreducible to repentance, punishment, retribution, or salvation, forgiveness as thought by Derrida is similarly inseparable from, and haunted by the notion of, perjury. It calls into question the inexpiable (Jankélévitch) as much as reconciliation (Hegel) or ethics itself.

If the political dimension of forgiveness was already very much in evidence throughout the seminar's first year, it stands out in particular during the second year against the background of the Truth and Reconciliation
16 Commission sessions in South Africa, of President Clinton's regret concerning slavery in Africa or concerning American policies in South America, notably in Chile, or again in relation to the Monica Lewinsky scandal, which Derrida followed closely, and which culminated in the impeachment and attempted removal of the American president.[13] One can also note im-

13. Derrida traveled to South Africa in 1998 and spent several weeks there, giving lectures and seminars in several universities: Western Cape, Capetown (meeting with Nelson Mandela on August 11), Stellenbosch, Pietermaritzburg, Potchefstroom, Johannesburg, and Pretoria (see Derrida and Malabou, *Counterpath*, 294 [*Contre-allée*, 288]). He participated in the "Refiguring the Archive" seminar series at the Graduate School for the Humanities and Social Sciences of the University of the Witwatersrand in Johannesburg (see "Archive Fever [a Seminar by Jacques Derrida, University of the Witwatersrand, August 1998, transcribed by Verne Harris]," in Carolyn Hamilton, Verne Harris, Jane Taylor, Michele Pickover, Graeme Reid, and Razia Saleh, eds., *Refiguring the Archive* [Capetown: Springer Science and Business Media, 2002], 38–54). The seminar was centered on *Archive Fever: A Freudian Impression*, trans. Eric Prenowitz (Chicago: University of Chicago Press, 1998) [*Mal d'archive* (Paris: Galilée, 1995)], notably on questions of memory, of the preservation and destruction of the archive in political, historic and psychic terms; an exchange with seminar participants that took place following Derrida's address is also transcribed in *Refiguring the Archive* (56–80). On the trip to South Africa see also *Counterpath*, 273 [*Contre-allée*, 269]. The film *Derrida*, directed by Amy Ziering Kofman and Kirby Dick (2002), was being made during that time, and the crew followed Derrida as he moved from place to place: two sequences show him visiting Nelson Mandela's cell in the Robben Island prison, and during exchanges with students in a seminar on the question of forgiveness. The *Annuaire de l'EHESS 1998–1999* also mentions several "visits, lectures or seminars, notably at New York University, the New School for Social Research, Cardozo Law School, Turin, Ma-

portant parallels in the construction of the seminar: if the first year began with sessions in which Derrida reflected on the questions of forgiveness and the absence of a statute of limitations (*l'imprescriptibilité*) for crimes against humanity in the European context of the Shoah and the years following World War II, the second, for its part, dedicates the first three sessions to the questions of apartheid and the Truth and Reconciliation Commission. Derrida underlines there the importance of the change of geographical focus from Europe toward another "scene" (in the theatrical sense, to which he remains attached),[14] that of South Africa. For, as he insists below, "everything, within a certain sequence that is of interest to us here, stems from modern Germany and speaks German,"[15] and it is for him a matter of thinking through a certain historical articulation, precisely where the history of forgiveness undermines that historicity all the way to the concept of history itself. In that respect Derrida follows closely the text by Walter Benjamin, "The Meaning of Time in the Moral Universe," in which the latter evokes what is for Derrida "forgiveness without reconciliation," which, as Derrida writes, is "another time, the time, the time of the storm of forgiveness, the tempestuous and untimely storm of forgiveness," a time that takes the form of a violence that "puts an end to time within time."[16] It is in relation to

17

---

drid, Valence, Oslo, Stanford, UC Irvine, Reading, Bordeaux, Athens, Istanbul, etc. Lectures in Arles (Assises de la traduction), London (ICA), and Brussels (International Parliament of Writers), etc." (*Annuaire*, 572). Note also, finally, the sign of the international reception and recognition of Derrida's thinking in the form of four honorary doctorates received during the two years of this seminar: University of Katowice in 1997, University of Western Cape in 1998, University of Turin in 1998, and University of Athens in 1999. Moreover, certain addresses given on those occasions, relating to the seminar, exist in print: "Le don, le pardon et la grâce (L'Université sans condition)," *Rivista di estetica* 38, no. 9 (1998): 209–18; *Inconditionnalité ou souveraineté: L'Université aux frontières d'Europe*, bilingual edition, trans. Vanghélis Bitsouris, Blanche Molfessis, and Aliki Keramides (Athens: Editions Patakis, 2002), 16–66 ["Unconditionality or Sovereignty: The University at the Frontiers of Europe," trans. Peggy Kamuf, *Oxford Literary Review* 31, no. 2 (2009): 115–31].

14. That is the case for this seminar as it will be for that on the death penalty, which follows it. See in this regard Derrida's note appended to "*Versöhnung, ubuntu*, pardon: quel genre?" Cf. 3n8 below.

15. See 35–36 below.

16. See 23 below. Derrida quotes the Benjamin fragment in the French translation, "La signification du temps dans le monde moral," trans. Jean-François Poirier and Christophe Jouanlanne, in Rolf Tiedemann and Hermann Schweppenhäuser, eds. *Fragments philosophiques, critiques, littéraires* (Paris: PUF, 2001), 107–8 ["The Meaning of Time in the Moral Universe," trans. Rodney Livingstone, in Marcus Bullock and

this "other time" of forgiveness, precisely, that Derrida asks to what extent the history of forgiveness is "Europe-centered, or whether, in the current globalization of confession, in the theatre of confession, it affects Europe, deporting, exporting, reporting, repatriating or expatriating it, reappropriating, expropriating or exappropriating it."[17]

In moving from the German word *Versöhnung* to *ubuntu*, Derrida also puts emphasis on insoluble problems of translation, remaining suspicious of the Christian connotations of "restorative" or "redemptive justice" that mark this notion used by Desmond Tutu. Always vigilant in the face of the political dimension of translation, Derrida underscores how that "can appear as a form of violence, no doubt well-intentioned, with the best intentions in the world, but an acculturating — not to say colonial — violence that is not limited to a superficial question of language and semantics."[18]

We similarly note that Derrida pays heightened attention during this second year to the theatrical dimension of these judicial scenes, whose importance he recalls several times in his extemporaneous remarks, constantly finding "additional reasons — but I am always finding new ones — for organizing everything we are talking about on the basis of theater, as a theatrical scene."[19] That theatricality was certainly present during the first year, but it here takes on a special dimension inasmuch as the organization of the seminar doubles with a mirroring effect the stakes of witnessing and swearing that are analyzed in it. From the outset Derrida asks this concerning forgiveness:

18   Must forgiveness [*pardon*], whether requested or not, granted or not, be
      named, and even heard, audible, visible, phenomenal? Or, on the contrary,
      secret, silent, mute, unuttered, unspeakable, inapparent, solitary? In other
      words, is there or is there not, should there or should there not be, a *scene*, a
      theatricality, a staging, or even a potential obscenity of the scene of forgive-
      ness? Must it be presented or must it withdraw, unpresentable, offstage from
      any scene; that is to say, from any theater, or even from any public space?
          Let's go to the theater, then; that's where we are. Let's watch and listen.[20]

Derrida then speaks of these four men — Hegel, Mandela, Tutu, and Clinton — who are protagonists in the seminar, characters, even appealing to

---

Michael W. Jennings, eds., *Selected Writings*, vol. 1 (1913–1926) (Cambridge, MA: Harvard University Press, 1996), 286–87].

17. See 16 below.
18. See 66 below.
19. See 83n56 below.
20. See 1 below.

the "voice off" of Hegel's ghost, waiting in the wings. Of course, if the protagonists in these scenes of public repentance are men, Derrida does not for all that forget the voices of women throughout this history of forgiveness, beginning with the voices of victims who witnessed before the Truth and Reconciliation Commission in front of their tormentors, or that of Antjie Krog, whose book *Country of My Skull* is referred to in the First Session and discussed much further in the Third Session, or those of the "sinners" Mary Magdalene and Monica Lewinsky. As he notes, that whole economy of stagecraft is far from anodyne, for "we are in the theater of theory and politics."[21]

Finally, as was the case in the first year of the seminar, where "works that seem to be more literary"[22] played a determinant role — notably during the four sessions of the 1997–98 year dedicated to *Confessions* — the second year gives an equally important place to texts by Rousseau and Augustine, to Blanchot, Kafka, and Shakespeare, and more especially to Henri Thomas's *Le Parjure*, which not only brings the year to a close but also ends the whole of the "Perjury and Pardon" cycle (one will also note the salience of works by Paul de Man, whose presence here remains at the heart of analyses constituting an "uninterrupted dialogue").

In a discussion session from this second year, on March 17, 1999, Derrida comes back to the question of forgiveness more generally by accentuating three of its aspects that matter especially to him.[23] First, forgiveness should interrupt "the course of history," as he demonstrates on the basis of Jeremy Rifkin's *The End of Work*,[24] and "consequently work in all its forms (labor, the work of the negative, process), and everything associated to work in the words 'reconciliation,' 'redemption,' 'healing.'" Derrida notes that "if there has to be a sort of revolutionary lightness in forgiveness, an end to work, this doesn't for all that mean that forgiveness is ludic, play." Forgiveness never allows itself to be contained within this opposition between work and play: "Forgiveness is a serious thing and will always remain something serious — if there is such a thing."

19

21. See 19 below.

22. *Annuaire de l'EHESS 1997–1998*, 554.

23. This discussion session is the only one for which we were unable to locate a recording. A preliminary transcription of the session was undertaken by Olga Rodel on the basis of cassettes belonging to Professor Makoto Asari that are now lost. We thank Professor Yuji Nishiyama for providing that transcription to us, allowing us to quote here certain passages of particular interest.

24. See Fourth and Fifth Sessions below.

The second aspect concerns the question of sovereignty. Derrida outlines therefore one of the investments that traverse this series of seminars:

> For us the difficulty would be to draw a fine, very fine, very fragile, very precarious limit between unconditionality — which we would say is forgiveness itself, that it is implied in every pardon worthy of the name — and sovereignty, which, however close to unconditionality it be, is nevertheless what corrupts all forgiveness. Forgiveness as affirmation of sovereignty is no longer forgiveness.

Coming back to his analysis of *The Merchant of Venice* and the right to pardon in Kant, dealt with in the first year of the seminar,[25] as well as to that of the pardon as exceptional right accorded the sovereign (president or governor), he underscores the following:

> This right to pardon in its sovereign form has something about it that obliges us think more carefully the distinction that I propose — a difficult distinction, I grant you — between unconditionality and sovereignty. Wherever forgiveness is affirmed as sovereignty, as a form of sovereignty, wherever I have the power to forgive, forgiveness is no longer forgiveness. As a consequence, forgiveness must conform to a sort of unconditionality, unpower, non-power. And that is where the theological heritage of the right to pardon, or the theological heritage of the concept of sovereignty is interrupted, or else transformed.

In his third remark Derrida analyzes the sacred or theological heritage of sovereignty that gets transferred from the divine right of the king to a sovereign people. He recalls the story of Daniel in the Book of Kings, where it is a matter of God's silent manifestation to the prophet Elijah. Isn't God's omnipotence (and hence, that of the sovereign), the fact of appearing silently, discreetly, "in such an inapparent way that his image is no longer that of an all-powerful God"? This "voice of silence" — something that Roger Laporte and Maurice Blanchot also pick up on — makes this silent manifestation a voiceless voice, the moment of interruption that is what interests him: "it is therefore in this sort of dead time, one of im-potence [*impouvoir*] and silence that perhaps leads us to think of a difference between sovereignty and unconditionality, that is to say a type of absolute. And forgiveness must be absolute if it is to be forgiveness, an absolute without power, an absolute that divests itself of the attributes of power." Derrida doesn't fail to note, immediately following, that this renouncing of the attributes of sover-

25. See *Perjury and Pardon*, vol. 1, 45ff., and 18–19, 161, 193–94 [*Parjure et pardon*, vol. 1, 79ff., and 47–48, 216, 254].

eignty could always simply be "a more cunning, more subtle affirmation of the same sovereignty, more irreducible, more indestructible." Forgiveness therefore pertains to "this time that is barely a time," an interval in which all of a sudden "space and time open without there being space and without there being time." Derrida concludes his remarks by making clear that if he has insisted on referring to this biblical text, it is because the latter gave "an idea of difference, which I well know is inconsistent, between unconditionality and sovereignty," and which forgiveness calls into question in a very serious manner.

The present volume reproduces the written seminar text read by Derrida   *21* in the eight sessions that took place at the EHESS in 1998–99. As always, all the sessions were entirely written out. Unlike previously published volumes of the EHESS seminars, such as *The Death Penalty* (1999–2001) and most of *The Beast and the Sovereign* (2001–3), which remained to a great extent unpublished, several sessions from this seminar have appeared in print. In addition to the first three sessions, mentioned above, the Eighth Session was also published by Derrida, as were brief sections that appeared in books and collective works.[26] The seminar "Perjury and Pardon" allows the reconstitution of the original sequence of those different texts, and a better understanding of the coherence of Derrida's thinking by putting side by side the published work and that developed "live" in the course of the seminar. In this way the reader will be able to compare the first draft of the texts and the final published version.

26. See xivn5 above. Cf. Derrida, "Le parjure, peut-être ('brusques sautes de syntaxe')," *Études françaises* 38, nos. 1–2 (2002): 15–57 ; and in a "slightly modified version," as Derrida explains, in *Cahier de L'Herne Derrida*, 577–600 ; finally as the book *Le Parjure, peut-être ("Brusques sautes de syntaxe")* (Paris: Galilée, 2017); see also pp. 21–25 of the First Session, published in "Leçon," in *Comment vivre ensemble*, 202–10, as well as passages from the Third Session that were reworked in the interview with Michel Wieviorka, "Le Siècle et le Pardon," in Jacques Derrida, *Foi et savoir, suivi de Le Siècle et le Pardon (entretien avec Michel Wieviorka)* (Paris: Seuil, 2000), 116–19. [Translator's note:] In English, see "'Le Parjure,' *Perhaps*: Storytelling and Lying ('abrupt breaches of syntax')," trans. Peggy Kamuf, in *Without Alibi*, 161–201; "Avowing—The Impossible: 'Returns,' Repentance, and Reconciliation: A Lesson," trans. Gil Anidjar, in *Living Together*, 18–41; and "On Forgiveness," trans. Michael Hughes, in Simon Critchley and Richard Kearney, eds., *On Cosmopolitanism and Forgiveness* (London: Routledge, 2001), 25–60.

We worked on the basis of the typescript that Derrida used in his semi-nar, the corresponding computer file, and the texts appended to them (press cuttings, photocopies of quoted passages, etc.). For this edition we relied on the so-called "American" seminar, housed in the Fonds Jacques Der-rida at the Institut Mémoires de l'édition contemporaine (IMEC) and now also held at the Princeton University Library in two versions, one including handwritten annotations and photocopies of newspaper articles.[27] We have taken those annotations into account in cases where they do not relate solely to Derrida's improvised translation given for his American audience. One also finds certain annotations concerning the organization of the American seminar, or relating to omitted or deleted passages; we have indicated those only when they directly concern the 1998–99 seminar. In rare cases where differences exist between the typescript and the computer file, we have in-dicated the same. Because the Fifth Session existed in two printings, we compared those versions and the different annotations relating to each. We also had at our disposal complete audio recordings of all regular sessions of the seminar, which allowed us to monitor how they proceeded. Thus, the Fourth Session, which included two different beginnings, was reworked in the seminar of January 20, 1999: Derrida replaced the beginning of the manuscript with that found on its final page; moreover, the last pages of that session (121–23) were crossed out and not read during the seminar, but instead held over for the beginning of the following session.

With regard to the sequence of the seminar, we note that it begins a little later than normal, in December, and ends earlier, at the beginning of April, as announced by Derrida the previous year, as he began his "retirement."[28] In opening the First Session Derrida recalls that announcement: "As I an-nounced last spring—those of you who were here will remember—because I am now, as one says, on 'administrative retirement,' I have decided, as I

---

27. The typescript is contained in an orange folder including the handwritten nota-tion (not written by Derrida) "Parjure Pardon 98–99 / Séances 1–8." It includes the eight sessions so numbered, classified separately in blue folders (the Eighth Session's folder is orange). Sessions 2–7 have the note "Photocopies of quoted passages missing." In another orange folder marked "Copie 2," there is a second printing of the Fifth Ses-sion. See Fonds Jacques Derrida, IMEC, file "Documentation: 'Le Parjure et le par-don,'" 239 DRR 240.1. The original typescript is now found in the Collection "The Library of Jacques Derrida," Firestone Library, Princeton University, Department of Rare Books and Special Collections (File 4, Box B-000262). Several files housed there include documents related to this seminar (periodicals, articles, press cuttings).

28. Editors' Note, *Perjury and Pardon*, vol. 1, xxii [*Pardon et parjure*, vol. 1, 19].

said then, neither to leave nor to stay."[29] That decision also implies a change   23
in the actual format of the seminar: beginning in 1998–99, "restricted" sessions are no longer held as they had been in preceding years, "since those
sessions were dedicated to presentations, specially reserved for presentations of research [that he was] supposed to be directing; there will be no
more restricted sessions, all sessions will be 'open.' Just that, from time to
time, as in the past, we will have a discussion session dedicated solely to
discussion or to presentations."[30] Those sessions took thenceforth the form
of open discussion sessions, during which student presentations might also
be given. According to the attendance register that we consulted in the
Derrida archive at IMEC, five such sessions took place during the 1998–
99 year: December 16, 1998, and February 10, March 3, 17, and 31, 1999.[31]
For the session of March 17 we were unable to locate either a typescript
or a recording, the only trace being the partial transcription quoted above.
In conformity with previously published volumes, the restricted sessions
and discussion sessions have not been transcribed for the present edition.
However, because Derrida alludes, during certain regular seminar sessions,
to two contributions prepared by him, we have transcribed and presented
them here as appendices. The first concerns the contaminated blood scan-   24
dal (discussion session of February 10, 1999) and the second, the war in
Kosovo (session of March 31, 1999).

We have verified quoted extracts and bibliographical references (they
are most often clearly indicated in the typescript in abbreviated form), and

29. Derrida continues by explaining the organization of the seminar for this year:
". . . simply, while continuing to hold this seminar as long as will prove possible for you
and for me, I am going to shorten it by starting a little later—as you see, we are beginning on December 2—and ending a little earlier, that is in the second week of April,
well, after the first week of April. So, the seminar will run from today to April 7 or 8"
(First Session recording, December 2, 1998).

30. First Session recording.

31. In an annotation made in the typescript (see 64n1 below) Derrida mentions the
dates February 3, March 3, and March 24 as intended for presentations. Because we
found no recording for the March 3 and March 24 sessions, although those dates are circled in the typescript (which is not the case for the third date) and they are not included
in the attendance register, it is reasonable to believe that it was a matter of suggestions
made by Derrida that didn't eventuate, unlike that of March 3. The recording of the
February 10 session confirms that the February 3 session was canceled. Presentations
were as follows: Jean-Philippe Pastor ("Le Pardon inattendu/impromptu"), February 10;
an unidentified woman ("*L'Épître du pardon* d'Abū al-ʿAlāʾ al-Maʾrrī"), March 3; Joseph Cohen ("La question de la révélation et du secret), March 31, 1999. We were unable to identify the other presenters.

provided any that were lacking. Unless otherwise stated, all notes are added by the editors. We had recourse to the very volumes that Derrida used and consulted in the collection held in the Princeton University library, which in 2015 purchased the philosopher's own library. We also consulted the inventory of Derrida's library in Ris-Orangis established by Marie-Joëlle St-Louis Savoie in 2009–11, in order to verify the editions used. We verified, and where necessary corrected the text of, quotations included by Derrida in his text, rectifying without notification obvious errors of transcription but bringing systematically to the reader's attention translations that he modified. A certain number of texts quoted were not transcribed into the typescript; they exist in the form of photocopies from books (French texts, translations, and texts in the original), showing numerous signs of close reading (underlined passages, circled words, various marginal annotations) that were inserted by Derrida in his typescript in the places where he planned to read and comment on them. Hence, in transcribing those passages, we indicate the commentaries made by Derrida in brackets, directly within the quotation; whenever he has himself transcribed the passages into the typescript, we so indicate with a footnote.

As with previous published volumes of Derrida's seminar, we had recourse to audio recordings of the sessions in order to establish the precise limits of quoted passages and in order to transcribe annotations intercalated by Derrida during his reading of the typescript. Those recordings also allowed us to clarify what was in fact said during the seminar, which doesn't always correspond exactly to the typescript. In carefully preserving the orality of this text, we also reproduce the various pointers that Derrida inscribes in the typescript, including reminders that he gave himself such as "(Blackboard)," "slowly," or "read and comment on," announcing a quoted passage or an excursus that he would then — but not always — develop extemporaneously. Where possible, we have transcribed the content of those significant additions in footnotes reconstructed on the basis of the audio recordings; we have similarly transcribed the numerous and often long translations that he directly submitted to his listeners on the basis of cited works, several of which had not yet been translated into French, such as the autobiography of Nelson Mandela, the book by Antjie Krog, or the cuttings from American newspapers commented on by Derrida throughout various sessions.[32]

32. [Translator's note:] Where such works exist in English (e.g., Mandela and Krog), I have provided the published translation; in other places, where Derrida is simulta-

As with previously published volumes of the seminar, we have tried to reduce as much as possible our modifications of the typescript. Whenever changes were deemed necessary for reasons of comprehension, we have systematically signaled each of those additions or modifications. Missing words are inserted between chevrons.

The text of the seminar is complete. On rare occasions we have made minimal adjustments to such things as proliferating diacritical signs (parentheses, brackets, dashes) that made it difficult to follow the syntax of the argument.[33] We corrected typographical errors in the typescript, several of which Derrida himself changed during his reading. Because several sessions of this seminar were reviewed by Derrida with a view to publication, we have kept his italics as they appear.

In his typescript Derrida frequently uses initials for the names of authors   26
he is quoting; we have always written those names in full. Finally, as is his custom, certain shorthand indications concerning matters he planned to take up during the session or in a following one are found at the end of each session; we have not reproduced those notes in this edition.

We offer warm thanks to George Leroux for checking the use of Greek terms, and Patricia Dailey for her help in verifying a reference. We thank André Derval, collections director; François Borde, deputy director for research; and all the personnel of the Institut Mémoires de l'édition contemporaine (IMEC) for their assistance during our time spent conducting research in the Derrida Collection. Because audiotapes for this year's seminar were held neither by IMEC nor at UC Irvine, we are grateful to those who provided them to us: Yuji Nishiyama, professor at Tokyo Metropolitan University and Japanese translator of Derrida's seminars, who also put us in touch with Makoto Asari, former professor at the Université Bordeaux-Montaigne, and Takaaki Morinaka, professor at Waseda University, who had copies of the tapes in Japan. We thank David Wills, English translator of these two seminar volumes, for his attentive remarks, as well as all our

---

neously translating from a text in another language (e.g., German), I have so indicated, while nevertheless providing references to published English translations.

33. [Translator's note:] Here and below I have omitted brief mentions in the French Editors' Note that are not relevant for the English translation.

colleagues on the editorial team for their commentaries and close rereading of our work.

Finally, and especially, we thank Jean Derrida and Pierre Alferi for their confidence in and support for the project from the beginning. We keep especially in our thoughts Marguerite Derrida, who died on March 21, 2020, and pay respectful and affectionate tribute to her memory.

Ginette Michaud, Nicholas Cotton, and Rodrigo Therezo

TRANSLATOR'S NOTE

As discussed in my Translator's Note to the first volume of *Perjury and Pardon*, the title of this seminar poses a problem for the English translator. French has a single word, *le pardon*, and its cognates (*pardonner*, etc.), for different usages of "forgiveness" and "pardon" in English, even if they coincide in a case such as *pardon* ["pardon me," or "sorry"/"excuse me"]. I have consistently used "forgiveness" rather than "pardon" as the general term throughout the seminar. A similar problem concerns the word *parjure*, which I have often translated as "perjury" even though that legal sense is more rare than the everyday "lie/lying." For reasons explained in the first volume, I have also chosen to keep the transliteration of Derrida's French title, "Perjury and Pardon."

I am sincerely grateful to my colleagues in the Derrida Seminars Translation Project Workshop—held via Zoom in July 2020—for their invaluable suggestions and assistance in the preparation of this volume: Geoffrey Bennington, Pascale-Anne Brault, Ellen Burt, Katie Chenoweth, Peggy Kamuf, Kir Kuiken, Michael Naas, and Elizabeth Rottenberg. Special thanks are also owed to Nicholas Cotton, Ginette Michaud, and Rodrigo Therezo for their generous assistance in answering my queries. I am also grateful to Barry Trachtenberg and Daniel Fisher-Livne for assistance with Hebrew transcriptions.

Editions used by Derrida are identified at the point of their first reference, preceded by, in almost all cases, the English translation I have relied on. For texts used repeatedly, page references are thereafter given in the main text, separated by a slash. The first page reference is to the quoted source (usually the English text), the second to the original.

Where Derrida provides page references in his typescript, I have refrained from repeating the information following the quoted passage unless the reader might be confused. In such cases Derrida sometimes adds letters or numbers, or both, presumably as a notation system for locating quotations in his own copy of the text. I have simply repeated those notations in the form in which they appear.

December 2, 1998

(Very slowly)

Last year, I opened the first session by saying—without further context, not even a sentence—*"pardon."*[1] A single word, *pardon*, a common noun, just that noun alone. The rest followed. I won't return to it.

Must forgiveness [*pardon*],[2] whether requested or not, granted or not, be named, and even heard; audible, visible, phenomenal? Or, on the contrary, secret, silent, mute, unuttered, unspeakable, inapparent, solitary? In other words, is there or is there not, should there or should there not be, a *scene*, a theatricality, a staging, or even a potential obscenity of the scene of forgiveness? Must it be presented or must it withdraw, unpresentable, offstage from any scene; that is to say, from any theater, or even from any public space?

Let's go to the theater, then; that's where we are. Let's watch and listen.

Act 1, Scene 1. The cast: four men, four proper names, four metonymies or pseudonymies, four figures, four characters,[3] some from our time, contemporaries, some from another time, but perhaps, for all that, no less contemporary nor more anachronistic: G<eorg> Wilhelm Friedrich Hegel, Nelson Mandela, Bill Clinton, and Desmond Tutu, in other words, the dialectician and philosopher of absolute knowing, heads of state from North America and South Africa, and the theologico-political priest, eminent representative of the Anglican Church.

30

---

1. See Derrida, *Perjury and Pardon*, vol. 1, 1 [*Parjure et pardon*, vol. 1, 27].

2. Extracts from the opening that follows (1–3), and several other passages from this session (7, 16) were filmed for *D'ailleurs, Derrida* (Safaa Fathy, 1999), which was in production in fall 1998. Derrida alludes to the filming during the session (see 20 below).

3. [Translator's note:] Word in English in typescript.

Note that they all belong, in one way or another, to the Christian faith, and are Protestants.

Other Christian characters are on the roster for later scenes,[4] the prosecutor Ken Starr, for example.[5] We won't rule out an appearance by the pope also (both head of state and theologico-political priest), with a speech about repentance to come concerning the Shoah and the Inquisition, but he hasn't arrived yet, being unwell. It is reported that after canonizing Edith Stein,[6] he called on Christianity, and I quote, "to revisit with an open mind . . . the problem of the Inquisition [which] belongs to a troubled period of the Church's history," at the same time warning against, and I quote again, "images of the past spread by public opinion, since they are often charged with an intense emotionalism that prevents calm, objective analysis."[7] To that end, he is reported to have charged a commission of historians with the task — the play that is about to begin once the curtain rises will be greatly concerned with commissions, and with the question of knowing whether these questions of repentance, forgiveness, conscience-searching, memory, etc., should or shouldn't be entrusted to commissions such as the South Af-

4. The typescript has this marginal annotation: "K<ier>k<e>g<aard> S. 4 <illegible word>."

5. Kenneth Winston Starr, American attorney, former judge of the federal Court of Appeals and 39th solicitor general of the United States (1989–93). First appointed to inquire into the suicide of White House counsel Vince Foster, and investments made by Bill Clinton in the Whitewater Development Corporation, he used his power as independent counsel to exploit Bill Clinton's liaison with Monica Lewinsky for partisan purposes. Starr was a member of the Republican Party. In the dossier of the Derrida archive at IMEC, there is a letter from Jacques Lang, at that time representative for the Loir-et-Cher in the French National Assembly, dated September 15, 1998, inviting Derrida to sign a text written on Lang's initiative, and that of writers William Styron, Gabriel Garcia Márquez, and Carlos Fuentes, denouncing the "arbitrary and unjust procedures" undertaken by Starr. Derrida was a signatory to that letter ("Contre les procédures arbitraires du procureur Kenneth Starr," *Le Monde*, September 24, 1998, 3). Concerning Starr, see further 93 below.

6. Edith Stein (1891–1942), renamed Saint Theresa Benedicta of the Cross, converted Jewish philosopher and Carmelite nun, born in Breslau, deported to and murdered in Auschwitz, beatified in 1987, then canonized by Pope John Paul II on May 1, 1998, an action that gave rise to controversy.

7. Pope John Paul II, "Address of the Holy Father Pope John Paul II to an International Symposium on the Inquisition," October 31, 1998: https://w2.vatican.va/content/john-paul-ii/en/speeches/1998/october/documents/hf_jp-ii_spe_19981031_simposio.html. See Jean-Paul Ferran, "Inquisition: Le pape prépare un *mea culpa* pour l'an 2000," *L'Humanité*, November 2, 1998, 13.

rican Truth and Reconciliation Commission. The pope, who hasn't yet arrived, and who perhaps won't make it before his visit to Iraq or who knows where, Babylon or Babel, has thus asked a commission to provide a historical reconstitution that takes into account the context of the era of the Inquisition so that the Church may judge, as he says, with full knowledge of the facts. But the pope, who is unwell, isn't yet here, nor is the Grand Inquisitor Kenneth Starr. Never mind, the four characters present, Hegel, Mandela, Clinton, and Tutu, all know a wee bit about forgiveness, amnesty, perjury, repentance, reconciliation, etc. We'll listen to their testimony.

But the curtain hasn't yet risen. Still in preview [*Hors d'oeuvre*]. Prologue [*Exergue*] (a voice is heard, off, before recommencing; it speaks German, of course).[8]

Das Wort der Versöhnung: "the word of reconciliation[9] [*Das Wort der Versöhnung*: not the word "reconciliation" but the reconciliatory word, the word of reconciliation, that is to say, the word by means of which one sets reconciliation in train, one offers reconciliation by being the first to extend one's hand, making the first move; it is the word one utters when one makes the   32

---

8. These pages (up to "a case of giving one's word," [22]) were published by Derrida, with some alterations, under the title "*Versöhnung, ubuntu, pardon: quel genre*," in *Le Genre humain* 43 (2004): 111–56, and in *La Solidarité des vivants et le pardon*, 61–120. Derrida adds in a note: "This text is the (very slightly revised) transcription of a seminar session on 'Le parjure et le pardon' (EHESS, 1998–99). I had then just returned from a trip to South Africa. The seminar was 'composed,' or even 'dramatized,' staged somewhat like the theatrical scene of a tribunal to which were successively summoned, as witnesses, four *men* (*not a single woman*) who were also *Protestants* (Hegel, Mandela, Tutu, Clinton). One will recognize here the traces of and justifications for that *mise en scène*. The seminar was expanded, in the years following, around the 'Death Penalty.' An analogous apparatus: four witnesses, four people sentenced to death; but on that occasion, with different religions and sexes (genders): Socrates, Jesus, Al-Hallaj, and Joan of Arc" ("*Versöhnung, ubuntu, pardon*," 154n*; *Solidarité des vivants*, 61n1, Derrida's emphasis). In fact, the revised version is drawn from not one, but three sessions of the second year of the seminar (see Second and Third Sessions, below), and reorganized in an unusual way, with subtitles for each part, and often including substantial additions.

[Translator's note:] Here and below I use "voice off," with overtones of a theatrical, or even Shakespearean stage direction, to render "*voix* off," meaning "offstage voice," "voice from the wings."

9. G. W. F. Hegel, *Phänomenologie des Geistes*, in *Werke*, vol. 3, ed. Eva Moldenhauer and Karl Markus Michel (Frankfurt: Suhrkamp Verlag, 1970), 493 [*Phenomenology of Spirit*, trans. Terry Pinkard (Cambridge: Cambridge University Press, 2018), 388 (§670); *Phénoménologie de l'esprit*, vol. 2, trans. Jean Hyppolite (Paris: Éditions Aubier Montaigne, 1941), 168].

first move ([*prendre les devants*]: extraordinary expression isn't it, *prendre les devants!*)[10] unilaterally, dissymmetrically, when one takes the initiative in favor of peace, forgiveness, or reconciliation, hence the act, the speech act[11] by which, with a word, by speaking, with what is a spoken word, one initiates reconciliation, one offers reconciliation by addressing the other. By means of this spoken word, one therefore makes peace, one declares peace, practices reconciliation. Reconciliation here works through the word addressed to the other, but a word that, for being a spoken word, is not mere words [*parole verbale*], as one says mockingly, rather it is an actual utterance, a spoken word that does what it says, a performative as it is called: "*Das Wort der Versöhnung*" here visibly designates a performative speech act: the act that operates, does, the *doing* of reconciliation, the gesture joined to the word, the gesture in the word.]"

The voice off begins again in German. "*Das Wort der Versöhnung*," "The word of reconciliation is the *existing* spirit [the spirit *being there*: der *daseiende* Geist: *daseiende* is underlined by Hegel (*Blackboard*)],"[12] whose voice you recognized: the word of reconciliation is the *being-there* of spirit; it is by this word of reconciliation addressed to the other that spirit is manifested *there*, it *is there*, it comes on stage, it is in its *being-there*, the *there*. What signifies, through the word "*there (da)*," both existence and phenomenal and actual presence, is *situated*—or is *situating*—in this word of reconciliation, and nowhere else. Reconciliation takes place, it finds room, as does an event, it situates *itself*, it is situated in this word, which situates it, but it is also situating; reconciliation *makes place* for this word. Spirit (which is not a *Witz*, a witty remark [*mot d'esprit*]), *Geist* takes place, makes place, it brings about [*fait arriver*] in this word and nowhere else; its being-*there* works through this word of reconciliation addressed to the other. Which means, at least, that before this word there was war, certainly, opposition or hate, division or dissociation or separation, and suffering and trauma, wounding, wounds (*die Wunden*); and that, because of that, during the time of those wounds, spirit *wasn't there*, *not yet there*, *as such*, not yet conscious and gathered in itself, not yet present to itself. It wasn't yet, it was in its *not-yet*, it was awaiting itself. It perhaps was, but in no way yet *there*, present in its *being-there*. Not at all

33

---

10. [Translator's note:] The phrase *prendre les devants*, with its unusual plural usage of *devant*, meaning "what is in front," "front leg," was originally a term for a tactic by which hunters try to get ahead of a prey whose scent they have lost. It means more generally "get out in front," "preempt," "jump the gun."

11. [Translator's note:] The words "speech act" in English in typescript.

12. Hegel, *Phänomenologie*, 493 [*Phenomenology*, 388; *Phénoménologie*, vol. 2, 198].

existing. Not at all on stage in history. It wasn't yet presenting itself. Not it-self to itself. Not being on stage, it whispered in the wings, rehearsed its role, wove its text in the prehistory of its first act.

We hear the specter of Hegel, the voice off of Hegel's ghost, even before he himself returns to the theater masked, we hear it wondering, no doubt, noting today, on this very day, the expanding range of scenes—at least mimed—of repentance, of forgiveness requested and of reconciliation, won-dering whether this globalization of confession is not at last the presentation of spirit, the being-there of spirit declaring itself in the world, as world, that is to say, as progression to revealed (Christian) religion, and, from there, to absolute knowing. For, as we shall later make clear,[13] that passage appears at the end of the chapter on "Spirit," which is going to open onto religion, then, at the end of the three moments of religion, onto absolute knowing as truth of revealed religion, that is to say, of the Christian religion.

And that also means that the *there*, the being-there, the event, the place, the taking-place in presence as being-*there* of spirit, would not be thought without what is pronounced [*le prononcé*], without thinking the proffering of this word of reconciliation. This would mean that I, an 'I,' accedes to the being-there of spirit—*I* make(s), the *I* make(s) spirit exist, *I* allow(s) it to take place and to present itself—only by offering reconciliation by means of a word, a phrase, an address made to the other; and actually proffered. It doesn't mean that I know beforehand what "spirit" means, what "being-there" and "being-there of spirit" mean, and that I subsequently understand that, thanks to grace [*grâce à la grâce*], to forgiveness, thanks to a word of reconciliation, I accede to this *being-there* of spirit. No, it could on the con-trary imply that if I want to accede to what spirit is, to what spirit itself sig-nifies when it is *there*, if I want spirit to respond when I ask of it "spirit, are you there?," if I want to accede to what *being-there* of spirit then can mean, to what existence or presence of spirit as spirit can mean, there must be, there will have to have been, the word of reconciliation, the word, the phrase that offers reconciling, and for that it is necessary not only that I learn what the concept of reconciliation, what the word "reconciliation" (and hence "spirit," and then "being-there of spirit") means, but also that I learn to reconcile in fact, to take the initiative for it, myself, to offer the gift of it, and the gift as gift of a word to the other. The word of reconciliation is given to the other. Is this gift a forgiving? Does it imply some oath, and hence the possibility of perjury? Is this word of reconciliation, to the extent that it is given, also a case of giving one's word?

34

13. See 17–18 below.

It is too early to decide that.

Let us keep close watch [*Veillons*] on just two signs, or rather let us note two *vigil effects*, even before beginning, though Hegel's ghost has already spoken, has had its voice heard even before presenting itself, before being *there* on stage, for we must still wait for it. Two *vigil effects*, two assurances that we must keep watch over, on the eve [*la veille*], before it all begins; two presuppositions, two premises or postulations that seem to decide it all before all else, surreptitiously, seeming to predestine the scene.

One of the two would touch on the *wound*, trauma, lesion, hurt [*tort*].

The other would take at its word the word "word [*das Wort, parole*]," the spoken word that, in this passage from *The Phenomenology of Spirit*, Hegel determines as "the word of reconciliation (*das Wort der Versöhnung*)."

1. The wound, first of all. Whatever else one thinks of the wound, of the concept of the wound or of the word "wound [*blessure*]" (certain etymologies take it back to Middle German *bletzen*, "to patch," from *Bletz*, the piece of leather used for patching, whence, paradoxically, "to tear to pieces"; and thus we would have at the same time in the same word — this is my interpretation, the one I'll hazard — two contrary but inseparable meanings: the double experience of what tears to pieces and patches up, what cuts and sews up, what injures [*lèse*] and repairs,[14] opens and sutures, wounds and bandages, wound and scar, wrong and reconciliation, the negative of separation and the labor of reparation; it would each time be a matter of tearing to pieces though trauma while patching over with a work of healing: the wrong and its remedy, sickness and treatment), whatever one thinks, moreover and in any case, of the wound, of the concept of wound or the word "wound," we always have to presume that a wound affects some vulnerable *living being*; and even if it is said to be a mortal wound, it is so only to the extent that the wounded one [*le blessé, la blessée*] remains alive. A dead person is no longer wounded. Of course, we spare a thought for any wound inflicted on the dead, about the wrong that can still be done to a dead person, but that is another way of keeping alive the specter or the memory of the dead, it is a way to resuscitate the dead, to have them live or breathe (breathe or exhale in us, breathe in us in spirit, in *psychē*, in soul, or in phantasm — *phantasma* in Greek is also "specter," "ghost" — to breathe or suffer in us). Some may do that out of love for the dead one, others out of hatred for the dead one, making the dead one survive in them, sustaining the dead one within them-

---

14. During the session, Derrida adds: "I think of circumcision, but simply because, at the end of this session, if you have the patience to wait, we will be concerned with Mandela's circumcision." See 29–31 below.

selves like a specter, just to be able to hound the dead and continue to insult them, persecute them, judge or even kill them. One could cite so many ex-amples of scenes (and perhaps all judgments derive from such a scene) in 36 which people continue judging the dead by buttonholing them more or less directly, doggedly making the case against them, as if the dead person had to be alive enough, present enough, there, or at least awakened from death just enough, just enough to hear the evil that is said or thought about them, the wrong that one would still like to do to them. You also know the scenes, physically real this time, where a person condemned to death is saved from a suicide attempt, saved and revived just long enough to be executed while still alive and conscious.[15]

But if we were to liberate ourselves, supposing it were ever possible, from all those phantasms and hence from that whole logic of spectrality, then we would say, in all good sense, and most irrefutably, that only a living person is wounded, can receive and feel a wound, even if it be a so-called mortal wound that he or she suffers, a wound that will, in the future, fatally bring about death. Lesion, blow, wound, trauma, gash, cut, abrasion, graze, muti-lation, incision, excision, circumcision, burn, concussion, contusion, sprain, fracture, dislocation, every imaginable wounding is inflicted on living tissue only by leaving, at least in its moment proper, a scar. And even if "wound" is a biological figure for speaking of psychological, moral, spiritual, or phan-tasmatic wrong or suffering, there is sense to forgiveness and reconciliation only where wounding has left, has been able to leave, a memory, a trace, hence a scar to be healed or salved. Bandaged.[16]

So, what does Hegel's ghost tell us, with its voice off, shortly before the paragraph that begins with "*Das Wort der Versöhnung ist der* daseiende *Geist*"?

It says, still in German: "*Die Wunden des Geistes heilen, ohne daß Narben bleiben* [The wounds of the Spirit heal, without scars remaining, and leave 37

---

15. During the session, Derrida adds: "I saw things like that, I knew about them at the end of the war. I think that was the case with Pierre Laval, who tried to com-mit suicide and who was cared for, no effort spared to revive him, in order that he could be executed." Pierre Laval (1883–1945), French politician and principal overseer, under Pétain (1856–1951), of the policies of state collaboration with Nazi Germany. Condemned to death for high treason by the High Court, he attempted suicide by swal-lowing a cyanide capsule on the day of his execution (October 9, 1945). Doctors brought him back to life, and gave him a stomach pump, so that, once well enough to walk, he could be executed by firing squad on October 15, 1945.

16. [Translator's note:] *À panser*, "to (be) bandage(d)," and homonymically, "(still) to be thought [*penser*]."

no scars behind]."[17] It doesn't say that wounds of the spirit don't give rise to scars; it says more precisely that the scars of the spirit don't last, don't remain, don't abide: *"Die Wunden des Geistes heilen, ohne daß Narben bleiben* [The wounds of the Spirit heal, and leave no scars behind]." Hegel doesn't say that they remain invisible or unconscious, he says that they don't remain. Not at all. They die as scars and don't abide. We endure here the double, contradictory injunction of every forgiveness worthy of the name: on the one hand, to forgive is not to forget, a forgiveness worthy of the name must keep intact the memory of the harm and keep alive the suffering; on the other hand, a forgiveness worthy of the name harbors no resentment, and at the outside no trace of the wrong, not even the memory of itself. Forgiving must erase everything, all the way to self-consciousness as forgiveness.

"Die Wunden des Geistes heilen, ohne daß Narben bleiben [The wounds of the spirit heal, without scars remaining, and leave no scars behind]." All that is found in the last pages of the main section on *Der Geist* (in the *Phänomenologie des Geistes*), just before the last section on "Religion," between spirit and religion therefore, and before the chapter on "Absolute Knowing," which follows that on religion (natural religion, art-religion, revealed religion). At the beginning of the chapter on "Absolute Knowing," the moment of pardon (*Verzeihung*) will indeed be recalled — and a certain relation between absolute knowing and forgiveness is what will no doubt matter to me here, later on. In the current process of the supposed globalization of acts of memory and reexamination[18] of the past of crimes, of confession, of repentance, of forgiveness requested, etc., is there not a certain posture or postulating of absolute knowing, of knowing [*science*] as absolute consciousness [*conscience*], that is now commanding this planetarization of the right of man, of the relation of the human to what is proper to the human as right?[19] As right beyond the political, but also radicalization and extension of the

17. Hegel, *Phänomenologie*, 492 [*Phenomenology*, 387 (§669); *Phénoménologie*, vol. 2, 197].

18. During the session, Derrida specifies: "I don't want to cite examples, they appear every day. You open any newspaper at all, every day you have a scene of reexamination, of having to remember, of forgiveness being requested, sometimes between an institution and a community, sometimes between one state and another. The most recent example is between China and Japan, I think, but they happen every day. I'm not going to weigh us down with examples, there are too many of them."

19. During the session, Derrida adds: "On the basis, as we talked about last year, of this fundamental — so obscure and fundamental — concept of crime against humanity, which commands this whole scene, absolutely." See *Perjury and Pardon*, vol. 1, 7–8, 321–22 [*Parjure et pardon*, vol. 1, 34, 413].

political beyond the nation-state form of sovereignty that has dominated and structured the political up to this point?

Let's leave that question as is for the moment and come back briefly to Hegel, and to the chapter on "Absolute Knowing" in *The Phenomenology of Spirit*. Hegel recalls there how, in forgiveness, hardness (*Härte*) renounces itself (*"sich selbst abläßt"*).[20] (*Blackboard*)

The hardness of what is hard lets go of itself, it forsakes itself, it departs from itself, it abandons itself and exits from itself, and in this way external-izes itself, alienates itself (*sich entäußert*); it becomes other than itself, for-eign to itself.

What does that mean? What is Hegel here calling *hardness* (*Härte*) when he says: "But we have seen how, in forgiveness (*Verzeihung*), this hardness (*diese Härte*) lets go of itself and goes out of itself, is externalized [alienated, becomes foreign to itself]." We will shortly see him call that hardness the hardness "of iron [*eiserne*]." And if one wanted to play on words, but not too much, between one language and another, one might say in French that, as you are going to hear, *le fer est porté dans le faire* (Handeln),[21] in operating, action, acting. The *"iron* effectivity (eiserne *Wirklichkeit*)" of duty is formed against the operation of *doing* (*Handeln*).[22] How to make it so that iron, the hardness of metal, is opposed to doing, to action?

The unbending [*inflexible*] hardness that bends in this way, the hardness of iron that lets itself be bent, is not simple empirical insensitivity, it is al-ready the hardness of duty, of the conviction that I act out of obedience to duty. I know, I am conscious—and I say so—that I act out of duty. How so? In the logic of this movement, which describes the different moments of a reconciliation of spirit with its own consciousness and self-consciousness, one understands that the history of spirit is nothing other than the history of a reconciliation. Reconciliation is spirit, the essence of spirit, the history of the essence of spirit, and history as the essence of spirit. Reconciliation is not a moment, it is coextensive with the whole process of spirit to the extent that it gathers itself (*zusammensetzt*) with its own consciousness [*con*science]

39

---

20. Hegel, *Phänomenologie*, 578 [cf. *Phénoménologie*, vol. 2, 298]. [Translator's note:] Cf. *Phenomenology*, 457, §793: "However, in forgiveness we saw how this hardness itself drains itself and then relinquishes itself."

21. [Translator's note:] Literally, "iron is transmitted in(to) doing," *fer* and *faire* being homophonic in French.

22. Hegel, *Phänomenologie*, 578 [*Phénoménologie*, vol. 2, 298], Derrida's emphasis. [Translator's note:] Cf. *Phenomenology*, 457, §793: "forms an ironclad actuality confront-ing action [*eine eiserne Wirklichkeit gegen das Handeln bildet*]."

("*mit seinem eigentlichen Bewußtsein*").[23] I underline *science* in "*con*science."
Becoming consciousness, for spirit, involves sublating an opposition and
reconciling itself. Everything that analyzes absolute spirit, in the *Encyclopedia <of Philosophical Sciences>* for example (§553ff.),[24] describes a movement of reconciliation. Spirit is reconciliation, it is sublation, sublated scission, opposition, and *sublated, aufgehoben* negativity. And forgiveness is an
essential moment of that sublation. Sublation is forgiveness, forgiveness is
sublation, *Aufhebung* of spirit as presentation and being-there of spirit.

Yet the moments of this process are singular, *einzeln*, and so separate,
dissociated, and it is their spiritual unity alone that constitutes what Hegel
calls "the force of this reconciliation (*die Kraft dieser Versöhnung*)."[25] But only
the last of these moments gathers them all into the strict figure of reconciliation as such, as finally worthy of the name. The first moment of spirit as
self-knowledge consists in "declaring (*Aussprechen*) that what it does, what
it has done (*tut*), it has done out of duty, out of a conviction of duty (*nach
Überzeugung von der Pflicht*)."[26] A Kantian moment. And that is the moment of hardness.

Hegel insists strongly on this language, and more explicitly on the speech
act, on the enunciation as such. In this first moment the language of spirit as
expression of a conviction makes action,[27] operation, its *Handeln*, equivalent

---

23. Hegel, *Phänomenologie*, 578 [*Phénoménologie*, vol. 2, 297]. [Translator's note:] Cf.
Phenomenology, 456, §793: "the reconciliation of spirit with its own genuine consciousness composes itself."

24. G. W. F. Hegel, *Philosophy of Mind, Hegel's Encyclopaedia of the Philosophical Sciences (Book 3)*, trans. W. Wallace (Oxford: Oxford University Press, 1971), 292ff. [*Encyclopédie des sciences philosophiques*, trans. Maurice de Gandillac (Paris: Gallimard, 1970),
478ff.].

25. Hegel, *Phänomenologie*, 578 [*Phenomenology*, 456, §793; *Phénoménologie*, vol. 2,
297].

26. Hegel, *Phänomenologie*, 578 [*Phénoménologie*, vol. 2, 297]. [Translator's note:] Cf.
Phenomenology, 457: "express[ing] that what it does, it does out of conviction of duty."

27. In Derrida's typescript a handwritten note is inserted here (after sheet #9). It is a
draft of his speech on the occasion of the honorary doctorate that he received from the
Pantion University in Athens, on June 3, 1999. It includes these lines: "To express my
gratitude to the university, to colleagues, to so many dear friends who honor me today,
I think that the moment is less than ever one for conventional words and the rhetoric
of circumstance. To give in to such formalities, to treat this honorary doctorate as a
ceremony, a tradition or ritual piously inherited from times past, would be not only to
sign on to an ingratitude but also to do injury to what is being said in present times, and
concerning the responsibilities <illegible word> that—in my view, today in Europe
more than elsewhere, in Greece, <in> Athens in a perhaps more exemplary way than

to simple enunciation in language. The value (*Gelten*) of the act, as duty, is   *40*
equivalent to the declaration [*énonciation*] of conviction. Of course, there is,
in this presumed equivalence of saying and doing, a unilaterality and a separation. *Handeln* is thus the first act that consists in separating oneself from
oneself (*das erste* ansich*seiende Trennen*), "the first division existing-*in-itself*
of the *simplicity* of the concept,"[28] the first separation to interrupt and so divide the simplicity of the concept, but also, by the same token, through that
separation, it already cuts into [*entame*] the return (*Rückkehr*) by means of
that separation; and as a result, it cuts into, begins [*amorce*], and so already
at least announces a second moment. From the first moment the second moment comes into play, for there is already in the first moment an element
of recognition (*Anerkennen*)[29] within which the consciousness of duty, the
knowledge of duty, posits itself as simple (as undivided, then) over and against
difference and division, doubling (*Unterschied* and *Entzweiung*). In action
or operation, *Handeln*, there is necessarily difference and doubling, scission
and division. Well, consciousness of duty opposes an effectivity[30] of iron [*fer*]
(f.e.r.) (*eine eiserne Wirklichkeit*) to this division and this difference of doubling (*Unterschied, Entzweiung*) that is implied by every action, all doing   *41*
[*faire*] (f.a.i.r.e.). It is trial by iron in contrast to doing. Duty, consciousness
of duty, the discourse of duty, is hardness itself, unbending, intolerant, unilateral, monolithic, indivisible, with respect to action. But in the recognition
of this separation (*Trennen*) between duty and action, between *fer* and *faire*,
a separation that cuts into the unilateral simplicity of the consciousness of
duty, a second moment is already announced, one that begins to bend the

---

elsewhere—are those of the University, and within it those of p<hilosophy> and of the
humanities. The idea of the university is a European idea (however enigmatic those two
words—'university' and 'Europe'—be or become today)." There follow some shorthand annotations for the rest of the speech, in which Derrida expresses for the first
time publicly, and in an academic setting, his position on the war in the Balkans involving ethnic Serb and Albanian inhabitants of the Serbian province of Kosovo, and the
NATO bombing of Serbia in response to that conflict. See Derrida, "Unconditionality
or Sovereignty: The University at the Frontiers of Europe," 115–31 [*Inconditionnalité ou
souveraineté. L'Université aux frontières de l'Europe*, 16–66]. On the conflict in Kosovo,
see 226–30 below.

28. *Phänomenologie*, 578 [*Phenomenology* 457, §793; *Phénoménologie*, vol. 2, 297],
Derrida's emphasis.

29. During the session, Derrida writes the German word on the blackboard and
adds: "I would have liked to follow this concept in Freud with you, but we don't have
time just now."

30. The typescript has "affectivity" for this and the following use of the word.

unbendable, to soften the iron. And that is the movement that is going to continue right up to the last moment, that of reconciliation in forgiveness, which is therefore at the other extreme from duty, albeit in the same process of dialectical development.

Immediately after saying that the first movement flows into the second, at the point where the element of recognition (*Anerkennen*) is posited as *simple*, undivided knowledge of duty over and against the difference and doubling that reside in doing (*Handeln*) as such, and form in that way an iron effectivity against doing, in the next sentence, Hegel says: "*In der Verzeihung sahen wir aber, wie diese Härte* von sich *selbst abläßt und* sich *entäußert* [But we have seen how, in forgiveness, hardness lets go *of itself*, forsakes *itself*, departs from itself and externalizes itself, goes to the outside of itself]."[31]

Let's pay close attention to this "of itself," "itself," this reflexivity. (Reread.) It is what renders the process dialectical. And it is this reflexivity that will be inscribed in the essence and moment of forgiveness. Hardness goes out of itself by itself [*d'elle-même d'elle-même*]; it is its own movement, here that of duty, which pushes it, from inside, to go out, itself to be and to do more than itself, therefore, to leave itself to go outside. It forsakes itself, it departs from itself, it leaves itself, it abandons itself, but that separation from itself was as it were prescribed on the inside of duty, which commanded it in a hard way to go right to the end of itself and so to soften or bend itself.

42   It is thus its iron inflexibility that bends the inflexibility, that inflects — by reflecting it, by reflection — iron inflexibility in doing. It is inflexibility, then, that inflects itself by reflecting itself, by self-reflection, and that goes out of itself by reflecting itself. When I say or admit that I am hard, that I act in a hard way out of duty, I begin to soften, to bend, I am already less hard. Hardness reflects itself, it bends itself [*se fléchit*], it bends by bending itself, it folds itself on itself, it goes beyond duty out of duty, it *ought* [doit] to go beyond duty and debt, it owes itself to go beyond what it ought, beyond obligation [*devoir*] and debt. So, it affects *itself* with its other, by commanding itself to go out of itself; it is reflection that pushes it to abandon itself and to go out of itself, to externalize itself, to become its other. This inflecting [*fléchissante*] and reflecting auto-affection is what will bring about the transition from the first to the second moment; this auto-affection, affect in duty,

---

31. *Phänomenologie*, 578 [*Phénoménologie*, vol. 2, 297], Derrida's emphasis. [Translator's note:] Cf. *Phenomenology*, 457, §793: "However, in forgiveness we saw how this hardness itself drains itself and then relinquishes itself."

mercy [*miséricorde*], heart, entrails of compassion, is also the dimension of *rahamîm* that we spoke of last year.[32]

[You see, I tell you in an aside or from the wings of what I am staging by hastily prompting [*en soufflant promptement*] the actors' lines even though they already know them by heart, you can well see what I am doing, precisely, between more than one language. I probably have to declare it; I don't say "admit" to it because it isn't necessarily an offense, and I am in the process of trying, in just terms, to justify it. To begin with I am taking Hegel literally, and in the spirit of his dialectical demonstration, I am taking the figure of hardness (*Härte*) seriously (it being a sensible, not a spiritual figure: a spirit or consciousness, a law even, could not literally be either hard or soft, inflexible or flexible; only a sensible thing — iron, for example, or wood — can be hard, opposite to "tender." That is why one sometimes says that he or she has a wooden heart or a heart of iron, in describing someone who has no heart.) Even taking literally Hegel's insistence — which is moreover classic, conventional — on speaking even of a hardness of iron or steel (*eiserne*), of an iron effectivity ("*eiserne Wirklichkeit*") in this hardness of duty, I didn't simply play on two French words that are almost homophones (*fer* and *faire*), but transported this metaphor or trope into my language, and transitioned, as if naturally, from the hardness of iron to the idea of inflexibility, and so to the inflecting of the flexible, and thence to the whole machine — moreover strongly Hegelian and dialectical in spirit — of inflecting, of specular or speculative reflecting, of *self-inflecting* in self-reflecting, in self-affecting with reflection. This law of speculative reflection is itself literally and overwhelmingly Hegelian; it is speculative dialectics itself and speculative idealism itself. As is well known, Hegelianism is a philosophy of reflection. And the quasi-deduction of forgiveness, of the law of a forgiveness that obeys and disobeys the iron law of duty, that deduction itself seemed impeccable, inflexible, inescapable, and unmistakable: irrefutable.[33] Although the logic of forgiveness is the antinomy of the logic of duty, it obeys its law, the same

43

32. Derrida, *Perjury and Pardon*, vol. 1, 138–39 [*Parjure et pardon*, vol. 1, 186]. During the session, Derrida adds: "In a Hebraic context, it's the heart in duty, in the heart of duty."

33. During the session, Derrida comments: "Hegel shows us irrefutably how one must move from duty to forgiveness, out of duty though, how to deny duty, finally, to sublate duty. And, in fact, one has there the whole contradiction of the history of forgiveness: one forgives out of love, through grace, not through duty. But that is also a commandment: it is the commandment to forgive, but the commandment to forgive not out of duty but out of love. The duty to forgive beyond duty."

law, etc. I forgive beyond duty, but I am duty-bound to forgive beyond duty. I forgive out of a duty that is beyond duty. That dialectical treatment of antinomy, which seems to be directed against the Kant of the categorical imperative, of duty or of what Hegel nicknames precisely the *"beautiful soul,"*[34] is also, as always with Hegel, a way of thinking what Kant should have thought had he been still more inflexible with his inflexibility, if he had been still more steadfast with the inflexibility of the categorical imperative. If Kant had radically thought what he thought he would have been Hegelian; and he would have forgiven Hegel in advance for saying it in that way, for correcting him or reforming him in that way.]

So, spirit, what is here called spirit, spirit in its being-there, in its existence, spirit that replies, "I am here," is what supposes and no doubt suffers division, wounding, and reconciliation, precisely for being there, but it is also what removes even the trace of the wound, even the lasting or surviving of the scar, probably not the memory of the wound, but what makes that memory a scar, the scar of a wound. That disappearance of the scar is what Hegel calls healing, cure, *heilen* (*"Die Wunden des Geistes heilen, ohne daß Narben bleiben"*).[35]

Heilen is a very rich word, and we'll come across it again in English ("to heal," "healing away") from the mouths of Mandela and Tutu, for example; it is a word that relates to the whole semantic family that I recalled and interpreted (forgive me this self-reference designed for economic convenience) in "Faith and Knowledge: The Two Sources of 'Religion' at the Limits of Reason Alone" (in *Religion*)[36] by putting it into relation with salvation (*Heil*), and *heilig*, holy,[37] the sacred, safe, unharmed, immune, and even — we'll speak more of this terrifying and inevitable possibility — of autoimmunity, the immunity that the living organism turns, inflexibly, as if by self-destructive reflection, back on itself. Between the being-there of spirit and the cure without trace, healing without lasting scar, immunization, process of restoration of immunity, there is supposedly an essential

34. Hegel, *Phänomenologie*, 484 (see also 491) [*Phenomenology*, 381, §658 (see also 386–87, §668); *Phénoménologie*, vol. 2, 168], Derrida's emphasis.

35. Hegel, *Phänomenologie*, 492 [*Phenomenology*, 387 (§669); *Phénoménologie*, vol. 2, 197].

36. Derrida, "Faith and Knowledge: The Two Sources of 'Religion' at the Limits of Reason Alone," trans. Samuel Weber, in Derrida and Gianni Vattimo, eds., *Religion* (Stanford: Stanford University Press, 1998), 1–78 ["Foi et savoir. Les deux sources de la 'religion' dans les limites de la raison," in *La Religion. Séminaire de Capri sous la direction de Jacques Derrida et Gianni Vattimo* (Paris: Seuil, 1996), 65–69ff.].

37. [Translator's note:] Word in English in typescript.

affinity,[38] and it is this affinity that is referred to as *Das Wort der Versöhnung*: the word of reconciliation would say not only "I forgive," "let's forgive one another," "let's reconcile," "I am ready to be reconciled," but also, for the reconciliation to be effective, to exist, lest the word remain a merely verbal and abstract word, we have both to heal the wounds and also to heal them effectively and radically enough to eradicate them, so that the scars don't even appear, no longer even appear. It is that logic, a very strong, even irrefutable logic moreover, that we will question again and again.

2. As I announced just a moment ago, I wanted, before even beginning, simply to draw attention to two things, two considerations to watch out for, one relating to the wound (which I have just developed), the other taking at its word the word "word," the word *parole* (*das Wort*), which Hegel defines in *The Phenomenology of Spirit* as the element of the universal. No sooner do I speak — if I can present things in this pedagogical way — no sooner do I speak than I abandon the element of singularity or particularity: the concept and the word exceed from the outset every pure singularity. Even when I say "I," the absolute singularity of the "I" is uttered as the most broadly shared element of the universal: each of us knows, every "I" knows what "I" means. "I" means this: the subject of the enunciation designates itself, which each of us can do in saying "I." Words belong structurally to the element of the universal, even when they designate the pure this, or the Now and Here of singularity (cf. the beginning of *The Phenomenology of Spirit*, concerning sense-certainty, etc.). Besides, a little earlier in the chapter we're in, on *Das Gewissen* (*Blackboard*) — "moral consciousness" for Hyppolite, "moral certainty" for Labarrière, "moral conviction" for Lefebvre[39] [however one translates it, and each of these translations is better than the next, one must recall this essential reference to knowledge, *Wissen*, or to knowing [*science*], consciousness [*con-science*]], "the 'beautiful soul,' evil and its forgiveness (*Die schöne Seele, das Böse und seine Verzeihung*)"[40] — Hegel recalls

45

---

38. During the session, Derrida adds: "And everything that is happening today, naturally, as much in what I called the globalization of confession as in the processes of an international law that removes criminal immunity in order to put those criminals on trial, is about just that."

39. Hegel, *Phänomenologie*, 464. [Translator's note:] Derrida's French sources, which give *conscience-morale*, *certitude-morale*, and *conviction morale*, respectively, are: Hegel, *Phénoménologie de l'esprit*, vol. 2, trans. Hyppolite, 168; *Phénoménologie de l'Esprit*, trans. Gwendoline Jarczyk and Pierre-Jean Labarrière (Paris: Gallimard, 1993), 549; *Préface de la Phénoménologie de l'esprit*, trans. Jean-Pierre Lefebvre (Paris: Aubier, 1991), 581. Cf. *Phenomenology*, which has "conscience" for *das Gewissen* in the chapter title (365).

40. Hegel, *Phänomenologie*, 464 [*Phenomenology*, 365; *Phénoménologie*, vol. 2, 168].

that language is the being-there or existence, the *Dasein* of spirit. It is the same formula, literally. Just as he will later say, "*Das Wort der Versöhnung ist der* daseiende *Geist*,"[41] so here, fifteen pages earlier, "*Wir sehen hiermit wieder*

46 *die* Sprache *als das Dasein des Geistes* (We therefore see, we therefore consider *language* again here as the *Dasein* of spirit)."[42]

If, as seems necessary, we put together these two formulas that both define the *Dasein*, the being-there of spirit, first through language, second through reconciliation, then we have to think that the speech act par excellence, inasmuch as it makes spirit *being-there*, inasmuch as it makes spirit be there, is the word of reconciliation. Language in its essence and in its performative essence, in its act, would be reconciliation. To speak would be to begin to reconcile, even if[43] one is going about declaring hate or war or vituperating and insulting, wounding. As soon as one speaks, speaks to another, a process of reconciliation is set in train. On condition, of course, that one speaks to the other. As long as I am speaking, as soon as I speak, even if I am doing harm, speaking evil, even if I am speaking ill or cursing the other, the word addressed already opens reconciliation, it confesses that it is seeking reconciliation. I begin to reconcile with the other as soon as I speak to them, albeit to declare war or confess to hating them.

I'll break off arbitrarily what Hegel's ghost is saying here,[44] for the economy of our production [*mise en scène*], I'll interrupt his voice off, his European, Germano-French voice, since we would have to wonder, concerning this whole history of pardon, to what extent it is Europe-centered, or whether, in the current globalization of confession, in the theater of confession, it affects Europe, deporting, exporting, reporting, repatriating or expatriating it, reappropriating, expropriating or exappropriating it. But there is no doubt that we'll have to let him, that is, Hegel, speak again later.

For the moment the curtain still hasn't risen. Now it does. It is rising. We find ourselves outside Europe but in a culture that is broadly if not exclusively European, and predominantly Christian, in North America and South Africa: Clinton, Mandela, and Desmond Tutu address each other through

47 microphones and cameras. They are together, but communicate only through

---

41. Hegel, *Phänomenologie*, 493 [*Phenomenology*, 388, §670; *Phénoménologie*, vol. 2, 198].

42. Hegel, *Phänomenologie*, 478 [*Phénoménologie*, vol. 2, 184]. [Translator's note:] Cf. *Phenomenology*, 376, §652: "Here again we see *language* as the existence of spirit."

43. During the session, Derrida adds, "And Hegel wasn't unaware of that, far from it: nobody was better than him at thinking evil and negativity and death."

44. During the session, Derrida adds: "Clearly at just the right moment." [*Laughter*]

all these intervening wires [*fils*], films, and filters. As the curtain slowly rises one hears the conclusion of the Hegelian soliloquy:

> *Das Wort der Versöhnung ist der* daseiende *Geist, der das reine Wissen seiner selbst als* allgemeinen *Wesens in seinem Gegenteile, in dem reinen Wissen seiner als der absolut in sich seienden* Einzelnheit *anschaut, — ein gegenseitiges Anerkennen, welches der* absolute *Geist ist.* [The word of reconciliation is spirit *being-there*, the being-there of spirit that sees (or intuits, contemplates, considers: *anschaut*) the pure knowledge of itself as *universal* essence in its opposite, in the pure knowledge of itself as *singularity* that is absolutely in itself — mutual or reciprocal (*gegenseitiges*) recognition (*Anerkennen*), which is *absolute* spirit.][45]

In other words, the word of reconciliation, the reconciliation that starts in a word, with a word, in speech addressed to the other, is the presence or presentation of absolute spirit, inasmuch as it also reconciles two contradictory postulations within the same pure knowledge, universality and singularity. Reconciliation is universality in singularity, the reconciliation of those two opposites: universal essence "*in seinem Gegenteile*," in its opposite; and the reciprocity, the mutuality of this recognition, of the cognition (*Wissen*, *Erkenntnis*) that becomes reciprocal recognition (*Anerkennen*), that's what gives you absolute spirit as it becomes present, there, existing. I can't forgive without postulating reciprocity, whereby the other confesses,[46] repents, asks for forgiveness, or forgives me in turn through a process of specular identification. It is that schema of conditioning reciprocity that we questioned and contested so intently last year. We'll come back to it again.

So you are expected to keep in mind, for what follows in the play, not only each element of these speculative propositions, of speculative idealism itself, of this unity of the heterological and tautological, but especially this schema of reciprocity, of the reciprocity of recognition that we aren't done with, far from it, wherever the subject is forgiveness, repentance, and reconciliation.

If I grant such a status to Hegel and to a certain architectonics or structure of *The Phenomenology of Spirit*, and so to that of the phenomenology of

48

45. Hegel, *Phänomenologie*, 493 [*Phénoménologie*, vol. 2, 198]. [Translator's note:] Cf. *Phenomenology*, 388, §670: "The word of reconciliation is the *existing* spirit which immediately intuits in its opposite the pure knowing of itself as the *universal* essence, intuits it in the pure knowing of itself as *singular individuality* existing absolutely inwardly — a reciprocal recognition which is *absolute* Spirit."

46. During the session, Derrida adds: "We worked on this motif a lot last year." See *Perjury and Pardon*, vol. 1, 10–11, 44–45, 103–4 [*Parjure et pardon*, vol. 1, 37, 78, 148].

reconciliation, it is with a hypothesis or suspicion in mind, one that would concern, let's say, some configural affinity: between, on the one hand, the current globalizing of confession, the Christianizing *globalatinization* of this process, and, <on the other hand,> the figure (a figure beyond every figure) of absolute knowing, which, as you know, comes in *The Phenomenology of Spirit*, or of reconciliation, to fulfill philosophy as truth of religion, that is to say, of revealed religion, *"die offenbare Religion,"*[47] which is the Christian religion, Good Friday before the speculative Good Friday, the final phase and truth of religion via its two preceding moments, *"die natürliche Religion"*[48] and *"die Kunst-Religion."*[49]

I won't say that reconciliation in and of itself is a Christian or essentially Christian motif. That would be false and absurd. The theme of reconciliation is also a Jewish theme, for example, as I'll come to in a moment. But one can't ignore a certain insistence on reconciliation, a certain centrality of the moment of reconciliation, in the process of fault and forgiveness, a certain specificity in the reconciling mission of the Messiah, in the figure of Jesus as reconciler of God with man, or of man with man. In so many Christian texts "reconciliation" is almost always the word that designates the return of the sinner or heretic to authentic faith. That is true of Christianity in general, of Lutherism in particular (and one can't read Hegel without remembering that he is Lutheran and that in *explicit, philosophical* terms he grants Protestantism a prominent philosophical role). But because, without going back one more time over the globalization of confession and all the scenes of repentance that are multiplying throughout the world, we are getting ready to raise the curtain on a South African landscape, we need to be reminded that Afrikaners, who played the role you are aware of in instituting apartheid, then accepted, or asked, at the end of the period of apartheid — we'll talk about this — to begin a process of amnesty and reconciliation, Afrikaners are above all fervent and strict Calvinists of Dutch origin. Now Calvin made reconciliation in the body of Christ, and through the death of Christ, a major theme of his thinking, and of the four-volume work entitled *Institutes of the Christian Religion* (1536/1744):[50] "if [we seek]

49

---

47. Hegel, *Phänomenologie*, 545–74 [*Phenomenology*, 430–53; *Phénoménologie*, vol. 2, 258–90].

48. Hegel, *Phänomenologie*, 503–12 [*Phenomenology*, 396–403 ("Natural Religion"); *Phénoménologie*, vol. 2, 212–22].

49. Hegel, *Phänomenologie*, 512–44 [*Phenomenology*, 403–30 ("The Art-Religion"); *Phénoménologie*, vol. 2, 223–57].

50. First published in Latin in 1536 with the title *Institutio Christianae Religionis*, the book was translated into French and published in four volumes in 1561. The date

reconciliation," he says, for example, "[it lies] in his descent into hell" (p. 405);[51] or again: "we were reconciled [to God] through Christ's death" (p. 388).[52] More interesting and unusual still, it even happens that Calvin dissociated, in exceptional cases, repentance and reconciliation, as when the *time* of repentance wasn't given, when repentance was preempted by death — presented by him as an exceptional case — but that leads us to think that, if every death is premature and if finitude or mortality always interrupts a repentance that should by right be infinite (I would never finish repenting, and that can also explain my desire for eternity, commensurable with my faults, my sins, my debts, or my deceits: "My God, let me live eternally so that I can repent as I ought, and for that I need infinite time" — you can imagine the scene, one of sincerity or hypocritical cunning — the strategy of a dying person who would make the priest wait and make the moment of confession last endlessly in order to put off the deadline, the permission to die following communion, the sacraments, or absolution; I believe in the profound truth of such a scene, but we'll leave it at that), so then, if reconciliation is no longer conditional upon an exhaustive repentance, well, between promised reconciliation, or even promised forgiveness and accomplished, fulfilled repentance, hence repentance itself, there is no longer an essential link; repentance would no longer be, in fact if not in principle, the absolute condition of forgiveness and reconciliation. That would have far-reaching consequences. Calvin writes: "Let those who in time of penance depart from this life be admitted to communion without reconciliatory laying on of hands" (P. 1171).[53]

50

End of the prologue, then, and of the voice off. We are in the theater of theory and politics. And of religion. And we are going to proceed as if we were opening the first sitting of a new commission, the "Perjury and

1744, noted here by Derrida, refers to *Lettres de Calvin à Jaques de Bourgogne, sieur de Falais en Brabant* (Amsterdam, 1744). Derrida quotes Calvin from Émile Littré, *Dictionnaire de langue française* (Paris: Librairie Hachette et Cie, 1877), particularly vol. 4, entries for *réconciliatoire*, 1516, and *réconcilier*, 1517 (references, 2623). See John Calvin, *Institutes of the Christian Religion*, trans. Ford Lewis Battles, vol. 1 (Louisville: Westminster Press, 2006) [*Institution de la religion chrestienne* (Geneva: Imprimerie Jacques Bourgeois, 1561)].

51. Calvin, *Institutes*, vol. 1, 527–28 [*Institution*, 405].

52. Calvin, *Institutes*, vol. 1, 506 [*Institution*, 388]. [Translator's note:] Calvin is here quoting Augustine.

53. Calvin, *Institutes of the Christian Religion*, trans. Ford Lewis Battles, vol. 2 (Louisville: Westminster Press, 2006), 1462 [*Institution*, 1171]. [Translator's note:] Calvin is here quoting the Council of Orange.

Pardon" Commission, in tribute to the South African Truth and Reconciliation Commission (abbreviated to TRC). And so in our commission, whose proceedings are archived, filmed, even televised, like those of the TRC, we would summon today at least these four Christian witnesses, these four metonymic or pseudonymous informants [*indicateurs*]: the figures of Hegel, Mandela, Clinton, and Tutu.

[54][It is by means of what I am staging here that I try at the beginning of each seminar, each year, or each week, more or less clumsily, as you will have understood, to resolve the recurring problem: how to recommence, how to begin while continuing? How to go backward while beginning and going forward? How can a turning-back toward the past, *over* the past, move things forward? (And to go back *over* the past is not simply to go back *toward* the past or go back *to* the past. It isn't simply an act of memory, even when it is commanded by what is so facilely called today a duty to remember. It is also a change of direction, already a conversion. To go back *over* the past is to bring about a movement of turning back that transforms or transmutes the perspective or interpretation, and which, by means of regret, remorse, or repentance, lights a path that could have, that should have been otherwise, and therefore calls for a new way or a recommencement. The great Judaic tradition of the Return (*teshuvah* [*Blackboard*], return as repentance, transformation through repentance and request for forgiveness, etc.) combines those two movements, going back *toward* and going back *over*, recalling and recommencing.)[55] We'll study that tradition, notably on the basis of texts by Hermann Cohen (*L'Éthique du judaïsme* [Paris: Cerf, 1994]; you should read in particular the two chapters on "The Concept of Reconciliation" and "The Day of Atonement"). Cohen makes special reference to the famous eighteenth chapter of Ezekiel, which treats of responsibility, of a collective responsibility, either transgenerational or not, and ends with an appeal to repentance, to *teshuvah*, to return as "going back over [*revenir sur*]." He recalls that "the Hebrew term for repentance, *teshuvah*, means "turning"—a turning from evil, a re-turning to the good, or a turning inward, into oneself" (136).[56] Associating forgiveness with the motif of purification,

54. The bracket that opens here is closed several pages further on (26). During the session, Derrida announces: "An aside, once more." Elements of this section were published in "Avowing the Impossible," *Living Together*, 36–37 [*Comment vivre ensemble?* 202–10].

55. We close here the parenthesis opened eleven lines above.

56. Cohen, *Reason and Hope: Selections from the Jewish Writings of Hermann Cohen*, trans. Eva Jospe (New York: W. W. Norton, 1971), 206 [Cohen, *Éthique du judaïsme*,

Cohen declares that "reconciliation . . . is the express purpose of all teaching [of the Torah]."[57] He quotes Ibn Ezra and Maimonides: "The world rests on three things: Torah, the worship of God—which means repentance—and loving deeds (good deeds)."[58] And in "The Day of Atonement" he goes as far as to say that "without my own moral effort and repentance even God cannot redeem me" (148).[59] Since Cohen quotes Maimonides, he could have recalled that, for the latter, *teshuvah*, repentance, also means, as return, the end of exile.

52

I refer you also to Leo Baeck, who affirms in *The Essence of Judaism* (1922, [French] translation 1993) that "the true meaning of the idea of atonement in Judaism is that the life of man can begin again" (255),[60] and that "in the Messianic doctrine the idea of atonement finds its completion."[61] (Of course, we will ask ourselves whether forgiveness must presuppose repentance and a request for forgiveness, as we did last year[62] and <as I> recalled just now, but also what "messianic certainty" means, whether messianicity is compatible with certainty.)

But I refer you also to the text by Levinas on forgiveness in "Four Talmudic Readings" ("Toward the Other: From the Tractate 'Yoma,' pp. 85b–87a–b"). Levinas there speaks of *teshuvah* also, "healing of the self by the self": "the effort the moral conscience makes to reestablish itself as moral conscience, *teshuvah*, or Return, is simultaneously the relation with God and an absolutely internal event."[63] In that very complex text, which I would like

---

trans. Maurice-Ruben Hayoun (Paris: Éditions du Cerf, 1994), *136*]. [Translator's note:] For the reference to Ezekiel, see *Reason and Hope*, 201.

57. Cohen, *Reason and Hope*, 209 [*Éthique du judaïsme*, 142].

58. Cohen, *Reason and Hope*, 209 [*Éthique du judaïsme*, 142], Cohen's parenthesis. [Translator's note:] The parenthesis does not appear in the English translation.

59. *Reason and Hope*, 212 [*Éthique du judaïsme*, 148]. During the session, Derrida adds: "Well, there we have the opposite of what Calvin says. It isn't possible to dissociate forgiveness or reconciliation, on the one hand, from repentance, on the other. Even God, God himself would not be able to forgive me if I didn't repent. That is very radical: God himself is powerless to forgive someone who doesn't present himself to God as blameworthy, that is to say, who doesn't repent."

60. Leo Baeck, *The Essence of Judaism*, trans. Victor Grubwieser and Leonard Pearl (London: Macmillan and Company, 1936), 187 [*L'Essence du judaïsme*, trans. Maurice-Ruben Hayoun (Paris: PUF, 1993), 255].

61. *Essence of Judaism*, 260. [*L'Essence du judaïsme*, 336].

62. See *Perjury and Pardon*, vol. 1, 27, 27n44, 34ff., 45 [*Parjure et pardon*, vol. 1, 57 and 57n2, 66ff., 78].

63. Emmanuel Levinas, "Toward the Other: From the Tractate 'Yoma,' pp. 85a–85b," in *Nine Talmudic Readings*, trans. Annette Aronowicz (Bloomington: Indiana

to follow closely one day,[64] Levinas mentions in passing, and too quickly, the complication that the unconscious can introduce into this problematic; but he mentions also too quickly, in my view, an opinion preserved in the Gemara, that of Rabbi Judah Hanassi, who speaks of a pardon—during Yom Kippur—or a purification without *teshuvah*[65] (without repentance) (p. 24. Calvin?).[66]

53   At that outside limit, at the improbable limit of the im-possible (forgiveness without repentance, or even without reconciliation), I would also situate a certain unpublished—I mean posthumous—text by the Benjamin of the 1920s (two brief pages written in 1921),[67] which goes so far as to evoke a process of forgiveness without reconciliation. And you know (some of you know) that, since last year, it is this im-possible possibility of dissociating forgiveness from confession, from repentance, but also from reconciliation—*within, inside*, but also *against* the dominant tradition of forgiveness—it is the possibility of this dissociation that has been captivating us. Now the Benjamin of this text (which for the moment I have in English

University Press, 1990), 17 ["Texte du traité 'Yoma' (85a–85b)," *Quatre lectures talmudiques* (Paris: Éditions de Minuit, 1968), 38].

64. See Derrida, "Avowing—the Impossible: 'Returns,' Repentance, and Reconciliation: A Lesson," in Elisabeth Weber, ed., *Living Together: Jacques Derrida's Communities of Violence and Peace* (New York: Fordham University Press, 2013), 36–37 [*Comment vivre ensemble*, 209–10].

65. Levinas, *Nine Talmudic Readings*, 17 [*Quatre lectures talmudiques*, 39].

66. During the session, Derrida adds: "An idea somewhat analogous, *mutatis mutandis*, to Calvin's. He speaks of a forgiveness without *teshuvah* and hence without repentance. It is alluded to and cited by Levinas, as if there were nothing to it, on p. 24, whereas, naturally, that statement is to my mind absolutely explosive."

67. In the margin of the typescript Derrida writes: "Find English text!" Photocopies inserted in the typescript are from Walter Benjamin, "The Meaning of Time in the Moral Universe," trans. Rodney Livingstone, *Selected Writings*, vol. 1 (1913–26), ed. Marcus Bullock and Michael W. Jennings (Cambridge, MA: Harvard University Press, 1996), 286–87. The editors note: "Fragment written in 1921; unpublished in Benjamin's lifetime." The reference to Atē and to the *Iliad* (19.87ff.) is explained in a note. Derrida inserts a photocopy of Benjamin's text in German, "Die Bedeutung der Zeit in der Moralischen Welt," *Gesammelte Schriften*, vol. 6, ed. Rolf Tiedemann and Hermann Schweppenhäuser (Frankfurt: Suhrkamp Verlag, 1991), 97–98; cf. "La signification du temps dans le monde moral," *Fragments philosophiques, politiques, critiques, littéraires*, 107–9.

translation only, and I thank Patricia Dailey[68] for pointing it out to me), the Benjamin of this text dares to dissociate, in a sentence left hanging at the end of his text, forgiveness and reconciliation. I'll sum up the argument that leads to that conclusion: Benjamin sets human law, which obeys the logic of retribution, in opposition to divine law and the profound logic of the Last Judgment. The significance of the Last Judgment does not pertain to the world of human law as law of retribution but only to what he calls the "moral universe," where forgiveness alone permits a reaching beyond the logic or economy of retribution. Referring to the *Iliad* and to the story of Atē, daughter of Zeus, who pursues the evildoer through time, Benjamin maintains that time does not, then, signify waiting and delay in the perspective of retribution, of punishment, sometimes from one generation to the next. Time conceived on the basis of the possibility of the Last Judgment signifies another time, the time [*temps*] of the storm [*tempête*] of forgiveness, the tempestuous and untimely storm of forgiveness. This figure of the storm signifies bursting without forewarning, it is a sort of raging violence that interrupts the calm of fine weather [*du beau temps*]. But it is still time, this bad weather, it is tempest and inclement weather [*intempérie*]. And the time of the Last Judgment signifies this time, this tempestuous precipitation of time, but it is another experience of time that does not wait for the calculation of retribution. And so puts an end to time within time. On several occasions Benjamin insists on this figure of the storm and thunder and lightning to speak of forgiveness. As always, when he speaks of divine justice,[69] he invokes a certain violence, and forgiveness is also, in this respect, understood as interruption of the human law of retribution, a form of violence. You are going to hear that; I am translating from his conclusion in the English version:

54

68. Patricia Dailey, a professor of English and comparative literature at Columbia University, was at the time a doctoral student at the University of California, Irvine.

69. During the session, Derrida specifies: "This is also found in his text 'Critique of Violence,' which we talked about a lot in this seminar; it is a text that is very contemporaneous to this one." See Benjamin, "Zur Kritik der Gewalt" [1921], in *Gesammelte Schriften*, vol. 2.1, ed. R. Tiedemann et H. Schweppenhäuser (Frankfurt: Suhrkamp Verlag, 1977), 179–303; "Critique of Violence," in *Selected Writings*, vol. 1 (1913–26), 236–52. On this text by Benjamin, see Derrida, unpublished seminar, "Politiques de l'amitié," EHESS, 1988–89, sessions 9–12; and Derrida, "Force of Law: 'The Mystical Foundation of Authority,'" in Drucilla Cornell, Michael Rosenfeld, and David Gray Carlson, eds., *Deconstruction and the Possibility of Justice* (New York: Routledge, 1992), 3–67 [*Force de loi: Le "fondement" mystique de l'autorité* (Paris: Galilée, 1994)].

As a purifying hurricane [comment on the motif of purification, recall Cohen] accelerates through thunder and lightning, God's anger growls through history in the storm of forgiveness,[70] in order to sweep away [or carry off] everything that would be consumed [burned] forever in the lightning or thunderclaps of divine anger [forgiveness is divine wrath, God getting carried away, God flies into a rage, off the handle, etc.[71] Comment.]

55   Benjamin continues:

What we have expressed here figuratively must be able to be formulated clearly and distinctly in a conceptual form: the significance of time in the economy of the moral world. In it, time doesn't only erase the traces of all misdeeds but also—because of its duration, beyond every memory and all forgetting—contributes, in totally mysterious ways, to completing the process of forgiveness, but never of reconciliation.[72] [Comment: erasure of traces, and of scars: still Hegelian? spiritualist? dialectical? while seeming to be radically Jewish and irreducible to Christian dialectics?][73]

Speaking of these bibliographical references, concerning all these questions around *teshuvah* and *tikkun*, which signifies "amends," I also invite you to read the various texts that have just been collected and published by Annick Charles-Saget, in a collective volume entitled *Retour, repentir et constitution de soi*, which is just out (Vrin, 1998). This valuable collective work helps reconstitute a whole trajectory going from *teshuvah* and more generally from a Judaic to a Christian tradition of repentance, conversion and

---

70. During the session, Derrida quotes the text in German and glosses, thus: "*so braust Gottes Zorn im Sturm der Vergebung [Vergebung* isn't *Verzeihung*, forgiveness, it is *Vergebung* and not *Verzeihung* here] *durch die Geschichte.*"

71. [Translator's note:] Cf. Benjamin, "The Meaning of Time," 287: "As the purifying hurricane speeds ahead of the thunder and lightning, God's fury roars through history in the storm of forgiveness, in order to sweep away everything that would be consumed forever in the lightning bolts of divine wrath."

72. [Translator's note:] Cf. Benjamin, "The Meaning of Time," 287: "What we have expressed here metaphorically must be capable of being formulated clearly and distinctly in conceptual form: the meaning of time in the economy of the moral universe. In this, time not only extinguishes the traces of all misdeeds but also—by virtue of its duration, beyond all remembering or forgetting—helps, in ways that are wholly mysterious, to complete the process of forgiveness, though never of reconciliation."

73. During the session, Derrida comments: "Well, erasure of traces and of scars, that still resembles Hegel's text. Is this a spiritualist, dialectician Benjamin here, whereas his text, moreover to all appearances radically Jewish, is irreducible to Hegelian or Christian dialectics? So be it, that is the question that Benjamin pursues well beyond this passage, which I leave here."

metanoia. The first of those articles is "Retour et repentir dans l'Israël an-cien," by Hedwige Rouillard-Bonraisin (a name that recalls Ezekiel 18, precisely the chapter I referred to just before, which begins with these fa-mous words: "The fathers have eaten sour grapes [*du raisin vert*] / and the children's teeth are set on edge [*les dents du fils en ont été émoussées — ou en ont crissé*]").[74] This article by Hedwige Rouillard-Bonraisin goes back to the radical *shuv*, whose proper, physical sense is "to return, recommence."[75] The analysis follows a complicated path through the prophets, the Hellenistic period, the Pharisees, the Essenes, and the whole debate around the ques-tion of knowing whether *metanoia*, the Greek word for "conversion" in the Septuagint, is or is not a concept distinct from *teshuvah*.[76] I'll let you read this text, and all the others in this fine volume, which we'll delve into, no doubt.

As I was saying, then, continuing by recommencing, commencing by recommencing, recommencing without repeating, has been one of the dif-ficulties I encounter when picking up the seminar again each year. Some of you gathered here know the premises or the previous history of this semi-nar and hear those opening sentences with a certain memory — unevenly shared, moreover — of the past, but there are also those for whom this is the first session or the first word of a seminar that has lasted, under the title "Questions of Responsibility," for nearly ten years and, under the title "Per-jury and Pardon," for more than a year.

How to recommence and speak to everyone at the same time?

Take note that this sentence, the formulation of this question — "how to recommence and speak to everyone, how to speak singularly and univer-sally at the same time?"; remember Hegel's text that we were listening to a moment ago — comes across as (we'll see how it works, we'll confirm that) a rather good formulation of the question of pardon and perjury. Not only be-cause it concerns a certain relation to the past (what to do with the past? and how to recommence? recommence in the sense that, preserving the memory

74. During the session, participants propose a different translation: *agacées* ["irri-tated"]. Derrida responds: "*agacées* is just a current translation, but those I've quoted [Dhorme], I didn't invent it, it's *émoussées* or *crissé*. As for Chouraqui . . . let's not argue. No, it's precisely in Ezekiel 18, there is this famous saying: "The fathers have eaten sour grapes / and the children's teeth are . . ."" [*Laughter*] That's the question, then, of guilt, of transgenerational responsibility, you see, that gets figured as grapes [*qu'on figure par du raisin*]."

75. Hedwige Rouillard-Bonraisin, "Retour et repentir dans l'Israël ancien," in An-nick Charles-Saget, ed., *Retour, repentir et constitution de soi* (Paris: Librairie philos-ophique J. Vrin, 1998), 40.

76. Rouillard-Bonraisin, "Retour et repentir dans l'Israël ancien," 48–49.

57   of the past, for example, of past wrongs, it is a matter of recommencing, for example, following repentance, forgiveness, reconciliation, redemption), but also in the sense that forgiveness, whether requested or granted, must also each time be the singularity of a new beginning as recommencement. What's more, the question "how to address several, more than one singularity?" could figure the cross of forgiveness.][77]

Enter Nelson Mandela. Freed following approximately three decades of harsh incarceration, returning from Robben Island prison without resentment, without any apparent desire for vengeance and punishment, see him come on stage here to recall how the preamble to the Constitution of a new South Africa—for which he struggled so hard, with so many others, blacks and whites—begins, from its very first words, in a gesture of confession, repentance, and reconciliation, with what one might call a "word of reconciliation."[78] It is an extremely modern, democratic Constitution, one written by very experienced and expert jurists, incorporating all the gains of the constitutional law of this century's democracies—we'll come to that.[79] Well, something that is to my knowledge without equal in the history of humanity, this modern, democratic Constitution begins with an act of repentance and an appeal to *cure*[80] through reconciliation. With a word of reconciliation. The "we" with which it opens posits itself as a subject that recognizes past injustice and the need for repentance. So Mandela, on stage, recalls the very first words of his Constitution, its very preamble, and they are "words of reconciliation," and these words of reconciliation are, as in every constitution, performative commitments, pledges, sworn oaths that prohibit perjury. The preamble of this Constitution, as you will hear, "recognise[s] the injustices of [the] past" and calls for "heal[ing] the divisions of the past" (read and translate):

58   We, the people of South Africa,
    Recognise the injustices of our past;
    Honour those who suffered for justice and freedom in our land;
    Respect those who have worked to build and develop our country; and

---

77. The bracket opened at note 53, above, closes here.

78. This part of the session was published by Derrida, with modifications and additions, in "Versöhnung, ubuntu, pardon: quel genre?" *Le Genre humain*, 113–17; *La Solidarité des vivants*, 61–69.

79. See 43ff. below.

80. [Translator's note:] Derrida's word is *cure*, a psychoanalytic term usually translated as "treatment," but Derrida has italicized it, suggesting the English sense that relates more closely to "healing" in the Constitution.

Believe that South Africa belongs to all who live in it, united in our diversity.
We therefore, through our freely elected representatives, adopt this Consti-
tution as the supreme law of the Republic so as to
Heal the divisions of the past and establish a society based on democratic
values, social justice and fundamental human rights.
. . .
May God protect our people.[81]

I underline the last sentence for at least *two reasons*.

On the one hand, not all modern democracies mention God; and official
political speeches by democratic heads of state do so—name or invoke
God—only in very specific countries, I don't know how many, but those
places mark a very significant difference: between,[82] for example, a secular
democracy such as France, where God is not named in the Constitution
and where it is out of the question for politicians, especially the head of
state, even if they are personally religious (that is to say Catholic—I don't
think that there has ever been in France a head of state who was by origin
non-Catholic, before or after the Revolution), where it is out of the question, then, for politicians, especially the head of state, to ever allow themselves in this century to mention God in an official speech. It is completely
different in the United States, for example, where the president takes the
oath with hand on the Bible, and invokes God in every solemn official statement. That explains—but we'll come back to this—why perjury in general, and the perjury of a president in the exercise of his duties and in a
scene of witnessing under oath, takes on such gravity and sensitivity, but
also can be exploited, in the United States. Well, postapartheid South Africa is of the "United States type" from that point of view, assuming in that
way—among others, or especially—the Christian, Protestant, Anglican,
and particularly Calvinist heritage of the Afrikaners. And, *on the other
hand*—and this will therefore be of considerable importance for the problems that we'll speak of, and it has roots that go deep into the culture or
cultures of this nation-state—that is all the more remarkable in that "May
God protect our people" is immediately translated, in the lines that follow,
into three other languages, two African languages that I'll say more about

59

81. See "Preamble," Constitution of the Republic of South Africa, May 8, 1996:
https://www.gov.za/documents/constitution-republic-south-africa-1996-preamble,
Derrida's emphasis. During the session, Derrida translates, and notes, following the
words "united in our diversity": "You can hear the echo of many other constitutions,
improved, refined—the American example is very present."
82. Syntax thus in typescript.

in a moment, and Afrikaans, a language in its own right derived from Dutch, but whose idiom, to which the Afrikaners remain very attached, and which was stabilized some centuries ago, was lexically and grammatically formalized only during the nineteenth <century> if I'm not mistaken.

This remarkable Constitution recognizes—also something without precedent as far as I know—eleven official languages, and it does so starting from the "Founding Provisions"[83] of the Constitution: "The official languages of the Republic are Sepedi, Sesotho, Setswana, siSwati, Tshivenda, Xitsonga, Afrikaans, English, isiNdebele, isiXhosa, and isiZulu."[84]

Following that formulation of the official status of the eleven languages, the Constitution includes another act of repentance, for immediately after that one reads: "Recognising the historically diminished use and status of the indigenous languages of our people, the state must take practical and positive measures to elevate the status and advance the use of these languages."[85]

Much might be said about the official status given to eleven languages within one and the same nation-state, about what is happening in fact, namely, the growing dominance of the use of the English language, in education, in the press, etc. All that is known and easy to imagine. For the moment, then, I will insist only on what preoccupies us most, namely "forgiveness," and the language of "forgiveness," the semantics of forgiveness and of reconciliation.

What, then, could Mandela say to us in that regard, once he appears on stage, *in English*? First of all, that he, who was born in the Transkei, received his English name only once he went to school; that he, who was the son of a chief of the royal house of the Thembu tribe, married to four wives, a counselor to kings and a kingmaker (I'm speaking of his father: he, Nelson, who has just remarried at the age of eighty, has had three wives, but one after the other); he who, then, as he recalls in his memoir, *Long Walk to Freedom*,[86] was the son of a man with four wives, one of whom was the

83. [Translator's note:] These two words in English in the typescript, translated by Derrida during the session.

84. "Founding Provisions," Constitution of the Republic of South Africa: https://www.gov.za/documents/constitution/chapter-1-founding-provisions.

85. "Founding Provisions," Constitution of the Republic of South Africa. During the session, Derrida comments: "So, remorse for the suffering of these languages, the repression of these legitimate languages, and commitment to repair that evil by developing the usage, status, that is to say the dignity and usage of these languages."

86. Nelson Mandela, *Long Walk to Freedom: The Autobiography of Nelson Mandela* (Boston: Little, Brown, 1994). A new edition appeared in 1995 with a preface by President Bill Clinton, published in French as Nelson Mandela, *Un long chemin vers la liberté. Autobiographie*, trans. Jean Guiloineau (Paris: Fayard, 1995). The typescript includes

mother of Rolihlala, later given the name Nelson (Rolihlala means "one who shakes the branches of a tree," which in colloquial usage means "spoil-sport," "troublemaker"[87]); he, then, whose mother became a Christian under the influence of friends of his father, two amaMfengu, from the ama-Mfengu tribe, the most advanced group of the community and the first to convert to Christianity; he who, as he recalls, I'll let him speak: "It was due to their influence that I myself was baptized into the Methodist [or Wes- 61 leyan] Church and sent to school. . . . On the first day of school, my teacher, Miss Mdingane, gave each of us an English name . . . [and] told me that my new name was Nelson. Why this particular name I have no idea."[88]

Now, Nelson would then say from the stage, I am going to tell you about my circumcision. (Read and translate pp. 15–16 NM, then NM (2), p. 14).

Chief Joyi said that the African people lived in relative peace until the coming of the *abelungu*, the white people, who arrived from across the sea with fire-breathing weapons. Once, he said, the Thembu, the Pondo, the Xhosa, and the Zulu were all children of one father, and lived as brothers. The white man shattered the *abantu*, the fellowship [companionship, brotherhood, the fact of "all living as brothers"], of the various tribes. The white man was hungry and greedy for land, and the black man shared the land with him as they shared the air and water; land was not for man to possess. But the white man took the land as you might seize another man's horse.

When I was sixteen, the regent decided that it was time that I became a man. In Xhosa tradition, this is achieved through one means only: circumcision. An uncircumcised male cannot be heir to his father's wealth, cannot marry or officiate in tribal rituals. It is not just a surgical procedure, but a lengthy and elaborate ritual in preparation for manhood.

The traditional ceremony of the circumcision school was arranged principally for Justice[89] [Justice is someone's name, the name of his friend of whom he said earlier, and I quote, "Justice was four years older than me and became my first hero after my father. I looked up to him in every way," etc. "he was extroverted, I was introverted; he was lighthearted, I was serious," "things came easily to him; I had to drill myself,"[90] etc. So, Justice was his friend and model and it was for him that the circumcision ceremony 62

---

photocopies of the illustrated and abridged version, *The Illustrated Long Walk to Freedom: The Autobiography of Nelson Mandela* (Boston: Little, Brown, 1996), which is the version he quotes and translates.

87. [Translator's note]: Word in English in typescript.

88. Mandela, *Illustrated Long Walk*, 9.

89. [Translator's note:] Derrida misconstrues the English text here and below, writing that the ceremony was organized principally "by" [*par*], rather than "for" Justice.

90. Mandela, *Illustrated Long Walk*, 11.

was organized.]. The rest of us, twenty-six in all, were there mainly to keep him company. Early in the new year, we journeyed to two grass huts in a secluded valley on the banks of the Mbashe River . . . the traditional place of circumcision for Thembu kings. . . . It was a sacred time; I felt happy and fulfilled taking part in my people's customs and ready to make the transition from boyhood to manhood.

At the end of our seclusion, a great ceremony was held to welcome us as men to society. Our families, friends and local chiefs gathered for speeches, songs and gift-giving.

The main speaker was Chief Meligqili, the son of Dalindyebo. He began by remarking how fine it was that we were continuing a long tradition. Then his tone suddenly changed. 'There sit our sons,' he said, 'the flower of the Xhosa tribe, the pride of our nation. We have just circumcised them in a ritual that promises them manhood, but it is a promise that can never be fulfilled. For we Xhosas, and all black South Africans, are a conquered people [so this promise cannot be attained]. We are slaves in our own country. We are tenants on our own soil. We have no strength, no power, no control over our own destiny in the land of our birth. Among these young men are chiefs who will never rule because we have no power to govern ourselves; soldiers who will never fight for we have no weapons to fight with; scholars who will never teach because we have no place for them to study. The abilities, the intelligence, the promise of these young men will be squandered. . . . These gifts today are naught, for we cannot give them the greatest gift of all, which is freedom and independence.'

Without exactly understanding why, his words began to work on me. He had sown a seed, and though I let that seed lie dormant for a long season, it eventually began to grow.[91]

. . .

63 The night before the circumcision, there was a ceremony with singing and dancing, and we forgot for the moment what lay ahead. At dawn, we were escorted to the river to bathe. Circumcision is a trial of bravery and stoicism; a man must suffer in silence. I felt as if fire was shooting through my veins; the pain was so intense that I buried my chin in my chest. We were looked after by a guardian, who explained the rules we had to follow if we were to enter manhood properly. He painted our naked and shaved bodies from head to foot in white ochre [here <in the book> there is a very fine photograph of this], symbolizing our purity. We were then instructed to bury our foreskins. The traditional reason for this practice was so that they could be hidden before wizards could use them for evil purposes, but, symbolically, we were also burying our youth. We lived in our two huts while our wounds healed. Outside, we were covered in blankets, for we

91. Mandela, *Illustrated Long Walk*, 15–16 [*Un long chemin vers la liberté*, 32–35].

were not allowed to be seen by women. It was a period of quietude, a kind of spiritual preparation for the trials of manhood that lay ahead.[92]

You have heard the word *abantu* (fellowship: brotherhood [*confrérie*], community); I would like to speak to you of the word *ubuntu*. It is the word used in the official discourse, at the end of apartheid, to translate the very mission of the Reconciliation and Truth Commission,[93] to translate "reconciliation" itself. Now, among the criticisms of this commission, presided over by the Anglican Bishop Desmond Tutu[94]—who did more than a little to Christianize its language, even its spirit and axiomatics—was that it took for granted the translation of African idioms (and those are not only questions of language, but of all the cultural and symbolic genealogies that fashion words). He was reproached, then, for translating the eleven African idioms into a single, dominant Anglo-Christian one.

For example, Mandela could say, in 1990, following his liberation, and the legalization of the ANC (African National Congress), when South Africans negotiated a Provisional Constitution in order to lead the country to its first democratic elections, it was first decided to extend immunity—amnesty, that is—to members of the ANC in exile, so as to allow them to participate in the negotiations. Those negotiations were often painful, in particular because they began bringing victims face to face with perpetrators.[95] And the two parties decided on an amnesty clause, which made the first elections possible.

64

92. Mandela, *Illustrated Long Walk*, 14 [*Un long chemin vers la liberté*, 35–36].
93. Thus in typescript.
94. Desmond Mpilo Tutu (b. 1931), Anglican archbishop of South Africa and campaigner against apartheid. Winner of the 1984 Nobel Peace Prize, he was president of the Truth and Reconciliation Commission from 1995 to 1998. In 1999 he published *No Future without Forgiveness: A Personal Overview of South Africa's Truth and Reconciliation Commission by Desmond Tutu* (New York: Random House, 1999) [*Il n'y a pas d'avenir sans pardon. Comment se réconcilier après l'apartheid?* trans. Alain Deschamps and Josiane Deschamps (Paris: Albin Michel, 2000)]. Derrida's dossier for *Perjury and Pardon* housed at the IMEC (Fonds Jacques Derrida, 219 DRR 240.1) contains an interview with Desmond Tutu by Frank Ferrari, entitled "Pas d'amnistie sans vérité. Entretien avec l'archevêque Desmond Tutu," translated by Christophe Reffait, which was published in the journal *Esprit* (12 [1997]: 63–72) [Frank Ferrari, "Forgiving the Unforgivable," *Commonweal* 124, no. 15 (1997): 13–18]. The interview is extensively annotated; see Derrida's commentary in the Second Session, below.
95. Derrida is here using the term from the "Publisher's Note" in Antjie Krog, *Country of My Skull: Guilt, Sorrow, and the Limits of Forgiveness in the New South Africa* (Johannesburg: Random House, 1998), vi [cf. *La douleur des mots*, trans. Georges Lory

To end, I'll read and translate the terms of that clause, in which you'll see the word *ubuntu* appear.[96] (Read-translate "Publisher's Note" from *Country of My Skull*, p. vi)

65   Busy with South Africa's future, they knew they had no choice but to deal with the country's past. They did so directly in the final clause of the Constitution. This clause, which stated that amnesty would be given, made the elections possible. It read:

> The adoption of this Constitution lays the secure foundation for the people of South Africa to transcend the divisions and strife of the past, which generated gross violations of human rights, the transgression of humanitarian principles in violent conflicts and a legacy of hatred, fear, guilt and revenge. These can now be addressed on the basis that there is a need for understanding but not for vengeance, a need for reparation but not for retaliation [and not vengeance, "a need for reparation but not for retaliation," not vengeance, not revenge], a need for ubuntu [the African philosophy of humanism][97] but not for victimization.
>
> In order to advance such reconciliation and reconstruction, amnesty shall be granted in respect of acts, omissions and offences associated with political objectives [that is the fundamental ambiguity of this Constitution, we'll talk more about that. Of course, this commission is not going to deal with common law crimes, but only "political" crimes, torture carried out, crimes against humanity.].[98]

(Arles: Actes Sud, 2004), in which the "Publisher's Note" is replaced by a "Preface" by Georges Lory, (9–13)]. Because Krog's book was not yet available in French translation in 1998, Derrida translated this and subsequent passages. During the session, Derrida comments on the word "perpetrator": "*perpétrer*, 'perpetrators,' and we'll come back to that, this story of perpetrators." [Translator's note:] References are to the paperback edition of *Country of My Skull* (New York: Three Rivers Press, 1999). The reference to "perpetrators" is in the Introduction by Charlayne Hunter-Gault, vi.

96. During the session, Derrida adds: "Which is a problematic translation precisely for all of that: forgiveness, reconciliation, the whole Christian conceptual framework. I am translating that from a text—which I also recommend you read—that I discovered during my trip to South Africa, a book by a South African poet called Antjie Krog, who is a great poet of Afrikaner origin, who agreed to chronicle the sessions of the commission, to provide a press and radio commentary, and who was shattered by all that she heard, by everything that she saw. She wrote about it in this book you must read, *Country of My Skull*, I recommend that you read it. So, at the beginning of this book, *Country of My Skull*, we have the text of this clause that I just spoke of, which includes the word *ubuntu*. I'll read this passage and we'll stop there."

97. This bracket appears in the text.

98. "Introduction," *Country of My Skull*, vi. The end of the audio-recording to which we had access is missing.

December 9, 1998

[1]In theater, as elsewhere, one mustn't enter by the wrong door, whether it be open or closed. Actors have to know that. There are always various exits, various doors, various ends, and they sometimes look so much alike that one can mistake them.

In theater. At the theater, the question of theater. Of theater in the theater. As a political question. "The play's the thing" is also a political question and a ruse designed to elicit a confession concerning the murder of a king or father.[2]

Is there an unconscious theater? And a theater of the unconscious? This old canonical question overlaps with that concerning confession, forgiveness, and repentance. We were wondering last time whether forgiveness, confession, repentance, etc., had to appear as such, present themselves, phenomenalize themselves or not, in other words, whether they do or do not belong to the possibility of the scene, or even of staging, or whether on the contrary they necessarily exclude the scene.[3]

---

1. In the typescript Derrida inserts a handwritten sentence between the session title and the first paragraph: "I am free," echoing the quotation from the autobiography of Nelson Mandela, "I am born free" (*Illustrated Long Walk*, 202 [*Un long chemin vers la liberté*, 644]), to which Derrida returns at the end of this session (see 61–63 below).

2. Cf. Shakespeare, *Hamlet* II.ii. See especially 155, 161ff. below, and *Perjury and Pardon*, vol. 1, 96, 120–26 [*Parjure et pardon*, vol. 1, 139–40, 166–73]. Derrida's French source is *Hamlet, Le Roi Lear*, trans. Yves Bonnefoy (Paris: Gallimard, 1978), 101.

3. See 1 above. Derrida makes this marginal handwritten addition to his typescript: "'Scene' connotes here not only visibility, the theatrical institution, but also dramaturgy, ritualization, the scene of confession, all of that." During the session, he adds: "I say 'scene' here in a very open sense. 'Scene' connotes here not only phenomenal visibility, the theatrical institution, but also all theaters, dramaturgy in general, and ritualization, that is to say, the scene of ritual confession, the scene of confession as it is staged

68   That is another way of asking whether one can imagine a confession, repentance, forgiveness that is unconscious. From the point of view of common sense and of the tradition, the response is no, clearly. From the point of view of the logic that we are attempting here, it would be almost exactly the opposite: given that they pass into consciousness and especially into language conscious of itself, confession, repentance, and forgiveness get involved in processes of identification and toward ends of reappropriation, through calculations that corrupt them. They end with language and consciousness even though they are said to begin there.[4] They should therefore not ever appear as such. If they appear as such, they disappear as such, and so every confession does the opposite of what it says, it lies not because it says this or that but quite simply because it avows, and, in avowing, it disavows. It perjures itself in avowing. In any case, between avowal [*aveu*] and disavowal, or rather between confession and the denial of confession, there would be a terribly permeable frontier.

Confession [*aveu*][5] and forgiveness should always remain outside the phenomenological field of consciousness. And that would be an objection on principle to a phenomenology of the Hegelian or post-Hegelian type, and no doubt to every philosophy of consciousness and intentionality, which nevertheless govern the very sense of confession and of forgiveness. Does that mean all the same that confession, repentance, forgiveness, reconciliation, etc., belong in their structural non-consciousness to what one calls — from a psychoanalytic point of view — the unconscious? And how does one define the relation between this non-consciousness[6] and its becoming-conscious? What is the status of that history?

69   The whole Hegelian concept of historicity, we shall see, is a certain logic of the becoming-conscious of the unconscious. And spirit, as spirit of reconciliation, is that. But, one will ask, from a psychoanalytic point of view,

---

[*mise en scène*], that is to say, ritualized, coded. The 'scene' is all that. So the question of an unconscious theater or a theater of the unconscious, that's not the same thing."

4. During the session, Derrida adds: "According to common sense, they begin there. In other words, there is no confession without language and no forgiveness without language. But from the point of view of the logic that we are attempting here, against that common-sense logic, which is also that of a most powerful tradition, it would be the opposite. Confession, forgiveness should not ever appear as such. Which is clearly some sort of madness, of course. What we are attempting here is a type of madness."

5. [Translator's note:] *Aveu* translates literally as "avowal" but is also used to convey "confession" in the broad sense. In *Perjury and Pardon*, vol. 1, Derrida claims to use *aveu* very sparingly, but as I note there (130n36), I do not especially find that to be the case.

6. During the session, Derrida adds: "Which is not necessarily the unconscious."

what is someone doing when they uncover, on the couch or elsewhere, murderous fantasies, or blameworthy drives of some kind? Are they confessing, repenting, asking for forgiveness, seeking reconciliation, etc.?

If I am linking these classic but unavoidable questions to that of the theater, it is probably because since last week we have been on a stage, in a scene and in front of a stage, but also because the link between theater and the unconscious is an old story. I am not talking solely about cathartic purging and hence a process of confession and recognition (the moment of recognition, *anagnōsis, anerkennen*, is structural to almost all theater, to a whole theatrics, an immense and dominant theatrical tradition in any case); nor am I thinking only of *mimesis* as identification. I am thinking above all of what, in the history of psychoanalysis, has linked the concept of the unconscious to the history of theater, from Oedipus to Hamlet ("the play's the thing") and to the structure of the scene, of the other scene, of the scene within the scene. In his *Oedipus and Hamlet* Jones wrote that each time there was a scene within a scene, as in *Hamlet* (about which we spoke at length last year), it had to do with Oedipus.[7]

All that is too well known for me to have to insist on it. But by tackling the questions of confession and forgiveness as we are doing here, there is perhaps a change of sign and landscape concerning how theater, scene, the passage or nonpassage to speech, and to what type of speech, and the relation between conscious and non-conscious or un-conscious, are determined. That is because Hegelianism—the Christian-Hegelian *telos* that is presumed to serve as basis *both* for the globalization of confession we are talking about, *and*, as a consequence, for the reconstitution of the scene we are moving toward with a view to analyzing it—the evangelical phenomenology of spirit as reconciliation, is also a concept of theater, a practice of theater, political theater in particular, and, by the same token, inextricably, a concept and politics of the becoming-consciousness of the unconscious.[8]

A voice off echoes once more, still in German, for I would like it to be inferred that everything, within a certain sequence that is of interest to us

---

7. See Ernest Jones, *Hamlet and Oedipus* (New York: Doubleday, 1954), 100–102 [*Oedipe et Hamlet*, trans. Anne-Marie Le Gall (Paris: Gallimard, 1967), 150–51].

8. [Translator's note:] Here and following, and somewhat in what precedes, the reader should be aware of play, in French, between the two meanings of *conscience*: "consciousness" and "conscience."

here, stems from modern Germany and speaks German. *"Das Wahre ist so der bacchantische Taumel, an dem kein Glied nicht trunken ist* [the true is thus the bacchanalian delirium (dizziness, drunkenness) in which there is no member that isn't drunk], and because each of them, to the extent of being isolated, is cut off (*sich absondert*), immediately dissolved, delirium is by the same token transparent and simple repose.[9] *In dem Gerichte jener Bewegung . . .* [In the tribunal of this movement . . .]," etc.[10]

So, there you have a drunkenness that is a tribunal, says the voice off, or a tribunal of history that is (like) a delirium or bacchanalian drunkenness, once it totalizes or is totalized, globalized. . . .

(To save time, I won't go back.)

We're interpreting. In the theatrical scene that we are by turns reconstituting, observing, analyzing, interrupting — or ourselves acting, interpreting the roles and speeches, identifying the voices off or those speaking on stage, quoting or paraphrasing published texts — you remember that the voice of *The Phenomenology of Spirit* echoed before the curtain rose (and we heard it speaking of the "word of reconciliation (*das Wort der Versöhnung*),"[11] speaking reconciliation, that is, doing what it was saying, speaking the discourse of reconciliation while explaining that discourse or language is reconciliation), its voice raising itself in the name of the spirit that is reconciliation, <in the name> of the wound of which spirit bears no scar, and in the name of the word "word" that always says yes to reconciliation and hence to the forgiveness that is always associated with it in Christian language (and you remember the discreetly dissonant voices of Rabbi Judah Hanassi who spoke of a forgiveness, on Yom Kippur, but without repentance (*teshuvah*); or of Benjamin's reflection that evokes a time of the Last Judgment, and thus of a certain Tribunal of History, where divine forgiveness would come

---

9. During the session, Derrida adds: "So, bacchanalian delirium, the true, is the bacchanalian delirium in which there is no member that is not drunk, all the members, all of them, are drunk, and so wildly, drunkenly agitated, but because each, as isolated from the rest, cut off from everything, *absondert*, immediately dissolves because it is only a part, well then, this agitation is in fact a calmness, *Ruh*, transparent and simple. We'll come back to that."

10. Hegel, *Phänomenologie*, 46 [*Phénoménologie*, vol. 2, 46, Derrida's translation]. [Translator's note:] Cf. *Phenomenology*, 29, §47: "The truth is the bacchanalian revel where not a member is sober, because, in isolating himself from the revel, each member is just as immediately dissolved into it — the ecstasy is likewise transparently and simply motionless. Judged in the court of that movement . . ."

11. Hegel, *Phänomenologie*, 493 [*Phenomenology*, 388 (§670); *Phénoménologie*, vol. 2, 198].

like a tempest and lightning to change time, interrupt time within time, but without reconciliation (*Vergebung* without *Versöhnung*)).[12]

[13]We are therefore on the theater, and in the theater, but also in front of the theater, at this moment when the question remains undecided, that of knowing whether the tribunal, the commission, the judging instance is human or divine, whether it is a matter of human judgment or the Last Judgment. It isn't certain that forgiveness still pertains to a logic of judgment, but presuming that were the case, it would be difficult to know, and it still remains difficult to know, who pardons whom, and for what, and whether God is or isn't the instance of final recourse. There is always this duality of orders: human and divine. That duality shares out or argues over the very concept of forgiveness and especially its moment of reconciliation. Reconciliation can come about between men and God, but it is true that most often the thematics of reconciliation, even when it comes about through God's mediation, always tends to humanize things, to soften the hardness of the verdict or of duty. And there is no doubt nothing fortuitous about the fact that the theme of reconciliation — which is certainly not absent from any of the Abrahamic traditions — appears as more Christian than Jewish or Islamic, in that the mediation of Christ or of God become man plays the role that we were recalling last time when we evoked Luther or Calvin, and when we recalled that our four onstage characters, Hegel,[14] Mandela, Clinton, Tutu, were Christians and Protestants, in spite of the more or less discreet differences that separate them, differences or disputes [*différends*] that will soon enough come out into the open.   72

But just as, last year, when we studied the right to pardon [*grâce*], and read *The Merchant of Venice* ("when mercy seasons justice," says Portia, the woman disguised as a lawyer, and representing the interests of the monarch, the Doge and the Christian theologico-political state, trying at the

---

12. See 3ff. above.

13. This part of the session was published, with significant changes and additions, in "*Versöhnung, ubuntu*, pardon: quel genre?" in *Le Genre humain*, 118–36, and in *La Solidarité des vivants et le pardon*, 71–94. Fragments from the session were also developed by Derrida in his interview with Michel Wieviorka, "Le Siècle et le pardon" (See Derrida, *Foi et savoir*, especially 114–16). [Translator's note:] The Wieviorka interview is published, without Wieviorka's questions, as "On Forgiveness," trans. Michael Hughes, in Simon Critchley and Richard Kearney, eds., *On Cosmopolitanism and Forgiveness* (London: Routledge, 2001), 25–60.

14. During the session, Derrida adds: "The only dead one among the four of them, which is why he speaks as a voice off, a specter." Mandela (1918–2013) was still alive at the time of Derrida's seminar.

same time to convince, to pretend to convince, to defeat, to deceive and convert the Jew, etc.),[15] as well as the text by Kant concerning the right to pardon inscribing the meta-juridical exception into the law and into the foundation of the law (I can't go back over that),[16] we tried to determine a place
(the right to pardon accorded the sovereign, the pardon accorded by the
sovereign) for the meeting of the theological and the political, the divine
and the human, the celestial and the terrestrial—a place that is all the more
remarkable for situating both an absolute exception, the inscription of the
nonjuridical in the juridical, what is beyond the law in the law, transcendence in immanence, and, by the same token, an exception that founds the
unity of the social body and the nation-state—well, so today, that remains
true, of course, wherever the right to pardon remains, but also through the
very notion of imprescriptibility,[17] and where the notion, the idea of imprescriptibility, is inscribed in the law, as has been the case in France since
1964 for crimes against humanity, becoming thus, beyond the notion, a juridical concept. For what does this concept of imprescriptibility signify? It
signifies that no human law in human time can exempt the criminal from
judgment. It isn't the opposite of the right to pardon, for a head of state can
still pardon a man convicted of a crime against humanity (and even do so
as Pompidou did for Touvier,[18] I think, in the name of reconciliation and
reconstituting the unity of the nation), but imprescriptibility is analogous to
the right to pardon—to the pardon whose opposite it appears to be—to this
extent, that in both cases the order and human time of law and judgment

73

15. Shakespeare, *Merchant of Venice* (IV.i); see *Perjury and Pardon*, vol. 1, 55 [*Parjure
et pardon*, vol. 1, 92].
16. *Perjury and Pardon*, vol. 1, 17–19, 161, 193–94 [*Parjure et pardon*, vol. 1, 46–48,
215, 253–54].
17. During the session, Derrida comments: "I recall, for those of you who weren't
here—because we already talked about that a lot: what is imprescriptibility?—that
this notion of imprescriptibility is in the law, in French law, as the rule according to
which, for certain crimes, one can be judged indefinitely, beyond any deadline; in English one speaks of a "statute of limitations," so cases where there is no "statute of limitations," as Americans call it. We say "imprescriptibility," "the law of imprescriptibility";
in France it dates from 1964 for crimes against humanity. See Derrida, *Perjury and
Pardon*, vol. 1, 7–10 [*Parjure et pardon*, vol. 1, 34–36].
18. Paul Touvier (1915–96), former collaborationist functionary in the Vichy regime.
Condemned to death in 1946 and 1947, he had his sentence commuted to life imprisonment on November 23, 1971, by President Georges Pompidou (1911–74). He is the
only French person to have been convicted of crimes against humanity. See *Perjury and
Pardon*, vol. 1, 148–49n2 [*Parjure et pardon*, vol. 1, 200n1].

are superseded by a transcendent instance.[19] Humans don't have the right to exempt someone or to exempt themselves from judgment, however much time has elapsed since the crime. In that respect, just as the right to pardon mimics the divine power that it derives from, and through which it is authorized, so the idea of imprescriptibility—a very modern thing, at least as a juridical phenomenon, and, to my knowledge, contemporaneous only with the similarly modern concept of a crime against humanity, which has been its correlate in France since 1964—the idea of imprescriptibility mimics the Last Judgment, it is carried forward toward an "until the end of time," hence toward a beyond time. It inscribes in time, and in the time of history, an instance that exceeds it, that exceeds every moment, all determinable time. In time, a beyond time or times: a time until the end of times.

But just as the order of the prescriptible or imprescriptible is not, as we have emphasized,[20] that of the forgivable or un-forgivable, these latter having nothing at all to do, in principle, with the judicial or the penal, so this hyperbole of the law nevertheless points toward a forgiveness that is either an excess within excess, a supplement of transcendence (one can forgive while still convicting for what is unforgivable in a court of law), or else a reappropriation, a re-immanentization of the logic of forgiveness.   74

This re-immanentization, if I can call it that, this humanizing reappropriation, is what always constitutes the stakes of a religious debate, a debate that cannot avoid working through religious sacredness, indemnity, immunity (*Heiligkeit*), and a religious debate among religions that, as do the separate Abrahamic religions, deal differently with reconciliation, with human mediation in the relation to God, with incarnation, the prophets, the Messiah and the Prophet. Jesus, the intercessor who asks God to forgive those who know not, is not everyone's Messiah, he is not the Messiah for the Jews and is merely a prophet for Muslims.

It is in order to question this potential planetary Christianization of current experience, what I am calling for short the globalization of confession, forgiveness, and reconciliation, following compensation [*indemnisation*], that we began by listening to Hegel. We began with him, and his spectral voice, not because he is the only dead man on stage (Mandela, Clinton, and Tutu are still alive) but because in his word spoken in the present, in the presence of his speaking, one can hear announced or recalled an absolute

---

19. During the session, Derrida adds: "And this transcendent instance is inscribed in the law: what exceeds the law is inscribed in the law."

20. See Derrida, *Perjury and Pardon*, vol. 1, 7, 8nn18–19, 15–16, 35 [*Parjure et pardon*, vol. 1, 34, 35n1, 35n2, 44, 67].

knowing that works through reconciliation, through forgiveness and God's death on the Cross, through the Passion of Christ and the speculative Good Friday. He was speaking German, and since we heard that Lutheran voice coming to us from Germany, I note in passing that since last week — within the daily mass of news concerning the frenetic and suddenly compulsive unfurling of processes of repentance, reparation, compensation (especially the restitution of goods, the return of plundered spoils, etc.) — well, I recall that if the great Willy Brandt[21] gave the first signal by kneeling and ask-

75 ing for forgiveness (at Auschwitz, I think) some decades ago, Volkswagen has of its own accord offered, just last week, fifty-five years after the fact, to compensate victims of forced labor in its factories during the war (including among them some fifteen hundred Jews, many of whom are now in Israel).[22] Everything seems to come out of Germany. Last year we read that letter from a young German to Jankélévitch, quoting Celan's poem "*Todesfuge*" in order to express his infinite guilt as a young German who was however innocent, like all those of his generation: "*Der Tod ist ein Meister aus Deutschland.*"[23]

You will also have noted, if you are interested in this Christian or Christianizing dimension to the current process, that in Chile, where at the beginning of the post-Pinochet period — Pinochet having been relieved [*relevé*] of his duties at the beginning of the democratization process and following elections, but sublated [*relevé*] in Hegel's sense, that is to say *aufgehoben*, having kept everything while being displaced, inasmuch as he remained head of the armed forces and a major voice in the country in spite of having given up power — at the beginning of the post-Pinochet era there was a general amnesty in Chile, well then, today it is the highest level of the Church that preaches national reconciliation. Granted, in 1973, following the assassination of Allende, Cardinal Raúl Silva Henríquez courageously declared that "human rights are sacred," before opposing Pinochet in his own way. But

21. On December 17, 1970, twenty-five years after the end of World War II, West German chancellor Willy Brandt knelt before the memorial to the victims of the Warsaw ghetto. On the same day he signed the German-Polish treaty that would lead to an opening with Eastern Europe. He received the Nobel Peace Prize in 1971.

22. See "Volkswagen confie à Shimon Peres le dossier des travailleurs forcés," *Le Monde*, November 16, 1998, 5.

23. Paul Celan, "*Todesfuge* [Death Fugue]," in *Paul Celan: Poet, Survivor, Jew*, trans. John Felstiner (New Haven: Yale University Press, 1995): "Death is a master from Deutschland . . . Death is a master aus Deutschland . . . Death is ein Meister aus Deutschland . . . der Tod ist ein Meister aus Deutschland." See Derrida, *Perjury and Pardon*, vol. 1, 26–27 [*Parjure et pardon*, vol. 1, 56–57].

today, old and ill, he has been *relieved* by the archbishop of Santiago, Monsignor Francisco Javier Errázuriz, who, this past November 20, insisted, and I quote, on the "necessity of forgiving."[24]

Is it excessive to recall that this archbishop had had postings in the Vatican and in Germany, that he belonged to one of the richest families in the country, and that his brother is an activist in the right-wing party called National Renewal?[25] One must always recall, since the situation is typical, that if the Chilean church is predominantly conservative (Chile counts among Christian countries where divorce is illegal), there were also priests who rose up against the dictatorship and paid for it with their lives. The same thing was true in South Africa, where, although there was a strong Calvinist theological association with the establishment, justification, and maintenance of apartheid, there were also theologians and a whole Christian movement that fought courageously against apartheid. Still on the subject of Chile, an article in *Le Monde* on November 26, entitled "The Church Seeks to Play a Major Role in National Reconciliation," recalls that, during Pope John Paul II's visit to Chile in 1987, the pontiff came out to greet the crowd, with Pinochet at his side, from the La Moneda palace balcony, where one could see, like scars, the impact holes of bullets and shells fired in the course of the 1973 coup. The pope was supposedly tricked by Pinochet: he was looking for the door out of the room where the interview had taken place, and it was reported that Pinochet maliciously steered him toward the window opening onto the balcony.

Enter Desmond Tutu. That the Church, the Christian Church, then, in its official statements, today proffers a discourse of reconciliation, offers the "word of reconciliation," that reconciliation is not only its language but the language into which all the worldwide discourses of reconciliation are translated, with or without the knowledge of the subjects of such discourses, is confirmed for us in a thousand ways and attested to by, among others, Desmond Tutu who has just come on stage, but as if to interrupt Mandela, or even to discreetly contest what he is saying.

24. See Christine Legrand, "L'Église veut jouer un rôle prépondérant pour la réconciliation nationale," *Le Monde*, November 26, 1998, 3. Cardinal Raúl Silva Henríquez is known for having publicly opposed General Augusto Pinochet during the military dictatorship (1973–90), and for having made such a statement in 1973, in the wake of the coup d'état against President Salvador Allende. Monsignor Francisco Javier Errázuriz (1907–99) was cardinal and archbishop of Santiago from 1961 to 1983.

25. The conservative Chilean political party Renovación Nacional was directed by co-founder Andrés Allamand from 1990 to 1999.

76

I have always wondered, having no answer within reach, what deep, se-
77   cret relationship existed between these two men who were no doubt allies in
a certain fight for justice and against apartheid, but whose coexistence one
might suspect to have been far from simple, for countless reasons, suspect-
ing also that there were probably things for which they had to forgive each
other once they appeared together and as allies on the public stage of political theater, which they are doing, however, over the course of a history that
distances them and perhaps separates them radically.

I am going to quote both of them; we'll hear from them. Mandela speaks
also of reconciliation. Tutu does, too. For example, he says this, which I am
quoting on the basis of an interview, the original of which I read in English
last year before going to South Africa, and which the journal *Esprit* published in translation in December 1997 with the title "No Amnesty without
Truth."[26] Later we'll reconstitute the whole interview and everything Tutu
says; I'll quote only this passage in which he speaks of both the Christian
idea of reconciliation that guides him as president of the TRC and, if not his
opposition to Mandela, at least his independence with respect to the latter's
political power, on a day, moreover, when Mandela himself, in the flesh,[27]
was present on stage for a session of the commission. The difference, or
even the virtual dispute between two men who were so close, is a discord
that is all the more subtle and difficult to locate, as you will hear, given that
what Tutu says about freedom and liberation (that of whites as much as of
blacks) overlaps identically, literally, with a statement by Mandela. (Read
and comment on *Esprit*, pp. 68–69, TT.)

> They never believed me, you see, when I told them this, when I said I am
> deeply committed to freedom. And it is freedom not for black people; it is
> freedom especially for white people. Because they are not completely free
> until we are free. Those are not just some slogans I like throwing around.
> They thought I was driven by political motives, and they believed that once
> you had this democracy, I would be seen holding down a particular posi-
78   > tion. I told them: "No, I am driven by my faith." [So, what he is marking
> here when he says "political" and "faith" is that, inasmuch as he is a man
> of faith, he is naturally above political ambition, above the politics of politi-
> cians. That said, we'll see that his Christian discourse of reconciliation is
> profoundly political in another sense of the word; it isn't that of a politi-
> cian.] So if something is wrong, I don't ask who has committed it, I say it is

26. Ferrari, "Forgiving the Unforgivable" ["Pas d'amnistie sans vérité. Interview
avec Archbishop Desmond Tutu"]. See 30n94 above.

27. During the session, Derrida adds: "Still the theater."

wrong. So they were surprised when I told President Nelson Mandela you can't have your gravy train. [He was appointed by Mandela, hence by one who held power, but as president of the commission, which is not a legal body but an independent one, like a tribunal, he claims absolute independence from power, and that's of course something one can respect.] We are even-handed, but some don't want to believe it. They decided long before the commission started that it was going to be a witch hunt. [That came from white people. Whites were not going to wait to accuse this commission. But as soon as this amnesty procedure had been requested, they very quickly accused the commission of accusing only whites, and hence of being a purge committee, a witch hunt. And Tutu, who wants to be just and evenhanded, defends himself against that accusation.]

A number in the white community hold on to the view despite the evidence. I said to the ANC, to no other party have I said I will resign if you hold on to a view that undermines our position. If that is how you feel about amnesty, I'll resign from this commission. I'm not here to play marbles. But I haven't said I will resign if you don't come before the commission. [Naturally, he summoned members of the ANC accused or suspected of violence, of terrorism, torture, etc., and he wanted to treat them in the same way as the guilty ones, the white "perpetrators" of apartheid, as we were calling them last time.] I was the chair when Mandela attended the hearing in Johannesburg. He arrived at a point when someone was accusing the ANC of atrocities in their camps. He sat through this tirade. We are independent. I was chosen because I was morally neutral. Any credibility that I might have comes from my fight against apartheid and against oppression. I don't make any apologies for that. They have a strange notion about what reconciliation is. They think that reconciliation is patting each other on the back and saying it's all right. Reconciliation is costly and it involves confrontation. Otherwise Jesus Christ would not have died on the cross. He came and achieved for us reconciliation. But he confronted people and caused division [this is obviously a most fundamental reference].[28]

79

As announced, before Tutu and Clinton, Nelson Mandela appeared in the flesh, and we heard him speak of the South African Constitution, of the place that it made for reconciliation and for the multiplicity of officially recognized languages, and then about his childhood, his conversion and circumcision, and the word *ubuntu*. He is still on stage, punctuating for us what is called his autobiography.

Why "autobiography"? I am here taking that word very seriously.

This autobiography recalls how, even before the word "reconciliation" was inscribed in the preamble of the Constitution that I quoted (last week),

28. Ferrari, "Forgiving the Unforgivable," 16 ["Pas d'amnistie," 68–69].

which spoke of "heal[ing] the divisions of the past,"[29] before a certain article I am going to read that recalls the act promoting national unity and reconciliation (1995), he, Mandela, had previously spoken of reconciliation, offered the word of reconciliation.

Even before this article of the Constitution entitled "National Unity and Reconciliation."[30] I'll just read it very quickly, but because it will also concern amnesty, I am emphasizing that its originality consists not so much in the content and intent of the amnesty, as in how it is formally and explicitly inscribed in the opening, and in the principle of a Constitution. In France, for example, on a number of occasions since World War II, highly placed political figures regularly used the same language: we must proceed to reconciliation through amnesty and so reconstitute national unity. This is a leitmotif in the rhetoric of *all* French heads of state and prime ministers since World War II, *without exception*. It was literally the language of those who decided, following the first moment of purging, on the great amnesty of 1951 for crimes committed during the Occupation. The other evening I heard Cavaillet say, in an archival documentary, which I am quoting from memory, that as a member of the National Assembly he voted for the 1951 amnesty law because it was necessary, and I quote, "to know how to forget,"[31] all the more so because at that moment—and there is always a strategic and political calculus in the generous gesture of one who offers reconciliation, we always need to integrate that calculus into all our analyses—and Cavaillet insisted strongly on this, the danger of communism was felt to be the most pressing concern, and it was imperative to bring into the national community all the anticommunists who, having been collaborators some years previously, risked remaining excluded from the political arena by a law that would have been too severe, and by a purging that didn't forget enough. Remaking national unity meant rearming with all the forces at one's disposal for a combat that would continue, only this time in peacetime or in the so-called Cold War. "National reconciliation" was also the explicit language of de Gaulle when he returned to Vichy for the first time and gave a famous speech there on unity and the oneness of France; it was literally

29. See above, Preamble to the Constitution of the Republic of South Africa, quoted by Derrida (27 above).

30. Sentence fragment in typescript.

31. Henri Cavaillet (1914–2013) had a long career as parliamentarian and legislator, serving thirty-eight years in elected office. Derrida is perhaps alluding to the documentary film that includes testimony by Cavaillet: Pierre Beuchot, *Les temps obscurs sont toujours là. Mémoires de la France de Vichy (1940–1998)* (France, 1998, 130 minutes, INA, PB Productions and La Sept ARTE).

Pompidou's discourse when he also spoke, in a famous press conference, of national reconciliation and of overcoming division at the moment of commuting Touvier's death sentence; and it was yet again the discourse of Mitterrand when he maintained, on repeated occasions, that he was the guarantor of national unity, and more precisely when he refused to declare France's guilt under Vichy (which he qualified as a nonlegitimate power appropriated by a minority of extremists).[32] Conversely, it is when the body of the nation can tolerate without risk a minor division or even find its unity reinforced by legal procedures or by the lifting of repression that different calculations dictate conceding in a more rigorous way to what is called the "duty to remember."

81

It is thus always a question, as in South Africa (but the analogy, however real, stops there, of course), of placing the unity of the national body that needs to be saved or cured (*heilen*, heal) over and above every other imperative of truth or justice. We could cite many other French examples. That said, this doesn't mean that those opposed to an amnesty, or even those who voted for the imprescriptibility of crimes against humanity (a law that, it must be noted, remained without effect with respect to French citizens, and defunct until it came to Papon,[33] since Barbie[34] was a foreigner), that doesn't mean that those who were opposed to an amnesty, or even those who voted for the imprescriptibility of crimes against humanity, were contesting this language of the health of the national body, of therapeutics, or indeed of ecology and of the necessary work of mourning. Quite simply, there are those who maintain within the same logic of health—hence of an indemnity to be restored,

32. François Mitterrand (1916–96), statesman and French president from 1981 to 1995, worked for the Vichy regime in 1942 [before joining the Resistance in 1943]. That episode, which remained unexplored for a long time, gave rise to considerable controversy throughout his presidency. Mitterrand refused to apologize on behalf of the French state for the fate of the Jews during World War II, alleging that Vichy did not represent the state, but simply the "*de facto* authority" of a provisional government. On July 14, 1992, he did, however, declare that the Vichy regime's participation in deportations was a prima facie fact, and in February 1993 he officially decreed July 16 as the "National Day of Commemoration of the Racist and Anti-Semitic Persecution Committed under the *de facto* Authority called 'Government of the French State (1940–1944).'" Concerning Mitterrand's declarations, see Gérard Courtois, "Rétrocontroverse: 1995, Vichy, c'était aussi la France," *Le Monde*, August 9, 2007.

33. Derrida already alluded to this trial in the previous year's seminar. See Derrida, *Perjury and Pardon*, vol. 1, 148–49n2, 154–57 [*Pardon et parjure*, vol. 1, 200, 205–9].

34. Nikolaus Barbie, known as Klaus Barbie (1913–91), Nazi SS officer, head of Section IV of the Gestapo in Lyon. His trial in 1987 was the first prosecution in France for war crimes. He was sentenced to life imprisonment for crimes against humanity.

of compensation—that the revelation of truth, the passage of justice, the sentencing of the guilty, etc., the "duty to remember," as it is also called, is a better therapy for the social or national body against the pathological effects of repression. And in fact, the same therapeutic logic may privilege opposing prescriptions—dare I say different medicines [*ordonnances*]—

82 opposing strategies from one moment to another in the history of the national body. What wasn't possible right at the time of the Liberation became possible and necessary six years later (amnesty); then what wasn't possible for decades (self-accusation or the indictment of this or that person) and until the last few years, now becomes possible and urgent. Up to a certain point and within limits that weren't to be exceeded (the so-called mutineers of World War I or <crimes against humanity in>[35] Algeria, for example).

One would have to develop long and subtle analyses there to show that successive and opposing stances often in fact depend on the same axiomatics: the good, the well-being, the smooth functioning of the body and social, state, and national machine, of the state and civil society in themselves, but also in their European and global environment.

Here now is the article of the Constitution on "National Unity and Reconciliation":

> Notwithstanding the other provisions of the new Constitution and despite the repeal of the previous Constitution, all the provisions relating to amnesty contained in the previous Constitution under the heading "National Unity and Reconciliation" are deemed to be part of the new <1996> Constitution for the purposes of the Promotion of National Unity and Reconciliation Act, 1995 (Act 34 of 1995), as amended, including for the purposes of its validity.[36]

83 So this is the act, the Reconciliation Act, duly confirmed and extended by the final Constitution that Mandela inspired, naturally gaining the approval of all parties then involved in the negotiation. For—this is what I wanted to come to—Mandela reminds us in his autobiography what his analysis, calculus, and duty were immediately after the first free elections of 1994. I am going to read (and translate) a long passage from that autobiography (completed with the help of all sorts of people, including writers such as

35. These words are added in the version appearing in *Le Genre humain* (125) et *La Solidarité des vivants et le pardon* (80).

36. Constitution of the Republic of South Africa, 1996—Schedule 6: Transitional Arrangements. See https://www.gov.za/documents/constitution-republic-south-africa-1996-schedule-6-transitional-arrangements#22. [Translator's note:] During the session, Derrida adds his translation of the paragraph.

Nadine Gordimer,[37] but begun in prison, secretly, under terrifying conditions, with extraordinary and moving forms of subterfuge to preserve it and smuggle it out of prison). I'll emphasize in this passage the imbrication of political calculus or reasoning, of historical conditionality and the logic of transcendent principle (liberty, justice, democracy, truth) in whose service this strategy says it is giving its consent. It is always by analyzing the status of forces, and relations of force, and with an eye to the integrity or rescue of the sociopolitical, or national-state body, that Mandela adjusts his political choices.[38] (Read and comment on *The Illustrated Long Walk to Freedom*, p. 200, including the right insert.)

Ten days before the vote, Mr de Klerk[39] and I held our single televised debate. I accused the National Party of fanning hatred between Coloureds [you know, "Coloureds" are not blacks, they are Indians, those who are neither black nor white] and Africans in the Cape by distributing an inflammatory comic book that said the ANC's slogan was "Kill a Coloured, kill a farmer." "There is no organization in this country as divisive as the New National Party," I declared. When Mr de Klerk criticized the ANC's plan to spend billions of dollars on housing and social programmes, I scolded him, saying he was alarmed that we would have to devote so many of our resources to blacks.

84

37. Nadine Gordimer (1923–2014), South African writer, critic, and publisher. Close to Mandela's ANC, she was involved in the struggle against apartheid and was awarded the Nobel Prize for Literature in 1991.

38. See Derrida, "Admiration de Nelson Mandela, ou les lois de la réflexion," first published in *Pour Nelson Mandela* (Paris: Gallimard, 1986); ["The Laws of Reflection: Nelson Mandela, in Admiration," trans. Mary Ann Caws and Isabelle Lorenz, in Peggy Kamuf and Elizabeth Rottenberg, eds., *Psyche: Inventions of the Other*, vol. 2 (Stanford: Stanford University Press, 2008), 63–86].

39. Frederick W. de Klerk (b. 1936) was then leader of the National Party. President from 1989 to 1994, he succeeded P. W. Botha, long-time defense minister, prime minister, then president from 1984 to 1989. De Klerk appeared before the Truth and Reconciliation Commission, and recognized that "apartheid was wrong," but he denied knowledge of the extent of human rights violations committed under his government. (See Timothy Garton Ash, "True Confessions," *New York Review of Books*, July 17, 1997, 33–38, especially 34–36 ["La Commission vérité et réconciliation en Afrique du Sud," *Esprit* 238 (1997), 44–62, especially 52–55]. Derrida's heavily annotated copy of Ash's text is housed in the Fonds Jacques Derrida, IMEC ("Le parjure et le pardon," 219 DRR 240.1). De Klerk, the last elected white president of South Africa, shared the Nobel Peace Prize with Nelson Mandela in 1993 for bringing about the end of the apartheid regime and laying the foundation for a new democracy in that country.

But as the debate was nearing an end, I felt I had been too harsh with the man who would be my partner in a government of national unity. "In spite of criticism of Mr de Klerk," I said, and then looked over at him, "sir, you are one of those I rely upon. We are going to face the problem of this country together." At which point I reached over to take his hand and said, "I am proud to hold your hand for us to go forward." Mr de Klerk seemed surprised, but pleased. [If you have seen the footage, from Washington, with Rabin, Peres, and Arafat, and the play of handshakes (which of them held out his hand, which of them hesitated, for how long, etc.),[40] you have there two scenes that it would be interesting to compare. So, who holds out his hand, who takes him up on it, in what time frame, with how much dead time, with or without haste? The difference between Rabin and Peres was spectacular, wasn't it: Arafat holds out his hand, like this. [*Laughter*] Rabin, on camera, wants to show that it's not that straightforward. Peres holds out his. Well, here, then, we have an analogous scene: Mandela holds out his hand.]

85   I voted on 27 April, the second of the four days of voting. I chose to vote in Natal to show the people in that divided [again, still the word "division," it is about healing divisions] province that there was no danger in going to the polling stations.

It took several days for the results to be counted. We polled 62.6 per cent of the national vote, slightly short of the two thirds needed had we wished to push through a final constitution without support from other parties [so they obtained a large majority, but not enough without relying on the support of other parties].

Some in the ANC were disappointed that we did not cross the two-thirds threshold, but I was not one of them. In fact I was relieved; had we won two-thirds of the vote and been able to write a constitution unfettered by input from others, people would argue that we had created an ANC constitution, not a South African constitution [there you have the calculus: happy not to be strong enough and so able to save national unity by passing a South African Constitution that whites will also be able to sign on to]. I wanted a true government of national unity.

On the evening of 2 May Mr de Klerk made a gracious concession speech. After more than three centuries of rule, the white minority was conceding defeat and turning over power to the black majority. That evening the ANC was planning a victory celebration at the ballroom of the Carlton

---

40. Derrida is alluding to footage that shows Yasser Arafat (1929–2004), leader of the PLO and president of the Palestinian Authority; Shimon Peres (1912–2016), Israeli statesman; and Yitzhak Rabin (1922–95), Israeli prime minister, during the signing of the Oslo Accords, previously called "Gaza-Jericho" Accords, on September 13, 1993.

Hotel in downtown Johannesburg. I went on stage at about nine o'clock and faced a crowd of happy, smiling, cheering faces.

From the moment the results were in and it was apparent that the ANC was to form the government, I saw my mission as one of preaching reconciliation. I knew that many people, particularly the minorities, whites, Coloureds and Indians, would be feeling anxious about the future, and I wanted them to feel secure. At every opportunity, I said all South Africans must now unite and join hands and say we are one country, one nation, one people, marching together into the future.[41]

86

But these strategic and politico-therapic[42] calculations, however entangled they be with the absolute and unconditional principle of freedom, do not prevent the call for reconciliation from claiming to be inspired by a transcendent ideal regarding all these conditional hypotheses, and, if we listen to Mandela himself, the passage to the unconditional was his experience and the place where his life, like his autobiography—through endurance of all the hardships in his combat for the liberation of his people, of an oppressed people—started out in advance along the path of reconciliation. Suffering itself allowed him to understand that the enemy, the white oppressor, was also a victim, also subjugated, also deprived in an obscure way of the same freedom. In my interpretation here I associate the endurance of suffering, the twenty-seven years of captivity (and if you could see what Robben Island and Mandela's prison cell were like, you would have an image of the "martyrdom"—I insist on that word—of a martyrdom and a passion that I refrain from describing in detail), I associate, then, the history of this suffering of martyrdom and passion with the story of his autobiographical narrative, precisely because of martyrdom, namely, of how pain is translated into testimonial language ("martyr" means witness; "martyrdom," testimony),[43] precisely because this testimonial language that I am here calling

41. Mandela, *Illustrated Long Walk*, 200 [cf. *Un long chemin*, 637]. During the session, Derrida gives his own translation of the passage. After reading and commenting on the passage, Derrida reads the caption under the photograph on the left of the page: "Before I entered the polling station, an irreverent member of the press called out, 'Mr Mandela, who are you voting for?' I laughed. 'You know,' I said, 'I have been agonizing over that choice all morning.' I marked an X in the box next to the letters ANC [that's how votes were cast] then slipped my folded ballot paper into a simple wooden box; I had cast the first vote of my life, like the woman pictured above."

42. The typescript has "*politico-thérapiques*," pronounced thus during the session.

43. On this question see Maurice Blanchot and Derrida, *The Instant of My Death / Demeure: Fiction and Testimony*, trans. Elizabeth Rottenberg (Stanford: Stanford University Press, 2000), 38 [*Demeure—Maurice Blanchot* (Paris: Galilée, 1998), 44]; and

autobiography and autobiographical writing—destined to leave the prison, destined for global space, having a universal destination—this becoming-discourse and address to the other is the immediate transmutation of the particular combat, of the particular figure, Hegel would say, of war for a finite cause (however broad it be), into a universal cause. That universal-ization of discourse and of the cause is the alchemy of language; and to re-translate that into Hegel's code, prior to his own appearance on stage, that is where language, the address to the other, even the language of political war, begins the process of reconciliation, offers the word of universal reconcili-ation, is the spirit from which *Dasein* effaces the scars of wounding. That is why I say that, even within the process of his terrifying but eloquent in-carceration, Mandela had already set out, politically and metapolitically, on his march to reconciliation as liberation, as march toward freedom, process in aid of freedom (*The Long Walk to Freedom*), when he proposes offering that freedom not only to his people in servitude, wounded, humiliated, ex-cluded, etc., but also to the oppressors, to the enemies, as you will hear him say, in the course of a war that he first wanted to be nonviolent (following the principles of Gandhi who, as you know, lived in South Africa and was thrown off a train in Pietermaritzburg for boarding a train or a car reserved for whites), a struggle that Mandela at first wanted to be nonviolent before having had to accept—faced with the brutal and relentless, merciless vio-lence of the power of apartheid—to prosecute it as a war, that is to say, by having recourse to violence.

Well, in the course of that war he understood, and this is his very lan-guage, that he also had to liberate the oppressor, liberate the master, and that his fight, his very concept of freedom, would have no sense unless it were to rise above the opposition, above the onesidedness, above war itself, by freeing the oppressor from his own servitude.

Before commenting further, before reading the words of reconciliation associated with those of freedom and liberation penned by Mandela, let's say that when it comes to this (both Christian and philosophical) gesture, the phenomenology of spirit in South Africa, one knows not whether its end, its *telos*, is *there*, attained, accomplished, whether it is merely adjourned, or whether that adjournment, which one can anticipate to be infinite, signifies the infinity of a regulative idea, of an Idea in the Kantian sense, or again an

"Poetics and Politics of Witnessing," in Thomas Dutoit and Outi Pasanen, eds., *Sov-ereignties in Question: The Poetics of Paul Celan* (New York: Fordham University Press, 2005), 75 ["Poétique et politique du témoignage," in Marie-Louise Mallet et Ginette Michaud, eds., *Cahier de L'Herne Derrida* (Paris: Éditions de L'Herne, 2004), 527].

SECOND SESSION ‡ 51

infinite that is thinkable but unknowable, or a limit that has to be thought   *88*
quite differently than through this Hegelian-Christian axiomatics.[44]

One more possible staging effect at the moment Mandela is about to
take the floor. At the moment he speaks, one could give utterance — in a
corner of the stage, or again as a voice off — to another Hegel, the same but
another, to the author of *Lectures on the Philosophy of World History*.[45] We
could lend our ear to what he says concerning Africa, comments that are both
famous and comical in the extreme (I performed a *mise en scène* of that in
Clang around what he says about the African fetish and won't go back over it
here).[46] But it is at the same time to be taken very seriously, at least inasmuch
as it is inseparable from the whole systematic machine of the dialectic and
speculative idealism — and from the dense motif of *spirit as reconciliation*. I
refer you to it, although I would have liked to reread the whole thing here,
but if I had to choose excerpts for our play, I would privilege the following
motifs:

1. First, the exclusion, dare I say the apartheid, with which Africa is branded
in this philosophy of history. Africa properly speaking, Hegel declares, has
remained for all time closed (*geschlossen*[47] *geblieben*) to the rest of the world.
It has no history because it is the golden land folded upon itself (this allusion to gold, *in sich gedrungene Goldland*), makes one think of South Africa,
although the history of gold and gold mining continues to explain, in the
area surrounding Johannesburg, a whole historicity of South Africa), but
not only is it the land of gold but also the land of childhood (*das Kinderland*)
that hasn't yet entered history, the dawning of history, come onto the stage
of history, of consciousness as history, precisely because it has remained,   *89*
like the color of Negroes (*Negern*), black, enveloped, buried, beyond the
dawning of a history conscious of itself in the dark night, in the black of

---

44. During the session, Derrida adds: "And my hypothesis, naturally, is that one
can't choose; that both are at work in Mandela, in the history that is Mandela."

45. In *Le Genre humain* and *La Solidarité des vivants et le pardon* version, Derrida
specifies in a note the reference for this passage. Cf. G. W. F. Hegel, *Vorselungen über
die Philosophie der Geschichte. Werke*, vol. 12, ed. Eva Moldenhauer and Karl Markus
Michel. (Frankfurt: Suhrkamp Verlag, 1970), 120 [Hegel, *Lectures on the Philosophy
of World History: Introduction*, trans. H. B. Nisbet (Cambridge: Cambridge University
Press, 1996), 173ff.; *Leçons sur la philosophie de l'histoire*, trans. J. Gibelin (Paris: Librairie
philosophique J. Vrin, 1945), 87ff.].

46. See Derrida, *Clang*, trans. Geoffrey Bennington and David Wills (Minneapolis:
University of Minnesota Press, 2020), 232ff. [*Glas* (Paris: Galilée, 2004), 232ff.].

47. Hegel's word is *verschlossen*, "cut off." Hegel, *Vorselungen*, 120 [*Philosophy of World
History*, 173; *Leçons sur la philosophie de l'histoire*, 75].

night; the dark continent, it also has that sense: "*es ist das in sich gedrungene Goldland, das Kinderland, das jenseits des Tages der selbstbewußten Geschichte in die schwarze Farbe der Nacht gehüllt ist.*"[48]

2. For that very reason Africa has not yet attained representation, the category of generality or universality (*Kategorie der Allgemeinheit*); and I underline this point because it is what will interest us in the text by Mandela. The African — not having attained universality, no more than he has attained God or the Law (*Gesetzt*) — has access neither to law or morality (*Sittlichkeit*), nor to the reign of right (*Reich des Rechts*); he knows only God's thunder (cf. Benjamin!!!)[49] and sorcery (*Zauberei*).

3. The Negro is ignorant of the immortality of the soul, even though one encounters phantoms of the dead (*Totengespenster*). It is true that, in Hegel's eyes, the cult of the dead indicates — whence the complexity of things and of his evaluation — an access by Negroes to something superior and the outlines of a sentiment of immortality. That is why he says that they are ignorant of the immortality of the soul *although* one finds ghosts among them.

4. But above all, and in this context the line along which I would let Hegel's ghost speak at greatest length is this: the essential trait of the Negro is slavery (*die Sklaverei*). The Negro doesn't yet have consciousness of his freedom. The black man *doesn't yet* have consciousness of his freedom, *not yet*. We need to insist on this "not yet," on the fact that unconsciousness is merely the "not yet" of consciousness and of the passage to consciousness, a simple delay, a simple anachrony in the process of a teleological time (*der Mensch das Bewußtsein seiner Freiheit noch nicht hat*); and that is why he falls to the level of a thing without value (*und somit zu einer Sache, zu einem Wertlosen herabsinkt*). And it is because he is a thing without human value, without freedom, without consciousness, that he becomes a commodity that Europeans reduce to slavery and sell to the Americans ("*Die Neger werden von den Europäern in die Sklaverei geführt und nach Amerika hin verkauft*").[50]

90

---

48. Hegel, *Vorselungen*, 120. [Translator's note:] Cf. *Philosophy of World History*, 174 [*Leçons sur la philosophie de l'histoire*, 75]: "it is the land of gold, for ever pressing in upon itself, and the land of childhood, removed from the light of self-conscious history and wrapped in the dark mantle of night".

49. During the session, Derrida adds: "Remember Benjamin's text where the moment of forgiveness is precisely the moment of God's thunder." See 24 above.

50. Hegel, *Vorselungen*, 125 [*Leçons sur la philosophie de l'histoire*, 75]. [Translator's note:] Cf. *Philosophy of World History*, 183: "The negroes are enslaved by the Europeans and sold to America. . . . Man is not yet conscious of his freedom, and consequently sinks to the level of a mere object or worthless article."

I am doubtless choosing these passages because we will shortly hear Mandela on freedom, and the paradoxes of an infinite liberation that can be only indefinitely deployed toward what it will have nevertheless been from the start, a freedom that was first and was originary, but also because, when Clinton comes on stage, this will be the moment when, without explicit contrition but with an admission of guilt, an avowal, a *nostra culpa*, he will recognize, on African soil, his country's failing, in the founding of the United States, namely the perpetration and perpetuation of slavery, in the course of a history that is the history of the United States itself, and a history that, well beyond the nineteenth century and the Civil War, and still today, continues to mark the whole of American culture and the air around it, the very element that one breathes there, even when one isn't unemployed as are the blacks who form the large majority of the unemployed and the excluded, and even when one isn't in prison like the vast majority of prisoners who are black within a country that has one of the highest rates, I think even the highest rate of incarceration in the world. You know that Clinton made that admission concerning the past crime of slavery during a trip to Africa this year — after, I think, having met Mandela.[51]

Faced with everything that seems today to deny and ridicule all these brutal and shocking statements, Hegel would not renounce them. He would maintain forcefully that it is precisely the transformation of Negroes by Christian civilization, their entry — thanks to colonization and slavery — into the European, American, and Christian world — that has brought them into history, onto the stage of history and consciousness, into the history of spirit as liberation, as access to freedom and emergence into the light of the free world, into consciousness, law, right, into the theater of the world, etc. The access to freedom and emergence into the light of the free world, into consciousness, law, right, is thus also the access to *reconciliation* — and

91

---

51. See *Perjury and Pardon*, vol. 1, 5n10, 7n13 [*Pardon et parjure*, vol. 1, 31n1, 33n2]. A newspaper clipping concerning Clinton's trip to Africa (March 23–April 2, 1998) was inserted into the seminar typescript. See Mimi Hall, "Clinton Ends 'Powerful' Africa Tour," *USA Today*, April 3–5, 1998, 1. Clinton was the first American president to visit Africa and during the trip he expressed his regrets for the role of the United States in the slave trade. On his photocopy of the *USA Today* article Derrida marked with an arrow the following paragraph in particular, underlining its last two words: "Clinton reiterated that theme throughout his trip during which he made a series of *near-apologies*" (Derrida's emphasis). It was only on June 18, 2009, more than ten years later, that the Senate passed a sense of Congress resolution condemning slavery and racial segregation, presenting a formal apology to the African American population in the name of the American people.

the reconciliation of South Africa freed from apartheid with a Christian discourse would be but further proof of that history of spirit. Moreover, if you reread closely, as I suggest that you do, at least this *Introduction to The Philosophy of World History*, what will you see there? In addition to some remarks that will make you die laughing, if I can say that, moments worthy of comic theater or farce, such as this sentence, for example, which, while denouncing Negroes' unleashing of arbitrariness (*Willkür*), of *sensuous* arbitrariness in politics—in opposition to freedom and the law, to right—the unleashing of arbitrariness that knows neither chain, "no[r] bond, no[r] restraint" (*Es gibt überhaupt kein Band, keine Fessel für diese Willkür*),[52] well then, in this unleashing of arbitrariness Negroes go as far as to depose their king and even to kill him: "if negroes are dissatisfied with their king, they depose him and execute him" (*Sind die Neger mit ihrem König unzufrieden, so setzen sie ihn ab und bringen ihn um*).[53] Well, just look at that. Hegel could have added, but he precisely doesn't: those Negroes behave like your garden-variety French or English. Rereading that sentence, I asked myself, in the context of the joyous global wave of confessions and declarations of past and collective guilt, where the right limit is to be found, if there is one. For example, must not France confess that the Reign of Terror and, to begin with, the Revolution, the decapitation of a king, were political crimes, or even, in the case of the Terror, a crime against humanity, and admit that all those horrors were not indispensable for the Declaration of the Rights of Man, which is nevertheless associated with them in such an assured manner? An enormous debate, as you know. All human rights declarations seem to have been bought at a very high price, I mean at the price of unavowable crimes. One wonders whether today all the revolutionaries (French or Russian), from 1789 and from 1917, might not be held accountable by international tribunals, their immunity lifted like that of some garden-variety Pinochet, their extradition demanded by émigrés, by the descendants of refugee émigrés in countries that have welcomed them. Pardon me for asking these sacrilegious questions, but good questions always risk being sacrilegious and dangerous. Right itself, and justice, have progressed only along the path of intolerable and nontolerated questions; unavowable questions. The condemnation of the death penalty, justly held to be an irrefutable

---

52. Hegel, *Vorselungen*, 126 [*Leçons sur la philosophie de l'histoire*, 78]. [Translator's note:] Cf. *Philosophy of World History*, 186: "Thus, the arbitrary will has no bond whatsoever to restrain it."

53. Hegel, *Vorselungen*, 126; *Philosophy of World History*, 187 [*Leçons sur la philosophie de l'histoire*, 78]. [Translator's note:] Syntax thus in typescript; see paragraph following.

advance in human rights, in Europe, and in France less than twenty years ago, would have prevented in 1789 the instituting of political and national tribunals and probably the Declaration of the Rights of Man—and, against that background, the first public condemnations of slavery.

In addition to numerous comments by Hegel such as that one, which will make you die laughing (Negroes dare to depose and kill their king!), make you die laughing because they can't be serious although they are stated with an imperturbable solemnity, you should reread—if only to celebrate in turn the Declaration of the Rights of Man—passages that complicate and clarify things, such as when Hegel not only condemns slavery but also denounces it as an injustice that must be abolished on the stage of history. He had first noted that the only connection that existed and continues between Negroes and Europeans was slavery, and that such slavery suits them, that they see in it nothing *unangemessen*, nothing unbecoming, improper, inappropriate, unsuitable, and that they even hold it against the English abolitionists who have wanted to put an end to trading in slaves, abolitionists whom the Negroes themselves, Hegel says, treat as enemies. Not only do Negroes like and cultivate a slavery that suits them, but they are ready to make war on those who claim to liberate them from it. "For it is a point of first importance with the Kings," Hegel says further, "to sell their captured enemies, or even their own subjects; and viewed in the light of such facts, we may conclude slavery to have been the occasion of the increase of human feeling among the Negroes (*die Sklaverei hat insofern mehr Menschliches unter den Negern geweckt*)."[54] Imagine a great philosopher saying that today, and you will no doubt understand what history is, but not necessarily a history that would exceed or contest the Hegelian concept of history, as we shall see. For there is a lesson (*Lehre*), Hegel adds, to be drawn from this condition of slavery. Moreover, this doctrine, this *Lehre* to be drawn, is the only interesting aspect of this for us ("*die allein für uns interessante Seite*"):[55] the only interesting side to slavery for us is the lesson in political philosophy that we can draw from it. What lesson? Well, first that slavery is a state of nature and that the state of nature (*Naturzustand*) is the state of absolute nonright, absolute injustice (*Unrecht*). Every intermediate

93

54. Hegel, *Vorselungen*, 128–29; *Philosophy of World History*, 98 [*Leçons sur la philosophie de l'histoire*, 79]. During the session, Derrida adds: "So slavery gave rise to more humanity because instead of killing prisoners they sell them as slaves, and if one seeks to prevent their doing that, well, they aren't happy."

55. Hegel, *Vorselungen*, 129. Cf. *Philosophy of World History*, 99 [*Leçons sur la philosophie de l'histoire*, 79]: "the only side of the question that has an interest for our inquiry."

degree, every intermediate stage (*Zwischenstufe*) between that state of nature or nonright and the rational state still includes moments and aspects
of *Unrecht* and *Ungerechtigkeit*, of nonright and of injustice. That is why
we encounter slavery even in the Greek and Roman states and encounter
serfdom (*Leibeigenschaft*) all the way to the most modern times (*neuesten
Zeiten*), in Europe, that is. But, Hegel then makes clear, when it exists *in* the
state itself, it constitutes a moment of progress (*ein Moment des Fortschreit-
ens*), in that it brings us out of isolated, purely material or natural existence,
and allows access to a certain degree of education, to a sort of participation
in the superior morality (*Sittlichkeit*) and culture (*Bildung*) that is attached
to it. In European states (Greek and Roman) slavery is a form of *Bildung*
and an opportunity to participate in morality. It remains, however, Hegel
declares just as firmly, that slavery is in itself and for itself an injustice, an
Unrecht, a nonright, for the being of man, the essence of man (*das Wesen
des Menschen*) is freedom, even though man must still become ripe for it
94   (*doch zu dieser muß er erst reif werden*).[56] So it is all about maturing; an immense question of maturation, of the time of maturation. (You remember
the beginning of Kant's text on the Enlightenment, *Was ist Aufklärung?* The
Enlightenment demands nothing other than freedom, and even the most
inoffensive of freedoms, making "*public use* (öffentlichen Gebrauch)"[57] of
reason; but that freedom, given to all men, presumes maturity, progression
beyond minority status (*Unmündigkeit*), out of being a minor, hence of an
enslavement, no longer having an appointed guardian,[58] something that can
be ascribed only to man. Man is accountable, responsible, guilty of this lack
of maturity that deprives him of responsibility and of freedom. Whence
the logic of rupture and of leap by way of mutation that seems to push

56. Hegel, *Vorselungen*, 129. Cf. *Philosophy of World History*, 99 [*Leçons sur la philosophie de l'histoire*, 79]: "but for this man must be matured." During the session, Derrida
adds: "That's his essence, but he must be ripe, he must mature to accede to that essence,
to be worthy of that essence, to accomplish that essence. Ripe, *reif*."

57. Immanuel Kant, "An Answer to the Question: 'What Is Enlightenment?'"
trans. H. B. Nisbet, in Kant, *Political Writings*, ed. H. S. Reiss (Cambridge: Cambridge
University Press, 1991), 55; Immanuel Kant, *Was ist Aufklärung?* in *Kants gesammelte
Schriften*, vol. 8 (Berlin: Walter de Gruyter & Co., 1923), 36 [*Vers la paix perpétuelle, Que
signifie s'orienter dans la pensée? Qu'est-ce que les Lumières? et autres textes*, trans. Jean-
François Poirier and Françoise Proust (Paris: Flammarion, 1991), 45].

58. During the session, Derrida adds: "Here, to remain a minor and not be mature
is something that can be ascribed to man; it is the fault of man if he remains a minor, and
so it is his responsibility to emerge from minor status or from enslavement."

Kant to say *"sapere aude"*: have the audacity, know how to dare,[59] have the courage to use your *own* understanding (*own* is underlined, *deines* eigenen *Verstandes zu bedienen*).[60] Make the leap that consists in freely ensuring your own freedom inasmuch as you already have it, originarily, inasmuch as it is only a lack of maturity, an age,[61] that still prevents you from appropriating what is already yours. In reading Mandela, we'll again find this logic of self-liberation, an interminable liberation, by a being and for a being that is, however, originarily free.) Kant's logic of rupture is and isn't—however paradoxical it be—that of Hegel speaking of slavery and freedom. Having just said that the essence of man is freedom, but that man must be ripe for what is nevertheless his essence, Hegel adds: "The *gradual* abolition of slavery is therefore wiser and more equitable (*etwas Angemesseneres und Richtigeres*) than its *sudden* removal."[62] The United States heard that lesson: not all at once, don't go too fast, and if you take a close look at the history of slavery and segregation, and civil rights, etc. in the United States, you will find a fine illustration of that progress, at the same time irreversible and interminably slow, or even interminably complicated and overdetermined. That interminability of liberation, starting from a freedom that is nevertheless presumed originary, is what we will talk about further in reading, in a moment, texts by Mandela. I note in particular that what is translated, in Hegel, as "sudden removal" (the abolition of slavery must not be a sudden suppression of it), is *plötzliche Aufhebung*. That indeed means a sudden suppression, but when one takes into account the difficulty of translating *Aufhebung* and Hegel's insistence on the dialectical character of that word—a stroke of luck for German given its affinity with dialectical speculative idealism,[63] namely, that *Aufhebung* means both suppressing and preserving, which I translate as *la relève*[64]—one can measure the ambivalence of this remark concerning the *Aufhebung* of slavery, of an *Aufhebung* (suppression/

95

---

59. During the session, Derrida adds: "One becomes mature all of a sudden, by a stroke of courage: it isn't finally a question of age, it isn't the passage from seventeen to twenty years old, one has to dare to be free, dare to be what one is, that is to say, free, in one fell swoop."

60. Kant, *Was ist Aufklärung*, 35, Derrida's translation. Cf. "What Is Enlightenment?" 54 [*Vers la paix perpétuelle . . . et autres textes*, 43].

61. During the session, Derrida adds: "Which isn't a matter of age."

62. Hegel, *Vorseļungen*, 129; *Philosophy of World History*, 99 [*Leçons sur la philosophie de l'histoire*, 79], Derrida's emphasis.

63. During the session, Derrida corrects himself: "Speculative dialectical idealism."

64. On the history of the translation of this word, see *Perjury and Pardon*, vol. 1, 58–59n18 [*Parjure et pardon*, vol. 1, 95–96n2].

preservation, *relève*) that must not be "sudden." (Transfer to "confession":

96 must it be sudden, must it interrupt the course or the process of a history, mark a revolution, or, on the contrary, take time, allow itself the time of a persistent transition?)[65]

One of the simultaneously essential, structural, and supplementary complications in this Hegelian logic or teleologic concerning Africa and its Negroes, is that, in spite of all the horrors that we have been hearing, Hegel is at the same time *for* the progressive, historic abolition of slavery; yet, whereas he simultaneously excludes Africa from history itself, he excludes it from what he himself calls the "real theater of universal history," the "actual theater of universal history."[66] A black African, *as such*, can never appear on the stage of universal history, and, should he appear there, like Mandela and Tutu, it is because he is already white, Christian, and not pure African. Indeed, immediately after pleading for a progressive disappearance of slavery, in opposition to a *plötzliche Aufhebung*, Hegel immediately leads into the following paragraph like this: "*Wir verlassen hiermit Afrika, um späterhin seiner keine Erwähnung mehr zu tun.*"

> At this point we leave Africa, not to mention it again. For it is no historical part of the World (*kein geschichtlicher Weltteil*); it has no movement or development to exhibit. Historical movements in it (*was etwa in ihm . . . geschehen ist*) — that is in its northern part [implication: in the South nothing has happened, even less history than in the North] — belong to the Asiatic or European World. Carthage displayed there an important transitionary phase of civilization; but . . . it belongs to Asia. Egypt . . . does not belong to the African spirit. What we properly (*eigentlich*) understand by Africa, is the Unhistorical, Unopened (*das ist das Geschichtslose und Unaufgeschlossene*) Spirit, still involved in the conditions of mere nature, and which had

---

65. During the session, Derrida comments: "Well, can one transfer all this logical, dialectical set of complications to confession? Can one say, for example, that confession must be sudden, as one often says, that it must interrupt the course or process of a history, mark a revolution — a confession is a revolution — or is it rather that real confession, actual confession, must take time, allow itself the time of a persistent transition, a repetition, marking time, the time of a confirmation, even a consolidation? Is confession, as passage to freedom, something done just like that — a decision interrupts the ordinary course of time, the course of ordinary things — or is it, on the contrary, an elaboration, a *perlaboration* that takes, that gives itself, all the time it needs?"

66. Hegel, *Vorselungen*, 129, Derrida's translation. *Philosophy of World History*, 99, has "the real theatre of History" [*Leçons sur la philosophie de l'histoire*, 80].

to be presented here only as on the threshold of the World's History (*an der Schwelle der Weltgeschichte*).[67]

And the following sentence, at the beginning of the next paragraph, names   97
the real *theater* of universal history, in short, the actual theater of globalization. "Theater" is Hegel's word: "Having eliminated this introductory element [Africa, that is black Africa], we find ourselves for the first time on the real theatre of [World] History (*Wir befinden uns jetzt erst, nachdem wir dieses von uns geschoben haben, auf dem wirklichen Theater der Weltgeschichte*)."[68]

Global theater is a theater of consciousness, theatrical globalization is a phenomenology of consciousness, namely, of spirit at home with itself and knowing itself. If one wants to analyze what is going on here, especially in political terms, one perhaps has to do that from another standpoint or another theater and another concept of the theater of the unconscious, another logic or another staging of theatrical unconsciousness or of the unconscious of the theater.

While the voice off of Hegel's ghost is developing its argument about Africa and its Negroes, here now is what Mandela says ([69]and it's the end of his autobiography, *The Long Walk to Freedom*; I take the title very seriously, and if we were to allow Hegel's ghost to speak one more time, in this theater of shadows, it would recall that the whole phenomenology of spirit is the justification of a figure of the road [*route*], of the speculative dialectical *method* as road, as path being made. The Hegelian dialectical mutation of the concept of method means that method is no longer an *organon*, a system of technical rules for following a path that already exists, no, method (*methodos*) *makes its way* [fait son chemin], it is process, the process, the way inasmuch as it is cleared and made; method clears its path and makes history.   98
tory. The Preface to *The Phenomenology of Spirit* contrasts this new concept of method — one that builds its road and is none other than the movement

<hr>

67. Hegel, *Vorselungen*, 129; *Philosophy of World History*, 99, trans. modified following Derrida's French modifications [cf. *Leçons sur la philosophie de l'histoire*, 80]. During the session, Derrida comments: "That is to say, in the "Introduction," after this, it's not talked about any more. Africa is on the threshold of a history, but that hasn't begun. When he says it is on the side of natural spirit, that means that there is a spirit, but as you know if you know Hegel a bit, natural spirit is spirit lost in nature, so it's not spirit, it isn't spirit as such, it's spirit in nature, hence before history."

68. Hegel, *Vorselungen*, 129; *Philosophy of World History*, 99 [*Leçons sur la philosophie de l'histoire*, 80]. Illegible annotations appear here in the typescript margin.

69. The parenthesis opening here does not close in the typescript.

of consciousness, of spirit becoming consciousness — with that old concept of method, the "philosophical method" that for Hegel "belongs to a bygone culture"[70] and seeks its model in mathematics. "Truth," he says, "is its own self-movement (*Die Wahrheit ist die Bewegung ihrer an ihr selbst*),"[71] in a sentence that comes just after he has once more spoken of the onstage entrance of truth, of the form in which truth must not or must *come on stage*, "auftreten *kann*": this figure of the entrance, appearance, coming on stage, of self-presentation, this figure is a typical and recurrent one in Hegel, and it again says something about historical theatricality, about history as theater and as tribunal — appearance and summons to appear [*comparution*].

[For if I am playing with staging a play, if I am playing without playing at staging a theater, with representing and interpreting theater, doing [*faisant*] or impersonating [*contrefaisant*] all the voices, it is also, as you will have understood, in order to enter into correspondence — both by setting it to work and by putting it to the test — to enter into correspondence with this profound, ontological theatricalism of Hegelian thinking, to which I am pretending to submit, to correspond where it corresponds with this determination of being as spirit and as spirit coming on stage, presenting itself, *Dasein*, in a language and in the word of reconciliation: the *Da-sein* of spirit; and so reconciliation is a type of scene, and a scene of judgment, and of Last Judgment, as we shall see.] Hegel contrasts, therefore, this speculative method with the old philosophical method, regulated according to the model of mathematical instrumentality, which is also to say, says Hegel, regulated on a dead space, a space of death. In that the movement of spirit constructs its method, its route as its very process and the clearing of a path, it is spirit as life itself that, through the endurance of death, is written, traced, traces its path as autobiography, writing of self by what lives. This is the famous passage, to which I refer you, in the Preface to the *Phenomenology of Spirit*, where the value of life is constantly associated with that of spirit, but a life as everything, the whole of life, of livingness [*vivance*], as "actuality and the living movement of truth (*die Wirklichkeit und Bewegung des Lebens der Wahrheit*),"[72] as bacchanalian revel (another theatrical

99

---

70. Hegel, "Vorrede," *Phänomenologie*, 47; "Preface," *Phenomenology*, 28 (§48) [*Phénoménologie de l'Esprit*, trans. Jarczyk and Labarrière, 106].

71. Hegel, "Vorrede," *Phänomenologie*, 47; "Preface," *Phenomenology*, 28 (§48) [*Phénoménologie de l'Esprit*, trans. Jarczyk and Labarrière, 106].

72. Hegel, "Vorrede," *Phänomenologie*, 47; "Preface," *Phenomenology*, 29 (§47) [*Phénoménologie de l'Esprit*, trans. Jarczyk and Labarrière, 105].

scene) in which there is no member that isn't drunk, but which is also rest to the extent that each isolated member immediately dissolves: both pure movement of life, hence of spirit as life—spiritual life and all authentic life is spirit, spiritual life—and transparent and simple rest (*durchsichtige und einfache Ruhe*). In this passage from the Preface, which you know well or which you should read and reread, I'll emphasize only the appearance, just after the allusion to bacchanalian revel, of the figure of the tribunal and of judgment (*in dem Gerichte*):

> Judged in the court [or before the judgment] of that movement, the individual shapes of Spirit (*die einzelnen Gestalten des Geistes*) do not stably exist any more than do determinate thoughts, but they are also equally positive, necessary moments just as much as they are negative, disappearing moments [*als sie negativ und verschwindend sind*: in other words, life is in the whole; death, the negative figures disappear, but they will have been moments of this history as path or method].[73]

Against the background of Hegel's voice off, let's now listen to Mandela, as announced earlier, at the infinite, nonfinite end, the unfinished finished end of his autobiography. I'll read and translate the final passages of the book in order to resituate this motif of reconciliation and liberation of the master oppressor, where, beyond calculation, it is a question of freeing freedom, of freeing the oppressor on the infinite road of a liberation; the question that remains being how to think this infinite, which is both that of *liberation*, rather than that of *liberty*, and of liberation as reconciliation (comment on the various possibilities: "I was born free," yet the path to freedom is infinite; Hegel: the infinite must be given for the indefinite to

100

---

73. Hegel, "Vorrede," *Phänomenologie*, 47; "Preface," *Phenomenology*, 29 (§47) [*Phénoménologie de l'Esprit*, trans. Jarczyk and Labarrière, 105]. Derrida writes the following in the margin of his typescript: "Spirit = specter ± life ± death!!!" During the session, he comments: "If one were simply to translate this history of spirit as reconciliation, then everything Hegel says to us would be: 'spirit is reconciliation, reconciliation is spirit.' It's very simple. If 'spirit' means what it has always meant (*spiritus, psychē*, life), then life, *c'est la vie*. And at the end of *The Phenomenology of Spirit* one can see being determined as life, spirit as life, not biological, genetic life, but life as spiritual life, which is life itself. At that point it goes without saying that life can be only reconciliation, that is to say, victory over scission, division, war, dissociation. Life is survival through reconciliation. To say that spirit is life is to say that spirit is reconciliation, in other words, something stronger than death, which is associated with dissociation, destruction, war, negative opposition, evil, etc. It is the surmounting of evil and death. What spirit as reconciliation and reconciliation as spirit means is all of that."

appear).[74] On the preceding page Mandela had declared that his mission (hence his duty, the conviction concerning his duty — remember the hardness of iron and doing that we spoke of last week)[75] was to preach reconciliation; here is what he says now: (Read and translate p. 202)

> I was not born with a hunger to be free. I was born free — free to run in the fields, free to swim in the stream that ran through my village, free to roast mealies [I don't know what that is][76] under the stars. As long as I obeyed my father and abided by the customs of my tribe, I was not troubled by the laws of man or God.
>
> It was only when I began to learn that my boyhood freedom was an illusion, when I discovered as a young man that my freedom had already been taken from me, that I began to hunger for it. At first, I wanted the transitory freedoms of being able to stay out late at night, read what I pleased and go where I chose. Later, I yearned for the basic freedoms of achieving my potential, of earning my keep, of marrying and having a family.
>
> But then I slowly saw that it was not just my freedom that was curtailed, but the freedom of everyone who looked like I did. That is when I joined the African National Congress, and that is when the hunger for freedom became the greater hunger for the freedom of my people. It was this desire for people to live their lives with dignity and self-respect that animated my life, that transformed a frightened young man into a bold one, that drove a law-abiding attorney to become a criminal [that's the moment when, in his work as a lawyer, he made the transition from nonviolence to violence], that turned a family-loving husband into a man without a home, that forced a life-loving man to live like a monk.
>
> It was during those long and lonely years that my hunger for the freedom of my own people became a hunger for the freedom of all people, white and black. I knew that the oppressor must be liberated just as surely as the oppressed. When I walked out of prison, that was my mission [he again uses the

101

---

74. During the session, Derrida comments: "'I was born free,' Mandela will say, as you'll hear, 'I was born free,' and, starting from there, I lost my freedom and the process of infinite liberation was set in train, of not only the oppressed but also the oppressors, of not only the slaves but also the masters — it is the slaves who are going to liberate the masters. And this infinite of freedom, what is it? Shall we think, like Hegel, that in order to think the indefinite movement of liberation, one must already have thought the infinite, that the infinite comes before the indefinite? That is the suit that Hegel brings against Kant: in order to speak of indefiniteness [*l'indéfinité*] you must already have thought the infinite, the infinite comes first. Or is it that the infinite is not given first, and the indefinite remains indefinite?"

75. See 13–14 above.

76. "Mealies" refers to ears of corn.

word "mission," the same word, you see] to liberate the oppressed and oppressor both. The truth is that we are not yet free; we have merely achieved
the freedom to be free, the right not to be oppressed. We have not taken
the final step of our journey, but the first step on a longer and even more
difficult road. For to be free is not merely to cast off one's chains, but to live
in a way that respects and enhances the freedom of others. The true test of
our devotion to freedom is just beginning.

I have walked that long road to freedom. But I have discovered that
after climbing a great hill, one only finds that there are many more hills to
climb. I have taken a moment here to rest, to steal a view of the glorious
vista that surrounds me, to look back on the distance I have come. But I can
rest only for a moment, for with freedom come responsibilities, and I dare
not linger, for my long walk is not yet ended. [So you see, schematically: *102*
"I was born free and the process of liberation that I then set in train is an
unfinished and virtually interminable process." Is this logic the same as that
we have identified or analyzed in others, Rousseau, Kant, Hegel, etc.? That
question remains very much alive.][77]

77. Mandela, *Illustrated Long Walk*, 202 [*Un long chemin*, 644]. During the session, Derrida translates the English text. The typescript for the session has these annotations at the end: "*slave master of the master, frees the master*" and "[his relationship with Tutu, mentioned by name once only, p. 160, then from there to Tutu, p. 69]."

January 13, 1999

[1]We are still in the theater this year, and the four characters in search of an author await us, either having already spoken up, as voice off, like Hegel, or having begun to speak in the flesh on the actual stage of history, like Mandela and Tutu. We're keeping Clinton waiting still, but in this case nobody, neither he nor we, loses anything by waiting.[2]

While Hegel's voice off continues to echo—we'll hear it again—here comes Desmond Tutu to take the floor on the stage of history.

[3]Like Mandela, as you remember, Desmond Tutu declares that the task of *liberation* (keep in mind this word "liberation," Hegel echoes it already in advance, if I can put it that way, in the wings from where his voice off reaches us, *Befreiung*, he says, "liberation,"[4] and *Befreiung* is a word that we could read in a passage of his so-called juvenilia on *The Spirit of Christianity and Its Fate*, precisely where he speaks of forgiveness; we'll listen to that more clearly a little later), Desmond Tutu declares, then, that the task of

104

1. The typescript has this notation before the session heading: "end of session → presentations—February 3, March 3, March 24." See Editors' Note, xxvn31 above.

2. [Translator's note:] *ne perd rien pour attendre*, also "will get what he deserves."

3. This session was published, with significant modifications and additions, in "*Versöhnung, ubuntu*, pardon: quel genre," in *Le Genre humain*, 136–54, and in *La Solidarité des vivants et le pardon*, 95–120. Fragments of the session were also recast by Derrida in his interview with Michel Wieviorka entitled "Le Siècle et le pardon" (reprinted in *Foi et savoir*), especially 116–19 [cf. "On Forgiveness," in *On Cosmopolitanism and Forgiveness*, 41–60].

4. *Der Geist des Christentums und sein Schicksal, Frühe Schriften*, in G. W. F. Hegel, *Werke*, vol. 1, ed. Eva Moldenhauer and Karl Markus Michel (Frankfurt: Suhrkamp Verlag, 1986), 357; Hegel, *The Spirit of Christianity and Its Fate*, trans. T. M. Knox, in *Early Theological Writings*, trans. T. M. Knox (Philadelphia: University of Pennsylvania Press, 1979), 241 [*L'Esprit du christianisme et son destin*, trans. Jacques Martin (Paris: Librairie philosophique J. Vrin, 1948), 64].

liberation assigned to the new leaders of South Africa, and more especially the TRC, consisted in liberating whites as much as blacks.

In the interview that I quoted from some weeks back (translated in *Esprit*, December 1997, p. 69), he affirmed: "They never believed me ... when I said I am deeply committed to freedom. And it is freedom not for black people; it is freedom especially for white people. Because they are not completely free until we are free. Those are not just some slogans. . . ."[5]

So not *freedom*, but a *liberation*, and not a unilateral, private liberation; liberation must be universal, universalizing, or not at all, it doesn't deserve its name and liberates no one.[6]

And the long development that I quoted last time ends, as you will perhaps remember, by invoking Christ on the Cross: "Reconciliation is costly and it involves confrontation. Otherwise Jesus Christ would not have died on the Cross. He came and achieved for us reconciliation. But he confronted people and caused division."[7]

This logic is not only a rhetoric. The logic of invoking Christ could, in itself, already seem strange coming from one in charge of a Truth and Reconciliation Commission destined to function in a country that is neither officially Christian nor in fact, far from it, composed solely of Christian citizens,[8] or even only Jews and Muslims. Apart from the fact that Jews and Muslims in South Africa form communities that are not necessarily in agreement with the Christian-Anglican interpretation of forgiveness (and I note that because we will have to come to the rich Jewish and Muslim traditions whose thinking and culture of forgiveness are not governed by the moment or model given by Christ's passion, which changes a lot of things), there is a broad segment of the South African population—and it is more than broadly represented among the victims of apartheid and of its executioners—having nothing to do with any of the three Abrahamic religions. The translation of *ubuntu*, which seems to imply "sympathy," "compassion," "recognition of the humanity of the other," etc., a notion that often appears in all the texts that served as premises for the TRC, Tutu's translation of *ubuntu* as "restorative

105

---

5. Ferrari, "Forgiving the Unforgivable," 16 ["Pas d'amnistie," 69].

6. During the session, Derrida adds: "One must liberate everyone or else one liberates no one."

7. Ferrari, "Forgiving the Unforgivable," 16 ["Pas d'amnistie," 66].

8. During the session, Derrida adds: "Because there are countries that aren't officially Christian, such as France, but inhabited by a majority of Christian citizens. That isn't the case in South Africa. There are Christians, Jews, and Muslims in South Africa, but not only."

justice,"[9] with the requisite Christian foundation for that determination of redemptive justice, can appear as a form of violence, no doubt well intentioned, with the best intentions in the world, but an acculturating—not to say colonial—violence that is not limited to a superficial question of language and semantics.

Nobody, then, tasked Desmond Tutu with acting, speaking and orienting things as a Christian, still less as an Anglican Christian, and, as you no doubt know, he has been reproached for his Christian activism, especially by the primary victims of apartheid. As a result, these different cultures of forgiveness (but can they be called "cultures of forgiveness" without already confirming a certain semantic authority of one over the other?), these different "cultures," these different "ethics," these different forms of *ethos*—even before, and in the prospect of settling or discussing their disagreements—would be required to reconcile among themselves, or even to forgive one another for trying, inevitably, to impose their own idiom on others.

But when I say "forgive one another," I am myself privileging one idiom. This drama of the imposition of idiom (an inevitable imposition, for there is no meta-idiom, and that absence of any meta-idiom is both a chance and an evil, which means that as soon as someone opens their mouth they have to be forgiven for—if I can venture to say so in my idiom—speaking their language.[10] Speaking one's language is the condition of an address, of course, but it is the beginning of a colonial aggression or of an anticolonial war, in any case of a colonial war—before any colonialism[11]—it is a *resistance*, in all the senses of that word). That means that every practice of an idiom, and especially of a nondominant idiom (neither English nor Afrikaans) in this story of the TRC, already constitutes in itself a contestation of the organizing principle, spirit, or letter of the TRC institution.

I shall take a single example, cited by Timothy Garton Ash in an article from the *New York Review of Books*, translated in the same issue of *Esprit*, p. 57 ("True Confessions").[12] It is the case of a black woman whose husband

106

---

9. Ferrari, "Forgiving the Unforgivable," 14 ["Pas d'amnistie," 66]; quoted in Timothy Garton Ash, "True Confessions," *New York Review of Books*, July 17, 1997, 33 ["La Commission vérité et réconciliation en Afrique du Sud," *Esprit* 238 (1997), 48].

10. During the session, Derrida adds: "As I just did now. When I say 'culture of idiom,' I am already saying 'I have to take back this expression because it imposes something on a culture in which the words "forgiveness" or "culture" don't have the same semantic weight as in the language that I am speaking.'"

11. During the session, Derrida specifies: "Modern colonialism."

12. The typescript has a marginal annotation, "True Confessions," referring to the title of Ash's article. See 47n39 above.

was kidnapped and killed. She is invited to attend and hear the testimony of the murderers, after which she is asked whether she is prepared to forgive. She speaks a local dialect and everything is mediated by interpreters, and I would be totally incapable of saying how well they performed their task. I read in the article that she is asked "if she could forgive." Well, she replies in her dialect the following, which I'll read in its English translation, then in French, hence with all the usual precautions that you can now imagine. She supposedly said, and I quote:[13] "No government can forgive." Pause. "No commission can forgive." Pause. "Only I can forgive." Pause. "And I am not ready to forgive."[14]

How to evaluate such an event? I am even incapable of having the slight- *107* est access to the event of translation that has imposed the word "forgive" to render what this woman meant to say in her language. No one can — no more than can I — have access to her suffering, to her experience, in her body and in her place. Nevertheless, in saying what is translated thus, she was indisputably doing something more and something other than saying, in a tragically contradictory manner, "I alone can forgive; but I alone am unable to, I am unable to do what I am able to do, and I am alone in that." In meaning that, she means something that goes beyond her unique and unspeakable suffering; she challenges the right or the sense of a "forgiveness" entrusted to a government or a commission, one entrusted to "no government," as she says, and to "no commission." She is also speaking *in general*, signifying that forgiveness is beyond the reach of every institution, that forgiveness has no commensurability, no analogy, no possible affinity with a juridical or political apparatus. The order of forgiveness transcends all law or all political power, every commission and every government; it does not allow itself to be translated, transported, transposed into the language of law and of power, it comes down to the pure singularity of the victim, to her sole, infinite solitude. But of course, when this woman reminds us that she alone can today forgive, but that she is precisely not prepared to do so, that means, or in any case it implies (for it is difficult to translate a "meaning-to-say [*vouloir-dire*]" here), it entails and implies more than one thing.

13. [Translator's note:] Derrida reads the French text, as follows: "*Aucun gouvernement ne peut pardonner.* [*Silence*] *Aucune commission ne peut pardonner.* [*Silence*] *Moi seule puis pardonner.* [*Silence*] *Et je ne suis pas prête à pardonner*" ("La Commission vérité et réconciliation," 57).

14. Ash, "True Confessions," 37 ["La Commission vérité et réconciliation," 57]. During the session, Derrida adds: "The text notes: 'Pause [*Silence*].' You can see the scene, this woman says in her language, 'No government can forgive.' Then a 'silence' that is translated into all the required languages."

Let us reread, then, these last two sentences as translated: "Only I can forgive." Pause. "And I am not ready to forgive." "Only I can forgive" — what
does that signify? It implies first of all that it is only from the side of a victim, and not from a commission formed by a government, that forgiveness
is *possible* (possible in the sense of "potential [*éventuel*]," able to be envisaged
and potentially worthy of the word "forgiveness," significant). *I*, I am a victim on the side of the victim, *we* are more than one victim in a single one,
and I am the sole surviving one of those victims; hence, it is from me alone
that forgiveness is possible, in other words that it would, could potentially
have a meaning, and that its meaning could be forgiveness, that it could be
worthy of the word "forgiveness." Yet this "I alone" also signifies that, alone
on the side of the victim, she is but one victim out of at least two victims,
including her dead husband. If she is alone, it is also because the absolute
victim, the first victim, is dead: *he*, the only victim able really to forgive, is
not there. From that point of view also, she may not feel she has the right to
forgive, alone as she is, a victim deprived of the other victim, her husband.
But when, following another silent pause,[15] she adds, let's read it: "And I am
not ready to forgive," which logically speaking is understood as "*yet* I am
not ready to forgive," that would call for another commentary and readings
that would multiply almost endlessly, especially if one doesn't have access to
what she said literally in her idiom.[16]

Since it is on the basis of that reasoning ("Only I can forgive." Pause.
"And I am not ready to forgive.") that she calls into question, or even puts
on trial, the politico-juridical logic, and the language (English or Afrikaans)
that is imposed on her, it would be necessary to determine what "not ready
to forgive" means. Does she want it to signify: "I am not in a position, I neither
can ever be, nor ever want to be disposed or ready to forgive"? Or rather:
today, not yet, where *not yet* can mean either "not in this situation," before
you,[17] or else "not yet" in time, not until I go down a certain path, work on it
somewhat, let's say undertake a labor of mourning, which I haven't yet done?

15. During the session, Derrida adds: "And the silence counts, and I don't know
what the translation of a silent pause into eleven languages is."
16. During the session, Derrida comments: "We are not the only ones, of course,
who don't have access to that idiom. Of course, we are here in Paris, we speak French,
I am reading that in translation, but where it was happening her words came by way of
translation for many members of the Commission, who had problems — if not the same
problems as ours — at least analogous problems."
17. During the session, Derrida adds: "In front of the murderer, who is there, the
murderer was there, present."

In truth, reading such accounts of the hearings with all these filters, we know nothing of what really happened, and we have to admit that. All the more so given that this irreducible screen of idioms (linguistic idioms or dialects, but also the singularity of the untranslatable suffering of a victim who is at the same time singular and also at the same time[18] united and divided, *109* a woman united with her husband and separated from him, like the survivor [*sur-vivante*] of one who has died, a survivor bearing someone dead within her outside her, both within her and outside her—and I insist on the fact that this is a woman, resolving to come back to that in a moment), this screen of idiom on the side of her who is being asked, following the testimonies and confrontations, whether she is ready to forgive, this screen that both filters and deforms, is opaque and nonopaque, a deforming, diffracting, and reflecting surface (what is the right metaphor for describing something that is neither a medium nor a means of communication?), this indescribable diffraction or distortion of the idiom on the side of the victim is multiplied or diffracted further in the idioms of the interlocutors—in the event, the commissioners—the men and women sitting on the commission, not to mention the interpreters and journalists and observers. When it comes to the commissioners, for example, according to the author of the article I was quoting from just now, "each . . . does it in his or her own way."[19] There is Tutu, the "fervent Anglican," "devout and passionate Christian," who begins his conversation with the author of the article with a prayer (there is a lot of praying in South Africa, and the Calvinist Afrikaners whom I met in Potscheftsroom precisely performed gestures of thanks [*actions de grâce*] before each meal, even in restaurants), so there is Tutu, the "fervent Anglican," "devout and passionate Christian," who, as the author says, "believes in forgiveness"—and in a moment we'll hear on what conditions he thinks that forgiveness is possible, namely, on the conditions of knowledge and of truth. But there are also commissioners who speak a totally different language. For example, the journalist quotes a "smartly dressed" black psychologist, Pumla Gobodo-Madikizela, who speaks to the victims in a language that is insufferable for the author of the article, and that's understandable, a language that, we have to admit, sometimes risks resembling our own, for he speaks to them, the victims, of "trauma" and of the way of "coping with trauma."[20]

18. Repetition in typescript, and during the session.
19. Ash, "True Confessions," 37 ["La Commission vérité et réconciliation," 57].
20. Ash, "True Confessions," 37 ["La Commission vérité et réconciliation," 57]. [Translator's note:] The French translation has "*discours . . . insupportables et condescendants*" for Ash's "insufferably condescending lectures." As adjective, *insupportable* takes

110 One can well imagine what the author of the article means when he finds that discourse intolerable; for it could be the discourse that we well know, that of professional shrinks and sociologists who have the statutory responsibility for helping victims or patients by giving them advice of this kind: "You know, now you have to get past it [*faire ton travail de deuil*], after the trauma that you've suffered somewhere in your unconscious or in your dominated woman's ego."[21] The author of the article, who isn't a journalist but a specialist of Central Europe and author of a book on *Germany and the Divided Continent* (Gallimard, 1995)[22] does not hide his antipathy either for the doleful piety that Tutu wears on his sleeve or for the black psychologist's show, expressing his preference for the behavior of those he calls white liberals (of neither black nor Afrikaner, but of English tradition) and among whose number he includes himself, writing: "The white liberals on the commission go for sober brevity and quiet, understated sympathy. There is no single moral style—in the commission, as in the nation it represents.[23] I prefer the understated sympathy myself, but then I'm a white liberal."[24]

Where is the truth? What is the truth? What is the essence of the truth?

Since in a moment we are going to take on board the question of *truth*, of what the word "truth" means in TRC, I would like to explain why, among the mass of examples and testimonies from which I could choose, I have *111* privileged, for economy and sobriety's sake,[25] but not only for that, the example of this woman who says, "And I am not ready to forgive." I made the choice for what this woman and wife says, of course, but also because she is a woman, a woman who speaks, and because we have to speak here

---

away from the force of the adverb in English, and does not quite have the nuance of English "insufferable."

21. During the session, Derrida adds: "One can imagine the exasperation, but one has to be careful not to speak in that way because when we speak a language, and often when we speak of trauma and of the work of mourning, we come right up to the edge of such language."

22. Timothy Garton Ash, *In Europe's Name: Germany and the Divided Continent* (New York: Random House, 1993) [*Au nom de l'Europe. L'Allemagne dans un continent divisé*, trans. Pierre-Emmanuel Dauzat (Paris: Gallimard, 1995)].

23. During the session, Derrida adds: "And it is true that few nations are as diverse as the South African nation."

24. Ash, "True Confessions," 37 ["La Commission vérité et réconciliation," 57]. During the session, Derrida adds: "It's a question of style. Difficult to find one's style in this situation. I won't say that ours is without reproach."

25. During the session, Derrida adds: "Since I am kind of a white liberal in my own way." [*Laughter*]

of sexual difference. Before coming back to this question of sexual difference, I note that the witnesses, on the side of the victims or allies of victims, were often women, wives, sisters, mothers, daughters; and that when Tutu sought to demonstrate that it was all done in view of forgiveness ("In South Africa," he says in a passage from the interview that I'll come back to, p. 65, "we are saying we genuinely want bygones to be bygones"),[26] when he wants to show that this forgiveness was in fact often granted, he also has recourse to an example, and there again it is the example of a woman:[27] (Quote and comment on *Esprit*, pp. 67–68 F)

[FERRARI]: . . . former deputy president F. W. de Klerk has said that the commission's activities and the way it is dealing with the past are rekindling polarization. Is the very reconciliation that you're trying to achieve threatened by the polarization coming out of the revelations of the past?

[TUTU]: No. One should ask people like de Klerk, "When you say it is opening up and exacerbating animosity, who are you talking about?" When we had the de Kock trial, some extraordinary facts emerged about the things done to our people.[28] Very few people attended that trial, even at the time when this guy was sentenced. Despite all of those revelations, that didn't egg our people on to an orgy of revenge. They had to accept that that is what the country did.   *112*

I noticed recently an article that referred to the mothers of the Gugulethu Seven.[29] I just want to point out that our commission counseled the mothers and told them that a video we had is quite harrowing. But they said they wanted to see it. When we were viewing it, they became so incensed that one

26. Ferrari, "Forgiving the Unforgivable," 14. [Translator's note:] Cf. "Pas d'amnistie," 65: "nous voulons sincèrement pardonner et clore le passé."

27. During the session, Derrida adds: "And of a woman who, this time, forgives. Not a woman who doesn't forgive, as we have just seen, but a woman who does forgive. It's always a woman."

28. Allusion to the trial of Colonel Eugene de Kock (1949–), which began in February 1995 before the Pretoria Supreme Court. For eight years, and under his orders, numerous murders were committed, as well as acts of torture and kidnappings (notably that of Tiso Leballo, former chauffeur for Winnie Mandela). Charged with 121 offenses, de Kock was found guilty of 89 crimes and sentenced on August 28, 1996, to two terms of life in prison plus 212 years for crimes against humanity. The Truth and Reconciliation Commission was not yet formed at the time of his trial, which meant he was not eligible for amnesty. He was freed on parole on January 30, 2015.

29. Name given to a group of seven ANC militants who were shot in a South African police ambush on March 3, 1986, in Gugulethu township, near Cape Town. [Translator's note:] The typescript gives "1996" as the date.

of the mothers threw a shoe at one of the police officers who was testifying. Afterwards they said it was horrible, horrible, horrible, but thank you because now we know what happened. . . . One of the mothers, whose son was dragged with a rope, was asked how do you feel about the police? What would you like to do to this policeman who shot your son? She said, "I don't want anything to happen to him. I don't want him to go to jail. I forgive him." This is not the only incident of that kind.

So I want to ask Mr. de Klerk, if it is a fact that the commission was exacerbating feelings of animosity, how come people can still live in squalor, wake up in the morning and go to work in town, mainly working for white people who are affluent and have beautiful homes, salubrious surroundings, and at the end of the day, those people go back to the squalor—all of this and that they shouldn't say we've had enough of this, we've just seen how horrible these people are, and now we want our payback. No way.

The article doesn't speak about people like Brian Mitchell, the police officer whose orders resulted in the death of thirteen people. The commission got him because he said he wanted to do something to help rebuild, rehabilitate his community, and he went before the commission. Initially it was a very difficult meeting, but by the time he left, the victims' kin were waving to him. I don't claim that that is our work. It is not our work in a proprietary kind of sense. The most that we have done is be facilitators. The people to whom we have to take off our hats are those who have been trampled underfoot, and by now are filled with anger and bitterness, and should be bent on revenge. And you see, just to add maybe one thing, many things have happened, many people have disappeared, but as a result of the amnesty applications, we've been able to find out where people who were secretly killed were buried. We've been able to exhume the bodies and help their families rebuild. The families have expressed remarkable appreciation, because it has helped a closure to take place. [So, we again find this problem of the wound, closed or not, of mourning. Tutu's project was not, of course, in essence, that of justice in the sense of retribution, still less vengeance or revenge, but that of making truth, making known, to the extent that "making known" or "truth" allowed wounds to be dressed. For example, identifying the place where the dead were buried, knowing what happened; hence, knowledge in the service of this work of mourning that closes the wounds.][30]

113

---

30. Ferrari, "Forgiving the Unforgivable," 15–16 ["Pas d'amnistie," 67–68]. [Translator's note:] The French translation has *aidait à fermer leurs plaies* [helped to close their wounds] for "helped a closure to take place."

You will therefore have noticed that it is again a woman who is being quoted, no longer she who says, "I am not ready to forgive," but she who says, "I forgive him." Forgiving or nonforgiving, in both of these typical cases the subject is a woman. I'm not emphasizing that in order to recall that the question of sexual difference, well beyond the great South African example or any possible example, has inscribed within it the question of forgiveness, which is something that must never be forgotten. And not only because one may think that the love or compassion that one associates more with forgiveness than with the rigor of justice seems naturally more feminine than masculine, as though the excess of forgiveness over law, over retribution, or even over vengeance, was something specific to women rather than to men. We'll shortly, or another time, look into texts from the Gospel discussed by Hegel in his early works on *The Spirit of Christianity and Its Fate*, texts in which the appearance of Mary Magdalene constitutes a grand scene of forgiveness, and where Jesus sets out, as it were, the essential link between love and forgiveness. The more love there is, the more forgiveness there is, and the more forgiveness there is, the more love there is, that is to say that there is more forgiveness and remission of sins for a woman sinner who loves more, as well as for a forgiver who loves more, who shows more *agapē* or *dilectio*, to cite the Greek and Latin translations. I am going to read this passage from <the Gospel according to> Luke right away, because we will need it when we come back to Hegel and what he says about the difference between Jew and Christian, between Pharisee and Christian, on the subject of forgiveness. The Pharisee is he who doesn't understand what it is to forgive because for the Jew, says Hegel, for the Jew who doesn't love, there is between trespass and pardon, between *Verbrechen* and *Verzeihung*, an "impassable gulf (*eine unübersteigliche Kluft*)" (p. 355).[31] We'll come back to that; and also, because Jesus's reasoning is rather interesting from the point of view that we'll call economic, both economistic and economistic still in its meta-economy.[32] (Read and comment on Luke 7:36–50, pp. 198–99, and Greek and Latin, p. 166.)[33]

114

---

31. Hegel, *Der Geist*, 355; *Early Theological Writings*, 240 [*Esprit du christianisme*, 62].

32. [Translator's note:] Syntax thus in typescript.

33. Luke 7:36–50. Derrida's biblical page references here are from these sources: *La Bible. Nouveau Testament*, trans. Jean Grosjean and Michel Léturmy (Paris: Gallimard [Bibliothèque de la Pléiade], 1971); *La Sainte Bible polyglotte, contenant le texte hébreu original, le texte grec des Septante, le texte latin de la Vulgate et la traduction française de l'abbé Glaire, avec les différences de l'hébreu, des Septante et de la Vulgate*, vol. 7, ed. Fulcran Vigouroux (Paris: A. Roger et F. Chernoviz Libraires-éditeurs, 1908), 288 and 290 for the Greek and Latin.

Then one of the Pharisees asked Him to eat with him. And He went to the Pharisee's house, and sat down to eat.

And, behold, a woman in the city, which was a sinner, when she knew that Jesus sat at meat in the Pharisee's house, brought an alabaster box of ointment,

And stood at his feet behind him weeping, and began to wash his feet with tears, and did wipe them with the hairs of her head, and kissed his feet, and anointed them with the ointment.

Now when the Pharisee which had bidden him saw it, he spake within himself, saying, This man, if he were a prophet, would have known who and what manner of woman this is that toucheth him: for she is a sinner.

And Jesus answering said unto him, Simon, I have somewhat to say unto thee. And he saith, Master, say on.

There was a certain creditor which had two debtors: the one owed five hundred pence, and the other fifty.

And when they had nothing to pay, he frankly forgave them both [so, he remits their debt, he forgives. As one says in the United States, "to forgive a debt." He remits their debt, he spared them (*leur fit grâce*)]. Tell me therefore, which of them will love him most?

Simon answered and said, I suppose that he, to whom he forgave most. And he said unto him, Thou hast rightly judged.

115   And he turned to the woman, and said unto Simon, Seest thou this woman? I entered into thine house, thou gavest me no water for my feet: but she hath washed my feet with tears, and wiped them with the hairs of her head.

Thou gavest me no kiss: but this woman since the time I came in hath not ceased to kiss my feet.

My head with oil thou didst not anoint: but this woman hath anointed my feet with ointment.

Wherefore I say unto thee, Her sins, which are many, are forgiven [*sont remis*]

...

And they that sat at meat with him began to say within themselves, Who is this that forgiveth sins also? [There, of course, you have the question of the Jew. Who is he? Who does he think he is? Who is it who would remit even sins? That's the big question, isn't it: who is he? "*Quis est hic qui etiam peccata dimittit?*"]

And he said to the woman, Thy faith hath saved thee; go in peace. [*Fides tua te salvam fecit: vade in pace*. So, the words for love are *agapē* and *dilectio*, and, for "are forgiven," it's *remittuntur*, or *apheōntai* in Greek.]³⁴

---

34. [Translator's note:] Luke 7:36–50. For the Latin and Greek, see the Polyglot Bible, https://www.sacred-texts.com/bib/poly/luk007.htm; and for Greek transliterations, Bible Hub, https://biblehub.com/byzt/luke/7.htm.

It isn't only for these basic reasons (woman and forgiveness, Christian figure of forgiveness as love and woman as love) that I emphasized that these victims' testimonies (forgiving or not) were often women's testimonies. It is also for other reasons. Nor is it only because the surviving witnesses are often women; rather because the scene of witnessing and truth, of the revelation of truth in a testimony that puts on stage the body of the witness who may also be a victim (for example, a woman who is a rape or torture victim), can raise new questions, notably that concerning violence done to the body *at the very moment of* the testimony and by means of the testimony, whether it be that a woman has for the first time to reveal on her unclothed body the trace of a wound (which certain of them, I emphasize, had never before done), or that she has to recount cases of rape, and so refuses to testify, is unable to testify to the truth because testifying would cause the original violence, about which she was being called to testify, to be repeated or increased. As is everywhere and often the case, and at a level that is difficult to measure, rape by police or militia forces was part of the torture. The question of rape was not an easy question for the TRC, nor was it just one question among others. Every violence is in a certain way, no doubt, a rape [*viol*] and a sexual violence, but there is what one calls rape literally and in the strict sense, the rape of a woman by a man, but also, let us not forget, of a man by a man (for it is always a man who rapes either a woman or man; and the problem of the frequency of sodomizing in prisons — which we'll talk about again — is also a problem of rape, although, as you will hear, men do not like to call it that); so rape is not just one form of violence among others. Now, without being able, or wanting, to keep adding moving examples and to restage them, I refer you to the book by Antjie Krog that I have already quoted from (*Country of My Skull*). Antjie Krog is herself a woman, a woman poet of Afrikaner origin, and she was present as a reporter and writer, so as a witness also, at the experience of the TRC, and her life was broken and changed by it, and she dedicated a chapter of her book, chapter 16, especially to the question of woman.[35]

Her chapter is entitled "Truth is a Woman," and it would be worth quoting it at length, for it is rich in examples and in distressing testimonies. At a given moment Antjie Krog asks the question: "Does truth have a gender?"[36]

116

35. Krog, *Country of My Skull*, 233–50 [*Douleur des mots*, 254–303]. In the French edition, chap. 13. The chapter title is "Le corps des femmes comme champs de bataille [The body of women as a battleground]."

36. Krog, *Country of My Skull*, 235. Derrida quotes the question in English before translating it.

And she invokes the testimonies of women activists[37] who recall suffering a

117 first humiliation reserved for women, a prerequisite humiliation as it were, which preceded and overdetermined every other violence: even before the risk of being raped or becoming the object of sexual aggression in general, being arrested and handed over to the special security services or the police, this meant being suspected of not being a true political activist but a prostitute.[38] The result of this double humiliation (not being recognized as a responsible activist but as a prostitute, and as a consequence being treated as such, being submitted to the sexual whims of the torturers), not only was that a double wound but also, third wounding, it made testifying on that subject before the commission impossible or particularly difficult. Some women were no longer able to *reveal* the truth, they became incapable of *manifesting* the truth of what had happened to them, precisely because the worst thing that happened to them was in the end being stymied, inhibited, prohibited in their very speech, in speaking publicly—and sometimes privately, in a familial setting—about those traumas, that trauma within a trauma: (1) not being recognized as a responsible activist, but as a whore; (2) consequently being treated as a whore and so exposed to sexual abuse; (3) therefore, not being able even to testify to it, especially not before the commission that was nevertheless called "Truth and Reconciliation." The condition both of truth and of reconciliation was destroyed in advance in those violent acts perpetrated against women. I'll translate, as one example among many, extracts from a speech given by the chairperson of a Gender Commission (Commission on Sexual Difference, if you wish) at the opening of a special hearing or testimony session reserved for women. The chairperson had herself been the victim of the violence she recounts, as you will hear, the worst violence, the furthest reach [*fond*] of violence being when violence implicates the very possibility of witnessing and/or truth. (Translate and comment on Krog, pp. 178, 179 T.)

118 Does truth have a gender?

"Rats would come into my cell at night to eat the soiled pads. They would try to get between my legs when I sleep."

37. During the session, Derrida clarifies: "Black women, activists fighting against apartheid; it happens that they are often black women, but there were also many whites, white, anti-apartheid men among those resisting within the ranks of the ANC, but the activist women in question were black."

38. During the session, Derrida adds: "This suspicion was, as all the women testified, implicit and immediate. Even before anything else whatsoever they were told: 'You're not a political activist, you're not a militant, you're in fact a whore.'"

"As women speak, they speak for us who are too cowardly to speak.

"They speak for us who are too owned by pain to speak.

"Because always, always in anger and frustration, men use women's bodies as a terrain of struggle — as a battleground," says Thenjiwe Mthintso, chairperson of the Gender Commission, in her opening speech at the special women's hearings held by the Truth and Reconciliation Commission in Gauteng. "Behind every woman's encounter with the Security Branch and the police lurked the possibility of sexual abuse and rape." Some activists say they sometimes didn't know which was worse — the actual assault or dealing with the constant fear in the confined and isolated space of a cell. "When they interrogated, they usually started by reducing your role as an activist. They weighted you according to their own concepts of womanhood.

"And they said you are in custody because you are not the right kind of woman — you are irresponsible, you are a whore, you are fat and ugly, or single and thirty and you are looking for a man.

"And when whatever you stood for was reduced to prostitution, unpaid prostitution, the license for sexual abuse was created. Then things happened that could not happen to a man. Your sexuality was used to strip away your dignity, to undermine your sense of self." You had to ask for toiletries like deodorant, soap, and sanitary towels.

. . .

Mthintso says a man who didn't break under torture was respected by the police. "There was a sense of respect, where the torturers would even say: 'He is a man' [so the black man who resists torture is a man and he deserves respect]. But a woman's refusal to bow down would unleash the wrath of the torturers. Because in their own discourse a woman, a black *meid*, a *kaffermeid* at that, had no right to have the strength to withstand them. [In other words: "the resistance shown by a man is worthy of respect, that shown by a woman is not."]"

Banning orders for women were treated differently. "Women were consistently peeped at and preyed on. They wanted to prove that you were a whore. Someone whose inclusion in the liberation struggle was simply to service the men. To tell you, 'You are not a revolutionary, you are a black bitch on heat.'"[39]

Having posed the question: "Does truth have a gender?" — a question to which she seems to reply with a pained yes, the word itself traumatized, — Antjie Krog provides as epigraph to the above development the quote from a victim, who says: (quote, translate, and comment on p. 178 R)[40]

119

39. Krog, *Country of My Skull*, 235–36.

40. The passage Derrida reads during the session is in fact found on p. 181 in the 1998 edition. [Translator's note:] My references are to the 1999 paperback edition (New York: Three Rivers, 1999)].

"Rats would come into my cell. . . ."[41]

[Why rats? Because of the following scene:]

There has been concern that so few women activists have come to testify before the Truth Commission. They have their reasons. "The day I became involved in the struggle . . . I made a choice and I fully understood the consequences of it. To run to the commission now just doesn't seem right." In an effort to draw in the experiences of women activists and get a fuller picture of the past, the commission creates special forums. At a hearing on prisons, Greta Appelgren . . . testifies. She is now known as Zakrah Nakardien:

"What bothered me were the rats. They were the size of cats and they were in the passage all the time. While I was eating, three of them would watch me. I took my clothes to block their access, but they ripped all that and came in, crawling up, until one night they reached my neck. . . . I screamed the place down and they found me in a corner eating my T-shirt. This is how berserk I was.

"Isolation for seven months taught me something. No human being can live alone. I felt I was going deeper and deeper into the ground. It felt as if all the cells were like coffins full of dead people.

"I had to accept that I was damaged. That part of my soul was eaten away by maggots and I will never be whole again."[42]

Why these rats, these rat women?[43] Because the common and widely reported experience of rats in prison cells signifies, symbolizes, and allegorizes— however real and terrifying it was—a certain loss of integrity, a certain destruction that comes of being devoured or threatened with being devoured that eats all the way into the possibility of being oneself, of a self speaking of itself, of testifying. (Translate and comment on p. 181 R.)[44]

A question of language and of semantics once more. Since the crime violates the body but by that same token violates the truth of the body as speaking body, rape could not be named as such, for many reasons: first, because

120

---

41. Krog, *Country of My Skull*, 235.

42. Krog, *Country of My Skull*, 238–39.

43. Allusion to Freud's famous case study of Ernst Lanzer, nicknamed "the rat man." See Sigmund Freud, "Notes upon a Case of Obsessional Neurosis (1909)," in *The Standard Edition of the Complete Psychological Works of Sigmund Freud, Volume X (1909): Two Case Histories ('Little Hans' and the 'Rat Man')* (London: Hogarth Press, 1955) [*L'homme aux rats: Journal d'une analyse*, trans. Elza Ribeiro Hawelka and Pierre Hawelka (Paris: PUF, 1974)].

44. During the session, Derrida does not read this (previously read) passage, moving on directly to the following paragraph.

if the Truth Commission[45] were to decide that there would be no amnesty
for rape, rapists would never admit to it; next, because the concept of rape
was improperly restricted to a particular violence performed by a man on
a woman (whereas there were rapes of men by men occurring in the prisons); next, because the women victims themselves didn't dare speak up, for
countless reasons that you'll hear about in detail; finally, because since the   *121*
commission had to deal not with common law crimes but crimes said to
have a political motivation, how was it to be decided whether or not a rape
had a political motivation? When it comes, then, to the semantic question
of rape,[46] to the concept of rape, the whole machinery of concepts and crite-
ria that construct the very axiomatic of the TRC finds itself compromised
or afflicted with ambiguity (public/private, political/nonpolitical, etc., testi-
mony/nontestimony, with or without repentance, etc.), along with the radical possibility of witnessing, of telling the truth. (Translate and comment
on pp. 181–82 V.)

> A seemingly simple question like "What is rape?" can derail a whole dis-
> cussion. South African law defines rape as occurring only between a man
> and a woman and involving the penetration of the penis into the vagina.
> Acts of forced oral or anal sex and penetration by foreign objects are not
> considered rape. But the Truth Commission has to establish whether one
> can rape with a political motive [because that is its criterion] and whether
> the raping of non-political women [those not presumed to be activists] to
> keep the comrades busy is indeed a political act. The Geneva Convention
> regards rape as a crime of war and prosecutions for rape in Bosnia have
> begun only because of its link to ethnic cleansing [so, a question of the status
> of rape].
>
> The Truth Commission might recommend that rapists should not be
> granted amnesty. But why would a rapist testify if he knows he won't get
> amnesty? Then again, few women have testified about rape, and fewer, if
> any, have named the rapists. So why would a rapist apply for amnesty at
> all? There seems to be a bizarre collusion between the rapist and the raped.
> Although rumors abound about rape, all these mutterings are trapped be-
> hind closed doors. Apparently high-profile women, among them cabinet
> ministers, parliamentarians, and businesswomen, were raped and sexually   *122*
> abused under the previous dispensation — and not only by the regime, but
> by their own comrades in the townships and liberation camps [so, raped not

45. Thus in typescript and during the session.
46. During the session, Derrida adds: "What is a rape? In relation to what concept
can one legitimately use the word 'rape'?"

only by white representatives of apartheid or the police, but also by their comrades in the struggle]. But no one will utter an audible word about it.

The silence is locked into loss and cultural differences, says clinical psychologist Nomfundo Walaza. "Women who have been raped know that if they talk about it now in public, they will lose something again—privacy, maybe respect. If you knew that a particular minister had been raped, what would go through your mind when you saw her on television? Another deterrent is that some of the rapists hold high political positions today—so if you spoke out you would not only undermine the new government you fought for, but destroy your own possibilities of a future. There is also a culture of not discussing these things with your own family." [In other words, one doesn't speak of that, even at home.]

"When they raped me, I was already torn and injured by electric shocks," testifies Thandi Shezi, "I hurt deep inside, I could tell nobody. My mother is sitting here—she is hearing it for the first time. . . . When I get involved with a man, I get scared. I didn't tell a single soul about it. I don't want them to pity me. I don't want them to call me names."

Men don't use the word "rape" when they testify. They talk about being sodomized, or about iron rods being inserted into them. In so doing [by not calling sodomy "rape"], they make rape a women's issue. By denying their own sexual subjugation to male brutality, they form a brotherhood with rapists [I don't know if that's clear: when men refuse to call sodomy "rape," well, they align themselves with the fraternity of rapists and make rape a question for women] that conspires against their own wives, mothers, and daughters, say some of those who testify.[47]

Let us return to the Gospels. When a raped woman testifies, and when the judges are men, she immediately risks being treated as a whore, and her accusation always risks resembling a self-accusation and the beginning of a repentance. The shadow of Mary Magdalene, the penitent, thus comes to haunt these scenes from the commission, especially when the president speaks all the time of Christ, and in the name of Christ, of Christ on the Cross and of the reconciliation that he sought and brought about. I'll quote him again: "Reconciliation is costly and it involves confrontation. Otherwise Jesus Christ would not have died on the Cross. He came and achieved for us reconciliation. But he confronted people and caused division."[48]

Invoking Jesus Christ here obeys a very ambiguous argument: on the one hand, of course, Christ came, according to Tutu, to bring reconciliation; in

47. Krog, *Country of My Skull*, 239–40 [*Douleur des mots*, 181–82]. During the session, Derrida translates from the French edition.
48. Tutu quoted in Ferrari, "Forgiving the Unforgivable," 16 ["Pas d'amnistie," 66].

that way he implies not only the reconciliation of man with God but also reconciliation among men. But, Tutu emphasizes, that reconciliation, that spirit of reconciliation was not able to manifest itself without provoking new confrontations (Christ "confronted people," Tutu says, thus reminding us that it didn't go well, that the reconciliation that Christ called for, by calling for forgiveness, produced new divisions; and, in a minor key, Tutu suggests more or less modestly that in his own work for reconciliation he made enemies, that reconciliation isn't easy; it is also a struggle; and he has us understand that he is ready to pay the price of that struggle).

Before coming back to the ground of this logic and argument, let us recall that certain people were quick to object to the very project of this Truth and Reconciliation Commission. They objected that, far from soothing and healing wounds, or the memory of wounds, it would reactivate the harm, even racial hatred, once it came to almost unbearable testimonies, and when it came, as it sometimes did, to encounters between victims and those who inflicted their suffering, the perpetrators (cf. what we said during the discussion session:[49] arguing for "forgiveness" prohibits or slows down the work of mourning—develop).[50] Here we touch on the difficulty of reconciling, in the first place, the two imperatives that define the task or responsibility of the TRC: *truth* and *reconciliation*.

What does "truth" mean here, and what is to be done when the said "truth" can impede reconciliation rather than lead to it? What does *truth* mean here?[51] It isn't a matter of establishing a scientific truth, a supposedly objective truth, such as a historian might claim to arrive at and determine,

124

49. Allusion to the discussion session of December 16, 1999.

50. During the session, Derrida comments: "And I recall what we said last time during the discussion session, namely, that, on the one hand, of course, forgiveness can obey a logic of the work of mourning, doing what is necessary for healing and the time of mourning, etc., but that, conversely, an unconditional forgiveness that interrupts the process of justice, reparation, punishment, retribution can prevent the work of mourning, although, on the contrary, justice (the fact of the criminal having to pay, facing charges, etc.) can be a part of a normal work of mourning. In other words, there are two logics in operation: the forgiveness that has as its purpose the work of mourning, or the forgiveness that is the polar opposite, which, just as it has nothing to do with right and justice, has nothing to do with the work of mourning. And so, precipitating a scene of forgiveness on the scale of a nation, of a nation-state, may, instead of bringing about reconciliation, disallow it, whereas justice, with its time, its weighing up, evaluations, sanctions, punishments, and also its work of truth, could function in the service of a work of mourning. So, we are inside that ambiguity."

51. During the session, Derrida adds: "Even beyond or even before this question of sexed truth."

nor is it a matter of an archive that would be constituted, reconstituted by being deposited in a safe place. (Concerning the archive, I note in passing, having heard it in Johannesburg straight from the director of the National Archives, that there was already a tension, indeed a conflict between the institution of the National Archives—which is in principle autonomous and independent of the government—and the government, on the other hand, over the matter not of the archive in general but of the archive of the sessions of the commission, an enormous quantity of sound and visual recordings, transcriptions, deliberations, etc., on the basis of which the commission wrote a report that already resulted in a selection and an interpretation, that report having recently been submitted to Mandela.[52] Knowing who will have that archive at their disposal, who will control access to it, who will continue to work on the interpretation of this history and of the narratives, testimonies, their interpretation, etc., obviously constitutes a serious question. The fact that the government itself is not ready to give up control over this archive may appear worrisome, even if it adduces in that regard a concern for appeasement and especially if it respects and follows through on the decision initially made, namely, to allow a limited time for the process of mourning and forgiveness.[53] Giving a finite time and a circumscribed place to a process of mourning may indeed seem "healthy" and necessary, from the psychic as well as the sociopolitical point of view (develop,[54] cf. Hannah

52. In "True Confessions," Ash makes clear that the hearings of the three main committees that made up the commission (Amnesty Committee, Committee on Human Rights Violations, Committee on Reparation and Rehabilitation) began in spring 1996 and that the committee was to "submit its final report and recommendations to the President by the end of March 1998" (Ash, "True Confessions," 34) ["La Commission vérité et réconciliation," 49n3].

53. During the session, Derrida adds: "And reconciliation. It was said from the beginning that the commission would sit from a given date until a given date, and following that, it was over, they stopped. Of course, by that date not everyone had testified about everything, but on that date they stopped. The condition governing a work of mourning is that past a certain point, it is over. One doesn't go back there anymore."

54. During the session, Derrida comments: "But of course, you can imagine, there are many aversions, repressions that this can leave open. Naturally, the people from that archive whom I met, who were not happy, rightly so—university people or in any case academic scholars independent of the government—claiming that as an archive, the archive had to remain available to historians. Otherwise, even if it isn't immediately made accessible, it must remain independent of the government. One finds there one of the themes that we addressed a long time ago in this seminar: the university. Hannah Arendt ended up saying, about political lies, that judicial institutions, but also university institutions, were the only ones able unconditionally to keep, to be keepers of the truth,

Arendt, Kantian tradition: unconditionality of the true, academic research   *126*
independent of the political . . . : truth and politics).)

The point that everyone agreed upon at the time of the creation and installation of the commission was that if the latter were to be original, and to be distinguished (I'll come to this in a moment) from precedents such as the Nuremberg tribunal or the procedure for a general amnesty in Chile, it had to be precisely in terms of truth, the concern for truth, the necessity of conditioning amnesty or forgiveness on the revelation and establishment, without concession, of truth. (Mandela said to me "evidence"; comment.)[55] As Tutu himself says, beyond a certain date the curtain had to fall on revelations, testimonies, the revelation of truth. It is he who had recourse to the theatrical metaphor of the "curtain," of the stage on which scenes, acts had to be played out, with their own duration, and with their finite, limited duration.[56] It is like a drama with a moment of recognition and of catharsis, for once the work was done, the scenario played out, the curtain had to fall. And the question of the open or closed archive, precisely like a wound (that wound which according to Hegel was removed, scar included, by spirit in

---

to the extent that the university, or in any case institutions dealing with research into truth, are independent from politics. That is what happens there: in an institution like a university, let's say a research-type institution that, without knowing that it does, claims to have the right to establish and control this archive, and hence the freedom of access to this archive, and the government. . . . You can imagine the stakes in such a situation." Derrida is alluding to the seminar "Refiguring the Archive," in which he participated at the Graduate School for Humanities and Social Sciences of the University of the Witwatersrand, in Johannesburg, in August 1998. See Editors' Note, xviiin13 above. On Hannah Arendt, see the lecture given at the Collège de France, Paris, in April 1977: "Histoire du mensonge. Prolégomènes," in Mallet and Michaud, eds., *Cahier de L'Herne Derrida*, 495–520, republished as *Histoire du mensonge: Prolégomènes* (Paris: Galilée, 2012) ["History of the Lie: Prolegomena," trans. Peggy Kamuf, in Peggy Kamuf, ed., *Without Alibi* (Stanford: Stanford University Press, 2002), 52–70].

55. During the session, Derrida comments: "The question is that of 'evidence' in English. If you'll allow me to bring up my meeting with Mandela, when we spoke of this commission, he said that what is important is 'the evidence.' 'Evidence' in English is obviously also proof. What counts is establishing the truth: not judging or punishment, retribution, but knowing what happened and producing 'evidence' of it, that is to say, at the same time evidential testimony but also proof, attestation. What is important, then, is the work of 'evidence'; with the ambiguity, you see, of this word 'evidence' signaling toward both a testimonial truth and proof."

56. During the session, Derrida adds: "That is one of the additional reasons—but I am always finding new ones—for organizing everything we are talking about on the basis of theater, as a theatrical scene, a question about theater—and politics."

the work of reconciliation), the question of the open or closed archive concerns the limitation to the theatrical time of this experience of truth and
reconciliation. If I have chosen to put on stage theatrical characters, such
as Hegel, Mandela, Tutu, and Clinton, it isn't only for the reasons that I
already gave in interpreting certain texts by Hegel; it is also because of this
127 scenography that is presumed to organize the place, the taking-place and
time, the finite and controllable duration, the staging of scenes and acts of
a revelation, of a testimony and of a work of mourning. Moreover, Tutu
himself explains that very well at the point where, in the same interview, he
tries to accentuate the originality of the TRC with regard to previous, and
supposedly analogous, institutions to which it could have been compared.
Those two institutions are the Nuremberg tribunal, and also Chile. Listen
to what he says: (Read and comment on *Esprit*, p. 65 P)

> What is happening at home in South Africa is that we are saying we genu-
> inely want bygones to be bygones, but not in a glib way that people don't
> take account of what has happened, because then they won't be bygones
> [in other words, what makes forgiveness possible is the fact that people
> know, realize, they realized what happened].[57] As Santayana said, those
> who forget the past are doomed to repeat it.[58] And there is a specific provi-
> sion in the law to do this over two years, *then the shutters come down. . . .*[59]
> After this period no one can come forward and say, just look at this horror
> story, because they've been given the opportunity of telling their stories.
> After this, the country can't be held to ransom by new revelations. [So there
> is a time of truth, truth must be kept within this time.] We are saying: We
> had the opportunity; we looked at cases to the best of our ability; we have
> unearthed the truth. [This expression isn't chosen by chance: "to unearth
> the truth" means that it has been exhumed, but at the same time, that the
> *body* of the victim, the body of evil has been located. It has been located,
> unearthed, one knows where it was, and now it is put back there, and one
> knows that the work of mourning was possible because the corpse was
> located.]

57. [Translator's note:] Derrida is referring to the French translation, which reads:
"*car alors, il n'y a pas de pardon possible* [for then there is no potential forgiveness]." Final
clause in English in typescript.

58. Cf. George Santayana, *The Life of Reason, or the Phases of Human Progress* [1905],
in Marianne S. Wokeck et Martin A. Coleman, eds., *The Work of George Santayana*,
vol. 7 (Cambridge, MA: MIT Press, 2011), 172: "Those who cannot remember the past
are condemned to repeat it."

59. [Translator's note:] Derrida's emphasis here, and his references to theater in the
preceding discussion, rely on the French translation, which reads: "*après quoi le rideau
retombera* [after which the curtain will again fall]."

It is not a general amnesty, but an amnesty on an individual basis. Perpetrators must apply and satisfy certain conditions: It must be a thing that happened between 1960 and 1994 [there are also dates, you see, for crimes]. It must have had a political motive [the question of rape that we were talking about just now: is it political?]. The policy of either the previous government or the liberation movement must have been behind it. And, sometimes people forget this: the amnesty is not automatic. There is also proportionality. If it is felt that what you did was out of proportion to your objective, then amnesty will be refused. Once amnesty is granted, the perpetrator is set free, and many have already been set free. Whereas the victims have to wait until we determine that they are a victim and then we make a recommendation to the president about the reparation that is to be made, and he has to ask Parliament. ("Reparation" is the term used in the act. We think it is instructive that the act does not use the term "compensation" [so, they distinguish "reparation" or "restoration" from "compensation" or "retribution"]. Compensation seems to say you can quantify suffering, compensate someone for the loss of a loved one. How do you compute this [so, "reparation" or "restoration," but not "compensation"]?)[60]

Wanting to dissociate the TRC from the Nuremberg tribunal, Tutu holds onto just one of its aspects, neglecting to recall that it was in the course of the process that gave rise to the Nuremberg judgments that the concept of "crime against humanity" was developed, a concept that will be constantly invoked by the TRC, as its basis (examining crimes against humanity for political ends). I remind you that the Interim Constitution of 1993 announced that "amnesty shall be granted in respect of acts, omissions and offenses associated with political objectives and committed in the course of the conflicts of the past."[61] That clause was what bound Mandela's government when he came to power in 1994. If Tutu refers to Nuremberg, it is because at the moment he is speaking the context in South Africa itself is already very sensitive to that reference, strongly marked by it. It happens that at the moment of making concrete institutional decisions to put into action the amnesty requirement established by the 1993 Interim Constitution, inquiries were made into more or less analogous precedents, in Chile, Argentina, Zimbabwe. Colloquia were organized on the topic and their proceedings published (*Dealing with the Past: Truth and Reconciliation in South Africa*,

128

129

60. Ferrari, "Forgiving the Unforgivable," 14, Derrida's emphasis ["Pas d'amnistie," 65].

61. See 32 above.

Boraine, Levy, Scheffer, Capetown, IDASA, 2nd ed. 1997).[62] Now, in beginning that preparatory reflection, some members of the ANC demanded what they themselves were calling "Nuremberg trials" for those guilty of the horrifying state racism that was apartheid. One of the proponents of such a Nuremberg trial was Kader Asmal, himself an international lawyer and anti-apartheid activist then in exile, who has since returned to South Africa where, I think, he is part of the current government.[63] He was author of a book, co-written with his wife, in which, while approving of the creation of the TRC as the best possible outcome, he explicitly compared apartheid to the Shoah, and that comparison produced a great deal of protest in South Africa. His book is called *Reconciliation through Truth: A Reckoning of Apartheid's Criminal Governance* (Cape Town, 1996).[64]

So, Tutu excludes as a model the Nuremberg trials, however present the reference to them may be. He excludes quite simply the idea of a trial; such trials are too costly, he says, and on top of that futile, as was shown by the example of the trial of General Malan (former minister of defense in the De Klerk government, accused with several other officials of the "deaths of thirteen people by death squad," all of whom ended up being acquitted).[65] So, no Nuremberg-type trial, but no automatic and general amnesty either, as in Chile. If you grant that general amnesty, says Tutu, you will confirm to the victims that they are, and will forever remain, victims.[66]

62. Alex Boraine, Janet Levy, and Ronel Scheffer, eds., *Dealing with the Past: Truth and Reconciliation in South Africa* (Cape Town: Institute for Democracy in South Africa, 1994; 2nd ed., 1997); cited in Ash, "True Confessions," 33n1 ["La Commission vérité et réconciliation," 47n1].

63. Derrida is here referring to a note in Ash, "True Confessions," 33n2, where Asmal is said to be "currently Minister for Water" ["La Commission vérité et réconciliation," 47n2].

64. Kader Asmal, Louise Asmal, and Ronald Suresh Roberts, *Reconciliation through Truth: A Reckoning of Apartheid's Criminal Governance*, preface by President Nelson Mandela (Cape Town: David Philip, 1996), cited in Ash, "True Confessions," 33n2 ["La Commission vérité et réconciliation," 47n2]. During the session, Derrida adds: "Reconciliation through truth, always, through truth. 'Reckoning'—that's a word I have a feel for, although I can never manage to translate it—bringing to account the criminal government of apartheid."

65. Ferrari, "Forgiving the Unforgivable," 14 ["Pas d'amnistie," 64n1].

66. During the session, Derrida adds: "Whence the idea that the TRC is absolutely original, absolutely groundbreaking. And it is, moreover, often treated as such, and Tutu is invited more or less everywhere in the world where this type of problem exists, and he is asked for advice concerning what now has to be done in Argentina, Chile, and many other places. It is interminable."

We had already begun to ask about this phenomenon of Christianization of the process. That Christianization proceeds not only through the slippage or translation of amnesty into forgiveness, a forgiveness preceded by testimony accompanied by repentance; the surreptitious Christianization is also, through this very process, through this becoming-forgiveness of amnesty, the attempt to impose a Christian model of forgiveness that seeks to prevail over other Abrahamic models of forgiveness (Jewish or Muslim), or other forms of reconciliation and compassion.

We'll come later to the question of forgiveness in Arabic and in Islamic culture. When it comes to the Jewish difference—which we already spoke about often last year,[67] and which we'll speak of further, a difference that is at the same time subtle, difficult to grasp, and yet, probably, quite pronounced—Hegel is often very eloquent. And while Tutu was speaking in the *Esprit* interview, invoking the Gospels and Christ's passion, one could have once more heard Hegel's voice off, from the wings, approving but all the while protesting: "But I already said that, and very early on!"

Very early on, that is to say before *The Phenomenology of Spirit*, in the passages that we read together, as early as the so-called juvenilia collected under the title *The Spirit of Christianity and Its Fate*.

As I took up the question of Hegel's Jew in *Clang*,[68] I won't go back over it, moving instead to places in these texts where Hegel deals with forgiveness. In particular in the fragments on *The Spirit of Christianity* from 1798–99. *131*

As you know—and I am recalling this because, for the reasons I gave, I need to privilege the theatrical reference—in the conclusion to *Der Geist des Christentums und sein Schicksal* (another fragment from 1798–1800), concerning "Der Geist des Judentums," Hegel concluded with a theatrical perspective.[69] He had compared the great tragedy of the Jewish people to Greek tragedy, and he had noted that the Jewish tragedy could inspire neither fear nor compassion (*"nicht Furcht noch Mitleiden"*) (p. 24 of the French translation published by Vrin, p. 297 in the *Frühe Schriften* of the Suhrkamp *Werke* in twenty volumes).[70] So, no pity, no compassion, no forgiveness or reconciliation with what happens to the Jews. Why? Because terror and

67. Derrida, *Perjury and Pardon*, vol. 1, 44–64, 151–53 [*Parjure et pardon*, vol. 1, 77–101, 202–5].

68. See 51n46 above.

69. [Translator's note:] "The Spirit of Judaism" appears as the first chapter of *The Spirit of Christianity and Its Fate* in *Early Theological Writings* (182–205).

70. Cf. Hegel, *Early Theological Writings*, 204–5: "The great tragedy of the Jewish people is no Greek tragedy; it can arouse neither terror nor pity . . . it can arouse horror alone"; and *Der Geist des Christentums*, 297 [*Esprit du christianisme*, 24].

pity are in general born from fatal error, faced with the fate of an unavoidable slip, the faux pas of a beautiful being *("eines schönen Wesens")*.[71] But there is no such thing with the Jews, which is why their tragedy doesn't inspire terror accompanied by compassion, but horror (so *Abscheu*, which is here opposed to *Furcht*, like repulsion, which distances, instead of the fear that produces an identification moved by pity, revulsion[72] instead of compassion). If there is a tragedy to which the Jewish tragedy can be compared, it isn't Greek tragedy but *Macbeth* (interesting, this reference to Shakespeare; last year in the same context we read Shylock from *The Merchant of Venice* closely, and the opposition that is brought to light there between the Christian theologico-political discourse of mercy [*grâce*] — "the quality of mercy" that "seasons justice," as Portia said — and Shylock's dogged but futile resistance).[73] Why this ruthless [*impitoyable*] repulsion, without pity or compassion, for the Jewish people? Because according to Hegel they themselves are without compassion, without love, as we shall shortly see; they themselves don't know how to forgive. In that period, the concepts of fate (*Schicksal*) and nature (*Natur*) were organizing Hegel's discourse on religion, and we shall soon see that the Christian religion conforms with love as with nature. Here, Hegel tells us:

> The fate of the Jewish people is the fate of Macbeth who stepped out of nature itself [*aus der Natur selbst trat*, and the whole Judaic movement, according to Hegel, is a movement of separation, dissociation, rupture, and not unification and reconciliation], clung to alien Beings, and so in their service had to trample and slay everything holy in human nature (*alles Heilige der menschlichen Natur zertreten und ermorden*), had at last to be forsaken by his gods (since these were objects and he their slave) and be dashed to pieces on his faith itself.[74]

It is within this history that Jesus appears prior to the final crisis for the Jewish people. He appears not in order to combat just one *part* of the Jewish

132

---

71. Hegel, *Der Geist*, 297 [*Esprit du christianisme*, 24]; cf. *Early Theological Writings*, 205: "the inevitable slip of a beautiful character."

72. In the typescript Derrida writes and crosses out "revolution." During the session he indeed says "revulsion."

73. See *Perjury and Pardon*, vol.1, 54ff. [*Parjure et pardon*, vol. 1, 91ff.].

74. Hegel, *Early Theological Writings*, 205; *Der Geist*, 297 [*Esprit du christianisme*, 24], French trans. modified by Derrida. During the session, Derrida comments: "It is with this fate shattered by a lack of love and by a movement of dissociation and separation, and servitude, subjection, enslavement, that one cannot empathize. One can't identify with that, one can't love that."

destiny but to oppose it in its *totality*, to raise himself (*erhaben*) above that destiny and raise up its people. But—and here is a remark that goes in Tutu's direction and anticipates him, as it were—Hegel notes that this effort by Jesus to raise himself above the totality of the Jewish destiny, taken as a whole, encounters first of all hostility and confrontation on the part of those closest to him. Whereas his aim is love and reconciliation, the hostility that Jesus provoked at first could be overcome, sublated (*aufzuheben*) only by valor (*Tapferkeit*), by courage, and neither conciliated nor reconciled by love ("*nicht durch Liebe versöhnt werden*") (25/317); the sublime attempt on Jesus's part ("*sein erhabener Versuch*") to overcome the *totality* of that destiny had to fail among his own people and Jesus had to become the sacrificial victim (*Opfer*) of that moment.[75] Jesus lost that war within his own people and found an entry, a welcome, an access, in the rest of the world, among people who had no part in that destiny and so had nothing to defend. So it is humanity, the beauty of nature, love, the unity of reconciliation, the heart and subjectivity that Jesus will set in opposition to Jewish dissociation, to obedience to the letter of the law, to pharisaism, etc., to the punctilious, mechanical execution of objective commandments.

133

Since it is late, and because next time I want to get closer to what Hegel then says about forgiveness, notably in connection with the Sermon on the Mount and the scene with Mary Magdalene, I'll stop there today, but not without having situated, as placeholders, two pieces that I would like to add to the dossier, things we'll come back to once Clinton comes on stage. They are two scenes, two theatrical sequences, as you are going to see and hear.

1. A. The first piece is made of two fragments, as if to put spirit (not the journal *Esprit*, but the *Geist* of Christianity according to Hegel) into opposition with Freud's *mot d'esprit* (*Witz*).[76] In his book on *Der Witz und seine Beziehung zum Unbewussten* (1905),[77] and still under the heading of humor and the irony of *Witz*, of language and joking, its mechanisms and economy, its techniques, there is first a passage from the "Analytic Part" where Freud puts on stage in his own way, naming it without naming it, the becoming-Christian of forgiveness as a response to aggression, and he describes it as a type of *economy* (as did Hegel, as we'll see, in his own way

75. Hegel, *Der Geist*, 297; *Early Theological Writings*, 205–6 [*Esprit du christianisme*, 25].

76. [Translator's note:]: *Mot d'esprit* or "witticism" (literally, "spirited word") is the French word for "joke" in the title of Freud's work discussed below.

77. Sigmund Freud, *Der Witz und seine Beziehung zum Unbewussten* (1905), in *Gesammelte Werke*, vol. 6 (Frankfurt: S. Fischer Verlag, 2000).

and in a completely different spirit, and as did Nietzsche in yet another way). I'll limit myself to reading the passage, you are going to hear that he is speaking about himself; I'll simply emphasize what Freud calls an analogy with sexual aggression (which was at the center of our session today), while at the same time analyzing a certain *economy* concerning such an aggression or its analogs. (Read and comment on *Le Mot d'esprit*, pp. 151–53 [*SE* VIII, p. 102–3].)

134   Here, from the outset, we come upon the same situation. Since our individual childhood, and, similarly, since the childhood of human civilization, hostile impulses against our fellow men have been subject to the same restrictions, the same progressive repression, as our sexual urges. We have not yet got so far as to be able to love our enemies or to offer our left cheek after being struck on the right [A Christian motif, but Levinas has things to say about the Jewish interpretation of this story of turning the other cheek].[78] Furthermore, all moral rules for the restriction of active hatred give the clearest evidence to this day that they were originally framed for a small society of fellow clansmen. In so far as we are all able to feel that we are members of one people, we allow ourselves to disregard most of these restrictions in relation to a foreign people. Nevertheless, within our own circle we have made some advances in the control of hostile impulses. As Lichtenberg puts it in drastic terms: "Where we now say 'Excuse me!' we used to give a box on the ears" [fantastic!]. Brutal hostility, forbidden by law, has been replaced by verbal invective; and a better knowledge of the interlinking of human impulses is more and more robbing us — by its consistent *"tout comprendre c'est tout pardonner"* — of the capacity for feeling angry with a fellow man who gets in our way. Though as children we are still endowed with a powerful inherited disposition to hostility, we are later taught by a higher personal civilization that it is an unworthy thing to use abusive language; and even where fighting has in itself remained permissible, the number of things which may not be employed as methods of fighting has extraordinarily increased. Since we have been obliged to renounce the expression of hostility by deeds — held back by the passionless third person, in whose interest it is that personal security shall be preserved — we have, just as in the case of sexual aggressiveness, developed a new technique of invective, which aims at enlisting this third person against our enemy. By making our enemy small, inferior, despicable or comic, we achieve in a roundabout way the enjoyment of overcoming him — to which the third person, who has made no efforts, bears witness by his laughter.

78. See Emmanuel Levinas, *Otherwise Than Being: Or Beyond Essence*, new ed., trans. Alphonso Lingis (Pittsburgh: Duquesne University Press, 1974), 111 [*Autrement qu'être ou au-delà de l'essence* (The Hague: Martinus Nijhoff, 1974), 141].

We are now prepared to realize the part played by jokes in hostile ag-   *135*
gressiveness. A joke will allow us to exploit something ridiculous in our enemy which we could not, on account of obstacles in the way, bring forward
openly or consciously; once again, then, the joke *will evade restrictions and
open sources of pleasure that have become inaccessible.* It will further bribe the
hearer with its yield of pleasure into taking sides with us without any very
close investigation, just as on other occasions we ourselves have often been
bribed by an innocent joke into overestimating the substance of a statement
expressed jokingly. This is brought out with perfect aptitude in the common phrase *"die Lacker auf seine Seite ziehen* [to bring the laughers over to
our side]."[79]

B. The second fragment is more theatrical still and puts on stage, as is
often the case in this book, the converted Jew Heine. Heine on his deathbed
and still in witty form. It is a remarkable scene or sequence at least because it exhibits, raises the curtain on, a certain automaticity of forgiveness,
a certain functional, professional and institutional machinality within the
mechanism of forgiveness (requested or accorded). But this trade [*métier*]
of forgiveness would be God's craft. What is remarkable is that, on the one
hand, Heine's comment on God's professional responsibility is addressed
to a priest, so to someone whose profession it is to forgive or transmit the
request for forgiveness; and, on the other hand, evoking analogous profes-
sions, those of a doctor or lawyer, he doesn't speak — and with good reason, but neither does Freud — about the psychoanalyst, about the sort of
doctor that the analyst is, and about whom one can't help thinking here.
The shrink as licensed forgiver, as the forgiveness "pro" or God's delegate
for forgiveness, the representative of the forgiveness boss [*patron du pardon*]
known as God. God sometimes does that work himself, like a master crafts-
man [*patron artisan*], and sometimes delegates it to his secretary-confidant-
confessor, the priest. Heine's remark is nevertheless quoted as that of a German Jew who says in French (Freud quotes it in French) something of the   *136*
Jewish point of view on forgiveness, and perhaps on Christian forgiveness.
(Read and comment on *Le mot d'esprit*, pp. 170–72 [*SE* VIII, p. 114].)

---

79. Sigmund Freud, *The Standard Edition of the Complete Psychological Works of
Sigmund Freud: Volume VIII (1905). Jokes and Their Relation to the Unconscious*, trans.
James Strachey (London: Hogarth Press, 1960), 102–3. *"Tout comprendre c'est tout
pardonner"* is in French in Freud's text [*Le mot d'esprit et ses rapports avec l'inconscient*,
trans. Marie Bonaparte and Dr. M. Nathan (Paris: Gallimard, 1971), 152].

It is on account of the allusion made by these pessimistic stories to the manifold and hopeless miseries of the Jews that I must class them with tendentious jokes.

Other jokes, which are in the same sense cynical and which are not only Jewish anecdotes, attack religious dogmas and even the belief in God. The story of the Rabbi's "*Kück*" [p. 63], the technique of which lay in the faulty thinking which equated phantasy and reality. . . . Heine is said to have made a definitely blasphemous joke on his death-bed. When a friendly priest reminded him of God's mercy and gave him hope that God would forgive him his sins, he is said to have replied [you know that he had converted]: "*Bien sûr qu'il me pardonnera: c'est son métier* [Of course he'll forgive me: that's his job]." This is a disparaging comparison (technically perhaps only having the value of an allusion), since a "*métier*," a trade or profession, is what a workman or a doctor has—and he has only a single *métier*. But the force of the joke lies in its purpose. What it means to say is nothing else than: "Of course he'll forgive me. That's what he's there for, and that's the only reason I've taken him on [in other words, 'I produced God, I gave him my expertise so he could pardon me, my crime produced it'] (as one engages one's doctor or one's lawyer)." So in the dying man, as he lay there powerless, a consciousness stirred that he had created God and equipped him with power so as to make use of him when the occasion arose. What was supposed to be the created being revealed itself just before its annihilation as the creator.[80]

2. The second piece that I would like to add to the dossier will announce the imminent entrance onto our stage of Clinton, in the next act, in the weeks to come. Why do I link that with these two texts by Freud? Because the document that I am going to read obviously concerns a plea for forgiveness on the part of the most powerful head of state in the world,[81] because this plea for forgiveness concerns, as in Freud's first fragment, an economy and rhetoric of sexual aggression, and, as in the second fragment, an almost private (half-private half-public) request for forgiveness, a request for forgiveness addressed to God via a profession and a profession of faith, via a religious institution, a priest and a religious community, an almost familial religious community. And in the newspaper article that I am going to read from (*New York Times*, October 23, 1998)—a public article concerning a pri-

---

80. Freud, *Standard Edition VIII*, 114–15 [*Mot d'esprit*, 171].

81. During the session, Derrida specifies: "No plea for forgiveness for what happened in Iraq, or elsewhere, but for the things you're aware of" [*Laughter*]. Derrida is alluding to the first Gulf War against Iraq (August 1990-February 1991), which ended in victory for the coalition of thirty-five states under the leadership of the United States.

vate letter whose actual words are not divulged, only the basic content—
one can observe the play of political strategy, of a public and juridical stratagem, a cleverly and professionally maneuvered functionality within the
scene of forgiveness, this time in the pious Protestant milieu of the American heartland, the very place, the same place from which there issues the
libidinal and inquisitorial aggression manifested by Kenneth Starr[82] and
the Republicans who manipulate him, of which the same Clinton is also
victim. The scene of forgiveness that I am going to read is situated on the
front between these two libidinal, theological, and political maneuvers and
countermaneuvers. (Read and comment on *NYT*, 10/23/98.)

> President Clinton has sent a letter to the members of his home church in
> Little Rock, Ark., expressing his repentance and asking their forgiveness
> for his sins.
>
> The two-page, handwritten letter was read aloud to the congregation of
> the church, Immanuel Baptist, at the close of morning services on Sunday
> by the pastor, the Rev. Rex Horne. A church staff member said Mr. Horne
> did not plan to release the contents of the letter because it was a private   *138*
> message about spiritual, not political, matters.
>
> "The President expressed repentance for his actions, sadness for the
> consequence of his sin on his family, friends and church family, and asked
> forgiveness from Immanuel," Mr. Horne said in a one-sentence statement.
>
> "It was the right thing for the President to do," Mr. Horne told the Ar-
> kansas Baptist Newsmagazine after the services.
>
> Mr. Clinton joined Immanuel Baptist Church in 1980 and has retained
> his formal membership there while living in Washington. The church is a
> member of the Southern Baptist Convention, the nation's largest Protestant
> denomination and one whose leadership has turned increasingly conserva-
> tive in the last decade.
>
> In the weeks since the President admitted to having lied about his re-
> lationship with Monica S. Lewinsky last August [we'll come back to this
> problem. The president has attracted a lot of notice in the press on this
> topic; he is famous for making this extraordinary statement: < In response
> to the question > "Was it a sexual relation or not?" he said, "It depends
> on what 'is' is!" That depends on what "is" is, on what "is" means.], top
> officials of the Southern Baptist Convention [*some* of them] have called on
> Immanuel Baptist to revoke Mr. Clinton's church membership.
>
> "How can President Clinton claim to be Southern Baptist and persist in
> this display of serial sin?" said R. Albert Mohler Jr., president of Southern
> Baptist Theological Seminary. . . .

82. See 2n5 above.

Mr. Horne has declined to respond to the calls to discipline the President but has emphasized Immanuel Baptist's autonomy.

The Rev. Michael Seabaugh . . . said of disciplining Mr. Clinton, "I don't see what would be gained." "He has confessed," Mr. Seabaugh added. "He has asked forgiveness, and forgiveness has been extended. [Next time we'll see what went on between them, because this letter is private, clearly, its content hasn't been made public, notwithstanding being made somewhat public in the *New York Times* at a time when that meant something. So, we'll come back to <this>. I wanted to quote it because it touches on all the parameters that we have spoken about today. There you have it.]"[83]

139

83. Laurie Goodstein, "Clinton, in Letter, Asks His Church for Forgiveness," *New York Times*, October 23, 1998, A19. Derrida translates the text into French during the session.

January 20, 1999

<hr/>

[1]Mary Magdalene. And Monica.

Who is the Mary Magdalene of our time?

You remember, the curtain is still up.

Desmond Tutu is still speaking; he repeats: "we want to forgive," "we want to forgive," and he recalls the conflicts ignited by the sacrifice of Jesus at the very moment when he was suffering on the Cross. . . .

And we hear Hegel's voice off asking: "Come now, I've already said all that, when will people in South Africa read my work? When will I personally be allowed to speak about forgiveness and Mary Magdalene, as I was already doing in my early works on *The Spirit of Christianity?* Will someone finally tell me who the Mary Magdalene of your time is?"

Mary Magdalene. And Monica.

Who is the Mary Magdalene of our time? Let's not be in a hurry to say her name—or to put her under house arrest, whether it be at the Cape of Good Hope, in Johannesburg (those names speak volumes) or in the White House, in South Africa or North America.

Africa and America, the South and the North of these great continents don't just situate parts of the world; they are places and metonymical names in the *theatrum mundi*. And we need to speak of globalization [*mondialisa-* 142 *tion*], of a global theater—and to know whether the world as city, as terrestrial politics, "globalized [*globalisée*]"[2] as one says in English for *mondialisée*,

<hr/>

1. The hard-drive file for this session includes two openings. The four paragraphs that follow here (up to the repetition of "Mary Magdalene. And Monica") were placed at the end of the typescript with the mention "(1) (read before beginning)." During the session, Derrida began by reading these paragraphs.

2. During the session, Derrida adds: "'Globalized, global' [in English]. The Globe is also a theater, as you know, and last year we met Shakespeare more than once along the way." Allusion to the Globe Theatre in London, built in 1599 and home to Shakespeare's

measuring the world in terms of the terrestrial globe, whether this world is the ultimate theater, the ultimate cinema. <(>For it won't have escaped you that the techno-globalization of theater works through cinema rather than through the stage, and everything that we are speaking of, from Tutu to Clinton, with Hegelian subtitles, is also cinema or television; everything we are speaking of would be impossible without cinema and radio-television.) So we have to ask ourselves whether this cinema is the ultimate cinema, the ultimate movement of images, or whether, behind or beyond the terrestrial cinematic city, there was a city of God, within or outside a Platonic-Augustinian cinematic cave.

Before the curtain rises on the next act of our historical play,[3] I would like today to specify or clarify *two paradoxes* whose macroscopic massiveness risks sometimes being lost from view. This or that analysis of details, this or that microscopy in the approach to certain texts or to certain historical sequences might hide the evidence writ large (as Plato says),[4] as when we can't see the forest for the trees.

These two paradoxes have a common trait. As paradoxes, they both treat of labor, of the relation between forgiveness and the economy of labor, of relations between forgiveness, the gift, grace, on the one hand, and the economy of labor (in the most unstable and plural sense of this word: painful labor, punishing effort [*peine*], working through, even the so-called work of mourning, act, *energeia*, energy, but also might [*puissance*], *dynamis* as potentiality and virtuality, dynastic and virtual power [*pouvoir*], practice, *praxis* and *poiēsis*, etc.), on the other. So, two paradoxes *more*, on the subject of the relation between par-don[5] and labor.

I say two "more [*de plus*]"—two supplementary paradoxes, two paradoxes "more"—because all thinking concerning forgiveness can proceed only through what exceeds *doxa*, opinion, the credible, even the possible and plausible [*vraisemblable*]; and I also say "more" because what is going to keep

143

---

theater company, The Lord Chamberlain's Men. On Shakespeare, see especially *Perjury and Pardon*, vol. 1, 44–64, 120–26 [*Parjure et pardon*, vol. 1, 77–101, 165–73].

3. During the session, Derrida adds: "And before Clinton appears, that will be next week. It's not that I'm waiting for the news [*Laughter*], it's pretty much known in advance, but I didn't want this to coincide with the State of the Union address." Clinton gave his State of the Union address on January 19, 1999, the evening before this session.

4. See Plato, *Republic*, vol. 1, books 1–5, ed. and trans. Chris Emlyn-Jones and William Preddy (Cambridge, MA: Harvard University Press, 2013), 159 (§368d) [*Oeuvres complètes, vol. VI. La République (Livres I–III)*, trans. Émile Chambry (Paris: Société d'édition "Les Belles Lettres," 1959), 64].

5. Word hyphenated in typescript in this and following instances.

us busy with these two more paradoxes in the relation between par-don and labor, is precisely the *more*, the *plus* that either exceeds the economy of all labor, or else—and here lies the paradox—inscribes *within* economy, inscribes in what is still the immanence of the economy of labor, a *plus* that isn't simply excess, but surplus value, profit, bonus [*prime*], the economic ruse of hyperbole, the strategy or stratagem of the aneconomic within economy.

1. First paradox, then: Christianization and globalization.

First, when I insist on speaking of a Christianization of the global process of confession and forgiveness, and when I point out the signs of it, taking into account as much as I can the differentiated complexity of things (Christianity, however irreducible it be, remains the child of Judaism, and Islam isn't simply the rejection of it; conversely, the multiplicity of moments of Christianity and of Christianities must be taken into consideration), it is not to have the said Christianization of the globalization of confession and forgiveness understood necessarily as the theme of a reductive and basically anti-Christian accusation. What I am saying is not anti-Christian. Not necessarily. In speaking of a Christianizing globalization, presuming my hypothesis is justified, or in any case makes some sense, I am not necessarily insinuating: look at what is going on, you can recognize something familiar there, there is a maneuver, a hegemonic strategy, an invasion of the world or the earth by these basically extraterrestrial powers that are Christian powers. I am not saying that and insinuating: well, there you go, we know what Christianity is (even if it is a complicated, differentiated, indeed contradictory thing), and we can identify its workings, stratagems, designs and advances. Or else: Christianity, the good news, the Passion and Crucifixion that Hegel and Tutu are talking about (to cite only the witnesses or characters or actors we have heard from in this context, in our theater) have taken place, we know what that is, and we are going to follow, or even shadow [*suspecter*] this Christian operation.

No, it's not so simple. And that is why, during a discussion session before Christmas, I insisted on the obscurity of the concept of world, of world in general and of world [*monde*] in what is called globalization [*mondialisation*].[6] Christians, men and women of faith and of Christian good faith, can always come and remind us that the said Christianization is not a process of conquest, a victorious strategy in a world, in an existing situation of the world [*mondanité*], in a sociopolitical or economic history, in a market, in languages and techniques of communication, so many things one often has in mind when speaking of globalization. No, Christianity as history of good news

144

6. Allusion to the discussion session of December 16, 1998.

and expectation of a new world, repetition for ever and ever of what Christ testified, etc., Christianity as world to come, is a globalization, is globalization; it will come about only according to and through that experience of universal reconciliation by means of the confession of sins, forgiveness, worldwide fraternization among brothers. There is no world outside the horizon of that globalization to come. In other words, there isn't Christianity—a Christianity allegedly known for what it is, imposing the law of what it is already in the world—instead Christianity itself would not yet have come about, it would be only a promise, the promise of what will have to happen, of what should happen to the world and to Christianity as Christianization, to Christianization as globalization. Christianity itself has to be Christianized,[7] its Christianization works through globalization, and vice versa. This globalization is the search for the Christian world that is altogether yet to come, and confession, expiation, repentance, the act of memory, the recollecting of sins, forgiveness, reconciliation, is the birth of the world, it is the becoming-world of the world.[8]

And that supposedly takes place, will take place, either in the form of absolute knowing and Hegel's end of history, or else in the form of Augustine's City of God ([9]and when Kojève declared—somewhat deadpan as he was wont to be, somewhat believing in it—that the end of history had arrived in the form of modern Japanese society,[10] he was perhaps omitting the fundamentally Christian dimension of Hegelian absolute knowing, and of the end of history according to Hegel, namely, of what tends to manifest itself today: a globalization whose realization works through absolute knowing as worldwide confession, the transparency of repentance, forgiveness, and universal reconciliation, all of that trumping, tending to trump, the frontiers between nation-states and those of the market. That history would be a manifestation of God, and I ask that you remember this expression— "history as manifestation of God"—we'll come back to it at the end of our trajectory.

Globalization as universal state, the free market, and immediate communication among all immaterial or virtual points, that is to say, among the

---

7. During the session, Derrida adds: "And that's not easy; remember Hegel's or Tutu's words—it involves conflict." See above, on Hegel, 50, 55–56; on Tutu, 66.

8. During the session, Derrida clarifies: "Or so a Christian discourse would say."

9. This parenthesis closes at the end of the following paragraph.

10. Alexandre Kojève, "Note to the Second Edition," in *Introduction to the Reading of Hegel: Lectures on the Phenomenology of Spirit*, trans. James H. Nichols, Jr. (Ithaca: Cornell University Press, 1980), 161–62n [*Introduction à la lecture de Hegel. Leçons sur la phénoménologie de l'esprit* (Paris: Gallimard, 1947), 434n1].

souls of the world, is also something that works by means of confession, re-pentance, cognizance and recognition of past evil, knowledge or conscious-ness that trumps labor, etc. I'll come back to the big question of labor in a moment.)

This globalization thus resembles also, or rather, the City of God, Augustine would say. From that point of view, not only should we not act as though we knew that a globalization is in train and taken over [*arraisonnée*] by a Christian hegemony; on the contrary, globalization would itself be a Christian promise, the promise of a world to come [*à venir*], of a world and a future [*avenir*] that presupposes or works through the confession of sins, through sanctification, forgiveness, and reconciliation. The part played by the papacy today, both in the orientation of this globalization and in this uni-versal awareness [*prise de conscience*] of past faults, in universal repentance, would be a sign of that Christialatinization or globalatinization [*mondiala-tinisation*]. Globalization, the becoming-world of a holy world, will, from that point of view, be Christian or not at all, a convinced Christian would say. Even if, and inasmuch as that still might seem impossible, <it> retains the figure, precisely, of the impossible.

146

There, since I just mentioned Augustine, not him of the *Confessions*, whose doctrine of grace and mercy we evoked last year,[11] but the Augustine of *The City of God* (which I would have liked to read with you at length, which I therefore invite you to read or reread since we can't do it here), allow me at least, for the moment, the freedom of an excursion into it. Too brief, but a little long for the time at our disposal, as Augustine will himself say at the end of his book. As I just said: "Globalization, the becoming-world of a holy world, will, from that point of view, be Christian or not at all, a convinced Christian would say. Even if, and inasmuch as that still might seem impos-sible," as I myself often speak of unconditional forgiveness as the impossi-ble, of what is possible only as impossible, as I often speak, concerning all the figures of the unconditional (hospitality, gift, forgiveness), of an experience of the impossible, well, that wouldn't have come as a shock to a Christian like Augustine, on the contrary. The becoming-world, globalization, is the impossible itself, but the impossible is the promise itself, the very promise that God made and that is manifested as manifestation of God. As the face of God. And what happens, what comes as future, the coming of what is to come, is the impossible itself. We should study closely—but I'll forgo that also—the analysis of what Augustine calls, at the end of the last chapter of

11. See *Perjury and Pardon*, vol. 1, 137, 140–41, 198–217 [*Parjure et pardon*, vol. 1, 184–85, 188–89, 260–82].

the last book of *The City of God* (XXII.xxx), impossibility, "the impossibility of dying," "the impossibility of sinning,"[12] the effect of what he calls the second "free-will."[13] The "first free-will, which was given to man when he was created upright," was the free-will of the possible, of the order of the possible: the possibility of sinning, being "able to sin" or being "able not to sin," whereas "this last free-will will be [all the] more powerful"[14] for being the power of the impossible: the impossibility of sinning as impossibility of dying. Man will remain free even as he will no longer be able to sin. That will be a supreme reward, the absolute reward: "to partake of God . . . [who] by nature cannot sin."[15] Man will remain free while at the same time no longer being able to sin. That inability [*impouvoir*], the nonpower of that impossibility, will not be negative, and it will be the effect of a grace: the grace of the impossible that leaves me free while forbidding me from doing evil. The "impossibility of sinning," like the "impossibility of dying," will be the effect of this grace, of God's gracious forgiveness, and that will be the time of the City of God, of a globalization of the holy, one and indivisible city, delivered from all evil. Before reading a passage from Book XXII (p. 355 of the third volume of the "Points" edition) on this matter, I'll emphasize the importance of this theme of the impossible in Augustine.

If God's grace — the grace that gives to us the impossibility of sinning and the impossibility of dying — accords us "this last free-will," it is also

12. Derrida adds this Latin above the two quotations in his typescript: "*non posse mori*," "*non posse peccare*." [Translator's note:] The English translation has "inability to die," "inability to sin" rather than "impossibility" (Saint Augustine, *The City of God against the Pagans*, vol. 7, trans. William M. Green [Cambridge, MA: Harvard University Press, 1972], 377 [XXII.xxx]). Derrida quotes from *La Cité de Dieu*, vol. 3 *(Livres XVIII à XXII)*, trans. Louis Moreau, rev. Jean-Claude Eslin (Paris: Seuil, 1994), 355.

13. Cf. Augustine, *City of God*, vol. 7, 377: "last [*novissimum*] free-will" [*Cité de Dieu*, vol. 3, 354]. During the session, Derrida adds: "If you're interested in that you could perhaps go and look at Blanchot speaking of time, of the impossibility of dying, and you could ask yourself whether there is a relation between the impossibility of dying that Blanchot talks about and the impossibility of dying that Augustine speaks of as the grace of God in the second free-will." See Maurice Blanchot, *The Writing of the Disaster*, trans. Ann Smock (Lincoln: University of Nebraska Press, 1995), particularly 68–71 [*L'Écriture du désastre* (Paris: Gallimard, 1980), 112–15]. See Derrida's commentary in "Maurice Blanchot est mort," *Parages* (Paris: Galilée, 2003), 288ff.; and *The Beast and the Sovereign*, vol. 2, trans. Geoffrey Bennington (Chicago: University of Chicago Press, 2011), 175–92 [*La bête et le souverain*, vol. 2, 256].

14. Cf. Augustine, *City of God*, vol. 7, 377: "this last free-will will be more powerful in that it will not be able to sin" [*Cité de Dieu*, vol. 3, 354].

15. Augustine, *City of God*, vol. 7, 377.

because God himself is capable of the impossible, of promising the impossible and of having it come to pass. In an extended discussion around Plato and Porphyry—who, Augustine says, "severally made certain statements, and if they could have shared these with each other, perhaps they would have become Christians,"[16] for "according to Plato the created gods were promised what is impossible by the God who created them"[17] (XXII.xxvi) he insists on the capacity to do what is "impossible" (*City of God*, XXII.xxvi and xxvii), to promise the impossible and to make it happen (at that point he is talking especially about the resurrection of bodies).[18]

148

But one must be attentive to this double value, this double (positive and negative) side to the impossible. The miracle, the unbelievable thing that God has occur, is that the impossible, the experience of the impossible, is not the experience of a limit but of a superpower, a hyperbolic power. For example: "We have already said much concerning his omnipotence, by which he does so many incredible things. If they wish to discover what the Almighty cannot do, they have it forthwith—he cannot lie" (XXII.xxv).[19]

That not being able to lie is a positive superpower [*surpuissance*], an omnipotence [*toute-puissance*] and not a lack of power [*im-pouvoir*], that is what we have to begin to think and believe. But this example of the impossibility of lying as truthfulness, manifestation of self, etc., inability to say anything

---

16. Augustine, *City of God*, vol. 7, 349 [*Cité de Dieu*, vol. 3, 344].

17. Augustine, *City of God*, vol. 7, 347 [*Cité de Dieu*, vol. 3, 343]. Derrida adds this Latin above the quotation in his typescript: "*qui eos fecit secundum Platonem quod est inpossibile fuisse promissum*" (*City of God*, vol. 7, 346). During the session, he comments: "Augustine also considered, like Pascal, that Plato was predisposed toward Christianity. Plato was almost a Christian. Plato and Porphyry, well combined, that makes a Christian." On Pascal, see Derrida, *Perjury and Pardon*, vol. 1, 57 [*Parjure et Pardon*, vol. 1, 94].

18. During the session, Derrida adds: "That's very interesting, like his discourse on women, on rape. We spoke about rape in South Africa last time. I refer you to Augustine's text on the rape of women and on the rape that doesn't put an end to virginity." Derrida is alluding to *The City of God* I.xvi: "the body becomes holy through the exercise of a holy will . . . no matter what anyone else does with the body" (*The City of God against the Pagans*, vol. 1 (books 1–3), trans. George E. McCracken [Cambridge, MA: Harvard University Press, 1957], 74–75 [*Cité de Dieu 1* (*Livres I–X*), trans. Louis Moreau, rev. Jean-Claude Eslin (Paris: Seuil, 1994), 55–56]).

19. Augustine, *City of God*, vol. 7, 343 [*Cité de Dieu*, vol. 3, 342]. Derrida adds this Latin above the quotation in his typescript: "*Si volunt invenire quod omnipotens non potest, habent prorsus, ego dicam: mentiri non potest*" (*City of God*, vol. 7, 342). During the session, he adds: "*Mentiri non potest*: the fact that God can't lie is a manifestation of his omnipotence."

other than the truth, isn't just one example among others. It is what links the essence of veracity (nonlying) to the essence of promise (*develop*)[20] as *149* profoundly as is required. For from the moment that I know that God can't lie, that he is the very one who, by reason of his omnipotence, cannot lie, cannot deceive me, that nonlying is what he is, that he is veracity, fidelity, sincerity, that that is what the name of God means, from then on I have to believe his promises, and precisely even when he seems to promise the impossible. Augustine continues:

> If they wish to discover what the Almighty cannot do, they have it forthwith—he cannot lie.[21] Then let us believe what he can do, by not believing the thing which he cannot do [the performative, the exhortation "let us believe" is, by means of the preceding "then," both a logical and theoretical consequence; it is a demonstration: "since . . . well then . . .].[22] So by not believing that he can lie let them believe that he will do what he has promised to do. And let them believe as the world has believed, for he predicted that they would believe [in accordance with the faith

20. During the session, Derrida comments: "The fact that God cannot lie means that when he promises I cannot but believe him. Even when he promises miracles, when he promises the impossible, the fact that he can't lie—that's his impossibility, he can't lie—when he promises the impossible, well, I cannot but put my faith in what he says. And in fact, that is a profound thinking that as good as links the theme of veracity to that of the promise because being truthful is already to keep a promise. To be truthful is to imply, when I speak to you, in an as it were *a priori* way, the following: 'I promise you the truth.' Even someone who lies says that, implies that, it is even the condition for the lie: 'I am telling you the truth, believe me, I am telling you the truth,' that's the condition for the lie. Well, the fact that in this situation, in this as it were originary promise that is the basis for language, the fact that in this originary promise someone *can* not lie means that I have to believe them all the time, I can't doubt their promise."

21. During the session, Derrida adds: "He wants to know what the Almighty *can* do. Positive statement: what can he do? Well, he *can* not lie. The 'He cannot' is a 'he can.'"

22. During the session, Derrida comments: "It's a performative exhortation and at the same time, with the *ergo*, a logical consequence. 'Since it's like that, let us believe!' In other words, it's a performative that calls to belief, but that recalls at the same time that you cannot not believe, it's necessary, it's a logical consequence. Since it's like that, *credamus ergo*! So let's then believe what he can without believing what he can't. So, you find associated in this *credamus ergo quod potest, non credendo quod non potest*, you have this subtle association, one could say a 'power grab' [*coup de force*], or, how else to say it, a subterfuge operation that links the performative to the constative, the order or exhortation to the logical consecution, to the syllogism."

that he has promised],[23] praised their faith, promised it and now shows it accomplished.[24]

There you have, as I see it, the most forceful Christian thinking of a thought *150* of the impossible, of the possibility of the impossible. Is it Christian only? Is Christianity the first, the major or irreducible revelation of it? Or is Christianity but one possibility of it among others? Or, yet again, and this would be something else, is it a reappropriation that writes off [*amortit*] the impossible within the sublime economy of the possible?[25] Let's leave those questions open — we'll encounter them again in a different form. And let's come back to that other figure of the impossible, to the grace that is granted us by God, by means of the second free-will, namely, not being able to sin and therefore not being able to die.[26]

Speaking of God's *gift* as an *order* (God gives us orders, but his orders are gifts: for God, *giving* [donner] and *giving an order* [ordonner] come down to the same thing — and this equivalence between giving and commanding is a serious question), Augustine writes this, and in order to understand it properly, remember that sin is death, mortality: being able to sin means being able to die, and not to sin is to be immortal. The inability to sin is therefore the inability to die:

23. [Translator's note:] Derrida's gloss refers to the French translation, which renders this sentence as follows: "Believe according to the faith of the world, according to the faith that he predicted, according to the faith that he praised, according to the faith he promised, according to the faith that he accomplishes before your eyes" (cf. *Cité de Dieu*, vol. 3, 342); cf. *City of God*, vol. 7, 342: "*et sic credant sicuti credidit mundus, quem crediturum esse praedixit, quem crediturum esse laudavit, quem crediturum esse promisit, quem credidisse iam ostendit.*"

24. *City of God*, vol. 7, 343 [*Cité de Dieu*, vol. 3, 342]. Derrida adds this Latin above the quotation in his typescript, and inserts it into his reading: "*Credamus ergo quod potest non credendo quod non potest . . . sicuti credidit mundus*" (cf. *City of God*, vol. 7, 342).

25. During the session, Derrida adds: "With this rhetorical logic that surreptitiously slides to *ergo* following on from *credamus*, does Christianity constitute a reappropriation of a thinking of the impossible that cannot be so easily domesticated, as it were, and repatriated into the order of requisite faith?"

26. During the session, Derrida adds: "One following the other. Not being able to commit a mortal sin, in contradistinction to a venial sin inasmuch as Christianity opposes venial sin — a sin that is easy to forgive — to mortal sin. And clearly, when he says that the impossibility of dying is the impossibility of sinning, naturally he is putting into close association sin and death by means of the category of mortal sin."

God by nature cannot sin, while he who partakes of God receives from him the inability to sin.[27] Moreover, there had to be steps in the divine gift—a first gift by which man should be able not to sin, and a last gift by which he should not be able to sin, the former that he might gain merit, the latter that he might receive the *reward* [I underline the word "reward" *<praemium>*].[28] But since that first nature sinned when it was able to sin, it is freed by *a more generous grace*, that it may be led to that liberty in which it cannot sin [I underline "a more generous grace *<(largiore gratia)>*": economy of retribution for the reward, excess with regard to the economy, gift beyond economy in the overabundance of grace, what Augustine calls "more abundant grace," more abundant than the grace that rewards, but an overabundant grace as reward, a disproportionate grace, and the whole difficulty of this accounting will come down to trying to reconcile the idea of a reward—which comes back repeatedly—with that of disproportion. What could an overabundant and disproportionate reward be? What is this surplus value of capital that gets back more than it invests?] For just as the first immortality which Adam lost by sinning was the ability not to die, and the last will be the inability to die, so the first free-will was the ability not to sin, the last the inability to sin.[29]

And immediately following that, in a very consequential way, Augustine describes the holy city, the world, in short, that will be the world delivered from evil, that impossible world of the impossible become possible:

> For the desire for godliness and righteousness will be as impossible to lose as the desire for happiness. For surely in sinning we retained neither godli-

27. During the session, Derrida adds: "Whoever partakes of God receives from God, as a gift, the fact of not being able to sin. And I insist on 'receiving,' as you'll see the role that it plays, *accepit*, that's the word."

28. During the session, Derrida writes the words on the board and adds: "That's so as to put him to the test: 'Because you'll sin, you won't sin, you're free. Here you'll do wrong, test, there reward, you won't be able to sin and so you won't be able to die.' Some might see that as the very form of hell, but that's not the case for Augustine. [*Laughter*] So I underline this word 'reward,' which will play an important role in how we lay things out." [Translator's note:] Derrida's commentary refers to the French translation, which renders the sentence as follows: "Now, that order had to be followed in the divine gift, in that man received through the first free-will the power not to sin; and through the second, the inability to sin; one as test, the other as reward" (cf. *Cité de Dieu*, vol. 3, 354–55).

29. *City of God*, vol. 7, 377 [*Cité de Dieu*, vol. 3, 354–55], Derrida's emphasis. Derrida adds this Latin above the quotation in his typescript, and inserts it into his reading: "*Deus natura peccare non potest . . . accepit . . . ut primum daretur liberum arbitrium . . . praemium . . . largiore gratia liberatur . . . prima inmortalitas*" (cf. *City of God*, vol. 7, 376).

ness nor happiness, but though we lost happiness we did not lose the desire
for happiness. Surely, though God himself is unable to sin, no one should   *152*
for that reason say that he does not have free-will.[30]
   Thus the free-will of that city will be one present in all, and inseparably
fixed in each individual. It will be freed from every evil[31] and filled with
every good, enjoying incessantly the delight of eternal joys; it will forget
past sins and punishments, but still will not for that reason forget its liberation and so be ungrateful to its liberator. [Insist on the word "liberator
<*liberatori suo*>," recall Hegel, Mandela, Tutu: universal liberation.][32]

In God's city to come, once deliverance, expiation, and redemption have
wiped away the sins, Augustine also sees the announcement of the end of labor, absolute rest, modern themes if ever there were. As you know, the process of globalization is often associated with the end of work, with working
remotely such as marks the end of work as labor, suffering, regimentation
of the body, sweat on one's brow; the becoming-virtual of work that light-
ens the load and the workplace aspect of work (I refer you to studies that
are in the process of becoming classics, such as Jeremy Rifkin's book on *The
End of Work* [that's the title], Dominique Méda, *Le travail: une valeur en*   *153*
voie de disparition? [Aubier, 1996], André Gorz, *Métamorphoses du travail.
Quête du sens*;[33] cf. *Les Temps modernes*, special issue on "The Mutation of
Work" [no. 600, July–September 1998]).

30. During the session, Derrida adds: "What is this naïve thinking that considers
that the fact that God can't sin represents a limit to his freedom? No, God can't sin, he
is free."
   31. During the session, Derrida comments: "*ab omni malo liberata*: that's the theme
of freedom, that's why I emphasized at length in Mandela, in Tutu, this theme of freedom [*liberté*] as liberation. See 50, 55ff. above.
   32. *City of God*, vol. 7, 377–379 [*Cité de Dieu*, vol. 3, 355]. Derrida adds this Latin
above the quotation in his typescript, and inserts it into his reading: "*voluntas pietatis et
aequitatis . . . erit inamissibilis . . . felicitatis . . . ab omni malo liberata . . . liberationis . . .
liberatori suo*" (*City of God*, vol. 7, 378). During the session, he adds: "Evil is forgotten
without leaving a scar, like spirit in Hegel, no scar, but the deliverance and the liberator, the liberation and the liberator won't be forgotten. We are therefore in the same
Hegelian logic as the process of liberation that we encountered in Hegel, in Mandela, in
Tutu, etc. And universal liberation: the process of globalization is a process of liberation
like that of *The City of God*.
   33. Jeremy Rifkin, *The End of Work: The Decline of the Global Labor Force and the
Dawn of the Post-Market Era* (New York: G. P. Putnam's Sons, 1995) [*La fin du travail*,
trans. Pierre Rouve (Paris: La Découverte, 1997]. Cf. Derrida's commentary in "The
University without Condition," in *Without Alibi*, 225–28 [*L'Université sans condition*,
54ff.]; Dominique Méda, *Le travail: une valeur en voie de disparition?* (Paris: Aubier,

I am not going to involve myself further in this problematic of the so-called "end of work," which wasn't altogether absent from certain texts by Marx and Lenin. As for the latter, he associated the progressive shortening of the workday with a process that would lead to the complete disappearance of the state (*The State and Revolution*, Éditions Sociales, p. 175).[34] Rifkin, for his part, sees in the third technological revolution currently in process (following that of steam, coal, steel, and textiles (in the nineteenth-century), then that of electricity, oil, and the automobile (in the twentieth century), two revolutions that each time opened up a sector into which the machine hadn't yet penetrated, and where human labor, not that of the machine or that which is replaceable by the machine, was still available),[35] well, following those two technological revolutions—ours then, the third, that of microcomputing and robotics, and where a fourth zone that would put the unemployed to work does not seem to exist—Rifkin sees in the third a saturation by machines that announces the end of the worker and hence the end of work.

I am not going to go into the objections that can be made regarding those discourses and what they say in general, nor will I deal with the so-called "end of work" any more than with so-called "globalization." In both cases, which are moreover closely associated, if I had to deal with them head on, I would try to distinguish, in a preliminary way, among the hard-to-dispute phenomena that are registered by these words and the use the words are put to in the absence of a concept. Indeed, something is happening to work, to the reality and concept of work, in this century, and that something has to do with technology and with a certain tendency to reduce asymptotically the time of work and work done in real time and localized in the same place as the body of the worker; work, then, in the classic forms that we have inherited; and concomitantly, something is indeed happening in the experience of frontiers, of virtual communication, the speed and extent of communication, something that goes in the direction of a certain globalization. All that is hard to contest and quite well known. But between, on the one hand, those phenomenal indices—which are partial, heterogeneous, unequal in their development, and call for subtle analysis and no doubt new concepts—

154

1996); André Gorz, *Métamorphoses du travail. Quête du sens. Critique de la raison économique* (Paris: Galilée, 1988).

34. Vladimir I. Lenin, *State and Revolution*, ed. Todd Chretien (Chicago: Haymarket Books, 2014), 159 [*L'État et la révolution* (Paris: Scandéditions/Éditions Sociales, 1984), 175]. The passage to which Derrida refers is found in chap. 6, sec. 3.

35. We close here the parenthesis opened four lines earlier.

and, on the other hand, the doxic usage, what others would call the ideo-
logical inflation, the rhetorical and often nebulous complacency with which
one gives in to the words "end of work" and "globalization," there is a gap
that not only would I not want to bridge in some facile way but whose facile
bridging must, I think, be denounced, especially when it tends to obfuscate
zones in the world, populations, nations, groups, classes, individuals who
are excluded en masse, or are even victims of this movement referred to as
the "end of work" and "globalization," victims either because they don't
have the work that they need, or else because they work too hard for what
they receive in exchange, their so-called recompense, and that is happening
in absolute figures more than ever in the history of a humanity perhaps further than ever from the globalizing or globalized homogeneity and "out of
work" status that is often alleged or given credence. Humanity is "out of
work" where it wants work, or more work, and it has too much work where
it would like to have less.

Having taken that precaution as a matter of principle, I'll be content to
note, for the purposes of our discussion, that the work being considered in
this way is not activity, but the labor that allows one to live by the sweat of
one's brow, hard, backbreaking [*douloureux*] work, *tripalium*, instrument of
torture, punishing work in its biblical dimension. Now it is this work that
is presumed to come to an end in *The City of God*, at the same time as deliverance, redemption, and the impossibility of dying and sinning. This is
the work one would be freed from. In forgiveness in general one can see the
end of labor in general, of the labor of the negative, of the work of mourning, of the historical process as labor. The end of the City of God, the end
of the book entitled *The City of God*, which in fact describes the world to
come, the world finally reconciled with its liberator, is also a long descrip-   155
tion of rest, of eternal repose in a world redeemed by Christ's expiation and
suffering. What predominates in those final pages, which I'll leave you to
read, is the advent of nonlabor, of rest, in a world that becomes what it had
to be, a kingdom that will in the end be without end, in the repose of the
sabbath. Here are just a few passages to show how the motifs of merciful
forgiveness, grace, and rest are tightly woven together (incidentally, grace,
in the most general sense of the term, is the opposite of work, of toil: a
movement of grace is a movement that excludes every sign of work, every
painstaking tension [*crispation laborieuse*], every toil [*peine*], everything that
weighs down [*pesanteur*], every usage of a force of work: what is graciously
given is given in absolute lightness, it neither weighs nor pains). Moreover,
Augustine—like the modern discourse that puts knowledge and science
(and, by hyperbole, absolute knowing) in opposition to work (it's science,

techno-science that frees us from work)—Augustine speaks of a holy knowledge, hence of an absolved and absolute knowing that knows what has to be known and knows how to ignore and forget evil. And just as there is a second free-will, after grace ("inability to die," "inability to sin"), there is a second forgetting (following expiation, forgiveness is the second forgetting, about which Hegel will say in short that it erases in spirit, as spirit, everything up to and including the scar of the wound):[36]

> It is according to this second kind of forgetfulness that the saints will forget past evils [hence sanctification, becoming-holy works through forgetting, the second forgetting, gracious forgetting], for they will be so unvexed by evils that evils will be completely erased from their senses. But by the faculty of knowledge, which will be strong in them, they will know not only their own past, but also the eternal misery of the damned. Otherwise, if they do not know that they were once wretched, how will they "sing the mercies of the Lord for ever," as the psalm says? Surely nothing will be more pleasant in that city than this song to the glory of the grace of Christ, by whose blood we have been freed.[37]

156   Let's hold on to this classic, but here decisive argument. In this expiation and this grace there was a payment; Christ paid for us, and the mainspring of this economy of sacrificial exchange will be in the end what renders the impossible possible, and especially, together with grace, with merciful forgiveness, makes possible the end of work. Twisted minds might translate that as saying that Jesus's suffering worked for us, that he put something aside, saved up, saved us, saved us work, prepared for our retirement at a time when, with the end of work, the pension coffers risk being empty. Augustine continues:

> Surely nothing will be more pleasant in that city than this song to the glory of the grace of Christ, by whose blood we have been freed. There will the

36. See 8, 14, 36, 50 above.

37. Augustine, *City of God*, vol. 7, 379–81 [*Cité de Dieu*, vol. 3, 355–56] (Augustine quotes Psalms 89:1). Derrida adds this Latin above the quotation in his typescript, and inserts it into his reading: "*non erunt memores sancti praeteritorum malorum*" (*City of God*, vol. 7, 378). Following the quote, this sentence is found in the typescript margin: "Even if the [French] translation is adding a little to the literal sense by using the word 'ransom' for *cuius sanguine liberati sumus*, the idea of a 'ransom,' of a price to pay in redeeming, is indeed there." During the session, he adds: "Christ's blood bought us back; we have been liberated, bought back and redeemed by Christ's blood. So the idea of ransom is indeed present there even if the word is a bit strong if taken literally: Christ paid with his blood."

words be fulfilled: "Be still and see that I am God." That will truly be the greatest sabbath, a sabbath that has no evening. This sabbath God commended in the account of creation, where we read [Gen. 2:2]: "And God rested on the seventh day and hallowed it, because in it he rested from all his works which God began to make." We ourselves shall be the seventh day. . . . There we shall be still and see that it is he who is God. . . . Restored by him and perfected by greater grace we shall rest for ever, and see always that he is God, and we shall be filled with him when he himself shall be all in all.³⁸

This end of work, this rest, will be a universal liberation (I insist on that for its resonance with what we were hearing from the mouths of Hegel, Mandela, and Tutu), a liberation from enslavement and servile labor: "For even our good works, at the moment when they are known to be his rather than ours, are at once imputed to us in order that we may gain this sabbath. For if we ascribe them to ourselves they will be servile works, while it is said of the sabbath: 'Ye shall not do any servile work.'"³⁹

Servility is therefore that of the subject who wants to find a relation between his labor and his merit, who wants to attribute and reappropriate to himself the origin and price of his labor, to *retribute* himself, whereas liberation consists in attributing to the other, to God's grace, the rest that we thus earn, that we don't in truth earn but which is graciously given us by the overabundance of divine mercy. This world of the end of the world without end, this Christian globalization comes on Sunday, it is Sunday, the Lord's Day, the becoming-dominical of the sabbath, the second sabbath. Following the speculative Good Friday, on the eve of the absolute knowing that Hegel speaks of, here—skipping a day is all it takes—comes the Sunday rest, the becoming-Sunday of a world reconciled, following expiation, and devoted to rest without end. Becoming-world would be Sunday, dominicalization;

157

---

38. *City of God*, vol. 7, 381 [*Cité de Dieu*, vol. 3, 356] (Augustine quotes Psalms 46:10 and Genesis 2:2). Derrida adds this Latin above the quotation in his typescript, and inserts it into his reading: "*Vacate et videte quoniam ego sum Deus . . . maximum sabbatum non habens vesperam . . . in primis operibus mundi . . . requievit . . . Dies enim septimus etiam nos ipsi erimus. . . . Ibi vacantes videbimus quoniam ipse est Deus. . . . A quo refecti et gratia maiore perfecti vacabimus in aeternum, videntes quia ipse est Deus . . . erit omnia in omnibus*" (*City of God*, vol. 7, 380).

39. *City of God*, vol. 7, 381–83 [*Cité de Dieu*, vol. 3, 356] (Augustine quotes Deuteronomy 5:14). Derrida adds this Latin above the quotation in his typescript, and inserts it into his reading: "*opera bona nostra . . . servilia. . . . Omne opus servile non facietis.*" During the session he comments: "It is a matter of the end of servitude and of servile labor, a liberation."

it would be the becoming-holy, becoming-City-of-God of the secular city [*cite séculière*], the becoming-holy world of the secular world, that of the ages [*du siècle*]. That's what it would be, the successful globalization of confession, expiation, universal forgiveness, the next Sunday, Sunday with all the next ones:[40]

158

"It is not for you to know the times which the Father has fixed by his own power." After this age God will rest, as on the seventh day, when he will cause the seventh day, that is, us, to rest in God himself. [So our future is not, tomorrow, to reach the seventh day, it is to become ourselves, in our being, following forgiveness, on the seventh day: there is no seventh day without forgiveness. Moreover, if you observe in devout Jews the extreme anxiety, the sometimes obsessive and aggressive nervousness of the vigilance that they apply to the sanctified repose of the Sabbath, to the extent of abstaining from any gesture that evokes, even in the slightest way, work, a productive labor or technique, one also needs to think, in order to understand the gravity of the observance that they thereby recognize—if one wants at least to understand the extraordinary anxiousness, the paradoxical nervousness of certain Jews on Saturdays—one has to take into account the fact that any transgression of this injunction against work is not only a sin in itself, it is also the sin of sinning, the risk of not expiating and not being forgiven every sin; it is the risk of being deprived of all exoneration (expiation, deliverance) for every sin. The sabbath is also like a day of atonement [*jour de grand pardon*] on which transgression becomes an aggravating confirmation of every other transgression. Augustine continues:] To discuss each of these separate ages studiously at this time is too long a task. But this seventh will be our sabbath, and its end will not be an evening.[41]

He doesn't say so, regarding this tradition of the seventh day that has no evening, no *grand soir*, but the revolutionary theme of the grand evening, of the ultimate grand evening that inaugurates an end to history, or the beginning of a new history without history, a classless society, a liberation that will liberate from servile work, all of that remains connected.[42]

---

40. [Translator's note:] *avec tous les prochains*, also "with all those nearest and dearest," or also, "with all one's fellows/neighbors."

41. *City of God*, vol. 7, 383–85 [*Cité de Dieu*, vol. 3, 357] (Augustine quotes Acts 1:7).

42. [Translator's note:] The term *grand soir* [literally "great evening," "grand evening,"], has the sense of a revolutionary night of reckoning. The term perhaps has biblical origins; it came into use in anarchist and millenarist circles in the late nineteenth century. See Maurice Tournier, "'Le Grand soir,' un mythe de fin de siècle," *Mots/Les Langages du politique* ("Batailles de mot autour de 1900") 19 (1989): 79–94.

But this seventh will be our sabbath, and its end will not be an evening, but the Lord's Day, an eighth eternal day, sanctified by the resurrection of Christ, which prefigures the eternal rest of both spirit and body. There we shall be still and see, shall see and love, shall love and praise. Behold what shall be in the end without end! For what else is our end, except to reach the kingdom which has no end?[43]

Having thus named the end, the end without end of the world as heav-   *159* enly kingdom, Augustine signs the end of the book. He signs, he says "I," there you have it, I've finished writing, this is the end of the book that I have just written. For what I have just read is found on the final page, almost at the very end of the book that has just announced to us the promise of the final end, namely, a kingdom without end, the end without end. Augustine, then, in the end, signs.

What does that mean, the fact that he signs, at the end of a book about the end without end? For us it means both that he calls it quits, says he is "acquitted," but acquitted (as when one is acquitted of a debt, of a writ or accusation, and so is pardoned), acquitted, then, with the help of the Lord; and, that he is all the same still asking for forgiveness, pardon for not hav-ing put it very well, which is to say here not having sufficiently measured his words, having said "too much or too little." As he is not in a position [*en mesure de*] to measure, to carefully measure his words, to find the right mea-sure, and because there again it is God alone who is in a position to find the correct measure of what is said, well, while saying that he has discharged the debt that he had to discharge with the help and grace of God, Augus-tine nevertheless asks for forgiveness. He asks forgiveness of the reader, of every possible addressee, but in truth once again of God who alone is able to inspire forgiveness on the part of the reader, of any addressee, that is to say of someone who, by reading, is presumed to be or become one of Augus-tine's brothers,[44] one of the sons of God the Father. So, by signing the end at the end without end, he asks for mercy [*grâce*] while at the same time

43. *City of God*, vol. 7, 385 [*Cité de Dieu*, vol. 3, 357]. Derrida adds this Latin above the quotation in his typescript, and inserts it into his reading: "*Ecce quod erit in fine sine fine. Nam quis alius noster est finis nisi pervenire ad regnum cuius nullus est finis?*" (*City of God*, vol. 7, 384).

44. During the session, Derrida adds: "This signature, which asks for forgiveness, is addressed to God and to any fellow man who cannot—if he reads well, by read-ing—but be called to become Augustine's brother. This is a scene or a process that I also analyzed in Saint Augustine's *Confessions*, where the reader, that is, the addressee, is a fellow man who is called to become—it is the other who is called to become the fellow man of the brother—son of God. And it works through forgiveness, through

giving thanks [*grâce*]. To *ask for* mercy while *giving* thanks, that is the double gesture of this signature,[45] a signature that is inscribed while being erased, that is erased while being inscribed, for finally he gives thanks to God for the ultimate responsibility for what he does. The good he does is what God gives and orders him to do, and for what he doesn't do well, or does badly, or not well enough, may God forgive him, or rather may the reader forgive him; God gives him his gift, he orders it of him, and in giving him thanks, Augustine asks him to give him forgiveness also. I quote:

> In my judgement I have, with the help of the Lord, discharged my debt of completing this huge work. May those who think it too little or too much, forgive me;[46] and may those who think it just enough rejoice and give thanks, not to me, but with me, to God. Amen. Amen.[47]

It won't only be said that this signature—which, all things considered, doesn't sign but tries to give back to God, to give thanks to God for having ordered the gift and forgiveness—breaks with the economy of symmetrical exchange. It breaks nothing, Augustine doesn't break that symmetrical economy and in the first place because the initiative for his decision and signature is not his. Let us say more rigorously that, without doing or breaking with anything, the signature inscribes itself, or instead rather it is inscribed beforehand in the dissymmetry of the gift without exchange. It acknowledges [*prend acte de*] what it *receives* and that acknowledgment is itself not an act but a *receiving*. In signing, it isn't a matter of giving but of receiving, of knowing how to receive what one knows one is receiving, what one knows and must know that one is receiving, as one must know what one receives, what is given to us, infinitely given. In signing it isn't a matter of

160

---

a signature in the form of forgiveness. See *Perjury and Pardon*, vol. 1, 117 [*Parjure et pardon*, vol. 1, 162].

45. During the session, Derrida adds: "And perhaps of every signature. If one analyzes what happens with the signature, perhaps Augustine would say that every signature is that: it is a performative that asks for forgiveness while thanking."

46. During the session, Derrida comments: "What is translated by 'forgive' is obviously a correct translation, but in fact the word is *ignoscant*, 'may they ignore [it],' 'may they not take [it] into account.' And that has the sense of 'forgiving': 'may they forgive me, may they not take it into account.'"

47. *City of God*, vol. 7, 385 [*Cité de Dieu*, vol. 3, 357]. Derrida adds this Latin above the quotation in his typescript, and inserts it into his reading: "*debitum, ignoscant*" (*City of God*, 384). During the session, he adds: "And here 'so be it [Amen]' takes on its full force; it isn't just a mechanical gesture, it is the performative of the signature, the subjunctive 'so be it [*ainsi soit-il*].' That's what happens in every signature: 'So be it.'"

giving, but of signing an acknowledgment of receipt. I myself am, in a manner of speaking, undersigned, an acknowledgment of receipt [un accusé de réception]. That signature itself signs itself with the sign of the cross ("So be it") in grateful [reconnaissante] memory of the gift that God gave us of his son on the Cross (remember Archbishop Tutu's remark);[48] and in a given passage in the same final book of The City of God where Augustine recalls that again, you are going to see this disappearance of work come into view, this end to the economy of work for the benefit [profit], if it can still be called that, of the freely given gift and forgiveness. Quoting Saint Paul (Romans 8:32), Augustine writes (Book XXII, chap. xxiv):

161

> Hence the Apostle says, speaking of those predestined to that kingdom: "He who spared not his own Son [Saint Paul doesn't say "like Abraham," but he speaks here as Tutu will], but gave him up for us all, how shall he not also with him give us all things?" [So, the gift of his son already being infinite, what else can he refuse us?] When this promise is fulfilled, what shall we be! And what shall we be like! What good things shall we *receive* in that kingdom [I am myself underlining this insistence on "receiving," on what one has to know that one *receives* and that one has to know how to *receive*], when we have already *received* such a pledge in Christ who died for us! [The gift of Christ, of the only son, was the gift of a pledge <pignus>, in other words "an advance," the gift of a promise, the gift of the promise of the impossible to come, and at the same time the present gift of a life.] What will man's spirit be when he has no vice at all—no vice to which he is subject, or to which he yields [so: liberation], or against which he struggles, in however praiseworthy a manner—but is perfect in the mastery of virtue [heavenly peace and not earthly peace]![49] How great, how beautiful, how sure will be the knowledge of all things there, without any error or toil, when we shall drink the knowledge of God from its proper source, with the greatest happiness, without any difficulty! What will the body be like, a body that will be in every way subject to the spirit, and being abundantly made alive by it, will need no food to nourish it! For it will not be an animal body but a spiritual body, having indeed the substance of flesh, but without any fleshly corruption.[50]

48. See 80–81 above.

49. [Translator's note:] Derrida's gloss refers to the French translation, which renders this clause as "will possess unchanging peace in perfection [possédera l'inaltérable paix dans la perfection]" (cf. pacatissima virtute perfectus! [City of God, vol. 7, 338]).

50. Augustine, City of God, vol. 7, 337–39 [Cité de Dieu, vol. 3, 340–41], Derrida's emphasis. Augustine quotes Romans 8:32. Derrida adds this Latin above the quotation in his typescript, and inserts it into his reading: "accepturi sumus . . . accepimus . . .

162   This experience which, in receipt of that asymmetrical gift and forgiveness, exceeds exchange and economy, must nevertheless be well calculated.[51] One needs to know how to calculate what exceeds calculation, and work toward the end of work. In that regard one could find examples — certain examples among others, for they are everywhere — in Christian discourse in general, in Saint Augustine in particular (and next time in Hegel), some samples of a sort of hypereconomism that comes as it were to doggedly persist, and with what difficulty, in transcending economics while compounding its accounting exercises, if I can put it that way. So as not to keep you for too long in this same place, and in order to limit myself to what touches on forgiveness or on the remission of a fault or a debt ("to forgive a debt," as one says in English), here are two such examples. One could choose many others, in particular in Paul's Epistle to the Hebrews, but I prefer James [*Jacques*] the Apostle, since it is he whom Augustine quotes on this subject. James, who was moreover often opposed to Paul and to Pauline influence, *Jacques*, then, writes in his Epistle, chapter 2, 12–13: "So speak ye, and do so, as they that shall be judged by the law of liberty. For he shall have judgment without mercy, that hath shewed no mercy; and mercy rejoiceth against judgment (*Sic loquimini, et sic facite, sicut per legem libertatis incipientes judicari. Judicium [krisis in the Greek] enim sine misericordia [aneleos in the Greek] illi, qui non fecit misericordiam: superexaltat autem misericordia [eleos in the Greek] judicium*)."[52]

    In other words, judgment doesn't forgive one who doesn't forgive (fair's fair [*donnant donnant*]; no fair / no fair; you give / I give; you don't / I don't), but forgiveness mocks judgment. Said differently still, judgment balances *163* pardoner and pardoned, it forgives only to the extent that the one who asks to be forgiven also forgives, reciprocally, symmetrically, in an exchange. That is what judgment (*judicium*), and sometimes justice, does;[53] but conversely, forgiveness mocks judgment, it mocks that balance, symmetry, measuring, or that economy, or even that justice.

---

pignus . . . sine errore aliquo vel labore"; he writes and underlines *Pignus* in the margin (cf. *City of God*, vol. 7, 338).

    51. During the session, Derrida adds: "One must calculate the incalculable."

    52. James 2:12–13 (Polyglot Bible [*Bible. Nouveau Testament*, 790; *Sainte Bible polyglotte*, 386]). See Augustine, *City of God*, vol. 7, 151, 163 [*Cité de Dieu*, vol. 3, 275, 280].

    53. [Translator's note:] As Derrida here suggests, Latin *judicium* may be closer to "judgment" than "justice" (cf. *judicia*). "Judgment" is the English translator's choice in Augustine's quote from James in the following paragraph, whereas Derrida's French text has "justice." I have retained "judgment" for repetitions of the quote below.

Augustine (XXI.xxvii, pp. 277–78) quotes James and even paraphrases him by saying that, for James, in the end "mercy triumphs over judgment."[54] Augustine then launches into a long and labored demonstration, quoting Matthew who says (6:12ff.), and this is The Lord's Prayer: "And forgive us our debts, as we forgive our debtors. . . . For if ye forgive men their trespasses, your heavenly Father will also forgive you: But if ye forgive not men their trespasses, neither will your Father forgive your trespasses." Augustine also quotes Matthew, who says: "Except your righteousness shall exceed the righteousness of the scribes and Pharisees, ye shall in no case enter into the kingdom of heaven."[55]

In the complex logic[56] of the argument that I am going to let you read (Book XXI, chap. xxvii), Augustine wants to retain at the same time the principle of conditionality, or in short that of merit, namely, calculable exchange, fair's fair, forgiveness for forgiveness ("if you don't forgive men, neither will your Father forgive you anything," or "if you remit men their wrongs committed against you, your Father will remit you your sin"), and, on the other hand, nevertheless, the aneconomic principle of a faith and a hope that obeys a logic of grace and not of merit, not of exchange. One must think first of all of one's own sins and not those of others, their grievous or venial sins. By means of the recommendations that I just quoted, the Lord supposedly doesn't teach us a principle of conditional, economic reciprocity between men, a contract of exchange (forgiver/forgiver) between men and guaranteed by God, but, beyond that calculation, which is at bottom that of priests of the ancient law, that of the Jews, he supposedly orders us, teaches us always to feel guilty before God, and exhorts us to depend finally— *164* beyond all calculus, beyond every forgiveness that is reckoned [*escompté*], earned, deserved—solely on God's grace. "This is the same instruction," says Augustine, "that God gave to the priests of the old law through the sacrifices that he commanded them to offer first for their own sins, then for the sins of the people."[57]

And yet, even the discourse on incalculable divine grace continues to find its model, or at least its pedagogical example, in a human and socioeconomic accounting system. Indeed, as you will hear, Augustine still speaks of

---

54. *City of God*, vol. 7, 163 [*Cité de Dieu*, vol. 3, 280].

55. Matthew 5:20; cf. *City of God*, vol. 7, 157 [*Cité de Dieu*, vol. 3, 278].

56. During the session, Derrida adds: "There we have the matrix of an extensive history of forgiveness between Judaism and Christianity, of which we've been seeing certain indices since last year. We'll come back to it."

57. *City of God*, vol. 7, 161 [*Cité de Dieu*, vol. 3, 279].

"reward as a matter of grace," and the example that he cites to explain that "reward as a matter of grace" is a human example, where a reward based on grace is in fact a reward based on merit. In other words, between the *two orders* (economic/aneconomic, calculable/incalculable, merit/grace, human/divine, etc.) the relation is not one of rupture or heterogeneity but rather one of analogy, of a still calculable proportionality. I quote:

> What the apostle James says also applies to the point, that judgement will be without mercy to him who has shown no mercy. Here no doubt that servant should be called to mind for whom his master forgave the debt of ten thousand talents, but later ordered him to pay them back because he did not have pity on his fellow servant who owed him a hundred shillings.[58]

This example, which comes from Matthew (28:23), and which I am going to read in the original, gives much to *reflect on*, to *reflect* God's relation to men *like* that of, *analogous* to that most hierarchical one of a free, rich lord toward his slaves, toward his "slave companions,"[59] a master who sets as condition for his unconditional forgiveness—for his gracious remittance of a debt, for his absolute liberalism—that the socioeconomic exchange contract, that the market be indeed the same down here, in the terrestrial city, as in the ideal heavenly city. Here is the text from Matthew, which is much more precise and eloquent than Augustine's summary:

> Therefore is the kingdom of heaven likened unto a certain king, which would take account of his servants [in this sentence, which speaks of analogy, of the relation based on proportion, "likened" is *assimilatum* in Latin, assimilated, similar, comparable, and in Greek, ὡμοιώθη <*ōmoiōthē*>; as for "account," it is *ratio* and *logos*, two words that could also express proportional reason, which means that *ratio* and *logos* designate *both* the accounts settled by the lord and by God *and* the law of proportion, the analogy between the two rules and the two reigns, celestial and terrestrial].[60] And when he had begun to reckon, one was brought unto him, which

---

58. *City of God*, vol. 7, 163 [*Cité de Dieu*, vol. 3, 279–80]. Derrida adds this Latin above the quotation in his typescript, and inserts it into his reading: "*non fecit misericordiam*" (*City of God*, vol. 7, 162).

59. [Translator's note:] Derrida refers to the words used in the French text of the quotation that follows, which has *esclave* for "servant" and *compagnon* for "fellow servant."

60. During the session, Derrida adds: "God as earthly lord settles his accounts with his creatures or his subjects, and this 'like' is basically a rule of proportion; it is still *ratio*/ *logos* operating twice, if you like: within each of the two situations and in the relation

owed him ten thousand talents. But forasmuch as he had not to pay, his lord commanded him to be sold, and his wife, and children, and all that he had, and payment to be made [Augustine doesn't relate this moment in the text]. The servant therefore fell down, and worshipped him, saying, Lord, have patience with me [*Patientiam habe in me* or μακροθύμησον ἐπ᾽ ἐμοί <*makrothumēson ep' emoi*>], and I will pay thee all. Then the lord of that servant was moved with compassion (*misertus*), and loosed him, and forgave him the debt [so there the lord seems to obey only compassion without exchange, only mercy; he is *misertus*. Still, it is saying a lot to say that there is no causality or exchange, for to be moved is to be affected, to suffer for the other, to exchange and identify with the other. But it's now that the things of interest to us are going to begin; and Augustine's version is a little cryptic in this regard, no doubt symptomatically, and for not insignificant reasons]. But the same servant went out, and found one of his fellowservants, which owed him an hundred pence: and he laid hands on him, and took him by the throat, saying, Pay me that thou owest. And his fellowservant fell down at his feet, and besought him, saying, Have patience with me, and I will pay thee all. [So there we have, in the terrestrial city of men, a second analogy, this time not between terrestrial and celestial cities but between two situations of human, terrestrial debt: lord/slave, slave/slave. The debt between slaves reproduces the situation of the debt between slave and master, given that in each case there is already a social hierarchy because the creditor is above the debtor; the debtor is always the obligated one — subject, liable, humiliated — with respect to the rich man who has lent him money. From top to bottom of these two analogies, of this series of analogies, there is a hierarchy between the terms and, on top, power always belongs to the one who possesses the capital, and who, on that count [*de ce chef*], is chief at the head of capital. For forgiveness, which is what we are talking about, it is basically the same thing, the forgiver is always on the side of capital: there is a capital relating to debt, a capital of the calculated remission of the debt; as it is today for third world countries, and this is a capital factor in globalization, its future and limits: how to deal with the debt of the third world and of poor countries, of these modern slaves of capital? I'll pick up the quotation again.] And his fellowservant fell down at his feet, and besought him, saying, Have patience with me, and I will pay thee all. And he [the slave] would not: but went and cast him into prison, till he should pay the debt. So when his fellowservants saw what was done, they were very sorry, and came and told unto their lord all that was done. Then his lord, after that he had called him, said unto him [and this, by analogy, is the voice of God, is it

166

_____

of analogy between the two situations, in the relation of proportion between the two situations."

not], O thou wicked servant, I forgave thee all that debt, because thou desiredst me: Shouldest not thou also have had compassion on thy fellowservant, even as I had pity on thee (*sicut et ego tui misertus sum*)?[61] And his lord was wroth, and delivered him to the tormentors, till he should pay all that was due unto him. So likewise shall my heavenly Father do also unto you, if ye from your hearts forgive not every one his brother their trespasses.[62]

The reference to the heart (to the compassion of the heart) is what is here supposed to break with the principle of an objective and calculable economy ("*Sic et Pater meus cælestis faciet vobis, si non remiseritis unusquisque fratri suo de cordibus vestris*").[63] But it is true — and, as I see it, this is the inextirpable root of all these paradoxes concerning economy, the ultimate resource of an economy, or even of an indisputable economism — it is true that compassion, mercy, the movement of the heart that impels one to take pity, to be moved, *misertus*, by the misfortune or fault of the other, such a movement includes an irreducible proportion of narcissism, of self-love, and must even do so in the most altruistic, the most *heteroverted*, the most generous and disinterested merciful compassion: "I suffer for you, with you, and instead of you, I take your suffering upon myself, in me, I am your suffering and so, by wanting to put an end to it, by forgiving you, by remitting your debt or your fault, by relieving you of your suffering-inducing guilt, I unburden myself, I alleviate my suffering, my love for you is inseparable from a self-esteem, a love for my self, a love of myself without which I wouldn't be able to love you." The economy, the law of the proper, is thus reconstituted in the heart of the heart, in the love of love, in the seemingly most gracious forgiveness. . . . [64]

Having made a cryptic allusion to this very ambiguous story, Augustine himself concludes in an ambiguous way, for in the lines that follow he is going to mix a logic of mercy and a logic of merit. And at the very moment when, on one side of this opposition, he is speaking of mercy, he says "reward." Having just summed up in a few discreet words (symptomatically

61. During the session, Derrida translates: "Shouldn't you have been moved like me? Shouldn't you have been merciful like me?"

62. Matthew 18:23–35; cf. Polyglot Bible [*La Bible. Nouveau Testament*, 61–62; *Sainte Bible polyglotte*, 86, 88]. During the session, Derrida adds: "So the threat remains, at every moment, going all the way up, namely that not only the earthly lord but also the divine lord can send you to the tormentors if you don't remit your fellow's debt, if you don't forgive your fellow."

63. Polyglot Bible [*Sainte Bible polyglotte*, 88].

64. [Translator's note:] Ellipsis in typescript.

omitting to speak of the cruelty of the lord who delivers the slave to the tormentors), Augustine writes:

> So in the case of those who are sons of the promise <and vessels of mercy>, the words of the same Apostle [James] in the same context apply: "But mercy triumphs over judgement." For even those righteous men who have lived in such holiness that they receive others also into eternal tabernacles (men who have gained their friendship by means of the mammon of unrighteousness, in order to be such as they are) have been freed as an act of mercy by him who justifies the unrighteous, reckoning the reward as a matter of grace, not of debt. For in their number is the Apostle who says: "I have obtained mercy, so as to be faithful."[65]

168

The Apostle he has just quoted is this time Paul, who says, in the First Epistle to the Corinthians, 7:25: "yet I give my judgment, as one that hath obtained mercy of the Lord to be faithful [*consilium autem do, tamquam misericordiam consecutus a Domino, ut sim fidelis*; γνώμην δὲ δίδωμι ὡς ἠλεημένος ὑπὸ κυρίου πιστὸς εἶναι <*gnōmēn de didōmi ōs eleēmenos upo kuriou pistos einai*>]."[66] (*Comment*)

That distinction between the logic of grace and the logic of merit will have the vast history you know about, notably in France with Jansenism, Pascal, etc., and up to the French Revolution or even beyond. But it has to be remembered that that history is rooted in a problematic of debt and forgiveness, and of mercy. And I think that the analogy I just insisted on — that which leads the aneconomic back into the economic in an abyssal way, leading grace back into a calculus that always tries to integrate the incalculable, etc. — keeps complicating, interminably, all the logics of rupture that have governed these debates between the earthly (political) city and the City of God, between earthly peace and God's peace. The immense posterity of *The City of God* often divides those who refuse from those who accept the division between the temporal order of politics and a gracious Providence that transcends history. As is recalled in the introduction to this edition of *The City of God*, the whole of modern political thought, starting with Machiavelli, Hobbes, Rousseau, Gibbon, the theoreticians of the French

---

65. Augustine, *City of God*, vol. 7, 163 [*Cité de Dieu*, vol. 3, 280]. Augustine quotes James 2:13, and 1 Corinthians 7:25. Derrida adds this Latin above the quotation in his typescript, and inserts it into his reading: "*Superexultat autem misericordia iudicio . . . ut fidelis essem*" (*City of God*, vol. 7, 162).

66. 1 Corinthians 7:25; cf. Polyglot Bible [*Bible, Nouveau Testament*, 544; *Sainte Bible polyglotte*, 92].

Revolution, Michelet, is anti-Augustinian.[67] But if one takes into account
the paradoxical analogy that I have just brought up, this opposition encounters a limit to its pertinence and it becomes difficult to divide the two orders
decisively—and to dissociate politics in general from Christian politics in
Augustine's sense—whence the repercussions for the concept of globalization. For the God of *The City of God* manifests himself in history and as
history. And the concept of "reward," which I never stop insisting on, is at
the center of this Augustinian theophany, of this thinking of the manifestation of God in history and as history to come. For example, at the end of the
final book, when Augustine glosses Jesus's comment (concerning "the face
of my Father who is in heaven")[68] and that of Paul who says, "now we see
in a mirror, dimly, but then face to face,"[69] he, Augustine, is insisting on the
fact that that face is not the visage, or face in that sense, but the manifestation of God in general, and his manifestation as reward: "Hence the words
of the Apostle, which I quoted a moment ago: 'Now we see in a mirror
dimly, but then face to face.' So that vision is kept for us as the reward of
faith, concerning which John [1:3:2] the apostle also spoke: 'When he shall
have appeared we shall be like him, for we shall see him as he is.'"[70] And
to that assimilation, that resemblance, that analogy (we shall be *like* him in
seeing him *as* he is: two values for "like": resemblance, similarity, analogy,
on the one hand, and, on the other, essence as such, as it is), Augustine adds
this clarification: "By God's 'face' we must understand his manifestation,
not any such bodily features as we have and call by the name of 'face'"
(p. 347, vol. 3).[71]

Naturally, when forgiveness based on mercy "triumphs over judgment,"
it is implied that it rises, as did Jesus, above the scribes and Pharisees, the

---

67. See Jean-Claude Eslin, "Introduction. L'Acte d'Augustin," Augustine, *La Cité
de Dieu*, vol. 1 (books VII–XX), and particularly in this regard, 18. During the session,
Derrida adds: "Precisely because they want to think the specificity of world politics, of
terrestrial politics, in opposition to a divine Providence, divine mercy."

68. Matthew 18:10, quoted by Augustine (*City of God*, vol. 7, 357–59 [*Cité de Dieu*,
vol. 3, 347]).

69. 1 Corinthians 13:12, quoted by Augustine (*City of God*, vol. 7, 359 [*Cité de Dieu*,
vol. 3, 347]).

70. *City of God*, vol. 7, 359 [*Cité de Dieu*, vol. 3, 347]; Augustine quotes 1 Corinthians
13:12, and 1 John 3:2.

71. *City of God*, vol. 7, 359 [*Cité de Dieu*, vol. 3, 347]. Derrida adds this Latin above
the quotation in his typescript, and inserts it into his reading: "*Facies autem Dei manifes-
tatio eius intellegenda est, non aliquod tale membrum, quale nos habemus in corpore atque
isto nomine nuncupamus*" (*City of God*, vol. 7, 358).

calculating Jews, "priests of the ancient law." You know that it is some-times said that Saint Augustine was the first political anti-Semite in history. I won't reopen that question. May it suffice to point out that although, in an overwhelmingly obvious way, *The City of God* is directed first of all against the pagan Rome of the time, the *globalatinization* that it inaugurates, which is a function of the new Christian Rome, is often a protest against econo-mism, or even Jewish literalist mercantilism, which is to say that it plays off one concept of reward against another. While taking to task the pagan Latin concept of forgiveness and Virgil's warlike expression from the *Aeneid*, "To spare the fallen and subdue the proud" (Book I, Preface, pp. 34–35),[72] Au-gustine often has in his sights the crime of Judas and his unatonable trans-action. For example, in relation to suicide, he has recourse to the following example:

(From here on, everything is held over for the beginning of the follow-ing session.)[73] (Read and comment on *The City of God*, vol. 1, Book XVII, pp. 77–79.)[74]

For if it is not right on individual authority to slay even a guilty man for whose killing no law has granted permission, certainly a suicide is also a homicide, and he is guilty, when he kills himself, in proportion to his in-nocence of the deed for which he thought he ought to die. If we rightly execrate Judas' deed, and truth pronounces that when he hanged himself, he increased rather than expiated the crime of that accursed betrayal, since by despairing of God's mercy, though he was at death repentant, he left himself no place for a saving repentance, how much more should the man who has no guilt in him to be punished by such means refrain from killing himself!

When Judas killed himself, he killed an accursed man, and he ended his life guilty not only of Christ's death but also of his own, because, though he was killed to atone for his crime, the killing itself was another crime of his.[75]   *171*

Then Matthew 27:5.[76]

72. Augustine, *City of God*, vol. 1, 13 [*Cité de Dieu*, vol. 1, 34–35]. Augustine quotes Virgil, *Aeneid* 6.853.

73. In the typescript Derrida has crossed out the final two pages (121–23), which were given during the following session (see 124–25, 129 below). During the session, he reads the passage from *The City of God*, ending the session immediately thereafter.

74. In fact, vol. 1, book I, chap. xvii.

75. Augustine, *City of God*, vol. 1, 77–79 [*Cité de Dieu*, vol. 1, 56]. The January 20, 1999, session ends here.

76. For the transcription of this passage see 125 below.

2. I announced a *second paradox*. It also concerns the a priori intrusion of economy into an apparent aneconomy, of work into nonwork, and of ruse into grace. I won't elaborate on it, simply recalling that in the two examples or series of examples that I used in concluding last time,[77] first the two passages from Freud's *Jokes and Their Relation to the Unconscious*, and then the *New York Times* article on Clinton, one could clearly see how the discourse of forgiveness was employed in the service of a calculus, a strategy; it "functioned" as a profession (the profession of faith being a profession, a *métier* as Heine said). But that investment of the same logic and the same economy of the reappropriation of surplus value set the unconscious working in one case—a whole topic and energetics, an experience of "work" in general—and politics, a modern politics of mass media in the other case.

Those two novel situations are not incompatible, quite the contrary, the strategy of mass media within politics putting into play the unconscious and requiring as a result new analyses and new categories. One question that remains to be answered concerns the role that can be played by the principle of a logic of the unconscious in globalization and in the analysis of the discourse *on* and *of* globalization. Is it significant that such a discourse is prospering at the moment we are witnessing a certain retreat *on the part of*, or even a certain reaction *against*, psychoanalysis in the world, and first of all in the United States? For you can well imagine that if we are interested, or getting around to being interested in Clinton, it isn't because Bill as a person, the individual, does or doesn't seem "likable [*sympa*]," but because what is going on there, and even when it appears in the *New York Times*, reaches us from the greatest global power, from a state that presents itself as the representative of democracy, of human rights, the self-appointed representative of the United Nations and of the Security Council whose decisions said state doesn't even wait for before taking on a mission, in Iraq and elsewhere, and where the question of forgiveness seems to concern the legitimacy, or not, the removal or not of a president of the United States before the eyes of his people, on the pretext of an internal, or even private [*intime*], domestic[78] and not international affair, one that doesn't concern the legitimacy of his political action in the world, the former being capable of providing an alibi for the latter.

How is that possible? How to explain that, at the heart of these new, very new problematics, that opened up by a logic of the unconscious and that of a twenty-first-century geopolitics, how to explain that the old notion

172

77. See 89–94 above.
78. [Translator's note:] Word in English in typescript.

of pardon—and of perjury, since with Clinton it will indeed be a question, more than ever, more explicitly and literally than ever, of pardoning a perjurer—how to explain that these old notions of pardon and of perjury still constitute an active heritage, one that signifies and has utility still? Why is that?

It is there that we might again find, as I announced last time, Mary Magdalene, Hegel's Mary Magdalene, and Monica, not *Santa* Monica (the saintly mother of Augustine, who, moreover, wasn't as saintly as all that and confessed the sins of her youth), but the less than saintly paragon of virtue [*moins sainte nitouche*] Monica Lewinsky,[79] and all the phantasmatic, economic, political, and other machines that she is prey to.

79. Monica Lewinsky (b. 1973) graduated with a major in psychology from Lewis and Clark College and was an intern at the White House in 1995 during President Clinton's first term of office. In 1998 she made headlines over her sexual affair with the president, who perjured himself by denying the affair, which led to impeachment proceedings against him.

January 27, 1999

What is work?[1]

1. There exist two typescript versions of this session. The first version includes a greater number of annotations and photocopies. The second version includes the hand-written mention "2) other printout" in the top right corner of the first page. Apart from the pagination, the annotations, and a poorly printed page 21 in the second version, the content of both is identical. We are here following the first version. Before beginning the session, Derrida reads an article from *Le Monde* as a preamble [the first part of the recording is missing]: "So, what I read yesterday in *Le Monde* is this, which will take us to five o'clock: 'At the 16th Street Foundry United Methodist Church, the pastor J. Philip Wogaman . . . suddenly . . . turned the discussion toward "the sad debate on Capitol Hill," "the most painful, the most disastrous of debates." . . . Reverend Woga-man, a respected theologian, is known as the customary pastor of the Clinton family, is he not? Isn't he one of the three official spiritual advisors of the president, who was slated to meet Pope John Paul II on Tuesday evening? "The subject [of the disastrous debate]," he said, "is an opposition between two conceptions of morality, two visions of life in society. It can be the occasion, for this country, to choose its values clearly. To define what constitutes its soul." On one side is the conservative clan [he is openly on the side of the Democrats, the reverend is the Clinton family pastor]: "Those for whom morality is above all a question of discipline, of the strict application of the law. That goes hand in hand with principles of authority, judgment and punishment." [That is the tone of Christ's condemnation of the Pharisees who favor justice, sanctioning, etc.] On the other side, the liberal clan: "Those for whom morality is a question of love and caring for others [there too, Hegel said the same thing when he described the relation between Christ and the Pharisees], those for whom the ideas of repentance, forgiveness and tolerance win out over those of sanction and vengeance." . . . In concluding the service, J. Philip Wogaman confirmed that he would continue to support Clinton, "in-defensible but not unforgivable [that's a new and interesting distinction!], a sinner and a sincere and trustworthy penitent." [*Laughter*] At the same time, on the west side of the city, in the Baptist Church of Jerusalem, Reverend Clinton Washington [his first name is Clinton, his family name Washington!] is welcoming the faithful for the 11:00 a.m. service. The really faithful, those who have crossed the whole city. . . . The imposing

And in what sense can one say that God plays dead [*fait le mort*]? (Read and comment on *The City of God*, vol. 1, <Book I, chap.> xvii, p. 56; then Matthew 27:5.)

If we rightly execrate Judas' deed, and truth pronounces that when he hanged himself, he increased rather than expiated the crime of that accursed betrayal, since by despairing of God's mercy, though he was at death repentant, he left himself no place for a saving repentance, how much more should the man who has no guilt in him to be punished by such means refrain from killing himself!

When Judas killed himself [this is a passage on suicide: Judas kills himself, hence without having really undertaken a repentance worthy of the name], he killed an accursed man, and he ended his life guilty not only of Christ's death but also of his own, because, though he was killed to atone for his crime, the killing itself was another crime of his.[2]

Then Judas, which had betrayed him, when he saw that he was condemned, repented himself, and brought again the thirty pieces of silver to the chief

---

Clinton Washington, with his huge smile, had a message to pass on. He read — just this once — the beginning of his sermon. "President William Jefferson Clinton is a sinner, but he isn't a criminal." He pauses . . . and catches his breath. "Removing a president because he is a sinner amounts to destroying the Constitution. Removing a president because you can't manage to defeat him in two elections is not only shameful, but perverts the 'rule of law.' Tens of millions of electors should not have their vote cast aside on the pretext that fewer than three hundred partisan politicians are not happy with the president those voters chose. We know the difference between crime and private sin." . . . For him, we have to denounce the trap set for Clinton, a president who is so close, he says, to the poor, the lowly, black people especially. "He is a president who looks after us, who loves us and resembles us. And that drives them [Republicans] mad. And they want to make him pay. . . . The downfall of Clinton would be quite simply our own."' There you have it, from *Le Monde* yesterday, and you see how it overlaps with what I would like, perhaps, to try to study today and again next time. There, it's now five o'clock, okay." (See Annick Cojean, "Baptistes et méthodistes, ils communient pour Clinton le pécheur," *Le Monde*, January 27, 1999, 1, Cojean's italics, my translation; available online at https://www.lemonde.fr/archives/article/1999/01/27/baptistes-et-methodistes -ils-communient-pour-clinton-le-pecheur_3532851_1819218.html.) Derrida next announces a launch in which he will participate, to take place the following evening at Le Divan bookstore, for a special double issue of *Cahiers Intersignes* (no. 13, autumn 1998, Casablanca: Éditions Toubkal) entitled "Idiomes, nationalités, déconstructions. Rencontre de Rabat avec Jacques Derrida," then begins reading his typescript. In both versions of the typescript Derrida has added the first sentence by hand. It exists in the computer file.

2. Augustine, *City of God*, vol. 1, 77 [*Cité de Dieu*, vol. 1, 56].

priests and elders, Saying, I have sinned in that I have betrayed the innocent blood. And they said, What is that to us? see thou to that. And he cast
down the pieces of silver in the temple, and departed, and went and hanged
175   himself. And the chief priests took the silver pieces, and said, It is not lawful
for to put them into the treasury, because it is the price of blood. And they
took counsel, and bought with them the potter's field, to bury strangers in.
Wherefore that field was called, The field of blood, unto this day. Then was
fulfilled that which was spoken by Jeremy the prophet, saying, And they
took the thirty pieces of silver, the price of him that was valued, whom they
of the children of Israel did value; And gave them for the potter's field, as
the Lord appointed me. [That is what I wanted to read last time in concluding the session; what I called the "first paradox."]³

2. You may remember that at the beginning of the previous session I
announced a *second paradox*.⁴ One *more* paradox, another paradox in addition. All the while explaining why thinking does not think here except
by involving us in paradox, inasmuch as every thinking of forgiveness can
progress only in what exceeds *doxa*, opinion, the credible, even the possible
and plausible [*vraisemblable*], all the way to the impossible, all the way to
what, for a long time, has been obsessing us, besieging us, even holding us
hostage, namely, the possibility of the impossible. And we also said "more"
because what is keeping us busy with these two paradoxes *more*, in the matter of the relation between par-don and labor, concerns as well the a priori
intrusion of economy into an apparent aneconomy, of work into nonwork,
and of ruse into grace, the reappropriation of excess as surplus value or bonus (*praemium*), as supreme reward. Of course, the intrusion of work into
nonwork also signifies the persistence, return, or insistence of work within
sabbatical repose (as described in *The City of God*) or in the both euphoric
and apocalyptic tableau of the era of the end of work that we were also
talking about last time and about which we'll have more to say: the endless end of work in the era of *The End of Work: The Decline of the Global
Labor Force and the Dawn of the Post-Market Era*.⁵ If this question of work,
176   of the asymptotic reduction in the time of work, interests you, notably in
its Christian history, in the history of that Christian theology of work, I'll
point to very particular input from a historian, very determinate input but
all the more rich in information, evidence, and useful references about the

---

3. Matthew 27:3–10 [*Bible, Nouveau Testament*, 94–95]. See 121 above.
4. Derrida here takes up pages 121–23 above, which he hadn't read during the previous session.
5. See Rifkin, *End of Work*. During the session, Derrida translates the English title.

medieval period: concerning the relation between work and *opus servile*, concerning a certain concept of work as paradisiacal, a certain secularization of the time of work, a medieval struggle—already—in favor of the lengthening, or conversely the reduction, of the workday, which came to a head, for example, in a case before the Parliament of Paris,[6] I would recommend that you read the opening chapter, entitled "Time and Work," in a collection of texts by my colleague Jacques Le Goff that is coming out this week with Gallimard ("Quarto") under the title *Un autre Moyen Âge*.[7]

Before adding a remark or two about Rifkin's book, following our rapid overview of *The City of God*, and just before coming back to Hegel and then welcoming Clinton onto the stage, I'll recall that in the two examples or series of examples that I noted in conclusion the time before last,[8] first the two passages from Freud's *Jokes and Their Relation to the Unconscious*, and then the article from the *New York Times* about the letter from Clinton to his fellow parishioners at the Immanuel Baptist Church, one could readily see how the discourse of forgiveness was being laboriously employed in the service of a calculus, a strategy; it "functioned," it worked as a profession (the profession of faith being a profession, a *métier*, as Heine said about God, whose "job," according to Heine quoted by Freud, was that of forgiving.[9] Human society can function only by having a functionary for forgiveness, an official [*préposé*] in charge of forgiveness, and that is God, God in the service of men.[10] On this view, God is there to forgive, engaged by men to attend to forgiving and to do his job as pardoner. He is paid and so exacts payment for that, a tax is imposed there, a value-added tax, and a salary: there is a sector, which is not the primary, secondary, or tertiary service sector, it would be the quaternary sector, that of the service performed by someone like God, the God of forgiveness, the God of mercy, private coverage and general insurance company for sins.)

177

6. The typescript has this annotation in the margin: "Or, on the contrary, for an increase in the duration of work." During the session, he adds those words, followed by these: "All of that was going on in the Middle Ages, a fight for reduction with court cases, etc., like today, and a fight for extending the time of work."

7. See Jacques Le Goff, *Un autre Moyen Âge* (Paris: Gallimard, 1999), in particular "Time and Work" (21–139). Derrida comments on Le Goff's book in "The University without Condition," in *Without Alibi*, 228–29 [*L'Université sans condition*, 61–64].

8. See 89–94 above.

9. See 91–92 above.

10. During the session, Derrida adds: "We referred very quickly to the situation of the psychoanalyst that remained unspoken in that scenario."

This investment of the same logic and the same economy of reappropriation of surplus value or value added set the unconscious working in one
case—a whole topic and energetics, an experience of "work"[11] in general—
and politics, a modern politics of mass media, in the other case.

These two novel situations are not incompatible, quite the contrary, the
capitalistic strategy of mass media in politics putting into play the unconscious and requiring as a result new analyses and new categories. One question that would remain to be answered concerns the role that can be played
by the principle of a logic of the unconscious in globalization and in analysis
of the discourse *on* and *of* globalization. Is it significant that such a discourse
is prospering at the very moment when we are witnessing a certain retreat
on the part of, or even a certain reaction *against*, psychoanalysis in the world,
a defensive offensive against psychoanalysis, and above all in the United
States? I am naming the United States because you can well imagine that
if we are interested, or are getting around to being interested in Clinton, it
isn't because Bill as a person, the individual, interests us as such, does or
doesn't seem "likable,"[12] because he does or doesn't need to be supported
as a historic individual caught up in a whole phantasmatico-political plot,
which extends from his own impulsive or libidinal frolicking in the manner of a sleepwalking adolescent who was never liked by the Washington
political milieu to which this provincial never belonged, all the way to the
political traps set for him by Republicans who conduct this affair by steering
the media this way or that, using as a brake the organized and moralistic
religious reaction that has been gaining momentum in the United States for
some time, while at the same time shifting gears in response to the conspi-
ratorial obsession of a relentless prosecutor, a Grand Inquisitor of modern
democracies who remains unperturbed by any scruple though displaying
all the same an imposing legal and rhetorical proficiency. No, that's not why
we are going to be interested in some supposed Clinton case, which would
deserve interminable analyses, but because what is going on there, and even
when it appears in the *New York Times*, reaches us from the greatest global
power, from a state that presents itself as the representative of democracy,

11. During the session, Derrida adds: "In the sense that psychoanalysis gives to that
word."

12. During the session, Derrida adds: "'Likable [*sympa*]' or more 'likable' than his
adversaries or not, it's complicated. As I was saying just before, the Clinton case is complicated. That is why I began just now by talking about the death penalty. He never
asked for forgiveness for doubling down on the death penalty in the United States, or
for Iraq or whatever else."

of human rights, the self-appointed representative of the United Nations and of the Security Council whose decisions said state doesn't even wait for before taking on a mission, in Iraq or elsewhere, and where the question of forgiveness seems to concern the legitimacy, or not, the removal or not of a president of the United States before the eyes of his people, on the pretext of an internal, or even private [*intime*], domestic,[13] and not an international affair, one that doesn't concern the legitimacy of his political action in the world, the former being capable of providing an alibi for the latter.

How is that possible? How to explain that, at the heart of these new, very new problematics, opened up by a logic of the unconscious and of a geopolitics of hegemonies in the twenty-first century, how to explain that the old notion of pardon — and of perjury, since with Clinton it will indeed be a question, more than ever, more explicitly and literally than ever, of pardoning a perjurer, of the link between pardon and perjury — how to explain that these old notions of pardon and of perjury still constitute an active, radioactive heritage, one that signifies and has utility still? Why is that?

It is there that we again find, as I announced last time, Mary Magdalene, Hegel's Mary Magdalene, and Monica, not *Santa* Monica, (the saintly mother of Augustine, who, moreover, wasn't as saintly as all that and confessed the sins of her youth), but the less than saintly paragon of virtue [*moins sainte nitouche*] Monica Lewinsky, and all the phantasmatic, economic, political, and other machines that she is prey to.

Before that, though, some additional remarks on this theme of the end of work, both to clarify what I said too quickly about it and to try to convince you that I didn't artificially juxtapose the motif of sabbatical rest from *The City of God* and the end of work following or during what Rifkin calls the "third industrial revolution."[14] First of all, this is indeed a question of life or death — and still one of possible or impossible forgiveness. For men and for God. When, for his part, Augustine addresses his fellows, his actual or virtual brothers within the Christian fraternity, when he speaks to them, and speaks to us of overabundant grace and of the second free-will accorded by an all-powerful God, who is incapable of lying, he is indeed speaking to us of the possible impossible, of the possibility of the impossible. God forgives and gives at the same time, and by remitting sins he remits, he gives *both* the impossibility of sinning as impossibility of dying *and* sabbatical repose, the seventh day that we *are* and don't just *have*, which would be available to us as an asset, an advantage, something that we could still work on

179

13. [Translator's note:] Word in English in typescript.
14. Rifkin, *End of Work*, 59–106 [*Fin du travail*, 91–152].

or that we would have to enjoy (I insist: "we ourselves shall be the seventh day"[15] is what we are told, because we are then participating in God's being and we become what we receive, the seventh day, the end of work: we are sabbatical, we are where we don't work, we don't work, therefore we are (people of God)). When Augustine explains that to us, he is indeed saying that God does the impossible. God promises the impossible and since he can't lie, as you remember, he keeps his promise and accomplishes the impossible, that is to say, what exceeds economy. But he does so by giving us the life and the blood of his son. And in that, salvation is tied to redemption, to buying back. His son, the life and blood of his son are what he gives us to redeem us, but clearly what is *given* is by the same token *bought back* by the resurrection of Christ and the resurrection of the body (an important theme in *The City of God*). And that resembles to a great extent what a man, a Jew, Abraham, was ready to do without calculating, out of pure obedience to God, namely, giving his son who, already, was given back to him. Last year we meditated a great deal on that scene,[16] which Augustine doesn't recall here, and we did so with reference to forgiveness, even with reference to the paradox of a forgiveness that, according to Kierkegaard, Abraham asked of God not for disobeying him but for having obeyed him. But let's leave that. What I wanted to point to from afar here is the strange equation linking or tying together for us these three threads [*fils*] in a single son [*fils*]: (1) absolute (that is to say unconditional) forgiveness; (2) the impossible; and (3) absolute death as death of God. If, as we often say here, absolute forgiveness, unconditional grace is the impossible, and if life itself must not then be the condition for forgiveness, if death is the impossible itself, God becomes the name for the impossible as death—and there is nothing surprising in seeing all these threads form a knot in the heart of the son, in the heart of the heart of what unties, for forgiveness consists in remitting, redeeming, releasing, absolving, undoing[17] obligation or debt. To approach things from another angle, one can ask what Augustine is talking about, or what we are talking about when we say "God." The question of God, before knowing whether God exists, before knowing what God is or who is God, means knowing what the name of God means. "God"—whom does that name? Or what? What are we saying when we say the name of God? Or rather when we call

180

---

15. Augustine, *City of God*, vol. 7, 381 [*Cité de Dieu*, vol. 3, 357]. See 110 above.

16. See Derrida, *Perjury and Pardon*, vol. 1, 85–115 [*Parjure et pardon*, vol. 1, 127–60].

17. [Translator's note:] These last three verbs (*délier, absoudre, défaire*) all have the sense of "untying."

him? What are we calling God? Who is it we are calling in this way, by this name?[18] The impossible. Here God names who or what promises and does the impossible, who above all makes the promise of the impossible (who *does* it — this promise — for a promise is a doing, it is a performative act, an event and an undertaking), and someone who, having made the promise of the impossible, does the impossible, keeps the promise; for what pertains to the name of God here is naming, calling someone who, by definition (the whole question is in this "by definition"), inhabits the impossibility of lying, inasmuch as a being that can't lie cannot not be sincere when he makes a promise and he is therefore before the fact in the kept promise.[19] A finite being, prior to sin, is a being that *can* lie, with the result that between the performative time of the promise and its fulfillment, an interval can be introduced, also a risk that the promise won't be kept, that lying, unfaithfulness, or powerlessness might cause the promise not to be kept. The finite creature may also, even without lying at the moment of promising, lack the means to keep a sincere, truthful promise, whereas in the case of God, no sooner is the promise made by this all-powerful being that cannot lie, than it is kept. Straightaway, already. No sooner said than done [*sitôt dit, sitôt fait*].[20] The good deed is in the very promise, giving and forgiving are in the very promise, analytically implied in the promising. It is in promising me the impossible that God gives it to me. Without waiting, without making me wait. For

181

18. During the session, Derrida adds: "An old, very old question. Who is it that we are calling thus, by this name? Well, everything here — in the context or logic or discourse that besets and constrains us — everything dictates this response: the impossible."

19. During the session, Derrida comments: "Serious [promise], that is to say, held in the promise that is kept. To be kept, therefore kept by him. Why? Well, there is a difference there, written in black and white: 'Whoever promises in a serious, sincere way is held in a promise to be kept,' but that doesn't mean that such a person can keep it. God is someone who not only makes a serious, sincere promise, hence one to be kept, but who keeps it. What does that mean?"

20. During the session, Derrida adds: "And, moreover, the word *tôt* — if you are interested in the word *tôt*, as I am — you know that it is a very interesting word in the French language. There are two possible etymologies. One goes back to *tostus*, which means 'grilled,' like toast [*Laughter*], that is to say, immediately flambéed, instantly, it catches fire, it's the suddenness of something that flames. The other etymology, more open to debate, probably unjustified, refers back to *cito*, speed, you see. We'll come across this word *cito* (c.i.t.o.), which means 'rapidly,' again. In any case, here it's absolute speed. As soon as he makes a promise, he keeps it. It is kept by the fact of being made. There is no time between the two, between the promise made and the promise kept." See 146 below.

God (and that is his essence, what defines him), there is neither difference[21] nor delay, between promising a gift, or forgiveness, and giving a gift or granting forgiveness. An impossible gift or forgiveness is no longer impossible on the part of someone who can do the impossible and who can't lie. What I need to hear is someone promising me the impossible. And the impossible is immediately [*aussitôt*] given. At an infinite speed, instantly. This, then, is a reflection on the promise, on the making [*le faire*] of a promise rather than a reflection on some subsequent act that would or wouldn't follow the promise. But it is also a profound reflection on the lie—and on the perjury that a lie always constitutes. On language and lying, language and perjury. When I speak or listen to someone who addresses me, I need to refer to a place of speech where lying is impossible. As we said when we read Kant "On a Supposed Right to Lie from Philanthropy,"[22] the essence of language, of addressing another, even where there is lying and even in order for the lie to make sense as lie, well, the essence of language implies that at the source there is a "believe me," "I'm telling you the truth," "I am sincere," "I am truthful." This constitutive requirement of language, inscribed in the heart of language or of address, signifies that I cannot have access to speech without implicitly referring to an absolute place from which lying is absolutely excluded and within which it is impossible, and where, between promising (the truth) and telling the truth, between making a promise and doing what is promised, no separation is possible, no difference/differance (with an *e* and with an *a*) and no delay, because in that place keeping a promise is promising: to make a promise is to keep it. And the name of God would name that, that absolute identity, that absolute synchrony between the promise made and the promise kept. That's what one could nickname the profession of faith, where professed faith, sworn faith, produces, while at the same time relying on it, that promise or that belief in the promise made as a priori fulfillment of the promise, covenant [*alliance*] or

182 (margin number)

21. During the session, Derrida adds: "With an 'e' or with an 'a.'"

22. See Immanuel Kant, "On a Supposed Right to Lie from Philanthropy (1797)," in *Practical Philosophy*, trans. and ed. Mary J. Gregor (Cambridge: Cambridge University Press, 1996) ["Sur un prétendu droit de mentir par humanité," trans. Louis Guillermit, in *Théorie et pratique—Droit de mentir* (Paris: Librairie philosophique J. Vrin, 1980)]. See also Derrida, "History of the Lie: Prolegomena," in *Without Alibi*, 43ff. [*Histoire du mensonge: Prolégomènes*, 42ff.]; unpublished seminar, "Le témoignage," EHESS, 1994–95, Third Session; unpublished seminar, "Hostilité/hospitalité," EHESS, 1995–96, Fifth Session; and *Of Hospitality: Anne Dufourmantelle Invites Jacques Derrida to Respond*, trans. Rachel Bowlby (Stanford: Stanford University Press, 2000) [*De l'hospitalité*, ed. Anne Dufourmantelle (Paris: Calmann-Lévy, 1997)].

pledge [*gage*]—call it what you will. What Augustine doesn't envisage is that to the very extent that God would wish to keep his promise infinitely, by remaining incapable of lying, he cannot keep it, or he can not keep it, inasmuch as the freedom of men, finite creatures, would come to remind him of his limit. What Augustine finds absurd is supposing a finitude for God, and starting out from that, starting from the finitude that would make me say the opposite, namely, that wherever the lie, wherever lying is impossible, veracity, sincerity, and the promise itself no longer make any sense; what he cannot admit, treating it as the absurdity of a false premise, is that we start from the axiom according to which only the becoming-possible of the impossible makes truth possible (namely, that God, who can't lie, can lie, that what for him is impossible becomes possible), that is, that on that condition alone there can be promise, veracity, etc. According to both hypotheses, however, according to both logics,[23] God is the name of the impossible. He does the impossible because it is impossible for him to lie and because that impossibility is not a negative limit, but an infinite surfeit of potentiality [*puissance*].

Why am I insisting here on this impossibility of lying, on this exclusion of the possibility of lying, of being able to lie [*du pouvoir-mentir*], an exclusion that simultaneously, immediately, always already, has the form of "having-not-to" as "not-being-able-to" (I cannot lie because I must not lie; God is the name of the absolute being for whom "being obliged not to lie" is immediately "to be incapable of lying, *mentiri non posse*")?[24] Why am I insisting on that so much? For the no doubt obvious reasons concerning the internal role that it plays in Augustine and in the theologico-politics of *The City of God*, of course, and all the more so in that Augustine is the author of two great books on lying (which we discussed here a few years ago—*Contra mendacium* and *De mendacio*),[25] but also, which is for the moment less apparent, because this is preparing us to think about what might constitute

23. During the session, Derrida adds: "Even if one engages in an interminable debate between, let's say, the infinitist and Christian logic of Augustine, and a logic such as I am developing in contrast to him, in both cases, according to both hypotheses, the common presupposition is that God is the name of the impossible."

24. Augustine, *City of God*, vol. 7, 342 [*Cité de Dieu*, vol. 3, 342; *De Civitate Dei / La Cité de Dieu (Livres XIX–XXII): Triomphe de la Cité céleste*, trans. Gustave Combès, ed. Bernhard Dombart and Alfons Kalb (Paris: Desclée de Brouwer, 1960, 678]. Augustine's Latin text reads "*mentiri non potest*."

25. See 132n22 above. Derrida quotes from Augustine's *De Mendacio* in "History of the Lie: Prolegomena," in *Without Alibi*, 35, 289n1 [*Histoire du mensonge: Prolégomènes*, 15n1].

a system within which, at a given point, which is also the capital head or capitol of the nation-state grouping, there must be (par excellence in the person of the king or head of state) a place where lying and perjury have to be impossible, that is to say, excluded from its principle, on principle, in this place of principle that is also the principal place of the prince, of the head of state or president. A certain impossibility of lying or perjury must ensure—at the head of the body of the nation or nation-state, par excellence a Christian nation-state, at the capital head of the City (as City of God)—a certain impossibility of lying or perjury must ensure in that place the unity or integrity of the spiritual body of a fundamentally Christian country, of a fatherland, of a kingdom or republic founded in the spirit or letter of a Christian tradition. You can see the Clinton case looming. This impossibility of lying, this exclusion of the lie, is an a priori part of the act of initial promise, that is to say, of the pledge that is sworn [*foi jurée*], the oath taken on the Bible by the American head of state, who, at the moment of taking the oath and in each public address, as president and as one speaking under oath, must in no way lie or perjure himself,[26] short of being as a result removed from office, prevented from exercising that function and that power. The president cannot lie as president any more than can God; he is the guarantor of everything declared under oath before the justice system of the country that he governs, incarnates, and represents. All the more so, and par excellence, when he himself, having already sworn under oath as president but also as citizen, finds himself obliged to testify under oath before a grand jury of his country. In the same way that a lying God wouldn't be God, wouldn't deserve the name God and should see himself demoted to the rank of idol and false God, so a sworn president who lies or perjures himself is not a president and deserves to be relieved of his function, prevented from continuing [*empêché*], impeached.[27] And if we were to risk speaking of a God who could lie or deceive us or fail in his promise, we wouldn't be speaking of God himself, we would be using the name of God as a *flatus vocis*, an empty word, a word that is only verbal, or again we would be speaking of a deposed God, an impeached God, a God we would

185

---

26. Derrida here—and often elsewhere—uses *parjurer* for "to perjure oneself" where the normal French verb would be the reflexive *se parjurer*. See *Perjury and Pardon*, vol. 1, 42 [*Parjure et pardon*, vol. 1, 74]: "I perjure myself as I breathe" ["*je parjure comme je respire*"].

27. [Translator's note:] This word in English in text here and, including cognates, below.

put on trial. Note that the trial of Christ,[28] who, all things considered, was accused of lying, of saying unbelievable things, accused of passing himself off as something he wasn't, king of the Jews, or of passing himself off as someone who could put himself above the laws of the land (like Clinton), or who could himself dispense justice, who could pardon, placing himself outside and above the laws in effect ("whom does he take himself for?" the Pharisees then ask), well then, this was a trial that resulted in Christ, king of the Jews, being impeached. And yet it is through that bloody impeachment procedure that God made the sacrificial sign of redemption, by means of which the truth, the veracity of his promise and his gift, was attested to, given as a pledge. That analogy shouldn't have us take Bill for Jesus, but I do believe in the structural, significant necessity of the analogy. The United States president swears on a Christian Bible. Moreover, when Clinton appears on our stage here, we'll indeed see that it isn't Monica or Paula[29] who are in play, it isn't a story of women, it's a story of swearing and forswearing [parjure] that threatens the foundations of the state and the Constitution at their head, and which must therefore be excluded as impossible, inadmissible. That is indeed where we'll find the meaning of the Republicans' accusation and the discourse of the accusation, the discourse of the prosecutor. *186* Just now, speaking in general, I was saying that this veracity, this nonlying under oath, guaranteed the city, the state, the political, up to the head of the person who is its head, the chief, prince, premier, whether he be king or president. I note simply, as a minor complication, which doesn't diminish the truth of this theologico-political truth, that Clinton's principal accuser in the Senate,[30] Henry Hyde (*Blackboard*), comes in a recent speech, both to confirm literally what I am saying, but also to add to it a secondary contradiction by distinguishing a democratic republic such as the United States is supposed to be from a monarchy based on divine right. I find the argument

28. During the session, Derrida adds: "I point out that Clinton has already been compared literally to the Antichrist in the press." He is perhaps alluding to numerous conspiracy theories circulating in the media in 1999, relating to the approach of the new millennium.

29. Paula Jones, a former Arkansas state employee, sued Bill Clinton in May 1994 for sexual harassment. The court found the suit lacking in legal merit, and it was settled out of court. [Translator's note:] It was in Clinton's deposition for the Jones lawsuit that he claimed not to have had sexual relations with Monica Lewinsky, a claim that led to charges of perjury and impeachment proceedings.

30. In his typescript, Derrida crosses out "in the Senate," and adds this clarification concerning Henry Hyde: "chair of the House Judiciary Committee." During the session he adds, "[House of] Representatives."

interesting but irrelevant to what interests us. What does Henry Hyde in fact say? I quote the translation, given by *Le Monde* in its January 23 edition, of his recent declaration. Hyde says this:

> This controversy began with the fact that the president of the United States took an oath to tell the truth in his testimony before the grand jury, just as he had on two prior occasions,[31] sworn a solemn oath to preserve, protect and defend the Constitution. . . . But I must say, despite massive and relentless efforts to change the subject, the case before you, Senators, is not[32] about sexual misconduct, infidelity, adultery. Those are private acts and are none of our business. It's not even a question of lying about sex. The matter before this body is a question of lying under oath. This is a public act. The matter before you is a question of the willful, premeditated, deliberate corruption of the nation's system of justice through perjury and obstruction of justice.[33]

187 And so, to reinforce this very serious accusation — in respect of which, as we'll see later, in what is also, but not only, the sort of gross and appalling stupidity that we are used to, it is deconstruction itself, deconstruction in America, the deconstruction of America that literally becomes, under its own name, the accused, I indeed say "under its own name" — to reinforce this accusation Senator[34] Hyde concludes his argument by denouncing another peril. In committing perjury, Clinton has not only undermined the foundations of the Constitution and of the judicial system of his country, he has thereby also done harm to the image of the United States in the world, and done harm precisely to the "trust"[35] — the word is important here — that one has in his country throughout the world. The United States doesn't occupy just any place in the world, if one thinks not only of a military and economic hegemony but of the fact that the application of international law, decisions made by international institutions, notably the United Nations and

---

31. During the session, Derrida adds: "So, this oath, which he swore before the grand jury, is analogous to the oath he took at the time of his inauguration."

32. During the session, Derrida adds: "So, the negative phrase, the denial."

33. Cf. "Pour les républicains, 'mentir sous serment est une insulte à la liberté,'" *Le Monde*, January 23, 1999, 4. [Translator's note:] I am quoting Hyde directly from the official record of January 16, 1999: US Senate, 106th Congress, 1st Session: "Proceedings of the United States Senate in the Impeachment Trial of President William Jefferson Clinton," vol. 2: Floor Trial Proceedings, 1188. https://www.govinfo.gov/content/pkg/CDOC-106sdoc4/pdf/CDOC-106sdoc4-vol2.pdf.

34. Here, and unless otherwise noted, Derrida has crossed out "Senator" in the typescript and substituted "Representative."

35. [Translator's note:] The word in French is *confiance*, "confidence."

its Security Council, depend for their effectiveness and implementation on the United States. By the same token, for that very reason, those institutions and decisions are sometimes overtaken by American initiatives that are improperly substituted for these international bodies in the manner of an executive power that doesn't even have to wait for the conclusions drawn by an assembly that deliberates, decides, and implements.[36] The United States often conducts itself as an executive power (that held by the president) that arrogates to itself the de facto executive power of the United Nations, of the world, and so would authorize itself by itself to intervene all over the globe on the way to globalization, without having to wait to receive instructions from the official and legitimate executive body. Whence the import of what Hyde says when he adds: "[Clinton] can no longer be trusted. And, because the Executive plays so large a role in representing the country to the world, America can no longer be trusted."[37] What Clinton's perjury threatens is   *188* the credit given to Americans in the world and hence American power in a world in the process of globalization.

Because of Clinton's lie, Hyde says, "Americans[38] can no longer be trusted." Americans in general. This discourse by a Republican congressman wants it to be understood that as soon as the president is removed, a new administration, preferably a Republican one, would restore that lost confidence: throughout the country and throughout the world. (I recall in passing that the institution represented by Starr, that of an independent counsel, was instituted following Watergate and the Nixon affair,[39] which wasn't more of a shining moment for a Republican administration.) But there is something still more interesting in Hyde's recent declaration. It is a very sophisticated attempt, in short, to confirm the theological logic of the oath and what links that whole system to the president's oath before God, hence to a condemnation of perjury as a sacrilege that is both political and religious, a blasphemy, while at the same time dissociating that political theology, that Christian political theology, as democracy, from divine right monarchies. It is as if he were distinguishing between divine right democracies and divine

36. During the session, Derrida adds: "Whence Hyde's reasoning: 'since this is the role we play, at least let's have people trust us, at least let our image be reasonably good.'"

37. Floor Trial Proceedings, 1189 [*Le Monde*, January 23, 1999, 4].

38. [Translator's note:] *Le Monde* has "Americans" for "America."

39. The so-called Watergate scandal is the name given to an electoral scandal that besmirched the second term of President Richard Nixon, a Republican. It began with a break-in at the offices of the Democratic Party during the electoral campaign. Despite having been reelected in 1972, President Nixon resigned on August 9, 1974, an unprecedented event in US history.

right monarchies. We are a religious nation, Hyde says in short, as you will hear, God is the ultimate witness of our politics, but we are a democracy and not a divine right monarchy where the sovereign is above the law. No one, and especially not the president, is above the law in a democracy such as ours. What value can be given to this argument, which is in the end quite subtle, and presents at its basis the absolute singularity of the United States as modern democracy founded on the Bible and before God, and within which no one, especially not the president, is above the law? Its intrinsic value or intent [*visée*]—which tends therefore to distinguish, from a certain point of view, between the absolute monarch by divine right and the elected president of a modern democracy, even if he takes the oath by swearing on the Bible and before God—that value or intent would presume at least two things:

189

1. *on the one hand*, that in the expressions "to be above the law" or "to submit to the law," "to be subject to the law," the distinction between the two is always clear and guaranteed (something that isn't sure inasmuch as a subject can *be* or *incarnate* the law, can be at the same time subject and superior to it, or both its subjected [*assujetti*] subject and its producer—which is the definition of Kantian autonomy and freedom, namely, the power to make for oneself the law to which one submits);

2. the value of the argument and of the distinction presumes, *on the other hand*, that the divine right monarch is simply above the law, which is far from being so simple. Beside those obvious presuppositions, Henry Hyde's argument, which I am quoting because it sums up very clearly the spirit and letter of the discourse and strategy of the charge made against Clinton, that argument has a consequence and another implication that is less immediately visible, a hidden political theology that comes to double, like Dr. Jekyll,[40] the discourse of Mr. Hyde. What is that? Before coming to it, I'll quote a passage from Mr. Hyde's speech:

> In recent months, it has often been asked—so what? What is the harm done by this lying under oath, by this perjury? Well, what is an oath? [Now there's a good question; it is ours. If he were free, we could've asked Mr. Hyde to come and do a presentation in our seminar, half an hour, no more.] What is an oath? [Dr.[41] Hyde's response:] An oath is an asking al-

---

40. The typescript has "Dr Jekill" for all occurrences of this name in the session. In Robert Louis Stevenson's novel, *The Strange Case of Dr. Jekyll and Mr. Hyde*, a solicitor, Gabriel John Utterson, investigates the link between Edward Hyde and Dr. Henry Jekyll.

41. Thus in typescript.

mighty God to witness to the truth of what you are saying. [Note that one could draw from this definition the consequence that perjury is as a result a matter between God and one who has sworn under oath, between God who sees into people's hearts and someone under oath who testifies before God, and that human justice has nothing to do with all that; as you can imagine, that is not the consequence drawn by Hyde, who immediately goes on:] Truth telling—truth telling is the heart and soul of our justice system. . . . Lying under oath is an abuse of freedom. Obstruction of justice is a degradation of law. There are people in prison for just such offenses. What in the world do we say to them about equal justice if we overlook this conduct in the President?[42]

190

There, as you see, the alleged logic is that of democracy: no exception for the citizen president,[43] respect for the law, equality of all before the law and equitable justice for all. But of course that democratic equality before the law is founded on an equality before God, to whom Hyde has just appealed, the God who, observing the president's oath and every oath in general, guarantees the law itself. Which means that the presumed autonomy of democratic law is founded on an absolute heteronomy, and that affects everything that follows in Hyde's speech as he now seeks to sing the praises of American democracy in contrast to divine right monarchy. Here it is: "That none of us is above the law is a bedrock principle of democracy."[44]

To attack that principle of equality before the law, as brothers before the father, before the Constitution drafted by the Founding Fathers[45] who are so often invoked in the United States, Hyde continues, "is to subscribe to a 'divine right of kings' theory of governance, in which those who govern are absolved from adhering to the basic moral standards to which the governed are accountable"[46] ("absolved [*absous*]" no doubt renders the idea of being "free from the obligation to adhere to basic principles," etc.). Hyde's rhetoric here abandons the theme of the oath to speak of basic morality, letting it be understood that the accused has disobeyed the law not by perjuring himself but by transgressing basic principles, such as conjugal fidelity or sexual abstinence during the exercise of his functions, etc. But let's leave aside that subsidiary point. What follows is more interesting. For Hyde next makes a provisional and hypothetical concession to the possibility that—in

191

42. Floor Trial Proceedings, 1190, 1191 [*Le Monde*, January 23, 1999, 4].

43. During the session, Derrida adds: "As is said today, no exception for ministers. Ministers must appear before the law—there are some who will be doing that soon."

44. Floor Trial Proceedings, 1190 [*Le Monde*, 23 January 1999, 4].

45. [Translator's note:] "Founding Fathers" in English in text here and below.

46. Floor Trial Proceedings, 1190 [*Le Monde*, 23 January 1999, 4].

the political philosophy of the lie since Plato and Augustine—has been called the helpful, officious (*officiosus*) lie (the very one that Kant judged unacceptable):[47] Hyde seems in fact to concede that in certain cases the head of state, for reasons of state, in the interest of the state (for example, in times of war), may dissimulate or twist the truth told to the people; but then that must be in the interest of the state and of the nation, in the interest of its citizens. One lies, in that case, to serve the interest of the receiver of the lie; one lies out of love for those to whom one lies and whose wellbeing one seeks. But that is by no means the case here, according to Hyde; Clinton's lie or perjury doesn't have such a justification. But, to demonstrate that, as you will hear, Hyde stumbles into a trap, for he is going to say that Clinton lied to "shade [*cacher*, I suppose that it is "hide" in the original, but I only have the translation here] the truth . . . for a private pleasure."[48] To hide the reality of a private pleasure, that is the sole purpose of Clinton's lie or perjury; which is to recognize what had been denied a moment prior to that, namely, that it is personal pleasure, the private sexual enjoyment of the president, that concerns the American people and unleashes or motivates or feeds or foments, that is to say, stokes the urgency of the accusation against the president made by the Republicans. Moreover, why would the president not invoke reason of state to dissimulate from the American people scenes from his private life that might harm civic morale or the morale of armies sent to Iraq or elsewhere? Here then, to be done with Hyde, is the conclusion of the passage. First the feigned concession to officious (*officiosus*) lying, the helpful or exceptional lie uttered by someone who is telling us, and hoping to be believed, that outside of those exceptional moments one must never lie and one does not ever lie in politics. Let us listen to Hyde:

192

> Morally serious men and women can imagine circumstances, at the far edge of the morally permissible, when, with the gravest matters of national interest at stake, a President could shade [*hide*, I suppose] the truth in order to

47. During the session, Derrida clarifies: "What is called the *officiosus* lie is the helpful lie. In certain cases, well, one has the right to lie in the interest of . . . etc. So there are people who believe in the helpful lie, such as Plato, and people who don't believe in it, which is the case with Kant. The *officiosus* lie is the very one that Kant judged unacceptable. One must in no case lie, even to save one's friend, and even when it is absolutely helpful."

48. The expression used by Hyde on January 16, 1999 is in fact "shade the truth" (see following quotation). *Le Monde*'s translation introduces the words "to lie" and "hide." (cf. Floor Trial Proceedings, 1191 [*Le Monde*, January 23, 1999, 4]).

serve the common good. But under oath [*mentir sous serment*], for a private pleasure?

In doing this, the Office of President of the United States has been debased and the justice system jeopardized. In doing this, he has broken his covenant of trust with the American people.[49]

What is vicious—and I mean vicious both in its logic and in its circular argument—both vicious and complicated in this argumentation is that, having admitted a certain exceptional legitimacy for the helpful lie in a case where that concerns the welfare of the people, Hyde says that that isn't the case here. Instead of concluding that the interest of Americans or of the nation has nothing to do with the president's personal pleasure, that that pleasure no more harms the health of the nation than serves it, that it simply doesn't interest and doesn't concern the American people, nor anyone else in the world for that matter, that it is neither for nor against their interest (I mean public interest, for in the so-called private sphere it can be otherwise), he nevertheless sees an offense in the fact of "hiding" (I suppose) that pleasure while under oath. Of course, it is always the oath and the covenant, it is the symbolic, then, that counts as final recourse, no attention being paid here to the fact that the threat weighing on the symbolic, on the pledge of good faith, on fidelity to the Constitution of our Founding Fathers, that what counts, then, what "matters,"[50] is that this threat takes the form of a sexual pleasure that is itself a perjury, the pleasure and perjury of a brother-son who should be the equal of all the citizen-brothers before the law, who, at the very moment when he is closest to the father, that is to say, gives himself over to a perjurious sexual pleasure that betrays another oath sworn before God, the marriage vow, the good faith conjugal pledge, and leaves traces of that pitiful perjured pleasure [*jouissance*] in the world, I mean stains that mar—with their testimony or their proofs, with their presumed "evidence"[51] or incriminating exhibits—the very purity of the oath in general as oath sworn before God. How to dissociate here two or three oaths taken before God, that of the citizen (Clinton in front of the grand jury), that of the husband on the day of his sacred marriage, and that of the head of state on the day of his inauguration, how to distinguish them as private rather than

193

49. Floor Trial Proceedings, 1191 [*Le Monde*, January 23, 1999, 4]. During the session, Derrida comments: "That couldn't be more clear. With Clinton, it isn't about perjury, it isn't just perjury, the law; he tried to hide his 'personal pleasure,' and, in order to hide his 'personal pleasure' he 'jeopardized [*mis en péril*]' all that" [*Laughter*].

50. [Translator's note:] Word in English in text.

51. [Translator's note:] Word in English in text. Derrida writes "evidences."

public, given that, in spite of all the obvious differences—for example, between family and state, private and public—those three oaths are sworn in public, on the Bible, before God, and that, de facto—but a de facto that is so overwhelming and constraining that it is equivalent to a de jure—we have never yet seen an American citizen-president who was not a husband, we have never seen a woman American president, or a bachelor or someone openly homosexual, nor even an American president who, the day of his inauguration, didn't take the oath in the presence of and under the gaze of his wife, with her, or practically hand in hand with his spouse?[52] That situation of a male heterosexual head of state, both husband and father, is moreover the most commonly occurring thing more or less throughout what are called the great Western democracies. Unless it be that, precisely at this moment, because of, among other reasons, what has transpired and come out of the Clinton affair, things are beginning gingerly, if not to change, at least to show the precursor signs of a possible change, which would perhaps be, along with the confused and symptomatic discourse that names deconstruction and takes it to task, a discourse that we'll talk further about, which would perhaps be, then, one of the subterranean historic signals sent to us by everything that we are talking about here, signals that would accompany, constitutively also, the so-called process of globalization. One of the signals that perhaps ventriloquize this poor Mr. Hyde (not Dr. Jekyll but Mr. Hyde, his evil, cunning double, after the meeting with the prostitute),[53] when Mr. Hyde, as a knowledgeable doctor, diagnoses the disease affecting the body and soul of his country. Mr. Hyde in fact declares that if the wicked President Clinton isn't impeached, well, and I quote, "then the Office of the Presidency has been deeply and perhaps permanently damaged."[54]

And, obviously in denial, he concludes with a declaration of love and not hate. Nobody hates Clinton, he says, we simply love the law, and having our fellows, that is to say, our brothers, be equals before it: "Some of us," he says, "have been called 'Clinton-haters.' I must tell you . . . that this impeachment is not . . . a question of hating anyone. This is not a question of whom we

---

52. [Translator's note:] Derrida appears unaware that James Buchanan, the fifteenth US president, was a lifelong bachelor.

53. Derrida is perhaps alluding to the character Ivy Pearson introduced into Rouben Mamoulian's 1931 film adaptation of *Dr. Jekyll and Mr. Hyde*, remade by Victor Fleming in 1941.

54. Floor Trial Proceedings, 1191 [*Le Monde*, January 23, 1999, 4]. During the session, Derrida adds: "the language of diagnosis, of medical diagnosis."

hate. It is a question of what we love. And among the things we love is the rule of law, equal justice before the law."[55]

It must be said, moreover, that if you read the texts by Clinton's attorneys, some of whom are quoted in the same article, you will see that they develop the same logic, the same axiomatics (it is finally the other side of the same discourse); it's just that Clinton's lawyers, and Clinton himself, whom we shall shortly hear from directly, speaking a homogeneous language conditioned by the same axioms, plead for the difference between the big picture and the details, and oppose Bill's testimony to that of Monica (but we'll come back to the discourse that is articulated on Clinton's side). Here, the lawyers declare that the president didn't lie "about the nature of his relationship [with Monica Lewinsky] but only about the details."[56]   *195* And to maintain the accusation of perjury, one of them says, "You must determine — forgive me — that he touched certain parts of her body, but for proof you have only her oath against his oath."[57] Back to our seminar on the difference between testimony and proof.[58]

What has led us here is an uneasiness about this thinking of the impossible, notably in Saint Augustine, and the becoming-possible of the impossible as such, that is to say the becoming-possible of the impossible having remained impossible. Wherever we name the impossible as the thing itself, the

55. Floor Trial Proceedings, 1192 [*Le Monde*, January 23, 1999, 4].

56. Floor Trial Proceedings, 1210; Charles Ruff, quoted in "Pour les défenseurs de la Maison Blanche, il s'agit d'une manipulation des faits 'concertée et partisane,'" *Le Monde*, January 23, 1999, 4. During the session, Derrida adds: "You know Clinton's famous statement when, having been asked whether his relation [with Lewinsky] was sexual, replied 'It depends on what the meaning of the word "is" is.' [*Laughter*] 'That depends on what "is" is, on what you mean by "is."'" It was on that basis that whatever he says is accused of being 'deconstructionist'! [*Laughter*] So, there you have it, he didn't lie about the nature of his relations, but about the details." See President Clinton's grand jury testimony of August 17, 1998: "It depends on what the meaning of the word 'is' is. If the — if he — if 'is' means is and never has been that is not — that is one thing. If it means there is none, that was a completely true statement" ("Clinton's Grand Jury Testimony," https://www.washingtonpost.com/wp-srv/politics/special/clinton/stories/bctest 092198_4.htm).

57. Floor Trial Proceedings, 1212; Charles Ruff, quoted in *Le Monde*, January 23, 1999, 4.

58. Derrida, unpublished seminar, "Le témoignage," EHESS, 1994–95.

impossible of the gift, of forgiveness, of hospitality, of absolute faith, of an economy, the possibility of this experience of the unconditional impossible indeed turns us to what we call God, but that God is also the name of death. Both because the unconditional removes all conditions, all the way to the economy of life, the economy of self as economy of the proper in general, and because this God who does and gives and is the impossible is the God who dies, who makes himself a gift of death [*qui se donne la mort*], who gives death to what he loves most in the world, his son. By doing the impossible, just as Abraham was getting ready to do, and in order to do the impossible, redemption through overabundant grace, God gives and enacts death, enacts being dead (the dead man-God), and since that death is the miracle, the condition for the miracle of the resurrection, the feint or sacrificial ruse is reintroduced and God plays dead by enacting death.[59]

God is, by playing dead, the dead time between infinite promise and its fulfillment in the very act of the promise. And since death is that repose, and, as Augustine was telling us, we are that seventh day, well, then, we are, or we participate in, this divinity that consists in playing dead. And it isn't necessarily blaspheming, cursing [*jurer*], or forswearing [*parjurer*] to say that God enacts death and plays dead. He is the impossible resurrection or resurrection as the impossible, forgiveness as the impossible, etc., but the possible impossible. And because all of that works through the Last Judgment (which we spoke about concerning Benjamin's strange text about God's forgiveness interrupting history in storm and tempest, without reconciliation),[60] it is not at all surprising that the tone of eschatology or apocalypse marks all these discourses. There is an eschatology or an apocalypse of work in all the discourses on globalization as the end of work, and on the end of work as endless end of the world. But there too, in the apocalyptic tone of discourses on the Last Judgment or the end of work, it isn't easy to decide whether economy does or doesn't approach its end and whether the sur-

---

59. [Translator's note:] The latter part of this sentence reads: "*Dieu donne et fait la mort, le mort (l'homme-Dieu mort) et comme cette mort est le miracle, la condition du miracle de la résurrection, la feinte, ou la ruse sacrificielle, se réintroduit et Dieu fait le mort en faisant la mort.*" It contains complicated plays on the differences between death [*la mort*] and a dead man [*le mort*], especially as used in conjunction with the verb *faire*, "to do," "make," "enact." In particular, note that *faire le mort* means "to play/act dead," "play possum," "lie low," by means of which Derrida suggests that Christ's death and resurrection is at the same time a miracle and a type of trick, that God repeats with his own son the complicated ruse that he forced upon Abraham.

60. Benjamin, "The Meaning of Time," 287 ["La signification du temps," 107–8]. See 24 above.

vival of economy and of work, survival *tout court*, doesn't rather remain "at work" in that end, in—let's not forget Augustine—what remains an end without end, in an end without end ("*in fine sine fine*"), in the seventh day, when God will rest, and which rest we will ourselves be ("*in die septimo requiescet Deus, cum eundem diem septimum, quod nos erimus, in se ipso Deo faciet requiescere* [God will rest, as on the seventh day, when he will cause the seventh day, that is, us, to rest in God himself]."[61]

This end without end of history, this eternal sabbath, this eighth day, this *197* dominical day that will be like an eighth day (*dominicus dies velut octavus aeternus*),[62] and which is the day of the promised and actual resurrection of the Lord, this strange "eight," this octave is the *without*. Octave is the without. It is within the "without" ([*sans*], *sine*) of the end without end that everything plays out.

If you want to be convinced of the apocalyptico-eschatalogical character of all that (and *eschaton*, as you know, is the last, the end, the ultimate), reread the Apocalypse of John. You will find all those themes there. There one can decline, conjugate death in the past and say: "He died [*il est mort*]" in the sense of "he has been dead [*il a été mort*] and he is living," "*qui fuit mortuus, et vivit* [These things saith the first and the last, which was dead, and is [however] alive] (*os egeneto nekros kai ezēsen*)" (Revelation 2:8);[63] "Blessed are the dead which die in the Lord from henceforth: Yea, saith the Spirit, that they may rest from their labours; and their works do follow them" (*Beati mortui qui in Domino moriuntur. Amodo jam dicit Spiritus, ut requiescant a laboribus suis: opera* [*erga*] *enim illorum sequuntur illos* [*sequuntur: akolouthei*: accompany, act in agreement (comment: heritage, minding [*garde*], etc.)]) (Revelation 14:13);[64] or again: "and there shall be no more death (*et*

---

61. Augustine, *City of God*, vol. 7, 382, 383 [*De civitate dei*, 716; *Cité de Dieu*, vol. 3, 357].

62. Augustine, *City of God*, vol. 7, 384; "the Lord's Day, an eighth eternal day" (385) [*De civitate dei*, 718].

63. Revelation 2:8; cf. Polyglot Bible; Bible Hub [*Bible, Nouveau Testament*, 867; *Sainte Bible polyglotte*, 476].

64. Revelation 14:13; cf. Polyglot Bible; Bible Hub [*Bible, Nouveau Testament*, 891; *Sainte Bible polyglotte*, 514]. During the session, Derrida comments: "In Greek, *sequuntur* is *akolouthei*, that is, 'to accompany': their works are in accord with them, follow them like a heritage, like a guard, right? 'Blessed are the dead which die in the Lord from henceforth: Yea, saith the Spirit, that they may rest from their labours; and their works do follow them.' So the end of labors doesn't mean the end of works; the works continue to be in agreement with them, to follow (*akolouthei, sequuntur*), to go along with them."

mors ultra non erit; *ho thanatos ouk estai eti*), neither sorrow (*luctus*), nor crying, neither shall there be any more pain: for the former things are passed away. . . . I will give unto him that is athirst of the fountain of the water of life freely [*gratis* in Latin, 'graciously']" (Revelation 21:4 and 6).[65]

And listen to all the repetitions of "Come (*veni, erchou*)" that open and close the address of the Revelation of Saint John, these "comes" express both the rupture of the economy of work, the end of the market, the coming of what Rifkin calls, in short, the Post-Market Era, and, immediately, simultaneously, the reaffirmation of that economy in the heart of a gracious aneconomy, the mercantile reaffirmation of *merces*, of merchandise or salary, the reintroduction of the market or bargaining or the mercantile, of "*merci*," in the very place where every mercantile dimension should be excluded or exceeded. For example, near the end, in chapter 22, verse 12: "And, behold, I come quickly;[66] and my reward is with me, to give every man according as his work shall be; *Ecce venio cito* [comment *cito*: quickly, immediately, at full speed], *et merces mea mecum est, reddere unicuique secundum opera sua*; *idou erchomai tachu, kai o misthos* (salary, guarantee) *mou met emou, apodounai ekastō ōs to ergon estai autou.*"[67]

But the promise of the imminent gift of grace, of the water of life given gratis, aneconomically, that promise is in fact so negligibly aneconomic that it—that promise, qua promise—is immediately accompanied not only by a mercantile reward (*merces*), but worse, by a threat. Those who don't hear this prophetic testimony, this attestation, because the apocalypse is an attestation, an oath, a testimonial "I sign," those who don't receive the testimonial, who don't subscribe to it, don't countersign it, those who don't countersign this book and still want to change something in it, add something to or subtract something from it, in short, those who wish to write, to write something different again, something more or something less, their name or in their name, for example, and so don't become brothers, well, those will be punished by God, and punished with death, that is to say, removed from the book, from the tree of life and from the City of God, the holy city. These

198

65. Cf. Polyglot Bible; Bible Hub [*Bible, Nouveau Testament*, 905; *Sainte Bible polyglotte*, 534].

66. During the session, Derrida adds: So, "quickly [*bientôt*] is *cito*, c.i.t.o., very fast, straightaway."

67. Revelation 22:12; cf. Polyglot Bible; Bible Hub [*Bible, Nouveau Testament*, 908; *Sainte Bible polyglotte*, 538]. During the session, Derrida translates: "to each his salary according to his work."

are even the final or penultimate words of this terrible Apocalypse, of this terrifying revelation (for as you know "Apocalypse" means *unveiling, revelation* of the truth). That is its terrible evangelical telemessage, the message delivered on the spot far away and at every distance, to all possible receivers, delivered to all the cities in the world by the angel, that is to say, by the *angelum*, the messenger, the bearer of news, the mail deliverer or spokesperson, the speaker:[68]

199

> I Jesus have sent mine angel to testify unto you (*marturēsai humin, testificari vobis*) these things in the churches. . . . And the Spirit and the bride (*spiritus et sponsa, pneuma kai ē numphē*) say, Come (*Veni, Erchou*). And let him that heareth say, Come. And let him that is athirst come. And whosoever will, let him take the water of life freely [*gratis, dōrean*: as a gracious gift]. For I testify [*contestor, marturō*: *contestor* doesn't mean "I contest," but "I attest," "I call to witness"] unto every man that heareth (*omni audienti*) the words of the prophecy of this book (*verba prophetiae libri hujus, tous logous tēs prophēteias tou bibliou toutou*), [and now comes the terrifying threat of punishment,[69] banking on the wages of fear] If any man shall add unto these things, God shall add unto him the plagues that are written in this book (*Si quis apposuerit ad haec, apponet Deus super illum plagas scriptas in libro isto*).[70]

So, if someone changes the text, if they add something to the book, God will inflict on them the punishment, the very plagues that are described in the book. So the book, as text of law and as promise, as sworn testimony, is also a prescription and a threatening description of the punishments that will rain down on those who don't read, don't know how to read, interpret poorly, in short on those who don't believe, in the sense of adding another text, altering the text by scribbling on it an additional text that they themselves sign without undersigning, without subscribing or countersigning, without trusting—in an act of faith—in the book such as it is given to them. That threat—addressed to those who, in short, write something else because they lack faith, don't show faith, or add their signs and their writing because they don't attach faith to the first text—that threat of an implacable punishment, without forgiveness or mercy, is the space opened to all

---

68. [Translator's note:] Word in English in text.

69. During the session, Derrida adds: "For those who don't listen or countersign, or wish to write in turn."

70. Revelation 22:16–18; cf. Polyglot Bible; Bible Hub [*Bible, Nouveau Testament*, 908; *Sainte Bible polyglotte*, 540].

the inquisitions to come, for there is supposedly in this very book, in which one must have faith as in a testimony given under oath, there is in this book the prescription and description of the punishment to be incurred by those who don't believe in the book, who add something to it. The punishment of unbelievers is part of the book; it is written, as one says. It is on the syllabus of the prescription, and it is also what one has to know how to read. And the punishment is none other, once again, than a death penalty for a deadly sin. The plagues [*plaies*] in question are plagues only if one adds something to the book, but they can become mortal wounds [*plaies*], wounds one doesn't recover from, once life is taken away, if one takes something away from the book. For the threat is aimed not only at those who add something to the book, but also at those who take something away from it. So then, those who take something away from the book, by omission or commission, those who lessen, those who *diminish* and don't respect the integrity of its total body, they will have their lives taken away, and taken away of course by God, by an implacable God. That will be the punishment, the terrible deadly retribution for the deadly sin. The diminution of the book will be paid for by the capital diminution that will lead to loss of life and more than life. I say "diminution" because that will be the Latin word in the text that I am going to read in a moment. If you diminish the text by reading-writing, if you make it lesser, if you do less with more, well, in such a diminishing reduction — or so says the text in short, this veil or revelation of the Apocalypse — you risk losing life and more than life: capital diminution. What I want to emphasize here, before reading these lines from the text, is that this death, this merciless capital punishment, this diminution that will provoke the taking away of life,[71] will deprive the sinner not just of life *tout court*, if I can say that, but, if I can further say this, of citizenship, of belonging to the holy city and to the holy community of the living. In divine punishment, in the penalty that is retribution for the diminution of the book, to lose one's life is the same thing, the same punishment, the same sanction as losing one's citizenship in the holy city. I'll read these few lines from the apocalyptic and eschatological conclusion of the Revelation of Saint John ("eschatological" because, at the end, it finishes with this ultimate death threat, that is to say, this threat of ending, of end without end, but this time end without end in the sense both of an end that doesn't last interminably

71. During the session, Derrida adds: "I'm insisting on this because I want to put it into relation with the death penalty, which we'll begin talking about today, the president and the death penalty." See 190ff. below.

as does the sabbath without evening, and of an end that lasts interminably, but as in hell, an infernal end without end, not a holy one):

> For I testify unto every man that heareth the words of the prophecy of this book, If any man shall add unto these things, God shall add unto him the plagues that are written in this book: And if any man shall take away (*diminuerit*) from the words of the book of this prophecy [*si quis diminuerit de verbis libri prophetiae*; *kai ean tis* aphelē *apo tōn logōn tou bibliou tēs prophēteias*: I underline the Greek *aphelē*, from *aphairō*, because this aphaeresis, this amputation, is expressed using the same vocabulary as the forgiveness that takes away, and remits and cancels the fault: *apheōntai sou ai amartiai*: your sins will be taken away, remitted, forgiven (Luke 7, 48), (so,) if someone diminishes the words of this book of prophecy God shall take away his part out of the book of life ("tree" of life is what the French translation says for *auferet Deus partem ejus de libro vitae*, the book of life, but *liber* is book because it is first of all the bark, *liber*, of the tree; the translator translates *libro vitae* as "tree of life," though it is also the book of life—and in Greek the word for *liber* is *xulon*, "wood," the wood of the tree, but this tree of life is also the tree or wood or book of the sanctified life)], God shall take away his part out of the book of life, and out of the holy city, and from the things which are written in this book (*auferet Deus partem eius de libro vitae, et de civitate sancta, et de his quae scripta sunt in libro isto*; *apheloi o theos to meros autou apo tou xulou tēs zōēs kai ek tēs poleōs tēs agias, tōn gegrammenōn en tō bibliō toutō*). He which testifieth these things saith, Surely I come quickly (*cito, tachu*). Amen. Even so, come, Lord Jesus. The grace of our Lord Jesus Christ be with you all [*avec tous*].[72]

This terrible punishment, you will have noticed, which is as implacable   202 as the fault of not hearing the testimony, of changing something in the book, of adding to it or subtracting from it, punishes without mercy an unatonable fault. One can hardly say that this merciless punishment for an unatonable sin concerns two acts or two wills—the sinner's and God's—which could or could not act this way or that, in this way and not otherwise. In truth, all that is comprehended analytically in the book, comprehended in the sense of being included, inscribed, prescribed, described. Textually. The punishment follows, as an inevitable consequence, a failing in reading the

---

72. Revelation 22:18–21; cf. Polyglot Bible; Bible Hub [*Bible, Nouveau Testament*, 908–9; *Sainte Bible polyglotte*, 540]. See also Luke 7:48: "And he said unto her, Thy sins are forgiven"; cf. Bible Hub [*Bible, Nouveau Testament*, 199; *Sainte Bible polyglotte*, 209]. The typescript has "*vous* [you]" instead of "*tous* [all]" as the final word of Revelation. During the session, he adds: "It is with these terrible threats that the Revelation of Saint John ends."

book that describes and prescribes the punishment for one who reads or understands poorly. The testimonial book says to the reader, in short: "If you read me poorly, if you interpret me poorly, if you don't hear, if you don't then believe my testimony as it is written in the book, well, it is written in the book that for that very reason you will be punished, plagues will rain down on you inasmuch as you added to the text; life and sanctified citizenship, life and belonging to the holy community will be taken away from you if you take away from the text. Everything depends automatically on the way in which you read and receive the text, the way in which you come to the testimonial text. As a result, 'come' means 'come' to the text, listen to and read the witness, come, and if you don't come, if you add or subtract anything, so if you don't come, you will suffer and even to death, and you will no longer belong to the *civitas sancta*, you will be excommunicated, in the strong sense of the term, you will excommunicate yourself, you will exclude yourself by yourself. You are forewarned by the text: if you don't come into agreement with [*convenir*] the text, if you don't believe it, if you betray the text, if, in short, you commit perjury in your very reading of the testimonial text, you are forewarned by the text, and in detail, about the punishment that your unatonable crime will deserve." It is in that way that the economy of sanctioning is reintroduced. What is here called the book[73] is a sort of Constitution that says to the citizen reader, the citizen by birth: "If you read or interpret poorly, if you betray the Constitution to which you are committed in advance; well, that same Constitution envisages the penalty you incur: suffering, plagues, and/or the death penalty, being deposed or removed from the holy city."[74]

203   Hegel's ghost is growing impatient. He would like to take the floor again as voice off in order to say, once more: "But I already said that, and I already analyzed that evangelico-apocalyptic economy, I already spoke of the trial of Jesus and about Mary Magdalene." We are going to keep him waiting a little longer, long enough for a digression to show that *The End of Work*, the book by Rifkin, and what it talks about, also ends in its own final and apocalyptic moment, by invoking the "fraternal bonds" of men.[75] To sum up too quickly: having defined the three technological revolutions, and ours especially, the third, "the information age," which, by means of "new, more sophisticated software technologies," will push civilization toward "a near-

73. During the session, Derrida adds: "The bark of life."
74. The typescript here contains several illegible marginal annotations.
75. Rifkin, *End of Work*, 292 [*Fin du travail*, 378].

workerless world," making it urgent to redefine "opportunities and responsibilities for millions of people in a society absent of mass formal employment,"[76] when "the only new sector emerging is the knowledge sector, made up of a small elite of entrepreneurs . . . professionals, educators, and consultants,"[77] Rifkin speaks of a "tragic toll"[78] in this "new phase in world history,"[79] and quite bluntly poses the problem of good and evil. He writes: (Read and comment on *The End of Work*, p. 16T)

> The Third Industrial Revolution is a powerful force for good and evil. The new information and telecommunication technologies have the potential to both liberate and destabilize civilization in the coming century. Whether the new technologies free us for a life of increasing leisure or result in massive unemployment and a potential global depression will depend in large part on how each nation addresses the question of productivity advances. In the final section, "The Dawn of the Post-Market Era," we will explore several practical steps for coping with productivity advances in an effort to mitigate the effects of mass technological displacement while reaping the rewards of the high-technology revolution.[80]

204

Yet when, in conclusion, following a trajectory whose content is most interesting, and which you must read on your own, in conclusion he comes back to the responsibilities needing to be assumed, well, to name what exceeds *both* the machine *and* the market, what defines the voice of salvation,[81] he returns to the Christian language of fraternity, of the virtue of fraternity and rebirth of the human spirit that will alone dictate nonmachinic solutions. In the passage that I am going to read, you will see reappear, not by chance, the lexicon of postmachinic and postmarket fraternity, the value of "the rebirth of the human spirit," and even the word "resurrection," and even the death knell [*glas*] with its apocalyptic connotation (you know the affinity that exists between the values of tolling, *gala*, and *apokaluptō* as revelation. I insist on that in *Clang* and in "Of an Apocalyptic Tone

76. Rifkin, *End of Work*, xv [*Fin du travail*, 13, 14].
77. Rifkin, *End of Work*, xvi–xvii [*Fin du travail*, 15].
78. Rifkin, *End of Work*, xvii [*Fin du travail*, 15].
79. Rifkin, *End of Work*, xvi [*Fin du travail*, 14].
80. Rifkin, *End of Work*, xvii–xviii [*Fin du travail*, 16].
81. The typescript has *voix du salut*, "voice of salvation." [Translator's note:] This may or may not be a slip of the pen. One would normally hear *voie du salut*, "way of salvation."

Recently Adopted in Philosophy"):[82] (Read and comment on *The End of Work*, pp. 378–79F)

Unused human labor is the central overriding reality of the coming era and the issue that will need to be confronted and addressed head-on by every nation if civilization is to survive the impact of the Third Industrial Revolution. [Don't think that I am discrediting this book, which is interesting and important, full of interesting information and such. I am trying to analyze the philosophy or ideology that caps it off, but that doesn't discredit the content.]

205   If the talent, energy, and resourcefulness of hundreds of millions of men and women are not redirected to constructive ends, civilization will probably continue to disintegrate into a state of increasing destitution and lawlessness from which there may be no easy return. For this reason, finding an alternative to formal work in the marketplace is the critical task ahead for every nation on earth. Preparing for a post-market era will require far greater attention to the building up of the third sector and the renewal of community life. Unlike the market economy [the sentence in French is "one has to know how to enter the economy of the market," but I am saying that within the economy of the market one has to quit the economy of the market], which is based solely on "productivity" and therefore amenable to the substitution of machines for human input, the social economy is centered on human relationships [that, moreover, is also the discourse of European socialism when it opposes an economist or monetarist concept of Europe. We have to build a social Europe: that is Rifkin's philosophy also], on feelings of intimacy, on companionship, fraternal bonds, and stewardship—qualities not easily reducible to or replaceable by machines. Because it is the one realm that machines cannot fully penetrate or subsume, it will be by necessity the refuge where the displaced workers of the Third Industrial Revolution will go to find renewed meaning and purpose in life after the commodity value of their labor in the formal marketplace has become marginal or worthless.

The resurrection and transformation of the third sector into a powerful independent realm capable of absorbing the flood of displaced workers let go by the market sector must be given urgent priority if we are to weather the technological storm clouds on the horizon.

. . .

82. Derrida, *Clang*, 220–24 [*Glas*, 220–24]; "Of a Newly Arisen Apocalyptic Tone in Philosophy," trans. John P. Leavey, in Peter Fenves, ed., *Raising the Tone of Philosophy* (Baltimore: Johns Hopkins University Press, 1999) [*D'un ton apocalyptique adopté naguère en philosophie* (Paris: Galilée, 2005)].

We are entering a new age of global markets and automated production. The road to a near-workerless economy is within sight. Whether that road leads to a safe haven or a terrible abyss will depend on how well civilization prepares for the post-market era that will follow on the heels of the Third Industrial Revolution. The end of work could spell a death sentence [*sonner le glas*] for civilization as we have come to know it. The end of work could also signal the beginning of a great social transformation, a rebirth of the human spirit. The future lies in our hands.[83]

Hegel, who can wait no longer, is soon going to hold the floor again, in more or less audible snippets. He is fidgeting in the wings. To reconstitute what he says you can go to different places in his earlier drafts of *The Spirit of Christianity and Its Fate*, notably to what relates to forgiveness, in the appendix (pp. 161ff.),[84] and especially, in the main text, the long passage on the Jewish Mary Magdalene, who commits, out of love, the single sin of putting herself above the law, of defying the juridical gaze of "*honnêtes gens*" (in the "foreign" French tongue in Hegel's text), the juridical gaze of "honest folk,"[85] that is to say, her fellows, the Pharisees or Jews. Next time we'll listen to him speak of the love of Mary Magdalene, the exceptional Jew, who was forgiven out of love by him who was able to raise forgiveness above the law or justice; but that was in the name of a superior economy, of the fullness and the *plērōma* of love (pp. 64ff.; German, p. 370).[86] *Plērōma* is the paradox of what fills by enveloping the limit, what completes and fulfills, what fills to the very top [*qui comble*] by fulfilling a promise, inasmuch as the fullest extent [*le comble*] is what fills to the brim but is also almost too much. The fullest extent of forgiving-forgiven love is the most absolute that both fills and exceeds, or fills up by overflowing.[87] Hegel uses the word "*plērōma*" when he says, for example, that the religious is the *plērōma* of love ("*Religiöses ist also das πλήρωμα der Liebe (Reflexion und Liebe vereint, beide verbunden gedacht*") [French, p. 75; German, p. 370; cf. also French, p. 34, German, p. 326].[88] On *plērōma* in Hegel you can also read Clang (p. 70), or

206

83. Rifkin, *End of Work*, 291–93 [*Fin du travail*, 378–79].

84. [Translator's note:] This appendix, "Projet original pour 'L'Esprit du christianisme,'" is not in the English version. See *Esprit du christianisme*, 161ff. [*Der Geist*, 306ff.].

85. Hegel, *Early Theological Writings*, 242; cf. *Der Geist*, 358.

86. [Translator's note:] Cf. *Early Theological Writings*, 242ff. [*Der Geist*, 357; *Esprit du Christianisme*, 64].

87. During the session, Derrida adds: "That's what Jesus is."

88. Hegel, *Der Geist*, 370, 326; *Early Theological Writings*, 253, 214 [*Esprit du Christianisme*, 75, 34]. During the session, Derrida translates: "The religious is therefore the pleroma of love, reflection and love united, the two of them thought, linked together."

the very fine book by Werner Hamacher, published in French translation in 1996 with a remarkable afterword by Marc Froment-Meurice: *Pleroma. Dialecture de Hegel.*[89]

207   Next time we'll begin by again hearing Hegel's voice off concerning this economy without economy of the *plērōma* (with the understanding that wherever forgiveness is requested and/or granted in love, there reconciliation, redemption, salvation retains (and is retained as) an economy of the self and of the proper, if only inasmuch as I can ask for forgiveness only by accusing myself and by repenting, and so by ceasing to be one with my guilty self, hence by saving myself, and inasmuch as I can forgive only by identifying myself through love with the one who saves themself in that way). But we'll come back to that also.

After hearing from Hegel we'll finally allow Clinton to appear in person or in the person of his representatives or lawyers. Clinton met the pope in Missouri yesterday.[90] Let's not forget that the pope is somewhat more than an extra in the globalatinization that we are interpreting. Before hearing from Clinton or his lawyers, we'll reflect on why today, in the United States, in the context of the Clinton trial, deconstruction is so often named, mediatized, called by its name, if not understood. By the press in particular—which is why I say "mediatized"—moreover, by a press that always situates deconstruction as a misfortune that befalls the United States, in Clinton's vicinity. Deconstruction is on Clinton's turf.

It is often said that, in the Senate, his lawyers "deconstruct"[91] the Republicans' arguments. A certain newspaper speaks—this is the title of an article in the *Los Angeles Times*—of "The Deconstruction of Clinton,"[92] while

89. See Werner Hamacher, *Pleroma: Reading in Hegel*, trans. Nicholas Walker and Simon Jarvis (Stanford: Stanford University Press, 1998); cf. *Pleroma: Dialecture de Hegel*, trans. Marc Froment-Meurice and Tilman Küchler (Paris: Galilée, 1996). [Translator's note:] The French title might translate as "Double-Reading" or "Dia-Reading of Hegel," with an obvious play on "dialectic(s)."

90. During a visit to Mexico and to the United States in January 1999, Pope John Paul II met Bill Clinton in St. Louis, Missouri, on January 26.

91. [Translator's note:] Word in English in typescript.

92. Neal Gabler, "The Deconstruction of Clinton," *Los Angeles Times*, January 3, 1999, M1, M6. The online version incorrectly has as title "The Destruction of Clinton" (cf. https://www.latimes.com/archives/la-xpm-1999-jan-03-op-59891-story.html). During the session, Derrida comments: "So clearly it's 'deconstruction'—one often plays on the syntax of the word—that is to say 'the deconstruction of Clinton,' it's deconstruction that deconstructs Clinton, or else deconstruction is put into operation by Clinton in order to defend himself."

another, in Alabama (*Tuscaloosa News*), concludes an analysis of Clinton's deceit, lies, and contortions of the truth by saying: "Polls change, truth does not. Not even in these deconstructed times."[93] Time isn't "out of joint,"[94] as Hamlet said, but in America we are living through a time of deconstruction, "in deconstructed times." And, as always, deconstruction is interpreted as relativism, skepticism, nihilism, ruination of truth and its foundations, etc., even sophist manipulation.

We will ask ourselves what is perhaps accurately conveyed through these symptoms and idiocies, which we are expected to get used to.[95]

208

93. Paul Greenberg, "Not Everyone Is Fooled," *Tuscaloosa News*, December 15, 1998, 7A. This article, preserved in the IMEC "Le parjure et le pardon: documentation" file (219 DRR 240), is heavily annotated by Derrida, who has added in his own hand: "*It depends on what is* is."

94. *Hamlet* I.v. Concerning this line from Shakespeare, see Derrida, *Specters of Marx: The State of the Debt, the Work of Mourning and the New International*, trans. Peggy Kamuf (New York: Routledge, 1993), 3, 19–21 [*Spectres de Marx: L'État de la dette, le travail du deuil, et la nouvelle Internationale* (Paris: Galilée, 1993), 21, 43–46].

95. The typescript includes a photocopy of a newspaper clipping: Thomas Geoghegan, "Lincoln Apologizes," *New York Times*, April 5, 1998. Derrida will return to this article in Session Eight, reading several passages from it. See 236n11 below.

February 10, 1999¹

... I wanted, in the time we have left—I was thinking we would have some time for <this discussion> because I don't know where else we might be able to come back to it in the seminar—to talk a little bit about what is happening with the contaminated blood trial that is now beginning. One can wonder—I suppose that, like me, like everyone, you are following things and reading the press reports, you are trying to understand what is going on—but to pose the question in a somewhat broad and unsubtle way: *who* is after *what* in this trial? What justice is at stake? What would it consist in? Is it a matter of reparation for what everybody agrees is irreparable? *Who* is repairing *what*? What is the difference between a political and a penal justice? Can someone at some point ask for forgiveness, can someone forgive? *210* What is it about? In other words, how would all the categories that we have been putting in play here for a year and a half be in keeping, or not, with this extremely complex, theatrical thing? It was theater that was on view

1. This presentation concerning the contaminated blood scandal was prepared and read by Derrida at the end of the discussion session of February 10, 1999. It followed a presentation by Jean-Philippe Pastor and a Q&A period. The contaminated blood affair affected several countries, in Europe and elsewhere, during the 1980s and 1990s, as a result of infections by blood products that hadn't been screened. In France the scandal erupted when journalist Anne-Marie Casteret (1948–2006) published an article entitled "Le rapport qui accuse le Centre national de transfusion sanguine" in *L'Événement du jeudi* (April 25–May 1, 1999), denouncing the fact that the Centre national de transfusion sanguine (CNTS) had knowingly distributed to hemophiliacs products contaminated with the AIDS virus between 1984 and 1985. One out of two hemophiliacs became infected in the course of a healthcare crisis that affected nearly two thousand persons. A first trial resulted in the sentencing of the former director of the CNTS, Michel Garretta, to four years in prison, and Jean-Pierre Allain, head of the CNTS Department of Research and Development, to four years in prison (two years suspended). See 173ff. below.

yesterday on television in the new set they have constructed for this trial. They constructed a set and displayed it, although it's invisible, there will be no direct TV in the courtroom, but they first showed us the wooden decor, the assigned seating, etc. Okay, I suppose you saw that on television, so, from the theatrical point of view it's extremely interesting: theater and politics. So there is lots to do there, a great deal of work to be done. At no point <did they evoke> the distinction between culpable and responsible. I don't know how that would have been said in German, for example, because people don't know how to translate *schuldig* in Heidegger,[2] or *Schuldigsein*; some translate it as "responsible," others as "guilty," because it means both those things. *Schuldig* means both those things; one can say, "I am responsible, not guilty." You know all that without my telling you, nevertheless, I would have liked us to talk a little about it here, it provides a huge example, which we could spend years on, but if someone wanted to talk about that, if you want to say something about it now, we have ten minutes, we could come back to it.

<A participant asks an inaudible question concerning the use of the term "contaminated blood trial," which seems inaccurate, since it isn't blood that is on trial, but certain government ministers.>

Indeed, we could begin there: it's that they don't know how to <name the thing>, and nobody knows, not even the presiding judge, not even the judge presiding over these strange proceedings is at ease with the structure of this thing. And then, we've never heard a presiding judge say: "What's happening is surreal [*surréaliste*]."[3] That's what he said, he said: "It's surreal," which is always an idiotic word. When someone says: "That's surreal," fine. . . . Nevertheless, he meant something. He meant, from the point of view of a jurist—he is one of the only jurists among those involved, I mean a professional jurist—that he doesn't recognize anything judicially normal and it's so abnormal, new, strange, that one in fact doesn't even know, as you were saying, how to *name* the thing. First of all, because there had already been criminal trials, like the series of cases, etc., in which there was a certain judicial normality. In the current case, we have a political instance that is constituted as it were ad hoc—right?—we don't know who

2. See 166–67 below.

3. Anonymous, "Le malaise ne fait que grandir au procès du sang contaminé, " *Le Temps*, February 26, 1999, https://www.letemps.ch/monde/malaise-na-grandir-proces -sang-contamine. The presiding judge, Christian Le Gunehec, indeed emphasized the "surreal" character of the procedure. See also Serge July, "Le procès du sang contaminé. Justice politique," *Libération*, March 10, 1999, https://www.liberation.fr/evenement/1999 /03/10/le-proces-du-sang-contamine-justice-politique_267127.

is on trial. Is it <Laurent> Fabius, Georgina Dufoix, or <Edmond> Hervé?[4] Or is some thing on trial? We don't even know whether it is a crime or not. The charge is second-degree murder [*homicide involontaire*] . . . the "contaminated blood trial": what is that strange metonymy?

<A participant asks an inaudible question concerning the figure of Oedipus, blood, and the technology of transfusion.>

No doubt, that said, this possibility, although it has appeared to be overwhelmingly linked to new techniques, is nevertheless not entirely new. One could contaminate blood before, without going back as far as Oedipus, don't you think, during this century one could contaminate blood, one could make a medical mistake where blood was contaminated by other pathogens. What is happening here—and I think that this is one element that responds to the question raised by this trial—is that this time the blood was contaminated by the state, which means that there was an anonymous, state responsibility in the decision that led to this relatively widespread contamination, and naturally an effort is being made to personalize that anonymity, but one well knows that, whatever the charges brought against these three ministers, there is a functioning of the state that is tied to the market and there is this state governmental structure that, at a given moment, is tied to mercantile interest according to mechanisms that I don't want to judge or analyze here. In the end, that is what is going on: they delayed, they allegedly delayed, let's be careful, in a negligent way, the practice of testing so that they could use a French product, with a French patent.[5] So, we are dealing with an offense [*une faute*], at least with an injury [*un dommage*], within the responsibility relating both to state and mercantile—that is to say anonymous—considerations. There was contaminated blood, anony-

212

---

4. Former Socialist prime minister Laurent Fabius, and former Socialist ministers Georgina Dufoix (minister of social affairs and national solidarity) and Edmond Hervé (secretary of state for health) appeared before the Cour de Justice de la République from February 2 to March 2, 1999, accused of "second-degree murder." The verdict of the court was to drop the charges against Fabius and Dufoix. The latter, who was president of the French Red Cross from 1989 to 1992, resigned following the scandal, and became known for inventing the infamous expression "responsible, but not guilty" during a declaration on national television channel TF1 on November 4, 1995. See 173ff. below.

5. In 1985 tracing of HIV-infected blood donors was delayed for five months because of competition between Diagnostics Pasteur and American company Abbott, which filed for a patent on its screening test in January, some seven weeks before the application filed by Diagnostics Pasteur. The health authorities waited for the French test to be ready, and approved it in July 1985, three days before approving the Abbott test. See 173 below.

mously; the victims can be named, but the guilty power is not clearly name-able and so it is now a question — in view of *what?* that is what I am asking — of incarnating and naming this state mercantile responsibility. *Who* person-ally took responsibility in the name of the state and the market, or in the name of the state tied to the market, for doing what happened?

<A participant asks an inaudible question concerning how to reestablish culpability for what took place.>

I agree, it's quite possible, but then that is why I am posing the question: *who* is looking for *what?* Because it is obvious that if they didn't have this trial, if there was nothing, if they said: "There you have it, a state and mar-ket dysfunction, the state tied to the market, to French research, etc., it has malfunctioned and that's a pity, they are going to do all they can to provide compensation, if they can, but who is to be punished? We don't know who to punish," it's obvious that without punishment something would be lack-ing. But then, who would be lacking it? Who would be lacking what? Nat-urally, one has to <know>, it is generally said, and one often hears upset-ting statements from victims, the family of victims or their representatives, namely, that they are not looking for revenge but want to know what went on — it's like in South Africa, as Tutu said, we have to know the truth, to know what went on — and in the access to objective and secure knowledge about what took place there is already reparation. Knowing that it hap-pened in that way, and that someone did something on such and such a date whereas they could have acted otherwise. So, having knowledge of it. Next, it is obvious that beyond that reparation there is no reparation. Is it a matter of a reparation that consists solely in establishing knowledge, in establishing an example, because — and that is understandable also — French citizens have to be able to tell themselves in the wake of such a cruel experience, cruel for the victims and, *mutatis mutandis*, cruel for those charged (second-degree murder, obviously none of them intended it, so irrespective of how the verdict turns out, they are of course harshly punished in a way), through the ordeal of this punishment, whatever it be, it is necessary to learn, it is necessary that politicians henceforth feel responsible, that they introduce changes and no doubt they will be more careful; they can do that. But what does that calculus mean? There are a thousand things to be calculated, and does the question of forgiveness still make sense, this calculating machine for reparations, examples, political lessons, etc.? I don't know.

<A participant asks an inaudible question concerning the reversal of moral responsibility.>

What is extremely significant in my opinion is that in fact, as you say, it is a matter of public health [*hygiène*], that is to say, immunity. Hygiene means what is sound [*sain*], safe [*sauf*], unscathed [*indemne*], immune, and to the extent that forgiveness can have as its mission—this is the problem—reestablishing immunity, reestablishing health [*le sain*]—*s.a.i.n*, or *s.a.i.n.t* (ύγιεινός) <hygiene>—it would be a matter at that point of using justice, whatever that be, to restore in the context of a hygiene problem a certain image, restore a certain figure of the public hygiene of the social body. Contamination of the social body cannot be tolerated, especially where the responsibility and competence are those of public health authorities. Contamination can perhaps be tolerated in Foreign Affairs, in the Department of the Interior (there it gets a bit complicated), but in Public Health, no. Moreover, Hervé is the person who is most liable in this whole story. In his case, it's that the person in charge of public health may have, as it were, opened things up to a type of "corruption" (I put that word in quotes: I don't think that Hervé is someone corrupt, but, all the same, along with others, he allowed the imperative of the market to infect decision-making, you see, there is therefore a seed of corruption in any case, of corruptibility), and so, for corruption to be introduced into the Ministry of Health, into the State Secretariat for Health, that is especially serious. And the question of forgiveness is indeed a question of health, one speaks of healing, reconciliation, immunity, and the concept of autoimmunity to which I often refer precisely interferes with the purity of what is immune, unscathed, where destruction gets reintroduced, autodestruction, as if there were an autoimmunity, an autoimmune process inside the Ministry of Public Health. That's what is intolerable. That is where we should be able to count on. . . . It's as if you weren't feeling <well>, you call the doctor, and it's the doctor who comes and gives you the flu. That won't go over well! [*Laughter*] I don't mind catching the flu from X and Y, but not from doctors! That's the whole thing going on in hospitals now, one can see that, with the big mess in how French hospitals are organized, there are more and more cases of hospitals that contaminate, where people no longer dare go into certain hospitals because they know that there are risks of contamination there, for example, not with AIDS but other infections, in hospital surroundings, specifically hospitals, and that's what is intolerable.

<A participant asks an inaudible question concerning structures that aim to reestablish immunity>

One hopes in the end to restore, it's purely phantasmatic, of course, the country is going to put on a show of restoring and of immunity, we'll get back our virginity, immunity, after punishing in one way or another, etc. It will be the same thing with Clinton. They won't be able to remove him from office, but he'll have a reprimand slapped on him and then they'll go get a makeover.

February 17, 1999

Act VI. Act VI of our scenario. "The play's the thing." Hamlet.[1] Theater within theater, a play within a play, deixis of theater at the theater, forgiveness that is always forgiveness of perjury, that is, in the theater, the thing itself, the stakes of performance. It is a question of knowing whether this is the place for making a scene with forgiveness or of putting forgiveness on stage. A pardoning of perjury always appeals to theater in the very place where, by always appealing to theater, it resists theater.

Last week we confirmed yet again both the necessity and impossibility of that theatricality of forgiveness, of that scene or staging of a visibility and phenomenality of forgiveness that we have been patiently analyzing since last year, from *The Merchant of Venice* to *Hamlet* ("The play's the thing"),[2] from references to theater made by Hegel and Desmond Tutu, to the two Medeas again last week.[3] I won't go back over that. On this theater within theater, which is also a theater without theater, a theater of the world, theater of history, political theater, theater of the court of justice, theater of the Last Judgment (Benjamin),[4] we never stopped hearing Hegel's voice off, and we saw and heard successively Mandela, Tutu, and we reconstituted many discourses, having them intersect with their biblico-Abrahamic or evangelical tradition, on the one hand, and with the large question of labor, on the other (the end without end of work, both in the register of Augustine's *City of God*, within which we analyzed the doctrine of sin, of mercy and the politics of sabbatical repose that knows no evening (neither

218

---

1. *Hamlet* II.ii [*Hamlet, Le Roi Lear*, 101].
2. On *The Merchant of Venice* see *Perjury and Pardon*, vol. 1, 44–64, 120–26 [*Parjure et pardon*, vol. 1, 77–101, 166–73].
3. Allusion to the discussion session of February 10, 1999.
4. See 22ff. above.

early nor late, *tarde*),[5] as end without end of history, the dominical Saturday of the second grace as impossibility of sinning and dying; and also, on the other hand, then, in the register of the problematic developed by Jeremy Rifkin concerning the end of work, in his recent book *The End of Work*).[6] Before continuing today by allowing Hegel his voice off for a moment, then by summoning Clinton onto the stage or to the stand, I would like, before even beginning, to emphasize three points that remained up in the air, suspended as if within an ellipsis [*comme des points de suspension*] during the last two sessions.

A. *Work, first of all*. If I insisted so much on the end without end of work, in those two contexts that seem so heterogeneous, those of Saint Augustine in *The City of God*, and of Rifkin's recent book on *The End of Work* within a process of globalization and in the time of what he calls the third technological revolution,[7] if I ended by marking in what respect the ethico-political, or even metaphysico-ideological discourse — which framed Rifkin's analyses, themselves very interesting and necessary, by the way — remained dependent on, inherited from the Christian tradition through its appeal (I am here using Rifkin's words) to "responsibility" with respect to a "resurrection," a "rebirth of the human spirit," a "fraternity," a distinction between good and evil and recourse to virtues that transcend the machine,[8] etc., if I thought it necessary to make that detour and to insist on it, it was for more than one reason.

1. On the one hand, it was to mark the sometimes scarcely visible continuity of a hegemonic Christian tradition (globalatinization);

2. On the other hand, it was because these discourses are typically discourses (as exemplary type, then, as much Augustine's as Rifkin's) *on the world*, on the concept of world and so-called globalization, given that our interest is in the globalization of expiation, repentance, request for forgiveness, etc.;

5. See 107–11 above.

6. See 105, 129, 150ff. above.

7. Thus in the typescript and in the corresponding passage in "Mes 'humanités' du Dimanche," *L'Humanité*, March 4, 1999, reprinted as "My Sunday 'Humanities,'" trans. Rachel Bowlby, in Derrida, *Paper Machine* (Stanford: Stanford University Press, 2005), 100–108 [*Papier Machine*, 331]. However, this indeed seems to be Rifkin's "third industrial revolution" (see Rifkin, *End of Work*, 59–89 [*Fin du travail*, 378], and 150ff. above; see also Derrida, "The University without Condition," in *Without Alibi*, 225–26 [*Université sans condition*, 56–57]). During the session, Derrida clarifies: "That of remote-working, etc., of robotization."

8. See 152–53 above. [Translator's note:] Rifkin's word is "qualities," which the French translation rephrases as "*vertus*." See *The End of Work*, 292 [*Fin du travail*, 378].

3. And finally, it was because what distinguishes the specificity of work from all sorts of associated values (work isn't simply activity, doing, *praxis*, production: one may act or do or practice without working, one may work without producing), what distinguishes the *tripalium* — the instrument of torture with three branches, the torture of work, punishment, the suffering of labor — is the consciousness and significance of an expiation, of an originary punishment that would have, from the beginning, sanctioned originary[9] sin and the experience of nakedness. Work is punishing [*une peine*], in the double sense of the word: it is hard [*pénible*], painful, difficult, as is a sentence [*une peine*], that is to say a punishment, a sanction that repays by means of a sentence a wrong committed [*un mal fait*][10] and not forgiven, an unremitted debt; a sanction that pays in order to repay the debt and see the punishment remitted, to buy it back as it were. In Genesis 3:16–20, two verses apart, there is no separation between the suffering of labor imposed on Eve, who will have to give birth in pain, in the hard labor of childbirth, and the suffering of Adam the farmer who will have to till the earth with the sweat of his brow.[11] For man as for woman, it's a form of parity for this pair of sinners, before any right to work, duty to work; the *tripalium* will signify the beginning of the world into which sin has thrown them or caused them to fall, and the beginning of an expiation — as if work had forever to retain the sense of a forgiveness implicitly requested for an always prior fault,[12] and in view of redemption, as if the price of work, a salary, were first of all the price not of a purchase but of buying back aimed at liberating from an always prior and inexpungible guilt, aimed at paying a debt, obtaining the remittance of a debt, releasing one from an obligation. Whence, among so many other meanings, that double movement that I spoke of last time[13] by calling to mind the medieval examples cited by Le Goff: centuries ago, like today, there were already demands both to limit the duration of the work day and, conversely, to obtain work, or more work. In both cases it is a matter of an economy of redemption or salvation, and of making it so that

220

9. Thus in typescript. During the session, Derrida corrects himself: "Original."

10. During the session, Derrida clarifies: "A misdeed [*méfait*]."

11. "Unto the woman he said . . . in sorrow thou shalt bring forth children. . . . And unto Adam he said . . . cursed is the ground for thy sake; in sorrow shalt thou eat of it all the days of thy life. . . . In the sweat of thy face shalt thou eat bread" (Genesis 3:16–19) [*Bible, Ancien Testament*, 11].

12. During the session, Derrida adds: "To work is to ask for forgiveness."

13. During the session, Derrida says rather "two weeks ago." See 127 above. On Le Goff's medieval examples, see Derrida, "The University without Condition," in *Without Alibi*, 228–29 [*Université sans condition*, 61–64].

a salary, a price paid for work, purchasing power, permits one to buy or buy back the most and the best at the price of the least expiation. My hypothesis is that one cannot set apart the politico-economic question of work in today's so-called globalization phase without reproblematizing that history, concept, and expiatory logic of a labor that always consists, in one way or another, in confessing while asking for forgiveness. (I note in parentheses, and in anticipation, since we shall soon come to the Clinton case, that among all the numerous, complex, and overdetermined reasons for his popularity — about which both the media and the Republicans understood nothing, a popularity thanks to which he no doubt escaped impeachment,[14] removal from office — there was economic prosperity, an apparently massive drop in unemployment, and job creation of similarly spectacular proportions (I won't go into here the difficult problem of knowing what those jobs were and how they were freed up or created). Clinton is perceived by lots of Americans as someone who was able to give work to job-seekers; that is no doubt one of the reasons why much was forgiven him.)

221   On the same track that links being bound to work to a history of sin and expiation, you might encounter or cross paths with a certain Kant, the Kant of *Religion within the Boundaries of Mere Reason*, who precisely proposes to put into perspective this conjoined history of work and sin dating from Genesis. Kant does that in the course of a long development that would merit our dedicating long sessions to it (something that I don't think I should do here for reasons of general economy), but I'll simply point to its architectonic place and main argument in the context of what interests us here. You'll then have to do the work yourselves. In the first part of *Religion within the Boundaries*, paragraph 3, Kant defined[15] what he calls radical evil, that is to say, an innate, originary evil in man that was however freely contracted by man, originary but born out of freedom, which allows an imputation to be made, for an evil has to be the effect of a freedom (it is a matter, then, of thinking an evil that is both originary, congenital, radical, from the root, and yet the act of a freedom like a "corrupt propensity (*verdebter Hang*),"[16]

14. After being impeached by the House of Representatives on December 19, 1998, Clinton was acquitted by the Senate on February 12, 1999. [Translator's note:] The word "impeachment" is in English in typescript.

15. During the session, Derrida adds: "And this has been an important place for us here since the beginning of the seminar." See Derrida, *Perjury and Pardon*, vol. 1, 18–19 [*Pardon et parjure*, vol. 1, 47–48].

16. Immanuel Kant, "Religion within the Boundaries of Mere Reason," trans. Allen Wood and George di Giovanni, in *Religion within the Boundaries of Mere Reason and Other Writings*, ed. Allen Wood and George di Giovanni (Cambridge: Cambridge Uni-

a propensity that isn't malice, isn't a bad will that would consist in the intention—as subjective principle of maxims—to incorporate evil as incentive into one's maxim, but rather a "perversity of the heart (*Herzensänderung, Änderung des Herzens*, change of heart),"[17] a bad heart that isn't incompatible with a good intention, but simply attests to a human nature that is too weak to observe the principles that it has adopted. In that interpretation of radical evil as perversion and not diabolical wickedness there is already a trait worth noting here, in anticipation of what we'll shortly read in Hegel on the relation between Christianity and Judaism. Kant, who moreover says in this same book that Christianity is the sole moral religion (because it is the only one that commands each person to do everything possible to become better without being concerned with favors from God—Kant distinguishes two types of religion, one that is a "mere cult"[18] (external and dedicated to calculating God's favors, becoming eternally happy without becoming better, through the remission of sins: hence, forgiveness and remission of sins: religion as simple cult), and the other, the Christian religion, purely moral, concerning itself only with the good conduct of man; cf. the end of the Remark following Part One, whose final note includes moreover a whole discourse on grace, the effects of grace and the means of grace);[19] so here is Kant naming as radical perversion and radical evil the gesture that consists in believing oneself to have lived up to the law to the extent that one has acted in conformity with the letter of the law; by observing the letter of the law without having respect for the law itself as sole motive; without doing anything contrary to the law one can then pervert the law and that radical perversion of the human heart is radical evil. It is indeed difficult not to recognize the conventional figure of Judaism in that accusation (one finds the same thing in the early Hegel: what he calls positivity, one might say the positivism of the Jew, which Jesus goes beyond, is immorality in that it is satisfied with conforming to the letter of the law (p. 44 of *The Spirit of*

222

versity Press, 1998), 56 [*Die Religion innerhalb der Grenzen der bloßen Vernunft, Werke*, vol. 6 (Berlin: de Gruyter, 1968), 32; *La religion dans les limites de la simple raison*, trans. Jean Gibelin (Paris: Librairie philosophique J. Vrin, 1952), 53].

17. "Religion within the Boundaries," 60 [*Die Religion*, 47; *Religion dans les limites*, 70].

18. "Religion within the Boundaries," 71 [*Die Religion*, 51; *Religion dans les limites*, 75].

19. "Religion within the Boundaries," 72–73 [*Die Religion*, 52–53; *Religion dans les limites*, 76–77].

Christianity in French)),[20] in the same way that one has difficulty thinking that Christianity (the letter of it, in any case, but so be it . . .)[21] consists in renouncing, in a purely moral way, in Kant's sense, every cultish religion and all hope of remission of sins).[22]

223   Having defined radical evil in the first part of this first section, well, in the second part of the same first section Kant tackles, at one point, what he calls a third difficulty, according to which, after the commission of a fault, no improvement on the part of the sinner, no conversion, no change in the man who has thus become different, can "wipe out" his debt — "original debt," says Kant, "that precedes" any good — which is what we call radical evil (Heidegger? and radical evil?).[23] Our "rational right" prevents us from considering that such a prior debt or fault can be wiped out either by

---

20. "Over against the positivity of the Jews, Jesus set man; over against the laws and their obligatoriness he set the virtues, and in these the immorality of 'positive' man is overcome" (Hegel, *Early Theological Writings*, 224 [*Esprit du christianisme*, 44]). During the session, Derrida comments: "In Hegel you could see analogous remarks that overlap exactly with Kant's here, where the one accused is really the Jew inasmuch as he is literalist and content to make the appropriate gestures, yes, conforming to the letter of the prescription and then feeling he has acquitted himself morally. That, right there, is radical evil." We close here the parenthesis opened four lines earlier.

21. [Translator's note:] Ellipsis in typescript.

22. We close here the long parenthesis opened thirteen lines into the paragraph.

23. Kant, "Religion within the Boundaries," 88–89 [cf. *Die Religion*, 72; *Religion dans les limites*, 88–89]. During the session, Derrida comments: "What precisely makes for the radicality of evil is that the transformation, or conversion, of the sinner is not sufficient to erase the debt. Last time, you remember, we were talking about Heidegger and the enigmatic impression given in *Sein und Zeit* such that the great discourse on originary *Schuldigsein*, on originary culpability or responsibility, is developed as a very powerful discourse that traverses the whole of *Sein und Zeit* without the question of forgiveness ever being posed, without the word "forgiveness" ever being uttered, as far as I know. We wondered why that was. One of my hypotheses is that he wanted, whether by denial or not, to avoid any Christian connotation. In any case, here Heidegger would intersect with the Kant who says that radical evil cannot be erased, that debt, sin, cannot be erased with respect to radical evil by whatever comes after, by a subsequent transformation of the sinner, by the sinner's becoming different. And Kant explains that our rational right, because constantly — as you know if you've read "Religion within the Boundaries of Mere Reason," but if you haven't, do it without delay, and as you know or should know, this extraordinary book whose status is very strange — constantly it consists precisely in explaining religion within the limits of reason alone, that is to say, in analyzing Christian revelation from the point of view of right, of nonrevealed reason, of reason without revelation, you see, of natural reason as it were, and in reading biblical accounts in such a way that in the weave of those narratives one deciphers as it

another or by the same man become other. For that debt is not transmissible like a financial debt that could be entrusted to a third party (*explain*).[24] It is here a matter of the most personal and least transmissible debt. Now, here we have the passage to the infinite (Read p. 99 I and comment):

> Now, moral evil (transgression of the moral law, called sin when the law is taken *as divine command* [that's not a biblical reference, it's a rational analysis]) brings with it an *infinity* of violations of the law, and hence an *infinity* of guilt [so the fault is immediately infinite][25] (though it is otherwise before a human court, which takes only the individual crime into account, hence only the act and anything related to it, not the universal disposition [in other words, the human tribunal deals with determinable, finite faults, and consequently is not concerned with the violation itself, the very intention to violate]), not so much because of the *infinity* of the highest lawgiver whose authority is thereby offended [so we wound the author of the law, God] (for we understand nothing of such intangible relations of the human being to the highest being) but because the evil is in the *disposition* and the maxims in general (in the manner of *universal principles* as contrasted with individual transgressions): consequently, every human being has to expect *infinite* punishment and exclusion from the Kingdom of God. [In other words, when it comes to radical evil, to the extent that it necessarily can't be transmitted, redeemed, bought back, and so is infinite, man would have to expect eternal punishment. If sin is what it is, namely, a debt, something always prior, original, innate, like radical evil, and yet a free act for which I am responsible and so it is imputable and carries with it a violation, infinite damage [*lésion*] to transcendent divine law, what can be done to avoid that eternal punishment? The rational conclusion is precisely that I will be forever culpable. In Heideggerian discourse, where *Schuldigsein* is part of the structure of *Dasein*, there is no redemption possible. That's how it is: I will be structurally guilty from the origin and forever. Well, there is a solution in Kant. And the solution to that difficulty is a reference that seems as if it wants still to be rational, that is to say to be without the authority of biblical revelation, although biblical revelation serves as an index for understanding

224

---

were ahistorical, rational and universal structures." Derrida is alluding to the discussion session of February 10, 1999. See 156–60 above.

24. During the session, Derrida adds: "As for me, I can't repay you, but another will repay you instead of me, which is something we can imagine when it is a matter of money. Or else, *I* can't repay you, I the guilty one, I can't repay you, but, become different, I will repay you, hence an appeal to a third party. But that's not possible, says Kant, it's contrary to the concept of radical evil and the rational right that is ours."

25. [Translator's note:] The French translation has *faute* [fault] for *Schuld*, whereas the English has "guilt."

what it is about. So, he is reading the Bible the whole time while saying: "Well, I am not relying on the Bible, the Bible isn't the authority, but if you want to understand what I am telling you, there is, in the Bible, a paradigm, a key, a rational key." And that is why the Christian religion is the only one that is moral, rationally moral. That is interesting for us. Because when we keep asking what is going on with Christianity, with what I am calling *globalatinization*, what is happening to Christianity, well, it's a religion that adjusts to rationality, that merges with the rationality of that historical becoming.][26]

The solution to this difficulty is an as it were rational reference to the event of the Passion and to the Son of God, whom Kant presents, as always in this book, as a sort of narrative figure who "personif[ies an] idea (*wenn wir diese Idee personifizieren*)" (p. 74).[27] (*Comment*)[28] The man who changes is a new man, the old man dies to sin—hence to all the dispositions that turned him away from the good—in order to live in accordance with justice. There then occurs "resipiscence (*Sinnesänderung*),"[29] return to reason and knowledge, which is what "resipiscence" means (a very interesting word for us, because it connects sense to repentance, knowledge and reason to remorse or repentance, to confession and request for forgiveness), resipiscence and also, by the same token, repentance, regret, change of heart and of sense; and resipiscence is abandonment of evil, exit from evil and entry into the good. But this resipiscence (*Sinnesänderung*) is not composed of two actions separated by a time interval: (1) "entry into goodness," and (2) "exit from evil (*Ausgang vom Bösen*)."[30] And it is in order to describe this unique movement of exiting evil and entering the good that Kant uses, within sin-

26. Kant, "Religion within the Boundaries," 89 [cf. *Die Religion*, 72; *Religion dans les limites*, 99].

27. Kant, "Religion within the Boundaries," 91 [*Die Religion*, 74; *Religion dans les limites*, 101].

28. During the session, Derrida comments: "Christ is a convenient personification of this idea of reason. And the whole book is constructed like that, which is obviously magnificent, fascinating, an extraordinary text. So, what is the idea that Christ personifies?"

29. Kant, "Religion within the Boundaries," 89 [*Die Religion*, 73; *Religion dans les limites*, 100]. During the session, Derrida adds: "Which is a magnificent word in French also." [Translator's note:] The English translation has "conversion."

30. Kant, "Religion within the Boundaries," 90 [*Die Religion*, 74; *Religion dans les limites*, 100].

gle quotation marks and parentheses (insist on these contrivances),[31] references to Christ. He says that *"[d]er Ausgang aus der verderbten Gesinnung,"* the exit from perverse intention so as to enter *"in die gute"* (into good intention) is (open parenthesis and insert single quotation marks): *"(als 'das Absterben am alten Menschen,' 'Kreuzigung des Fleisches')* [as death to the old man, crucifixion of the flesh]":[32] already in itself a "sacrifice *(Aufopferung)"* and the beginning of a long series of ills borne by "the new man *(der neue Mensch) in der Gesinnung des Sohnes Gottes* (according to the intention of the son of God)" [comment on the ambiguous status of these statements: justified by the status of Christ, "representative of humanity": moral and rational religion],[33] that is to say, solely for the love of the good; ills that returned and were intended for another "as punishment *(als Strafe)*," that is to say, intended for the "old man" (Jew?), for the one in question is morally another man [Maimonides and the different man — announce development to come].[34] (Read *Religion* p. 101 J.)[35]

226

31. During the session, Derrida adds: "And one must, when reading this text, pay close attention to the single quotation marks and parentheses. One has to be attentive to these contrivances of writing."

32. Kant, *Die Religion*, 74. During the session, Derrida includes his translation. Cf. "Religion within the Boundaries," 90 [*Religion dans les limites*, 101]: "(as 'the death of the old man,' 'the crucifying of the flesh')."

33. During the session, Derrida comments: "So there, once again, I'm insisting unduly on that, but I think it has to be done: these statements have a very ambiguous status since it is a question, on the one hand, of a rational discourse that takes as its paradigmatic illustration what happened with Jesus, but, on the other, it isn't only a pedagogical illustration because this ambiguity is justified by the status of Christ, who is the representative of humanity on earth, and by the status of Christianity, which, according to Kant, is a moral and rational religion."

34. During the session, Derrida comments: "You know, we'll probably come to this later in studying more closely a Judaic tradition, there are literally analogous things in Maimonides — and probably in others also — where the whole theory of repentance is tied to a discourse on transformation, on 'I become different, I am no longer the same, I am a new man,' and that is without reference to Christ. The Jewish sinner who asks for forgiveness is often presented — and it's a problem, an easy option that we've spoken about often here — as a new man: 'It's no longer me, there, it was I who did that but it's no longer me, forgive me since I am no longer the same.' And there are long texts by Maimonides on this becoming different, and new, of man."

35. During the session, Derrida comments: "Second part, first section: he has just explained, then, this death of the old man and the crucifixion of the flesh — it isn't the death *of* the old man, but dying *to* the old man: here the translation says 'death of the old man,' 'death of the old man' and 'crucifying of the flesh,' within quotation marks, and he says about it that it is 'in itself already sacrifice and entrance into a long train of

227

[I]lls which . . . are still fitting *punishment* for someone else, namely the old human being (who, morally, is another human being).—*Physically* ([i.e.] considered in his empirical character as a sensible being) he still is the same human being liable to punishment, and he must be judged [so, he remains physically the same and hence must be guilty, he is guilty, he must be judged, physically, *physisch*, in italics] as such before a moral tribunal of justice and hence by himself as well. Yet, in his new disposition (as an intelligible being [hence as a nonsensible, nonphysical being]), in the sight of a divine judge for whom the disposition takes the place of the deed, he is *morally* another being. And this disposition which he has incorporated in all its purity, like unto the purity of the Son of God—or (if we personify this idea [*wenn wir diese Idee personifizieren*]) this very Son of God—bears (*trägt für ihn*) as *vicarious substitute* [*Stellvertreter, Vertreter*: he comes in place of, he offers himself instead of the guilty one] the debt of sin for him (*die Sünden-schuld*), and also for all who believe (practically) in him: as *savior*, he satisfies the highest justice through suffering and death, and, as *advocate* [so, translation: Christ is an advocate, he replaces (*als Stellvertreter*), he is man's representative, lawyer, he represents the guilty one and is going to save him as such], he makes it possible for them to hope that they will appear justified before their judge. Only we must remember that (in this way of imagining) the suffering which the new human being must endure while dying to the *old* human being throughout his life is depicted in the representative of the human kind (*an dem Repräsentanten der Menschheit*) as a death suffered once and for all.—Here, then, is that surplus [this excess is what I want to insist on, because we are constantly going to encounter it as the aneconomical within economy, you see, *Überschuß*] over the merit from works for which we felt the need earlier [so, one can no longer evaluate merit by means of a sanction, there is no longer any correspondence between what one has done and the punishment, between the worth of one's works and the judgment, there is a surplus, an overabundance, *Überschuß*, which is going to be called "grace"], one which is imputed to us by grace (*aus Gnaden*). [So, we need to link this discourse on grace to what we were saying last year about political pardon [*grâce*] in Kant, but I won't go back over that.][36] For what in our earthly life (and perhaps even in all future times and in all worlds) is always only in mere *becoming* (namely, our being a human being well-pleasing to

---

life's ills which the new man undertakes' according to the mentality [according to the intention (*in der Gesinnung*)] 'of the Son of God, that is, simply for the sake of the good.' And he continues:"

36. See Derrida, *Perjury and Pardon*, vol. 1, 18–19, 193–94 [*Parjure et pardon*, vol. 1, 47–48, 253–54].

God) is imputed to us. . . . [You see: the status of the Son of God and of grace   *228*
beyond the worth of works.][37]

Yet it is in the course of this passage—which I entreat you to reread
closely (I've had to go too quickly here)—that, concerning punishment,
Kant speaks in a note of "work" as punishment or expiation.[38] And there
again, the status of this note and its logic is very curious, significant, and
decisive for us as we ask ourselves where and how the virtual limit runs
separating faith from knowledge, the discourse of secular reason from the
discourse of Christian revelation within this history of the globalization of
forgiveness, etc.[39] For Kant, to consider the evils man suffers as punishments
incurred for transgressions is not a commitment to a theodicy or priestly religion (a "cult" as Kant says), a revealed or positive religion; rather, beside
the fact that it is a universal understanding (that which makes work a punishment), too widespread to depend on a priestly religion alone, it answers
to a demand of human reason: namely, the demand that we tie "the course
of nature [back into] the laws of morality"; and thus, "we should seek to
become better human beings . . . before we can request to be freed from
the ills of life."[40] That idea of punishment for an earlier sin in the service
of progress is rational (Kant's progressivism).[41] Yet, in the same note Kant
adds: "Hence [because of rational reason] the first man is represented (*vorgestellt*) [a parenthesis again] (in Holy Scriptures (*in der heiligen Schrift*)) as
condemned to work [*zur Arbeit verdammt vorgestellt*: condemned, damned,
cursed, *con-damné* to work] if he wishes to eat, his wife [condemned also]
to bear children in pain, and both [are condemned] to die, *all on account of
their transgression* (Übertretung), although [Kant adds this strange remark]   *229*
there is no telling how animal creatures, fitted with their bodily limbs, could
have expected any other destiny (*Bestimmung*) even if these transgressions

37. Kant, "Religion within the Boundaries," 90–91 [*Die Religion*, 74–75; *Religion
dans les limites*, 101–2].

38. Kant, "Religion within the Boundaries," 90n [*Die Religion*, 78n3; *Religion dans
les limites*, 100–101n1].

39. During the session, Derrida adds: "And that's our question here, isn't it: given
the Abrahamic heritage of forgiveness, what happens in globalization, a globalization
that apparently no longer refers to that message, to that heritage, to that Abrahamic
testament? So this is the separating limit that interests us."

40. Kant, "Religion within the Boundaries," 90n [*Die Religion*, 78n3; *Religion dans
les limites*, 100–101n1].

41. During the session, Derrida adds: "It's the Kant of the Enlightenment speaking
here, speaking of punishment for sin and of work as expiation."

had not been perpetrated."[42] So, anyway, even without the biblical story it was normal, rational, that living animal creatures and animals of human likeness should be destined to suffer and work, to suffer in working. And to justify the universality of the structural logic, as it were, beyond the positivity of Christian "revelation" and the Bible, Kant recalls that "[f]or the Hindus human beings are but spirits (called 'Dewas') locked up in animal bodies as punishment for previous crimes,"[43] and that even a European and Christian philosopher, Malebranche, "preferred to attribute no soul, and hence no feelings, to nonrational animals rather than to admit that horses had to withstand so much torment 'without having ever eaten of forbidden hay.'"[44] (*Comment*)[45]

42. Kant, "Religion within the Boundaries," 90n [*Die Religion*, 78n3; *Religion dans les limites*, 100–101n1]. During the session, Derrida comments: "In other words, how is it one can't understand that even without sin, well, beings like us, constructed like us, etc., couldn't have had a different destiny? That's what is difficult to understand, that's where the question of the Bible, of biblical references obviously counts a great deal, along with the ambiguity of its status."

43. Kant, "Religion within the Boundaries," 90n. During the session, Derrida adds: "In other words, in non-Christian cultures, there is the same schema, namely, that man, the animal named man, who has the same conformation as we do, is captive, he is represented as imprisoned in an animal body as punishment or expiation for a former crime. So there is the same paradigmatic narrative."

44. Kant, "Religion within the Boundaries," 90n. The quote from Malebranche (1638–1715) is unattributed in Kant. Cf. Charles-Joseph Panckoucke, *Encyclopediana, ou dictionnaire encyclopédique des Ana.*, supplement to *L'Encyclopédie méthodique par ordre des matières* (Paris: Charles-Joseph Panckoucke Éditeur, 1791), 642 (my translation [DW]): "When it was put to Malebranche that animals were sensitive to pain, he replied jokingly: '*Apparently, they ate forbidden hay*; but a joke is not a reason.'" See also Nicolas Malebranche, *De la recherche de la vérité*, 1674–75, in *Œuvres I*, ed. Geneviève Rodis-Lewis and Germain Malbreil (Paris: Gallimard, 1979), book 4, chap. 11.

45. During the session, Derrida comments: "In other words, the trap for Malebranche involves imagining that animals have a soul, that horses have a soul, and thus having to explain, if animals have a soul, it has to be explained that, since they strive, work hard, draft horses, say, they suffer in working, it would then have to be because they ate the equivalent of the apple, so, forbidden hay. That's not possible, it's not possible. So for that reason Malebranche was led not to allow that animals have a soul. That isn't Descartes's reasoning, obviously, [*Laughter*] it's a different reasoning, isn't it. But the result is always the same: the animal doesn't have a soul, otherwise it no longer makes sense, or else one would have to consider the toil [*la peine*] of the animal—in the way one says 'workhorse [*bête de peine*],' 'beast of burden'—that the toil of the animal is in a sense work, and hence expiation, and therefore that the animal had committed a sin, possessing a soul that was free. And that's what is inadmissible. So Malebranche

B. *Work, then, and theater*. The second ellipsis point again punctuated the   *230*
theater thing. There is this drama of the theater: pardon for perjury appeals
to global theater (a pardon has to be manifested and not remain secret, it
has to be declared in a scene that isn't free from a virtual tribunal, and judgment) and at the same time it excludes visibility, manifestation, or even pub-
licity inasmuch as it should remain heterogeneous, if not to justice, at least to
the law, to the judicial and penal (we insisted on that a lot last time).[46] That
means that all the prominently political, public, and global examples that,
up to now, we have been privileging here—from South Africa to Clinton,
through all the examples of acts of public repentance that we refer to each
time—are theatrical, but also, perhaps, by the same token, foreign to every
rigorous experience of forgiveness, of pardoning a perjury. It remains that
even where theater and judicial theater should be excluded, theater is an
insistent presence, and what we are interested in when it comes down to
it is this impossible theater, this theater of the impossible, this theater that
contends with the impossible theatricalization that it is precisely a question
of staging, by inventing another scene, the detheatricalization of theater or
the theatricalization of what cannot be theatricalized. Last time, as the trial
of the three ministers was beginning, we began by observing, too quickly,
what was going on with the construction—itself mediatized—of a new   *231*
set with stages, chairs, and tables in an amphitheater and a new topology
designed for the so-called "contaminated blood trial"; and we began—we
should continue—to wonder what was happening there: for whom, about
what, to what end. Since we are talking about theater, contaminated blood,
and perjury, I invite you to read and reread—if you didn't see it while it
was playing at the Théâtre du Soleil—Hélène Cixous's extraordinary and
beyond sublime *Ville parjure*,[47] which will tell you more, and give further
food for thought, graciously, about all the topics that we are sketching out
here, laboriously, toiling away [*peinant*] at the task. We could and should
devote an interminable session to this so-called "contaminated blood trial"
in which all the motifs that make up our problematic are combined: on one

---

himself, a European and Christian philosopher, had to admit the universality of the
schema of guilty man, etc., having to work because of his guilt. There you have a first
ellipsis point."

46. Allusions here and following are to the discussion session of February 10, 1999.
See 156–60 above.

47. Hélène Cixous, *The Perjured City or the Awakening of the Furies*, trans. Berna-
dette Fort (London: Routledge, 2003) [*La Ville parjure ou Le Réveil des Érinyes* (Paris:
Théâtre du Soleil, 1994)]. The play was performed at the Théâtre du Soleil, Cartouch-
erie de Vincennes, in spring 1994.

side, the search for a free and personal responsibility, for a culpable act that can be attributed to a singular initiative, a wrong, with singular injuries and victims (at least implicit breaking of a promise or commitment, hence perjury and pardon requested or accorded beyond any judicial and penal retribution); on the other, the anonymous apparatus of the law, judicial calculus, the anonymity of the state, the conjunction between a state logic, more precisely a nation-state logic, and a market logic, a calculus and mercantile accounting on the way to, and in resistance to, globalization, relying on authorized knowledge or pseudo-knowledge provided by experts, scientists possessing, or dreaming of possessing, power (I am referring here to the French-American competition to develop screening tests, etc.: we can come back to that in discussion). Last time we tarried for a moment on a tendency to refrain from naming AIDS (in the context dubbed that of "contaminated blood," and concerning the African example that I alluded to (*develop*)).⁴⁸

232 Without going back over the different hypotheses that we formulated then, I'll make this much clear, from the point of view of the seminar. If it were said that AIDS is an illness that doesn't forgive, that formula could be understood not only in line with the current usage of "it's unforgiving," in the sense that AIDS is like a fatal illness, it kills, it is implacable, it seems at least like an implacable threat that isn't treatable, that in the end condemns to death, runs its course to the end like a death sentence ending in the execution of an unpardoned, "uncommuted" condemned person, etc.; but also, honing a little the way that "it's unforgiving" is heard, one can understand fault, culpability, the pitiless verdict of an illness that, before even condemning to death in the end, as would a natural organic process (and the destruction of biological immunity), condemns a failing and even an act of perjury. According to the common way of thinking, one contracts AIDS, one is contaminated by the AIDS virus only through the experience of illegitimate love and desire, outside legal and legitimate marriage. If AIDS is contracted inside a marriage between faithful spouses, or by means of a transfusion in a hospital setting, that is an accident, it shouldn't happen. The normality of AIDS, if one can say that, of the experience that contracts the virus, is outside any contract; it's sin, betrayal, anomaly, perjury. AIDS is interpreted as a fault or infamy, which bites back as an unforgiving sanction,

---

48. During the session, Derrida comments: "You remember, I only briefly mentioned it, it was about a poor African who was explaining that in his country, where AIDS is spreading like wildfire in proportions that are incommensurable with those of Europe, AIDS is never named as such, one says 'the illness,' etc. So, we asked ourselves why, and notably in the context of that trial, why AIDS isn't named explicitly."

precisely against the sinner, the perjurer, the guilty one. Someone stricken with AIDS is a guilty person for whom there is neither immunity nor pardon. The inhibition about naming is here the refusal to avow or blame an evil that, by reason of the affinity it retains with perjured love, or unavowable sexual transmission, has no relation to other viruses and other waivers of immunity (even if in the past certain illnesses, from the plague to syphilis, syphilis more than the plague, were manifestations of evil, the unavowable aspect of an evil or venereal perjury, that is to say an infidelity with respect to love, with respect to Venus). All the cultural progress and all the struggles concerning AIDS, for <almost> two decades now, have precisely tended to neutralize that shameful religious interpretation of the shame allegedly attached to this "contamination," and to render the thing not only treatable   *233* but nameable. We are still far short of the mark.

C. Third ellipsis point, following work, theater, and AIDS: Heidegger. Heidegger didn't experience AIDS. One day, perhaps, a distinction will be made between two eras, between pre-AIDs thinkers and those who were born or lived late enough to encounter AIDS in the world and to have inscribed its motif in their thinking or writing. (I won't make a list,[49] especially for those of my, or our, generations, but I'll recall, by way of an unusual sign of the generational disorder or difference in the process of aging and in the age of thinking, that Blanchot did, for example; he named and situated AIDS after the fact on the back cover of the re-edition of *Le très-haut* (1948, "renewed in 1975,"[50] but, it must be said—once one reads that back cover—re-renewed in 1988: 1948, 1975, 1988, forty years, one or two generations).) (Read back cover of *Le très-haut*, then epigraph.)[51]

---

49. During the session, Derrida adds: "Heidegger, clearly, is not included; he died too early. That said, I don't know what he would have done had he lived longer. I doubt—if one can make such an estimation—that had he lived longer he would have been in a position to inscribe this thing in his discourse."

50. During the session, Derrida adds: "This is an extraordinary edition, I recommend this edition because its margins and thresholds are very interesting. There is 'Éditions Gallimard, 1948, renewed in 1975': what does 'renewed' mean? And then there is 'Maurice Blanchot, novelist and critic. His life is entirely devoted to literature and to the silence proper to it.' [*Laughter*] What . . . well, all that has been republished in this paperback edition in 1988. So, there are three dates." See Maurice Blanchot, *Le très-haut* (Paris: Gallimard, 1988); *The Most High*, trans. Allan Stoekl (Lincoln: University of Nebraska Press/Bison Books, 2001).

51. During the session, Derrida adds: "I am going to read you the back cover because Blanchot may well have been 'devoted to literature and to the silence proper to it,' but he is nevertheless very attentive to what is going on in the world and notably to

Here reigns "Absolute Knowing" [in quotes, "Absolute Knowing": that's the theme of this seminar, no?]. Everyone is satisfied. There is nothing left to do.

The unsurpassable is reality.

234 In that sense, as a citizen of the universal homogeneous State, I am any man, other and the same, subject to the supreme law that I incarnate, invisible and faceless, beyond dispute because everything that disputes me confirms me.

But now comes someone—a woman no doubt—who exempts me from what I am and recognizes the Most High in this me that dissolves.

The Most High cannot be but its own negation. In a perfect society, when the plague breaks out, in such a way that those infected become the only rebels, when AIDS puts supreme law in danger, the Most High, beyond all divinity, is but a patient who dies without dying, unless he become the "Thing" itself, the terrifying nothing, the truth that always deceives and is deceived, the ultimate word that immortal death alone can finally have heard. [Hear Saint Augustine there, or what we were saying about Saint Augustine on the impossibility of dying, the possibility and impossibility of dying. And when he says: "the truth that always deceives and is deceived," the truth is what deceives, one is referred, as it were, to the book's epigraph, which says, in quotes, a text that I think is quite famous: *"I'm a trap for you. Even if I tell you everything—the more loyal I am, the more I'll deceive you: it's my frankness that'll catch you." / "Please understand: everything that you get from me is, for you, only a lie—because I'm the truth."*[52] Well, "I am the truth," it's Christ who says that, "I am the truth and the life." And that's perjury, the lie, it's proffered by, it proceeds from one who says, "I am the truth." One who says "I am the truth" cannot but lie.]

But you, reader, forget all that, for it is also Antigone, the pure virgin, uniting with her dead brother so that the incest taboo, henceforth suspended, subverts as much ideal law as natural law. Abjection is love, just as absolute freedom is absolute servitude.[53]

Concerning what "subverts as much ideal law as natural law," we now come back to Heidegger.

Last time[54] I alluded to the strange phenomenon—and food for thought—
235 namely, that in *Sein und Zeit*, in that powerful, original, and very conse-

---

AIDS. As you can imagine, in 1948, AIDS wasn't mentioned in the book, but the new back cover says this:"

52. Blanchot, *Most High*, n.p., Blanchot's italics [*Le très-haut*, 7]. This quote is the book's epigraph.

53. Blanchot, *Most High*, back cover.

54. Allusion to the discussion session of February 10, 1999.

quential discourse on the structure of originary culpability or responsibility, on the originary *Schuldigsein* of a *Dasein* that isn't determined within a morality or anthropology, as a subjectivity or human consciousness as such, at no point is any reference made to excuse or forgiveness, much less to expiation. I had begun to say something about that last time, namely, that the issue there was perhaps this: in his wish (in my opinion fruitless) to dechristianize a discourse on the Fall, the *Verfall*, etc., one that remains in its denial very Christian, Heidegger no doubt wanted to avoid what in the thematics of forgiveness was still in conversation with a biblical genealogy, like a too visible debt incurred toward the Abrahamic tradition (Judaic-Christian-Islamic). I won't go back over that point, which is also a very weighty one. By way of contrast, though, thinking of theater and the scene of the tribunal, of the visibility of judicial space and of judgment as theater,[55] or even of the tribunal of history, thinking also, once more, of the heterogeneity of forgiveness with respect to law and even ethics, to ethical, political, or legal norms and prescriptions, I'll recall what Heidegger does say about "moral conscience," *Gewissen*,[56] in the context of his description of its existential structure in *Sein und Zeit*. He attunes it closely to the register of the "call (*Ruf*),"[57] of the voice, the spoken word, hearing, listening, and he insists on excluding that reference to the voice, the call, or listening from all rhetoric, image, metaphor. Saying that "moral conscience" (*Gewissen*) is a call, that it is by no means a simple "image" (*Bild*), in the way that, Heidegger adds, "the Kantian representation of conscience [is somewhat like] a court of justice (*etwa wie die* Kantische *Gerichtshofvorstellung vom Gewissen*)" (p. 271).[58]   236

55. During the session, Derrida adds: "Where witnesses, that is to say, those accused, as well as the lawyers, and in any case witnesses must be present, they can't be represented by a cassette tape, a letter, or anybody else, the requirement is that a person testify. The question of testimony is very serious today, as you know, in this contaminated blood trial, where the victims or representatives of the victims are so seriously hindered in obtaining judgment."

56. During the session, Derrida clarifies: "That gets translated as 'moral conscience,' a complicated translation." See 15 above.

57. During the session, Derrida adds: "We often spoke of that here last year." See *Perjury and Pardon*, vol. 1, 12, 25 [*Parjure et pardon*, vol. 1, 39, 54].

58. Martin Heidegger, *Sein und Zeit*, in *Gesamtausgabe*, vol. 2 (Frankfurt: Vittorio Klostermann, 1977), §55, 360; *Sein und Zeit* (Tübingen: Max Niemeyer, 1963), 271 [*Être et temps*, trans. François Vezin (Paris: Gallimard, 1986), 327]. Cf. *Being and Time*, trans. Joan Stambaugh, rev. Dennis J. Schmidt (Albany: SUNY Press, 2010), 261: "The characterization of conscience as a call is by no means only an 'image,' like the Kantian representation of conscience as a court of justice." [Translator's note:] Derrida's inserted references here and below are to the Niemeyer edition of *Sein und Zeit*, cited above.

In other words, the theater of the tribunal is here presumed to be a representation of representation, an image that would consist first in a comparison or metaphor, and then in a metaphor that consisted in rendering visible, hence imaged, something that would be by no means that. Not that the call is audible, for that matter, in the sense of something accessible to the auditory sense, for we don't listen to it through the ear, insists Heidegger, and it could be uttered very quietly; and furthermore (but I am not going to go down that path, which we have explored previously, here in fact),[59] Heidegger here rejects any anthropological or theological approach to this existential structure of *Gewissen*. What is more important for us here is Heidegger's interpretation of this theatrical "representation of a tribunal"[60] in Kant. For Heidegger isn't content to say of this theater that it is "only an 'image (*Bild*),'"[61] a manner of speaking, a rhetoric that misjudges or tends to deny the invisible, nonsensible, and nonanthropological character of the call. One has also to account for the necessity that leads to that image or representation in Kant. The reason for this would be that Kant determines *Gewissen*, "moral conscience," as relation to a *law*, to a moral law or "*law of mores (Sitten*gesetz)."[62] According to Heidegger, what *Gewissen* listens to in the call does not in the first instance have the form of a law:[63] responsibility (the originary being-responsible, the originary *Schuldigsein*) is not in the first instance "before the law," it isn't "before," exposed, in front of something,[64] and in that sense there is no tribunal for it, nor is there theater, judicial situation, even as metaphor, that can account for this situation, and hence there is no theater if theater presupposes both the law and being-before, and finally judgment[65] (for if a judgment closes a judicial proceed-

237

---

59. See Derrida, "L'Oreille de Heidegger. Philopolémologie (*Geschlecht* IV)," in *Politiques de l'amitié* (Paris: Galilée, 1994), 341–419, especially 343–65, 367–90; cf. "Heidegger's Ear: Philopolemology (Geschlecht IV)," trans. John P. Leavey, Jr., in John Sallis, ed., *Reading Heidegger: Commemorations* (Bloomington: Indiana University Press, 1993), 163–218, especially 164–65, 167–79. See also unpublished seminar, "Politiques de l'amitié," EHESS, 1988–89, Sessions 4–8.

60. "'*Gerichtshofvorstellung*,'" *Sein und Zeit*, §59, 388, Derrida's translation; cf. *Being and Time*: "'idea of a court of justice'" (280) [*Être et temps*, 351].

61. *Sein und Zeit*, §55, 360; *Being and Time*, 261 [*Être et temps*, 327].

62. *Sein und Zeit*, §59, 388; *Being and Time*, 281: "moral *law*" [cf. *Être et temps*, 351].

63. During the session, Derrida adds: "That is why I related it to what Blanchot says here concerning what subverts as much ideal law as natural law."

64. During the session, Derrida adds: "Or someone."

65. During the session, Derrida comments: "Heidegger practically doesn't mention judgment in this analysis. And moreover, the force of this discourse is that it tries

ing and procedure, brings the sessions of the tribunal to a close, there is almost always a judgment also, a judgment of history coming at the end of a
theatrical performance, a Last Judgment). Further along in *Sein und Zeit*,
Heidegger comes back, then, with quotation marks, to Kant's use of the
expression *"Gerichtsvorstellung"* ("representation of a tribunal"; insist on *Vor-
stellung*: theatrical objectivity of being-before, *Vorhandenheit*). Heidegger
writes: "The fact that Kant takes the 'idea of a court of justice' as the key
idea for the basis of his interpretation of conscience is not a matter of chance,
but was suggested by the idea of *Sitten*gesetzes (§59, p. 293) (*Gesetz* emphasized, in italics), although his concept of morality was far removed from
utilitarianism and eudaemonism."[66] Immediately after that Heidegger will
similarly reject the theory of values or norms. In other words—and it is the
special force of Heidegger's gesture that interests me here—it is a matter of
marking in what way responsibility, listening to the call of what is here
called "moral conscience (*Gewissen*)," is the relation neither to a law nor to
norms or values. And that is what is implied by his contesting judicial theater or this profound rhetoric of the tribunal of conscience. Responsibility in
its essence is prior to, or irreducible to, juridical or political law (which is
what we are also saying here about forgiveness); and if in what the call of
moral conscience or responsibility dictates to me or calls me to decide, what
I am called to respond, or what I am called to answer for, if that is dictated
to me by a law or by norms, there is no longer any responsibility. We have
there the very strong and difficult idea that responsibility and decision, the
possibility of decision, presuppose (I am translating that into my language)
a rupture or an independence with respect to all law or all normativity. If I
do what I do because I know the law or the norm, because I know what I
have to do or what it is better to do, then at least to that extent, to the extent
that I am applying, or obeying, or bending to the law or normative value,
well then, I am carrying out a program, I am paying a debt, but I am not
acting freely in the full sense of responsible decision. I am irresponsible because I am obeying the law, prescription, or norm. In that there is an at least

238

to have us think a call, a 'moral conscience,' as one says, and thus a responsibility that
doesn't refer to any law and so doesn't obey anything. Because once one appears before a
law or submits to a natural or ideal law, or whatever its nature be, well, one knows what
has to be done: one has to obey, one has norms and laws. And at that point, responsibility
is dissolved. Here there is no law, in any case, no law before which one is. The law has
to be invented at every moment. So *Schuldigsein* is not exposed as if before some thing,
and there is no tribunal and hence no judgment for it."

66. *Sein und Zeit*, §59, 388; *Being and Time*, 280–81 [*Être et temps*, 351].

implicit critique (which I for my part have often tried to develop elsewhere, in a different way, in numerous places) of moral action as defined by Kant; not only that conforming to duty (*pflichtmässig*), and with which Kant is of course not satisfied, but even that which must be done, according to Kant— who recommends this—"from duty," really from duty (*"eigentlich aus Pflicht"*) or from pure duty (*"aus reiner Pflicht"*).[67] What I am suggesting here is that even what is done out of pure duty (that is to say finally in order to discharge a pure debt) cannot therefore derive from an absolute and absolutely responsible decision, a decision such as must be decided on the basis of the undecidable by inventing its decision and the event of its decision in the night of knowing, in nonknowing. Not that it is necessary not to know, on the contrary, but that there is and there must be, from knowledge to decision, and to responsibility, an infinite leap. If deciding is to have a sense, one must decide without knowing in advance what the decision should do, and to what law or norm one is subjecting oneself. One can say that, develop that logic, starting from this remark of Heidegger's directed against Kant, if you wish, but, more radically still—for it is already highly audacious in being directed against Kant—one can turn it around yet again, against Heidegger as well, where he continues to speak of *Schuld* or *Schuldigsein*, that is to say, of debt or culpability.[68] Even if that debt and culpability are incurred by nothing and with respect to nobody, and before or without reference to any original sin in the biblical sense. If I act by virtue of a debt or duty, from knowledge of a duty, by being conscious of a duty, there is no longer any responsible decision, simply an economy. And the law, the becoming-juridical of ethics, the theater of the tribunal, is the most visible form of that economy. Take particular note that, in the same passage from *Sein und Zeit* (p. 293, "§59. *Die existenziale Interpretation des Gewissens und die vulgäre Gewissensauslegung*," comment),[69] Heidegger makes a harsh and ironic remark about the inauthentic interpretation of being-there, as being-there before things, and about being as *Vorhandenheit* (being before one, in front

67. Immanuel Kant, *Grundlegung zur Metaphysik der Sitten*, in *Werke*, vol. 4 (Berlin: de Gruyter, 1978), 406; Kant, *Grounding for the Metaphysics of Morals*, trans. James W. Ellington (Indianapolis: Hackett Publishing Co., 1981), 19 [*Fondements de la métaphysique des moeurs*, trans. Victor Delbos and Alexis Philonenko (Paris: Librairie philosophique J. Vrin, 1980), 75].

68. Heidegger, *Sein und Zeit*, §58, 281ff.; *Being and Time*, 270ff. [*Être et temps*, 337ff.].

69. During the session, Derrida translates the chapter heading without further commentary: "The existential interpretation of *Gewissen* (of moral conscience), and the vulgar explanation of *Gewissen*."

of one's hand),[70] an interpretation that makes of the experience of moral conscience an encounter between a judge and a creditor — "moral conscience being like a judge and a creditor (*das Gewissen als Richter und Mahner*) with whom Dasein negotiates by haggling"[71] — the text literally says with whom *Dasein* deals, transacts (*verhandelt*, which refers both to the market and to manipulation, to maneuvering, manner, hand-play [*le jeu de main*], but also resonates with the *Vorhandenheit* of the being interpreted as being in front of the hand and near to hand [*sous la main*]: *verhandelt*): "*mit dem das Dasein rechnend verhandelt* [a judge or creditor with whom Dasein deals, transacts, bargains by counting, calculating, *rechnend*]."[72] So there is an indication there, both irrefutable and difficult to sustain, however, of a sense of responsibility or "moral conscience" that would exceed all economic or judicial calculus, all measure, all accounting. That goes a long way, all the way to thinking responsibility as extending beyond all law and all moral calculus (vengeance and retribution: the order of forgiveness, which we are talking about and which Heidegger doesn't speak of, would belong, like the impossible itself, to that incalculability). What extends beyond the judge and the creditor (Nietzsche . . .)[73] extends, then, beyond the law court and the theater of any tribunal, and finally even beyond judgment, and even beyond the Last Judgment [*develop*].[74]

240

So there you have the *three ellipsis points* that I wanted not to fill in or saturate but prolong, keep suspended for a little longer. Up to the point where, it

70. [Translator's note:] Stambaugh/Schmidt translates *Vorhandenheit* as "objective presence"; Macquarrie and Robinson (*Being and Time*, trans. John Macquarrie and Edward Robinson [New York: Harper and Row, 1962]) as "presence-at-hand."

71. *Sein und Zeit*, 388. [Translator's note:] Derrida modifies the French translation, which has *créancier* [creditor] for *Mahner* [*Être et temps*, 350]. Cf. *Being and Time*, 280: "Experience encounters conscience as a judge and an admonisher [*Mahner*] with whom Da-sein calculatingly deals."

72. *Sein und Zeit*, 388; *Being and Time*, 280 [*Être et temps*, 350].

73. During the session, Derrida adds: "Naturally there are in *The Genealogy of Morality*—all this is very Nietzschean—passages by Nietzsche that say the same thing in very strong terms, but as I've spoken about that elsewhere, in *The Gift of Death*, I won't go back over it here, but clearly, that's what it's about: negotiation, economic transaction." See Derrida, *The Gift of Death and Literature in Secret*, trans. David Wills (Chicago: University of Chicago Press, 2008), 112–16 [*Donner la mort* (Paris: Galilée, 1999), 154–57].

74. During the session, Derrida adds: "The logic of the Last Judgment that we were talking about in relation to Benjamin especially." See 23, 66, 144, 161 above. He then adds the long commentary that we have included as an appendix at the end of this session. See 193–95 below.

being a question of law and forgiveness, of law as right, of justice as right and of forgiveness, we will again find the trace of the Mary Magdalene whom we abandoned along the way some weeks ago (following our rereading of the Gospel, Augustine, and after having made a start on the question of "Monicagate" by reading the American newspapers that put on trial conjointly — in the same trial, therefore — deconstruction and Clinton).

Hegel's voice off, then: as for Mary Magdalene, I said everything there was to say in my early works. Hers is the feminine name for the moment of love when Jesus taught what, in merciful forgiveness, exceeds the law and its rabbis and goes beyond the order of justice of the Pharisees, the moment when Christianity, Christian forgiveness, takes a step beyond Judaism. There was an event where that was put in play,[75] represented, incarnated, taking shape, a beautiful, representable shape, the scene involving Mary Magdalene in the Gospels. Speaking of forgiveness, the vocation of forgiveness, the religion of mercy, would once again be both the thing most widely shared among Judaism, Christianity, and Islam, and the most widely shared along a dividing line, or even a war, a front, an enmity, an irreconcilable, inexpiable dissension: that of the unforgivable itself, as though the unforgivable were to consist here in not thinking, interpreting, determining forgiveness as should be done. As though one were to say to another:[76] "I don't forgive you for not knowing what forgiveness must or must not be." How to agree on forgiveness (develop the aporia; does forgiveness suppose agreement and consensus concerning the sense of forgiveness?)?

What does Hegel's voice off say to us? It explains what forgiveness for sinning is when it rises above right (*Recht*) and justice (*Gerechtigkeit*) (p. 331 of the German Suhrkamp edition);[77] when Jesus demands that in general one renounce the law in favor of love, that one break with what the laws say (*Gesetze*: anti-Kant, Heidegger?),[78] that is to say (conventional interpretation of this Judaic precept: "an eye for an eye, a tooth for a tooth"), reciprocity (*Wiedervergeltung*) and equality between crime and its sanction, also the principle of every state constitution (*Staatsverfassung*). Before bringing onto

75. During the session, Derrida adds: "I'm mimicking Hegel here, okay, I'm paraphrasing as it were, or reinventing."

76. During the session, Derrida clarifies: "Among the three representatives of the three monotheisms."

77. Hegel, *Der Geist*, 331 [*Early Theological Writings*, 218; *Esprit du christianisme*, 38].

78. During the session, Derrida comments: "*Gesetze*, because that's what it is, already; one encounters the question of laws, and so it's already Christian to say that one has to break with *Gesetze*, with laws. Not only Blanchot and Heidegger, it's Christian already."

the stage what he calls the beautiful example (*ein schönes Beispiel*) of Mary Magdalene,[79] the "beautiful example of a repentant sinner (*einer wiederkehrenden Sünderin*)" that occurs in the life of Jesus: "*die berühmte schöne Sünderin, Maria Magdalena*"[80] (and Hegel deliberately insists on beauty, because this whole, still very romantic discourse is a discourse on love and beauty, on life, on the reconciling force of nature and destiny through and in beauty): further along in the same context, quoting Christ, Hegel suggests in short 242 that the Jews and those who are surprised by Jesus's pardoning of Mary Magdalene are insensitive to beauty. That Jews are ugly and insensitive to beauty is a recurrent, organizing theme in the Hegel in question here. He notes that Simon and those who would have preferred to sell the perfume for three hundred pence and given the money to the poor, those who made that fine calculation "failed to grasp the beautiful situation (*die schöne Situation*)," they profaned "the holy outpouring of a loving heart."[81] "Why do you trouble her," says Jesus, "she has wrought a *beautiful* work upon me (*sie hat ein* schönes *Werk an mir getan*)"; and Hegel then notes: "and this is the only thing in the whole story of Jesus which goes by the name of 'beautiful' [*den Namen eines schönen*: where the name of something beautiful is pronounced (develop: beauty and forgiveness; beauty and femininity, femininity and forgiveness),[82] that is why Hegel chooses this episode, which he finds revealing]."[83] And Hegel adds this very curious remark, as if he were commenting both on the words, Christ's calling it "beautiful," and on Mary Magdalene's expression or gesture: "only a woman full of love (*nur ein Weib voll Liebe*) expresses herself, shows herself on the outside (*äüßert sich*) in such an unsophisticated, candid, naive (*unbefangen*) way, without seeking anything useful, without utilizing, utilitarist or instrumental purpose (*ohne*

79. In Hegel's text, the passage concerning Jewish insensitivity to beauty comes after the "beautiful example" of Mary Magdalene rather than before, as Derrida appears to suggest.

80. Hegel, *Der Geist*, 357 [*Early Theological Writings*, 242; *Esprit du christianisme*, 64]. [Translator's note:] The English has "returning sinner" for *wiederkehrenden Sünderin*.

81. Hegel, *Early Theological Writings*, 243 [*Der Geist*, 358; *Esprit du christianisme*, 65].

82. During the session, Derrida comments: "And this interpretation of Christ's forgiveness has an essential link to beauty. Forgiveness is beautiful, this forgiveness is beautiful or it is done in the name of beauty. And beauty is what reconciles life, it is the unity of life. And naturally: femininity, beauty, femininity, forgiveness. Femininity, forgiveness, beauty."

83. Hegel, *Early Theological Writings*, 243 [*Der Geist*, 359; *Esprit du christianisme*, 65]. During the session, Derrida adds: "Theatrically revealing."

Zweck irgendeiner Nutzanwendung: grace, gracious), neither in deed nor in doctrine (neither in "theory" nor in "practice," says the clumsy [French] translation, for in *Tat oder Lehre*: Mary Magdalene and Christ)."[84]

243

Beauty, love of beauty, love as beauty, there you have what is going to make possible both "reconciliation" (*Versöhnung*, the keyword for this text, along with *Vereinigung*, "reunification") and the ethic of Christian forgiveness when it rises above the law (understood as Jewish). This metaphysics of love as reconciliation, reunification, healing, cicatrization, is also a philosophy of life. Of life as love. For nothing can annihilate life, one can merely introduce into it opposition and scission, a negativity of division, but which is always found to be immanent to life. It is life that opposes itself by splitting and producing its other or its vis-à-vis. The annihilation of life (in murder), the "*Vernichtung des Lebens*,"[85] is not a nonbeing, a *Nicht-Sein*[86] of life, but splitting, separation (*Trennung*) of life; and the annihilation of life, rather than producing nonlife, non-being, produces hostility to life; it produces the enemy (*Feinde*). Death doesn't exist; what exists when there is murder is only life opposing itself. Life is immortal (*unsterblich*)[87] and, once killed (*getötet*), it appears, it reappears,[88] it makes a reappearance [*refait apparition*] as an apparition, as its own "terrifying ghost (*als sein schreckendes Gespenst*)" that deploys all its ramifications, all its branches, "let[ing] loose its Eumenides (*seine Eumeniden losläßt*)."[89] That could signify, among other

---

84. Hegel, *Der Geist*, 359 [*Esprit du christianisme*, 65], Derrida's modified translation. Cf. *Early Theological Writings*, 243: "So unsophisticated an action, an action so void of any intent to make useful application of deed or doctrine is the self-expression only of a woman whose heart is full of love." During the session, Derrida adds: "Neither as act nor as teaching, as theory. And that goes as much for Mary Magdalene as for Christ."

85. Hegel, *Der Geist*, 342 [*Esprit du christianisme*, 49]; cf. *Early Theological Writings*, 229: "nullification of life."

86. During the session, Derrida adds: "This term, isolated from its context, naturally has a Levinassian side to it. For Levinas, death is not a nonbeing. Well, I'm not going to confuse things because the context is completely different, but you have there the idea that death has nothing to do with nothingness."

87. In the typescript there is an annotation at the top of the page referring to this word: "Nietzsche: 'one can die from being immortal.'" Letter to Malwida von Meysenbug, end July 1888: "Man kann daran zugrunde gehn, '*unsterblich*' zu sein!" See Nietzsche, *Digitale Kritische Gesamtausgabe*, ed. Giorgio Colli and Mazzino Montinari, http://www.nietzschesource.org/#eKGWB/BVN-1888 [Georges Walz, ed., *La vie de Frédéric Nietzsche d'après sa correspondance* (Paris: Les Éditions Rider, 1932), 498].

88. During the session, Derrida adds: "And there we have theater again."

89. Hegel, *Der Geist*, 342 [*Esprit du christianisme*, 49], Derrida freely translating the German. Cf. *Early Theological Writings*, 229: "Destruction of life is not the nullification

things, that the logic of spectrality doesn't signify a pledge made to death
but just as much a salute to what in life remains indestructible. The ghost
is life still, not already something dead. Repressed life returning, something
of a return of the living repressed, a sign of life and not a death notice. "The
illusion of trespass [du criminel], its belief that it destroys the other's life   244
and thinks itself enlarged thereby, is dissipated by the fact that the disem-
bodied spirit of the injured life (der abgeschiedene Geist des verletzen Lebens,
wounded life) comes on the scene against the trespass, just as Banquo[90] who
came as a friend to Macbeth was not blotted out when he was murdered
but immediately thereafter took his seat, not as a guest at the feast, but as
an evil spirit," an evil genius (als böser Geist).[91] And you see, once more (we
have had many examples of this in Hegelian texts and contexts that are
absolutely different, for example, in the Lectures on the Philosophy of World
History), that the theatrical reference is absolutely unavoidable and dominant, the reference to <a> theater of judgment precisely, of the tribunal of
history. This whole thinking of immortal life that cannot but heal its wounds
(und das Leben kann seine Wunden wieder heilen)[92]—life "severed, hostile
(getrennte feindliche)" that "can return to itself again" and "aufheben" the criminal's misdeed, law and punishment (und das Machwerk eines Verbrechens, das
Gesetz und die Strafe)[93]—this life that is finally divisible but immortal, un-
breachable [inentamable], is what performs reconciliation and reunification,
these latter always having the form of an Aufhebung, a sublation. "Transgression, infraction (Übertretung), crime and punishment are not in a cause and
effect relation: punishment is not the effect of a crime where the determinant link between one and the other would be a law, something objective
(ein Objektives, ein Gesetz); in that case, if it were to be thus, cause and effect, as simply separate, as a cause and an effect, could never be reunified

---

of life but its diremption, and the destruction consists in its transformation into an enemy. It is immortal, and, if slain, it appears as its terrifying ghost which vindicates every
branch of life and lets loose its Eumenides." During the session, Derrida adds here:
"There we have theater again."

90. During the session, Derrida adds: "Still more theater."

91. Hegel, Der Geist, 342–43 [Early Theological Writings, 229; Esprit du christianisme, 49–50]. During the session, Derrida adds: "The victim always returns, they aren't
dead."

92. Hegel, Der Geist, 344 [Early Theological Writings, 230; Esprit du christianisme,
50].

93. Hegel, Der Geist, 344 [Early Theological Writings, 229; Esprit du christianisme,
50–51]. [Translator's note:] In Hegel's text a footnote follows, omitted from the English
edition.

(*vereinigt werden*)."[94] Now, on the contrary, they can and must be reunified by what, throughout this context, Hegel calls "fate (*Schicksal*)," according to which the law, "turning against the criminal" and against the fault, can, like fate, "*aufgehoben werden*,"[95] because the criminal has himself imposed this law. The separation — "the scission (*Trennung*)" that the criminal has himself produced, that he has introduced into life by creating hostility, by producing the enemy, enmity — this scission that he has himself made can be *vereinigt, vereinigt werden*: cicatrized, sutured, bandaged, healed ("*diese Vereinigung ist in der Liebe*").[96] The basis of the question of forgiveness — the word *Vergebung* will very soon appear in this religious and properly spiritual concept, rather than *Verzeihung* (recall the beginning of the seminar last year on this topic)[97] — will always be this: what do reconciliation and *Aufhebung* mean, *Aufhebung* as reconciliation, this *Aufhebung*, this *sublation* that is the major concept of all of Hegel's ontology, all his speculative idealism, his whole dialectic? We have been tracking this question since beginning to hear the Hegel of *The Phenomenology of Spirit*, at the beginning of this play, since beginning to hear Hegel's ghost explaining to us in short what a ghost is; and the fact that the phantom is life, resurrection and not death.

This love, as the reconciliation of life, in life and with fate, this concept of fate (*Schicksal*) is what bears the whole difficulty and carries the whole sense of this text.

What is fate? It isn't a foreign element, it has nothing foreign about it ("*nichts Fremdes*"),[98] says Hegel, unlike punishment, which comes from outside. Fate is not an actual and determined reality, as evil action would be for moral conscience. Fate is the consciousness of self (*das Bewußtsein seiner selbst*), but of self as enemy (internal enemy). Now the whole, the totality of the whole, can precisely produce the reconciliation of fate or with fate, the

---

94. Hegel, *Der Geist*, 344, note * [*Esprit du christianisme*, 51n[a]]. [Translator's note:] I am translating Derrida's loose translation of Hegel's footnote (omitted from the English edition).

95. During the session, Derrida translates: "Be sublated [*être relevé*]."

96. Hegel, *Der Geist*, 344, note * [*Esprit du christianisme*, 51n[a]]: "This union is [found] in love" [my translation, DW].

97. See Derrida, *Perjury and Pardon*, vol. 1, 4–5 [*Parjure et pardon*, vol. 1, 30–31].

98. Hegel, *Der Geist*, 346, note * [*Esprit du christianisme*, 53n[a]]. [Translator's note:] This note, omitted from the English translation, follows this sentence in *Early Theological Writings*, 232: "The trespass which issues from life reveals the whole, but as divided, and the hostile parts can coalesce again into the whole." The remainder of this paragraph, and that following, is Derrida's loose translation of the footnote.

whole (*das Ganze*) can restore friendship and consist, moreover, in friendship (*Freundschaft*) among the parts. This totalization of parts in one is life itself. The whole can restore friendship because it is the whole, that is to say, friendship; and so, as whole, it can come back, return, turn back to pure life, thanks to love. In this movement of totalization, friendship, love, reconciliation of life with itself, consciousness again becomes faith in oneself (*Glauben an sich selbst*); in other words, faith is this movement of gathering in love, "the intuition of self becomes other and fate is reconciled (*das Schiksal ist versöhnt*)."[99]

246

And that occurs par excellence—and indispensably, essentially—through forgiveness (here, *Vergebung*). But forgiveness of sins, Hegel insists, does not, at least not immediately, sublate punishments (*Vergebung der Sünden ist daher unmittelbar nicht Aufhebung der Strafen*). For punishment remains, it is something positive, real, actual, something that cannot be destroyed, no more than can bad conscience be *sublated* (*nicht Aufhebung des bösen Gewissens*).[100] But fate can find reconciliation through love; it is born either from our own act or from the act of another.

We have in that reconciliation through the forgiveness of love, which sublates neither punishment nor bad conscience, the event of Jesus's teaching. He teaches what is "the most incomprehensible opposite of the Jewish spirit (*das unbegreiflichste Gegenteil des jüdischen Geistes*)."[101] In all of these subtle pages—which I'll leave you to read—concerning the beautiful soul and the forgiveness of sins (pp. 56ff.; German, pp. 350ff.),[102] I'll underscore only, as I announced a fortnight ago[103]—the sublime and spiritual Christian economy that Hegel puts in opposition to the Jewish economy. For this philosophy of life and love as totalization and reconciliation through sublation is an economy. A potent one, the most potent, since it integrates noneconomy. Hegel explains quite clearly that "to save himself, the [Christian] man kills himself."[104] Granted, he puts himself to death, he renounces life, but that is in order to save himself (*Um sich zu retten, tötet der Mensch sich*).[105] What

99. Hegel, *Der Geist*, 346, note * [*Esprit du christianisme*, 53n[a]].

100. Hegel, *Der Geist*, 346, note *.

101. Hegel, *Early Theological Writings*, 241 [*Der Geist*, 357; *Esprit du christianisme*, 63].

102. Hegel, *Early Theological Writings*, 236ff.

103. Derrida is referring rather to the January 27, 1999, session, held three weeks previous. See 124 above.

104. Hegel, *Early Theological Writings*, 235 [*Der Geist*, 350; *Esprit du christianisme*, 56].

105. Hegel, *Der Geist*, 350.

247   is the meaning of his putting himself to death and losing himself in order to save himself? Well, he renounces appropriating for himself anything whatsoever, or saying, "This is my property, this is mine," and as a result he no longer has any enemy, he can no longer be either attacked, robbed, despoiled, or dispossessed (*und so vernichtet er sich, indem er sich erhalten wollte*).[106] He lifts himself "above fate entirely. Life has become untrue to him"; but he hasn't been untrue (*untreu*) to life, he has kept faith in life, even at the cost of losing it. Life can leave him, but he doesn't leave it, but keeps faith in it. And that is indeed Jesus's gesture when he recommends that his friends forsake their father, their mother, give their cloak to one who has taken their coat, cut off a limb that offends them. That liberation, that "highest freedom," is the "negative attribute" of the beautiful soul, Hegel notes, "i.e., the potentiality of renouncing everything in order to maintain one's self (*die Möglichkeit, auf alles Verzicht zu tun, um sich zu erhalten. Wer aber sein Leben retten will, der wird es verlieren*)." So, "supreme guilt is compatible with supreme innocence; the supreme wretchedest fate with elevation above all fate (*So ist mit der höchsten Schuldlosigkeit die höchste Schuld, mit der Erhabenheit über alles Schicksal das höchste, unglücklichste Schicksal vereinbar*)."[107] It is always this uniting of opposites that constitutes and saves economy, that economizes economy, here in its negative guise, which allows the soul, the *beautiful* soul, to rise above relations of right (*Rechtsverhältnisse*), beginning by renouncing its rights and by doing so in order to have nothing to forgive the offender, since the latter has not injured my rights, which I renounced in advance.[108] I give in advance, I renounce so as to not even have to forgive, I forgive in advance. "*Y a pas d'mal* [no harm done]," as we would say last year.[109] And that soul, that beautiful soul certainly isn't so proud as to demand of another that they ask for forgiveness and confess,

---

106. Hegel, *Der Geist*, 350 [*Esprit du christianisme*, 56]; cf. *Early Theological Writings*, 236: "and so he annihilates himself in wishing to maintain himself." During the session, Derrida translates: "And thus he destroys inasmuch as he wants to save himself." [Translator's note:] What follows continues to loosely translate or paraphrase this passage from Hegel.

107. Hegel, *Early Theological Writings*, 236 [*Der Geist*, 350–51; *Esprit du christianisme*, 56].

108. [Translator's note:] Cf. Hegel, *Der Geist*, 351; *Early Theological Writings*, 236: "A heart thus lifted above the ties of rights, disentangled from everything objective, has nothing to forgive the offender, for it sacrificed its right as soon as the object over which it had a right was assailed, and thus the offender has done no injury to any right at all."

109. See Derrida, *Perjury and Pardon*, vol. 1, 162–66 [*Parjure et pardon*, vol. 1, 216–22].

that they proceed to make a confession (*Bekenntnis*) in the sphere of the law.[110] There is indeed, then, in this analysis by Hegel, that powerful recognition of the gesture by means of which, following the teaching of Christ,   *248* forgiveness must be granted even before any requirement of the other's confession, and in accordance with the economy that has me renounce my right and my property, renounce my very immunity. It is once again an economy of life in love that leads me to that unconditional forgiveness that has renounced economy. Economy here consists — this can be interpreted as a sublime ruse or an infinite sacrifice — in renouncing economy and the right to property, renouncing one's own right, one's own *tout court*, one's self. Aneconomy isn't the opposite of economy; or at least the opposites are reconciled here, and this reconciliation works through forgiveness.

And that is confirmed in the following movement, which goes beyond this negative determination of the freedom of the beautiful soul, namely, when Jesus says that that first movement (forgiving the other by renouncing one's own right and one's own property, renouncing one's own and oneself in *abnegation*), that first negative movement of abnegation of self is the condition for you yourself being forgiven by God. Double economic calculus:

1. I renounce myself, my life, my own, my rights so as not to be injured by the other and so as not to have to suffer or punish, in order to be able to forgive, as it were, a priori;

2. I do that in order to be in turn forgiven by God. This second forgiveness, Hegel clearly says, results from the first. "Forgiveness [here *Verzeihung*] of sins, readiness to reconcile oneself with another, Jesus [he says] makes an express condition of the forgiveness [*Verzeihung*] of one's own sins."[111] That is why Jesus often repeats: "*So ihr den Menschen ihre Fehler vergebt, so wird sie euch euer himmlischer Vater auch vergeben* [For if ye forgive men their trespasses, your heavenly Father will also forgive you]."[112]

---

110. [Translator's note:] Cf. Hegel, *Der Geist*, 351; *Early Theological Writings*, 236: "On its side [that of the heart open to reconciliation] there stands in the way no hostile feeling, no consciousness, no demand on another for the restoration of an infringed right, no pride which would claim from another in a lower sphere, i.e., in the realm of rights, an acknowledgment of subordination."

111. Hegel, *Early Theological Writings*, 236 [*Der Geist*, 351; *Esprit du christianisme*, 57].

112. *Der Geist*, 351, note * [*Esprit du christianisme*, 57n[a]]. [Translator's note:] This note, which follows the previous quote, is omitted from the English edition. The biblical citation is Matthew 6:14.

(So . . . so, analogy, proportion, configuration, etc.: comment).[113] The world
below is caught — as global economy that renounces life in order to save
it — in a terrestrial-celestial economy. And ultimate forgiveness is in the
hands of the Father, as we are taught by the Son (recall all the examples
here, from Abraham, to Kierkegaard and Kafka).[114] Mary Magdalene is a
repentant prostitute who kneels before the Son and weeps with love for the
Son, she throws herself at his feet, weeps, bathes his feet with her tears, wipes
them with her own hair, kisses them, anoints them with balm made from
very expensive nard. All of that is very liquid, moist, humble, and humid,
it all flows from all sides and inundates memory and things with its moist
traces, and the memory of them is fresh, they are barely dry, the traces still
remain. It is a Jewess who rises above the Jews, above the legally minded
gaze of the honest folk, of the Pharisees, etc. And she is beautiful in so doing,
as Jesus says. She bears witness to that beauty of reconciliation, and not only
does Jesus forgive her but he also teaches forgiveness based on her example: there will be no trial, he says, neither prosecutor nor guilty verdict (I'll
leave you to read those pages).

The question *today* is no longer about knowing whether Clinton — who
asked for forgiveness (but why, and for what, we'll see) — knowing whether
he will be removed from office or pardoned, but whether he will forgive,
for his part, or whether he will take revenge. A mood of panic seems to
have come over the Republican camp in recent days. Not only because it is
possible that Judge Starr will in turn be sued by the White House but also
because, in the words of the leader of the Republican Party, Clinton supposedly intends to carry out, and I quote, a "politics of vendetta" (vengeance,
revenge, resentment, punishment, reprisals, backlash). The (conservative)
Wall Street Journal has entitled an article, "The Payback Presidency," and
invited Republicans to reflect on how they might protect themselves against
the vendetta. One of Clinton's advisers, James Carville, is even supposed to
have declared, "I'm not on the forgive-and-forget battalion."[115] Not very
Christian, all that.

113. During the session, Derrida comments: "That's the question: it's the question of
economy, that of analogy here, of proportion, of the configuration between the forgiveness
that I grant men a priori, and the forgiveness that I can then expect from God."

114. See Derrida, *Perjury and Pardon*, vol. 1, 96–105 [*Parjure et pardon*, vol. 1, 139–
49]; and *The Gift of Death*, 133–58 [*Donner la mort*, 161–209].

115. Quoted in "The Payback Presidency," *Wall Street Journal*, February 12, 1999,
A16.

Now that Clinton is finally coming on stage, we need to announce his   250
appearance by recalling several imposing pieces of evidence that therefore
risk being forgotten. First, like all the characters in our play—Hegel, Tutu,
Mandela—he is a Christian, and a reformed Christian, a Protestant. How
should we interpret that fact, and align it with the globalization of confession and repentance that I said was tied to a *globalatinization* (which would
instead be thought on the basis of Rome and things Catholic)? I have some
hypotheses on the subject, but the problem is too complicated, and we'll
come back to it in conclusion. Keep in mind simply, while thinking of the
recent meeting between Clinton and the pope, and what we said about
that[116] (the pope taking a position against the death penalty while actually
in the United States, where certain executions were simply postponed during his stay before being resumed with renewed vigor following that): the
United States isn't just a democracy that, though it presents itself as a model,
remains the only democracy in the world and in the West that not only
retains the death penalty in almost all of its states, but puts it into effect or
is restoring the practice of it on a massive scale. Yet Clinton, who asked for
forgiveness and has just been acquitted, was a governor who, having at his
disposal the right to mercy ("pardon")[117] that we spoke of, always refused,
for his part, to exercise that right.[118] Moreover, being firmly in favor of the
death penalty, he has even reinforced the mechanisms that allow capital
punishment to be applied more often and more rapidly. He has reinforced
the juridico-lethal apparatus, and is proud of it. It would also be necessary,
in order to establish the right scale, to recall all the actions in global politics that are far more serious than Monicagate (beginning with the conditions that led to, and especially those that followed, the Gulf War),[119] and
that would have required explanation, or even confession and repentance,
all the more so given that Monicagate—for reasons of public and international space, of mediatization and the role played by the United States in
the world—has never been a purely domestic affair, presuming that there
ever were such a thing.

Before even beginning, let us also recall that once Clinton was found not   251
guilty, while not asking for forgiveness for what was at the bottom of it all,
he nevertheless did publicly say "sorry [*désolé*]" (I suppose "sorry" was the

116. See 154 above.

117. [Translator's note:] Word in English in typescript.

118. Derrida expands upon this statement in "Le Siècle et le pardon," in *Foi et savoir*, 121.

119. See 92n81 above.

word). He said sorry—he weighed his words—for what he said and did to trigger these events and for imposing such an ordeal on the American people. To say "sorry" for that chain of events is not to ask for forgiveness, but neither is it something else; and as for the words "for what I said and did,"[120] they will be at the center of discussions we'll devote to them in the following sessions. We shall analyze the logic and rhetoric of a certain number of Clinton's speeches and certain newspaper articles in order to try to "deconstruct"—I am this time using this word intentionally—in order to try to deconstruct in them an insistent mediatic discourse on the effects and misdeeds of deconstruction, named as such, for once outside the university and academic world, in Monicagate.

120. "Text of Clinton Remarks Acknowledging Mistakes," *Los Angeles Times*, December 12, 1998, https://www.latimes.com/archives/la-xpm-1998-dec-12-mn-53315-story .html. See also the account of Clinton's February 12, 1999, acquittal reported in Patrice de Beer, "*Bill Clinton remporte au final un succès d'une ampleur inespérée*," *Le Monde*, February 14–15, 1999, 2, https://www.lemonde.fr/archives/article/1999/02/14/bill-clinton -remporte-au-final-un-succes-d-une-ampleur-inesperee_3536607_1819218.html; cf. https:// www.cnn.com/ALLPOLITICS/stories/1999/02/12/clinton/transcript.html.

Page 181, note 74

Since I don't have the time to talk to you about this for very long, I would like to point out a publication — I am doing so in the context of Heidegger — which has just appeared. It is the transcription of a course, a seminar by my friend Jacob Taubes, who is now dead: it is called *The Political Theology of Paul: Schmitt, Benjamin, Nietzsche, Freud.* Read it, he says things . . . he is someone quite extraordinary, who published very little, and died of cancer. He was dying when he gave this class, and I remember that shortly before he died, he was in Paris and he got word to me through someone (we had known each other for a long time, having met in Berlin, he was the son of a rabbi and taught at the University of Berlin, fascinated by Schmitt, a truly great expert on Saint Paul), he had someone tell me that he was going to die and was saying goodbye. Someone transmitted that message to me at the end of a seminar, I thought he was dramatizing as he often had periods of depression, etc., and then, he indeed died shortly thereafter. And just before his death, a few days before his death, he gave a seminar that was transcribed and is published here. You will find in it many things related to our interests here, and, in particular, as I am soon going to emphasize very briefly (I had already prepared it before reading this text, which I received yesterday), when I remark shortly that what Mandela, Tutu, and Clinton have in common is the fact of their being Protestants, that they are Protestant Christians, and that we have to reflect on that. How to connect that with what we were saying about globalatinization? And so, at a given moment, with a grain of salt, as they say, he says that he has a hypothesis about what united those Nazis, or quasi-Nazis or very-Nazis, big Nazis, namely, Heidegger, Carl Schmitt, and Adolf Hitler:

254

I have thought about the problem for a very long time and have found something in common — well, take this *cum grano salis*, but it is meant very seriously—something in common between Schmitt, Heidegger, and Hitler. Can you think of something? Then I will pose it as a riddle after all. There is a very profound commonality. What do Adolf Hitler as a person, Heidegger as a person, and Schmitt as a person have in common? I will tell you what I think without any if's, and's, or but's [it's a conversation; it's very much like that, off the cuff]. In this I am very concrete. My first thesis is: The German culture of the Weimar Republic and the Wilhelmine period was of a Protestant and somewhat Jewish coloring. This is a *factum brutum*. The universities were Protestant. I mean there were areas reserved for Catholics, somewhere there in Munich, a sort of counter-university and then, what do I know, Bonn, and so on, but that didn't really count, and certainly not in exegesis. *Catholica non sunt legenda*.

My second thesis is: All of them are Catholics gone stale. This is not a small thing. To talk now about the two intellectuals [that is Heidegger and Schmitt, and I repeat that, like Benjamin, Taubes was fascinated by Schmitt, in spite of the latter's antisemitism and Nazism; he corresponded with him, he had an ambivalent admiration for this man and that fascination stayed with him for his whole life]: They are not secure in the milieu of the German university and conquer a place for themselves with a gesture of destruction and annihilation of that which came before, that is, the Protestant-Jewish consensus, which had, for instance, in the name of Ernst Cassirer, an elegant, perfumed representative. These are people guided by a resentment, that's the first thing, but who with the genius of resentment also read the sources in a new way. Heidegger, the Jesuit pupil, read in a new way. He read Calvin, he read Luther [that is very important; one can't read Heidegger without hearing Luther and Calvin in the background], he read Kierkegaard [even more, clearly]. For us—I mean now, for you and me—this was an intellectual heritage [*Bildungsgut*], for us, so to speak, it came with the territory. One got a little worked up about Karl Barth's *Epistle to the Romans*....[1]

255

So, those are texts that should form part of our basic bibliography. Well, this history of Catholics versus Judeo-Protestantism plots out the global terrain that interests us here, don't you think? There are constantly alliances against Judaism and either Catholicism or Protestantism: the American and Israeli alliance is clearly a Judeo-Protestant alliance, and then, in certain cases, it is a Catholico-Judaic alliance. When it comes to forgiveness, one has

1. Jacob Taubes, *Political Theology of Saint Paul*, trans. Dana Hollander (Stanford: Stanford University Press, 2004), 103–4, translation slightly modified [Taubes, *La théologie politique de Paul: Schmitt, Benjamin, Nietzsche, Freud*, trans. Mira Köller and Dominique Séglard (Paris: Seuil, 1999), 148. Cf. *Die politische Theologie des Paulus* (Munich: Wilhelm Fink Verlag, 1993, 140].

to combine those axes constantly. And a bit further along, to lighten things up, a story:

> Let me tell you the following: The Jew, Emmanuel Levinas [this is a rabbi's son talking], now talked up so much in the media as a wise man and so on, told me the following. He was at the time in the circle of students who journeyed along to Davos [you know, that famous meeting], where Cassirer met with Heidegger. I mean these were, so to speak, medieval conditions. He came of course from Freiburg, phenomenology and so on. And the students organized an evening after the great disputation, at which, by the way, Heidegger refused to shake Cassirer's hand. It was a party, put on by the students, and Mr. Emmanuel Levinas, who had very thick black hair, which, however, could be powdered white, came on [Emmanuel Levinas, young student in Freiburg, etc., he has said a lot elsewhere about this Davos meeting] as Cassirer. His German was of course pretty weak, and he went across the stage and said only two words, always repeating them: "Humboldt, Kultur." And then came a howling that already took on Göringian proportions ("Whenever I hear the word 'culture' I cock my revolver"). That was Emmanuel Levinas. That's the atmosphere of 1931, that's what it looked like.
>
> With Schmitt it was the same thing. This wasn't a Jew. . . . [2]

He claims to have received from Schmitt, at the end of the latter's life, confidential information that he can't reveal. And I also invite you to read, and I'll be done with this text, what concerns Freud and Saint Paul and expiation, at the end. Freud's *Moses* is the expiation of a crime, of originary murder.[3] Read that for yourselves.

256

---

2. Taubes, *Political Theology of Saint Paul*, 104 [*Théologie politique de Paul*, 149].

3. Sigmund Freud, *Moses and Monotheism*, in *The Standard Edition of the Complete Psychological Works of Sigmund Freud*, vol. 23 (London: Hogarth Press, 1964) [Freud, *L'Homme Moïse et la religion monothéiste* (Paris: Gallimard, 1986)].

March 10, 1999

Ah, sovereignty!

One autumn afternoon Clinton declared, he found the words to say that he couldn't find the words to fully express his profound remorse: "Mere words cannot fully express the profound remorse I feel. . . ."[1]

That, one autumn afternoon, was a public declaration whose wording was carefully calculated and then released to the press. He began as follows, but we'll come back to it at length:

Good afternoon. [Every word counts: *bonjour, bon après-midi.* (*Laughter*)]

As anyone close to me knows, for months I have been grappling with how best to reconcile myself to the American people, to acknowledge my own wrongdoing [that's very hard to translate, but the stakes are very high, "my own wrongdoing," what I've done wrong or what harm I caused, what I was wrong to do. So, for now, that is the most neutral way to translate it] and still to maintain my focus on the work of the presidency.

Others are presenting my defense on the facts, the law and the Constitution. Nothing I can say now can add to that [so, to what my lawyers are doing for me elsewhere, to defend me on these questions of fact, the law and the Constitution, and nothing I say here can add to what they are saying. They have their function, their mission, to say, etc.]. What I want the American People to know, what I want the Congress to know, is that I am profoundly sorry [you can translate that as you wish: *navré, désolé, je regrette*] for all I have done wrong in words and deeds [again, hard to translate "wrong": if it is translated by "what I have done wrong in terms of words and actions," that already represents a decision, "what I was wrong to do," we'll come back to that, "what I was wrong to do by means of my language and my acts"].[2]

1. "Text of Clinton Remarks," *LA Times*, December 12, 1998. [Translator's note:] Ellipsis in typescript.
2. "Text of Clinton Remarks."

(*Translate*).³ We'll come back at length to this opening, and to what follows it, for each word counts and calls for infinite commentary.

Can a sovereign repent? Can a sovereign feel remorse? Profound remorse? A question of depth. Clinton twice says "profound" ("profound remorse," "I am profoundly sorry": it is because it is profound that, at such a profundity, words, simple words, can't reach it . . .).⁴

In a way Clinton is in the position of an elected sovereign. He represents at the highest level the sovereignty of a great sovereign nation-state, a nation-state, moreover, that claims its full and complete sovereignty on every occasion, like every self-respecting nation-state today, today when precisely sovereignty, which has always been problematic or in crisis, is so more than ever, in an explicit way and on all fronts. What's more, the United States claims its sovereignty so well that it regularly violates international law, resisting it and circumventing the United Nations and the Security Council when it judges that to be opportune and in conformity with the exercise of its sovereignty.

Clinton is by right the elected sovereign of a sovereign nation-state whose sovereignty he represents by means of his four-year electoral mandate. As in every supposed democracy, he is elected by the direct or, in this case, indirect but universal suffrage of a so-called sovereign people that delegates — in conditions, limits, and for a very determinate time — its sovereignty. In any case, this whole political field⁵ is dominated by the very thing that defines domination and superiority, namely, sovereignty.

Can a sovereign repent? And what relation might there be between this concept of sovereignty and the concept — so close to it, but which I nevertheless consider to be different — of "unconditionality" that is keeping us so busy here? The question is very difficult, but decisive for us. The sole difference between these two concepts, in such a close relation one to the other, is the difference of power, and I will try to show that bit by bit. In the purity — presuming there is such a thing — of giving, forgiving, hospitality,

258

259

---

3. [Translator's note:] During the session, Derrida freely translates the English text, adding the glosses inserted in brackets above. He adds at the end: "So, we'll come back at length to this opening, and to what follows it, for each word counts and has of course been calculated, and would call for infinite commentary. 'Ah, sovereignty!' as I said at the beginning."

4. [Translator's note:] Ellipsis in typescript.

5. During the session, Derrida adds: "Like every political field today, and like the political in a certain way."

mercy [*grâce*], etc., the requisite unconditionality must renounce all power,[6] hence all sovereignty. What threatens to corrupt forgiveness is precisely the transformation of unconditionality into an affirmation of sovereignty: "I can forgive you." This "I can" is the end of forgiveness. An "I can forgive" or a pure "may you be forgiven," presuming there is such a thing, must be unconditional but not sovereign. The frontier between them is subtle, per-meable, constantly open to crossover [*passage*], to crossing [*traversée*], trans-gression, or perversion, but it is absolutely essential, critical. It is "critical" in all senses of the word: it produces a decision, *krinein*, and it is always in a "critical state": precarious, under threat.

Note that, from the beginning of this seminar,[7] we have been interested in the globalization of confession, our guiding thread is indeed what happens to sovereignty, that is to say, at the moment, unique and almost without pre-cedent in history, when sovereign states or the heads of state who represent them bring themselves around to recognizing faults, crimes, even crimes against humanity, and bring themselves to ask for forgiveness, as it were, on the worldwide stage. These are serious things that are happening to sover-eignty, that affect so-called sovereignty, or by which it is auto-affected and more precisely hetero-affected. That is one of the signs by which one can recognize the crisis of the nation-state, and the painful transaction in which all nation-states, the most powerful or the least powerful, are involved in order to save what they are losing, in order to reaffirm[8] the sovereignty that they are clearly in the process—and this is globalization itself—of losing.

For a *major* historical lever ("*major*" is the word: the greatest possible, the highest possible, extreme and sovereignly sovereign), a historical lever that is major and determinant in what I call globalatinization [*mondialatinisation*]— which encompasses this globalization of confession or avowal marked by Romanness or Latinness—is indeed the concept and vocabulary of sover-eignty, the history of what has happened through sovereignty and to sover-eignty. As you no doubt know, the word "sovereign" comes from Latin, but from Low Latin. The word from which it is derived doesn't exactly have this form in ancient or classical Latin, but only in Low Latin; and that word

260

---

6. During the session, Derrida comments: "That is the possibility of, or the power to renounce all power, and so by the same token all sovereignty. Although the two things are very close, sovereignty is an unconditional power, but one has to think, if I can put it this way, an unconditionality without power."

7. Derrida, *Perjury and Pardon*, vol. 1, 7–8 [*Parjure et pardon*, vol. 1, 34], and in this volume, 5ff., 67ff., 97ff., 191ff. above.

8. During the session, Derrida adds: "To tense up about [*se crisper sur*]."

is, dare I say, superb, sublime, it is *superanus* (*blackboard*). Everything here issues from the *superanus*. *Superanus*—derived from *superans* (*blackboard*), which does exist in classical Latin, precisely meaning "superior," "predominant," just as *superantia* means "predominance"—*superanus* is the quality of what dominates absolutely, what is so high that it has nothing above itself, the peak, the lord, the sovereign, the king, the sovereign prince, the lord god, in a word, the first, over which there is nothing, and which is therefore absolutely independent. It is the supreme, the summit and the *summum*, "the supreme." Moreover, Latin *summum* is often translated by "sovereign," for example, in Augustine (*summa felicitas*: supreme or sovereign felicity). This divine sovereignty—for God's divinity, even and especially that of a merciful God, is sovereignty *par excellence*—this divine sovereignty was transferred to the absolute monarch by divine right, and then, through a fundamental mutation, but whose fracture has not, as I see it, cracked open the properly theological or theologico-political solidity of the semantics of sovereignty, through this mutation, in a republic or supposedly secularized democracy, divine or monarchic sovereignty was transferred onto the people. The people become the sovereign, one and indivisible, the absolute source of power and of right. Throughout the history of politics and of the political philosophy that bears and richly attests to this mutation, we could identify at least two reference points, the two prototypical authors of Confessions whose political thinking is in both cases centered either on the relation to the *City of God*, or on the human and earthly *Social Contract*. Well, if it is easy to imagine that divine sovereignty is the indispensable reference in *The City of God*, a certain theory of sovereignty is no less the centerpiece of a *Social Contract* that seems, however, to be purely anthropological. I will let you read and reread the very interesting theory of the sovereign and of sovereignty in *The Social Contract*. But I will quickly recall that the very signature of this great, and strange book, his *signature* (and that is why I reminded you that it was also, like *The City of God*, that of the author of the *Confessions*, saying "I" when he speaks of politics), the signature of the author justifies itself, positions and presents itself as that of a "member of the sovereign,"[9] a notion that he will nevertheless later define, in "On the Sovereign" (Book

261

9. Jean-Jacques Rousseau, *Social Contract, Discourse on the Virtue Most Necessary for a Hero, Political Fragments, and Geneva Manuscript*, trans. Judith R. Bush, Roger D. Masters, and Christopher Kelly, in *Collected Writings*, vol. 4, ed. Roger D. Masters and Christopher Kelly (Hanover, NH: University Press of New England, 1994), 131 [*Du contrat social et autres oeuvres politiques*, ed. Jean Ehrard (Paris: Garnier Frères, 1975), book 1, 235].

I, chapter vii, then in Book II, chapters i and ii), as inalienable and indivisible. That theory of indivisible sovereignty has, as you know, been broadly invoked on both sides—here implicitly, there explicitly—on both sides of the strange and flawed debate that has just been going on in France, without the least intellectual rigor, around what it has been thought necessary to call "parity."[10] Well, Rousseau first signs and authorizes himself to speak of politics as a citizen of a free state and "member of the sovereign." I refer you to the extraordinary beginning of this book, as extraordinary as that of the *Confessions*, and I would take from it just this extract, at the beginning of Book I, before Chapter i:

262

> I start in without proving the importance of my subject. It will be asked if I am a prince or legislator to write about Politics. I reply that I am neither, and that is why I write about Politics. If I were a prince or a legislator, I would not waste my time saying what has to be done. I would do it, or keep silent.
>
> Born a citizen of a free State, and a *member of the sovereign*, the right to vote there is enough to impose on me the duty of learning about public affairs, no matter how feeble the influence of my voice may be. And I am happy, every time I meditate about Governments, always to find in my research new reasons to love that of my country![11]

In this apparently secularizing and humanizing conversion of the theological concept of sovereignty (a concept, one is tempted to say, that belongs *par excellence* to the concepts of the political that Carl Schmitt said were secularized theological concepts),[12] in this apparently secularizing and human-

---

10. Allusion to the debate on gender parity that took place in the National Assembly and led to the adoption on March 10, 1999, of a change in the Constitution, namely, that "the law determines the conditions within which the equal access of men and women to electoral terms and elected office is organized." See the adopted text in the "Archives de la XIe législature," http://www.assemblee-nationale.fr/11//ta/ta0224.asp.

11. *Social Contract*, 131 [*Du contrat social*, book 1, 235–36], Derrida's emphasis.

12. During the session, Derrida comments: "I would like to develop that, but don't have time to do so. You know that, how the dominant concepts of political language are secularized theological concepts. The concept of sovereignty—I don't remember whether Schmitt speaks of this, probably, I haven't gone back to look at all that—like the concept of decision, it is probably exemplary in this regard, the concept of secularized theology. But, and I'll come back to this, secularization is an intrareligious and Christian process." See Carl Schmitt, *Der Begriff des Politischen* [1932] (Berlin: Duncker & Humblot, 1979) [*La notion de politique / Théorie du partisan*, trans. Marie-Louise Steinhauser (Paris: Flammarion, 1992)]. See also Schmitt, *Théologie politique (1922, 1969)*, trans. Jean-Louis Schlegel (Paris: Gallimard, 1988). In English, see *The Concept of the*

izing conversion being a citizen, having the right to vote, having a voice, as one says, a political voice, means being a member of, participating in the sovereign body ("Born a citizen of a free state, *and a member of the sovereign*," says Rousseau). What does that mean? Take a look at chapter vii of Book I, at the moment when, under the title "On the Sovereign," Rousseau defines the social contract as an association or reciprocal commitment between the public and individuals, but an as it were autonomous contract in which the individual contracts only with themself, but then finds themself involved in a double relation: as *member of the sovereign* and *toward the sovereign*. At the end of the preceding chapter, as he is defining the "social compact [*pacte social*],"[13] it is the notion of a people that implies that appeal to the notion of sovereignty—taking on a very acute sense—qualifying therefore the republic or the body politic (or the "public person," the republic being a new name for what was previously being called the "*City*"), a body politic that would be called state when it is passive and sovereign when it is active. And within the same body politic, in the same republic, individuals are collectively called people, a people of *citizens* inasmuch as they take part in sovereign authority, and a people of *subjects* when they submit to the laws of the state. But these are the same individuals in different relations, which is why, Rousseau says, one often takes one term for the other. In any case, sovereignty is implied in the definition of the republic, the body politic, and the citizen. I'll very quickly read a few lines:

> This public person, formed by the union of all the others, formerly took the name *City*, and now takes that of *Republic* or *body politic*, which its members call *State* when it is passive, *Sovereign* when active, *Power* when comparing it to similar bodies [*à ses semblables*].[14] As for the associates, they collectively take the name *people*; and individually are called *Citizens* as participants in the sovereign authority [so, the citizen is sovereign, member participating in the sovereign, but with a sovereignty that nevertheless remains, as we shall see, inalienable and indivisible], and *Subjects* as subject to the laws of the State. But these terms are often mixed up and mistaken for

263

Political, trans. George Schwab (Chicago: University of Chicago Press, 1996); *Theory of the Partisan*, trans. G. L. Ulmen (New York: Telos Press Publishing, 2007); *Political Theology*, trans. George Schwab (Chicago: University of Chicago Press, 2005).

13. *Social Contract*, 139 [*Du contrat social*, 244–45].

14. During the session, Derrida adds: "That is to say other states, foreign states, and—I'll come back to this in a moment—Rousseau leaves foreign policy completely to the side in the *Social Contract*. He doesn't talk about it, he makes a note, three lines at the end of the book, let's says that he doesn't have time, etc."

264   one another. It is enough to know how to distinguish them when they are used with complete precision.[15]

And chapter vii, which immediately follows, "On the Sovereign," explains the relation of obligation that binds the people as subject, which subjects itself as subject to itself as sovereign, even though one would be tempted to think that one cannot commit oneself with respect to oneself. (Read *Social Contract*, beginning of chapter vii, p. 245 C, p. 246 D.)

> This formula shows that the act of association includes a reciprocal engagement between the public and private individuals, and that each individual, contracting with himself so to speak, finds himself engaged in a double relation, namely toward private individuals as a member of the Sovereign and toward the Sovereign as a member of the State. But the maxim of civil right that no one can be held responsible for engagements toward himself cannot be applied here, because there is a great difference between being obligated to oneself, or to a whole of which one is a part [so, one is member of the sovereign, hence part of a whole, when one is engaged in the sovereign order, and although this is toward oneself, it isn't simply toward oneself. So, the clause from civil law that says that one can't be engaged with oneself doesn't work].
>
> It must further be noted that the public deliberation that can obligate all of the subjects to the Sovereign — due to the two different relationships in which each of them is considered — cannot for the opposite reason obligate the Sovereign toward itself; and that consequently it is contrary to the nature of the body politic for the Sovereign to impose on itself a law it cannot break. [That is very important: "it is contrary to the nature of the body politic for the Sovereign to impose on itself a law it cannot break." In other words, the Sovereign cannot impose a law on itself without being able to break it. In other words, there is no law above the sovereign.]
>
> . . .
>
> Now the Sovereign, formed solely by the private individuals composing it, does not and cannot have any interest contrary to theirs. Consequently, the Sovereign power has no need of a guarantee toward the subjects, be-
265   cause it is impossible for the body ever to want to harm all its members, and we shall see later that it cannot harm any one of them as an individual. The Sovereign, by the sole fact of being, is always what it ought to be.[16]

A certain number of consequences derive from that, and you could follow them in Book II, chapters i and ii, on the inalienable and indivisible

---

15. *Social Contract*, 139 [*Du contrat social*, 244–45].
16. *Social Contract*, 139–40 [*Du contrat social*, 245–46].

character of sovereignty ("1. That Sovereignty Is Inalienable," read p. 250 D, chap. i of Book II)

I say, therefore, that sovereignty, being only the exercise of the general will, can never be alienated, and that the sovereign, which is only a collective being, can be represented only by itself. Power can perfectly well be transferred, but not will.[17]

"2. That Sovereignty Is Indivisible" (read chap. ii of Book II, D, pp. 250–51).

For the same reason that sovereignty is inalienable, it is indivisible. Because either the will is general or it is not. It is the will of the people as a body, or of only a part. In the first case, this declared act of will is an act of sovereignty and constitutes law. In the second case, it is merely a private will or an act of magistracy; it is at most a decree.[18]

Read also chapter iv, "On the Limits of the Sovereign Power," which are not exterior limits, not foreign limits, but self-limitations, and in which Rousseau, defining what is properly an act of sovereignty ("What really is an act of sovereignty then?" he asks),[19] defines it as a "legitimate convention," because it doesn't bind the inferior to the superior, because it is equitable, as a result of which, recognizing that sovereignty isn't natural but conventional, hence fictive in a way, he can say that "as long as subjects are subordinated only to such conventions, they do not obey anyone, but solely their own will"[20] (will = freedom = power of freedom = sovereignty; sovereignty: free and self-determining will constituting "I can," "I can of myself, on my own behalf," *ipse*, and I underline this implication of "I can" and of "ipseity" for a reason that I will clarify later). Remember in any case what we were saying in previous years about the implication of capacity [*pouvoir*] or power [*puissance*], about the masculine mastery, even, of *hospes* and of the patron or husband, spouse, in the very etymology of *ipse* and of ipseity.[21] *Sovereignty* goes hand in hand, let me say, with the position of self as autoposition of power of masculine ipseity; the sharing of sovereignty in two equal parts will change nothing in that regard.

266

The single point that I really want to shed full light on, if there can be light here, in this immense problematic, is this onto-theological articulation

17. *Social Contract*, 145, trans. slightly modified [*Du contrat social*, 250].
18. *Social Contract*, 145–46 [*Du contrat social*, 250–51].
19. *Social Contract*, 150 [*Du contrat social*, 255].
20. *Social Contract*, 150 [*Du contrat social*, 255].
21. See Derrida, unpublished seminar, "Hostilité/hospitalité," EHESS, 1995–96, First Session; and *Of Hospitality*, 41, 149–50 [*De l'hospitalité*, 41, 131–32].

of the motif of sovereignty, an onto-theological, or anthropo-theological, or secular-biblical, or globalatinizing articulation, an always unfulfilled secularization (for the concept of secularization is itself a religiously Christian concept: the *seculum* [*siècle*] is (of) the world, in the Christian sense), hence, as secularization[22] in the betrayed tradition of the Bible, this republican democratization that transfers the attributes of sovereignty onto a people consisting of citizens and subjects, feels guilty. It feels vaguely guilty, blaming itself and asking forgiveness of the absolute sovereign, of the ultimate source of sovereignty, the only one that is thought to *be capable* of forgiving.[23] That is the place of every proceeding and every trepidation. The single sign of it that I will point out here, in the context of Rousseau (but enormous analogous work remains to be done in other contexts and with other corpora of discourses and political theories, and even in Bataille, who nevertheless attempts to separate sovereignty from mastery, in a purely terminological way, seemingly, and arbitrarily from the lexical point of view,[24] even though that arbitrariness must signify something nonarbitrary, inasmuch as he retrieves absolute sacredness in the sovereignty of ecstasy, laughter, sexual climax, etc., but let's leave that aside), the single sign that I will point out here, in the context of Rousseau, is the revealing insistence with which Rousseau recalls the sacred — in truth, religious — character of the *Social Contract*. Even when the right instituted by the social contract isn't natural but conventional — not natural as if from Adam, "King Adam" or Robinson Crusoe, who Rousseau said were "Sovereigns of the world"[25] because they were the sole inhabitants, like kings of humankind, not having to fear any enemy or "rebellions, nor wars, nor conspirators"[26] — even when the social contract doesn't come from nature but is founded on convention, "the social

22. During the session, Derrida adds: "No secularization has ever brought us out of Christianity, contrary to what many people think."

23. During the session, Derrida adds: "Because the position of forgiveness, and even the political position of pardon, *grâce*, in the United States is the position of sovereignty, the kingly right to pardon, it is naturally the right of the sovereign, he is not required to give an account to anybody, he is above the law."

24. During the session, Derrida adds: "He is the only one ever to have done that." See Derrida, "From Restricted to General Economy: A Hegelianism without Reserve," trans. Alan Bass, *Writing and Difference* (Chicago: University of Chicago Press, 1978), 251–77 [*L'Écriture et la différence* (Paris: Seuil, 1967), 373–80].

25. Rousseau, *Social Contract*, 133 [*Du contrat social*, 238]. See also in this regard Derrida, *The Beast and the Sovereign*, vol. 2 [*La bête et le souverain*, vol. 2].

26. *Social Contract*, 133 [*Du contrat social*, 238].

order is a sacred right"²⁷ (chapter i of Book I of the *Social Contract*). Every-thing that proceeds from "the will of the people or sovereign will, which is general"²⁸ (synonyms in chapter ii of Book III) is "sacred" and as a result "inviolable."²⁹ In *Letters Written from the Mountain* he declares that "the will of all is thus the order, the supreme rule, and that general and personified rule is what I call the Sovereign."³⁰

For even when Rousseau seems to posit limits on sovereignty, limits that aren't in fact limits because they are self-limitations that are the very ex-pression and the manifestation of absolute sovereignty, well, he recalls the sacred character—inviolable and indivisible because it is sacred—of said sovereignty. At the end of the *Social Contract* he may all very well exclude every Christian republic ("I am mistaken when I speak of a Christian re-public; these two words are mutually exclusive," chapter viii, before the "Conclusion"),³¹ but he must maintain the sacred nature of the social pact. (Read p. 255 of the *Social Contract*, chapter iv of Book II: "On the Limits of the Sovereign Power").

268

It is apparent from this that the Sovereign power, albeit entirely absolute, entirely sacred, and entirely inviolable, does not and cannot exceed the lim-its of the general conventions, and that every man can fully dispose of the part of his goods and freedom that has been left to him by these conven-tions. So that the Sovereign never has the right to burden one subject more than another, because then the matter becomes individual, and its power is no longer competent. [In other words, the limit to the general will is is the

27. *Social Contract*, 131 [*Du contrat social*, 236].

28. *Social Contract*, 170 [*Du contrat social*, 277].

29. *Social Contract*, 150 [*Du contrat social*, 255].

30. Rousseau, *Letters Written From the Mountain*, trans. Christopher Kelly and Ju-dith R. Bush, in *Letter to Beaumont, Letters Written From the Mountain, and Related Writings*, in *The Collected Writings of Rousseau*, vol. 9, ed. Christopher Kelly and Eve Grace (Hanover, NH: University Press of New England, 2001), 232 [*Lettres écrites de la montagne*, in *Oeuvres complètes*, vol. 3, *Du contrat social—Écrits politiques*, ed. Bernard Gagnebin and Marcel Raymond (Paris: Gallimard, 1964), 807].

31. *Social Contract*, 221 [*Du contrat social*, 333]. During the session, Derrida adds: "There is no 'Christian republic.' These words make me think of Heidegger who says that 'Christian philosophy' is like a 'square circle.' That said, he is as Christian as is Rousseau. As always." See Heidegger, "Phenomenology and Theology," trans. James G. Hart and John C. Maraldo, in William McNeill, ed., *Pathmarks* (Cambridge: Cam-bridge University Press, 1999), 53: "there is no such thing as a Christian philosophy; that is an absolute square circle [*ein 'hölzernes Eisen'*]" ["Théologie et philosophie," *Archives de philosophie* 32 (1969), 393; "Phänomenologie und Theologie," in *Wegmarken, Gesam-tausgabe*, vol. 9 (Frankfurt: Vittorio Klostermann, 1976), 66].

limit of the very generality. As soon as it is applied illegally to individuals, it is no longer general, it is no longer what it is. At that point, it comes up against a limit, but that limit is an internal limit, you see, it isn't a limit. In order to be what it is, it must remain a general, universal, inviolable, sacred and indivisible member.]32

You will have understood in passing that this secularization that remains a sacralization of the principle of sovereignty, of indivisible and inviolable sovereignty, this as yet unfulfilled secularization, by definition (for secularization, I repeat, remains a religious moment and will always remain a theological modification of the theological), this sacred secularization of sovereignty is nothing other than the constitution of what is called the citizen or legal subject [*sujet de droit*], political subjectivity itself; it is without any doubt the constitution of the subject, and I say "what is *called* the citizen" or "political" subject because there are perhaps other paths and other ways to come for thinking and interpreting and historically implementing citizenship and the political. For a certain process of deconstruction of sovereignty, which has always already begun, has already taken more determinate, even juridical forms during this century, which, as the century of crisis or of decline of the nation-state, as Arendt says, cannot but be a crisis of sovereignty.33 As you well know, so I won't waste our time on this, one could cite ten thousand examples of limitations on sovereignty that have been accepted, like it or not, recognized or not, by individual states.34 I will make do with evoking texts of international law that recommend—in cases where the sovereignty of countries still seems to reign sovereignly, namely, in international law, precisely—well, legal texts recommend limitations on or divisions of sovereignty with a view to peace, social and economic justice. That was already the case for the Hague Conventions of 1899 and 1907; then it was made more specific through the Covenant of the League of Nations, then through the United Nations Charter—and more recently with the project for the International Court of Justice (which the United States has refused to sign and which France signed with much reticence and foot-dragging precautions). And naturally, a *divided* sovereignty may always remain a sovereignty, as I was saying just now; otherwise, and this

269

32. *Social Contract*, 150 [*Du contrat social*, 255].

33. Cf. Hannah Arendt, "The Crisis in Culture," in *Between Past and Future: Eight Exercises in Political Thought* (New York: Penguin Books, 2006) [*La crise de la culture: Huit exercises de pensée politique*, trans. Patrick Lévy (Paris: Gallimard, 1972)].

34. During the session, Derrida adds: "I think that what is today called 'Europe' is only an experimental laboratory for this history, for this painful deconstruction."

is another "politics" altogether, another "ethics" altogether, another "law" altogether (presuming that law can bypass at least fictive reference to sovereignty, which is an enormous question), otherwise, *divided* sovereignty, then, in a totally different sense, is no longer sovereignty, which in essence is, or wishes to be capable of being, indivisible and inalienable. That ambiguity always remains. You would find it if you were to read the *Encyclopaedia Britannica* (vol. 11, p. 57) article on "Sovereignty," a Latin word incorporated into English, the royal road to globalatinization. You would see there that the pluralizing of "peoples" and "peoples of the world" will have, through that very worldwide pluralizing, called into question the principle of indivisible sovereignty, while all the time maintaining it as "divided."[35] And contrary to what Rousseau says, leaving questions of foreign policy and international politics completely out of question at the end of the *Social Contract* (read p. 336),[36] the article on sovereignty in the *Encyclopaedia Britannica* interests me on account of a certain logical turn that it performs, namely, by positing that, contrary to what is thought, and hence contrary to what Rousseau thinks here, laws themselves, far from depending on the principle of sovereignty,[37] would not be possible without limiting the principle of sovereignty.

270

I'll read, for example:

> The people [collective singular] of the world have recognized that there can be no peace without law, and that there can be no law without some limitations on sovereignty. They have started, therefore, to pool sovereignties to

35. "Sovereignty," in *Encyclopedia Britannica*, vol. 11, ed. Philip W. Goetz (Chicago: Encyclopedia Britannica, 1990), 57; cf. https://www.britannica.com/topic/sovereignty/Sovereignty-and-international-law.

36. During the session Derrida reads the "Conclusion" (Book IV, chap. ix) of the *Social Contract*: "After setting forth the true principles of political right and trying to found the State on this basis, what remains to be done is to buttress the State by its foreign relations, which would include the law of nations, commerce, the right of war and conquest, public law, alliances, negotiations, treaties, etc. But all that constitutes a new object, too vast for my limited purview. I should always have set my sights closer to myself" (224 [*Du contrat social*, 336]). He then adds: "The same one who says 'I,' etc., member citizen of the sovereign state, follows up by saying, 'foreign policy will be for another book.' [*Laughter*] That is what we are talking about, isn't it?"

37. During the session, Derrida adds: "As Rousseau says. For him there are no laws if there is no principle of sovereignty, just as for most politics. There are no laws if there isn't a principle of sovereignty. Well, this article from the *Encyclopaedia* suggests that, on the contrary, without limitation of the principle of sovereignty laws wouldn't be possible, that it is, as it were, sovereignty that prevents laws."

the extent needed to maintain peace; and sovereignty is being increasingly exercised on behalf of the peoples *of* the world [peoples and not the people; plural, peoples] not only by national governments but also by organs of the world community [allusion to all NGOs, principle of intervention].³⁸

271   Before abandoning somewhat this major, sovereign, question of sovereignty, I recommend that you read all the examples that you will find under the entries "Sovereignty" or "Sovereign" in the Littré dictionary; it is a goldmine, everything is there, the whole history of the word since the Middle Ages. But I'll extract from there just a single quote that I haven't verified in its original context. It is from a postrevolutionary and no doubt counterrevolutionary text by Villemain, from his *Souvenirs contemporains. Les Cent Jours* (chapter 7), which I haven't read. Villemain says this: "By means of these last expressions [the "interest" and "will" of the nation] the victor implies the sovereignty of the people, *the other type of divine right* that has no need of reasons and need not give any account, and can become the most outrageous and most irresponsible instrument of many things that justice condemns."³⁹

ᘜᏋ♥Ᏸᘖ

One autumn afternoon, then, Clinton declared that he couldn't find the words to fully express his profound remorse. Better yet, he declared that
272   "mere words cannot fully express the profound remorse I feel for what our

---

38. "Sovereignty," *Encyclopaedia Britannica*, vol. 11, 57, Derrida's emphasis. In a note Derrida indicates that the article is quoted by Richard Kearney in "Towards a British-Irish Council," *Céide* 2, no. 2 (1998): 11–13. During the session, Derrida translates the English text. [Translator's note:] The current online version has this wording: "Citizens and policymakers generally have recognized that there can be no peace without law and that there can be no law without some limitations on sovereignty. They started, therefore, to pool their sovereignties to the extent needed to maintain peace and prosperity . . . and sovereignty was increasingly exercised on behalf of the peoples of the world not only by national governments but also by regional and international organizations." https://www.britannica.com/topic/sovereignty/Sovereignty-and -international-law, accessed July 19, 2022.

39. Abel François Villemain, *Souvenirs contemporains d'histoire et de literature. Seconde partie. Les Cent Jours* (Paris: Didier Libraire-éditeur, 1864), 175, my translation [DW]. Quoted in Littré, *Dictionnaire de la langue française*, vol. 4, 2026, Derrida's emphasis.

country is going through, and for what members of both parties in Congress are now forced to deal with."[40]

What does that mean? What does he mean to say? Which words has he not been able to find, to say what? And which words has he not been able to find, given that, as he says in a few words, there are none ("mere words cannot," etc.)? And yet it works, these words have been found to say they can't be found. Found by whom? That will be one of our questions. I'll first read—beyond these first lines—the first few paragraphs of this declaration preceded by the words without words that I have just quoted and repeated. (Read [some English words], then translate in the "Text of Clinton Remarks Acknowledging Mistakes" up to "to deal with," then interpret the title [notably "mistakes": faults, errors, etc. "Work" twice: two strategies: more to be done, so reconciliation and labor of atonement].)[41]

Good afternoon.

As anyone close to me knows, for months I have been grappling with how best to reconcile myself to the American people, to acknowledge my own wrongdoing and still to maintain my focus on the work of the presidency.

Others are presenting my defense on the facts, the law and the Constitution. Nothing I can say now can add to that.

What I want the American people to know, what I want the Congress to know is that I am profoundly sorry for all I have done wrong in words and deeds.

I never should have misled the country, the Congress, my friends or my family [I should never have led astray, deceived, no, not deceived . . . led in this wrong direction. That's it, I should never have led in this wrong direction. It's a remarkably well-written text; I suspect others had their hand in it]. Quite simply, I gave in to my shame [I don't know how to translate that; the ambiguity is there in English, in French, I'm afraid it's . . . so, yes,

273

40. "Text of Clinton Remarks." Derrida's photocopy of this text is heavily annotated. See the dossier "Le parjure et le pardon: documentation," Fonds Jacques Derrida, IMEC, 219 DRR 240.1. [Translator's note:] Here and below Derrida reads, translates, and glosses the English text. I have conveyed those effects when deemed significant.

41. During the session, Derrida clarifies: "This is published by the Associated Press, it's a press agent who circulates Clinton's declaration under the title "Text of Clinton Remarks Acknowledging Mistakes"—well, "mistakes" is the problem: it means "fault," "error," "wrong," but everything is in play there, in the distinction between fault and error. So here is the text transcribed by the Federal Document Clearing House. I've already read it, but I'll reread this passage." He then proceeds to read the text, translating directly from the English version.

I am shamed. I have been shamed. What follows clarifies]. I have been condemned by my accusers with harsh words.

And while it's hard to hear yourself called deceitful and manipulative [those are the words used to describe me, deceiver, manipulator, those are the accusations], I remember Ben Franklin's admonition that our critics are our friends, for they do show us our faults.⁴² [So, he is hurt, but all the same, he remembers the great president who said that our critics are our friends, so "I won't defend myself" because critics shows us what our faults are. Well, "fault" is another very ambiguous word, "our wrongs, we'll come back to these words, "wrong," "fault," etc.]⁴³

274   Mere words cannot fully express the profound remorse I feel for what our country is going through, and for what members of both parties in Congress are now forced to deal with.⁴⁴

I'll already emphasize some of these well-chosen words, in order to come back to them later, very well chosen, no doubt with the vigilant assistance of expert attorneys, for this confession, which has the tone of immediacy, as if spoken from the heart, and claims to look the Americans, and in truth the whole world, straight in the eye, eye to eye, directly, this confession that

42. Benjamin Franklin (1706–90), signatory and co-creator of the Declaration of Independence, was one of the Founding Fathers of the United States [not a president, as Derrida's gloss states (DW)]. The saying attributed to Franklin by Clinton is an adaptation of the former's famous aphorism, "Love your Enemies, for they tell you your Faults" (Franklin, *Poor Richard Improved*, 1756), https://founders.archives.gov/documents/Franklin/01-06-02-0136.

43. The recording of this session to which we had access has a gap here while the tape is changed. It picks up again in the middle of a commentary by Derrida: ". . . he is going to insist on the fact that he has, however, done all he could to continue working. During this whole time, he insists twice on the work of the presidency, 'We all must return to the work. . . .' So the strategy is naturally the ambiguous language of these words that pivot among wrong, error, and fault—I'll come back to that in a moment—and then the insistence on work, which is not simply said to move hearts, to remind Americans of what is essential (what is essential, as he has said and repeated the whole time, is not these ridiculous attacks that I am subjected to, etc., it is the politics of the country that I am obliged to continue to lead: there are tasks to be done overseas, there is Iraq, etc., so I have to keep on with my work, etc.). So, this double reference to work is made not simply to move hearts and to recall what is essential, that is, to distract from the proceedings, from Monicagate, but it is also, as well—third advantage of this strategy—because work has an atoning value (and that is the theme of our seminar). Because I am working, perhaps at the end, when all's said and done, when you've seen the end of the proceedings, because I have continued to work. . . . Work has an atoning value, as we well know in this seminar. And hence, reconciliation."

44. "Text of Clinton Remarks."

feigns absolute proximity and defenselessness, invoking what those closest know of this penitent who is confessing ("As anyone close to me knows"), this theatrical confession, claiming to be unmediated, has not only been prepared, rehearsed, mediatized by a television screen and by a prompter[45] (the president is used less to speak than to read from a teleprompter that whispers the lines to him, as he moreover does during hours of speeches on the state of the Union while at the tribune when addressing Congress. That impels us to pose here the very general and radical question of the prompter of a whispered word:[46] inasmuch as a confession and request for pardon must repeat intelligible formulas, draw on a vocabulary and a grammar, be guided by the code included in every language, are not this confession or request for forgiveness from the outset—originarily, in order to emerge—*already* in a situation of *repeating*,[47] hence of reading from a prompter or a quasi-prompter on a <more or> less interior screen that whispers and dictates the words of the confession and request for forgiveness, and, to that extent, do they not break with or corrupt the pure sincerity, pure spontaneity, pure intentionality, the pure purity that is nevertheless adduced or claimed in the highest degree? There is always a prompter, a whisperer; one listens and reads when one speaks—even if one reads and listens to oneself alone, one reads and listens to another, one reads oneself and listens like another who is completely other—and that would suffice to introduce lying, nonveracity, bad faith, and disavowal into avowal, impurity into purity, etc. In other words, and this is one of the reasons why I am putting the question of theater at the heart of our reflection on pardon and perjury this year, if forgiveness must be put on stage, declare itself and have itself heard, be phenomenalized in the place where it also demands, on the other hand, nontheatricality, then its theater is a theater where, as in every theater, good and evil is—before the premiere or full dress—being rehearsed [*avant la première ou la générale, la répétition*]. What we are speaking of here is repetition, repeating in theater and as theater, and theater as rehearsal—or as I said last century, the *parole soufflée*);[48] I was saying then that this word whispered in one's ear or this puffed-up [*boursouflée*] word of Clinton's, this theatrical confession claiming to be unmediated, has not only been prepared,

275

---

45. "Prompter" and "teleprompter" in English here and below.

46. [Translator's note:] *la parole soufflée*, the word breathed in one's ear, spoken by a theatrical prompter [*souffleur*].

47. [Translator's note:] *répéter*, also "rehearsing."

48. See Derrida, "La parole soufflée," in *Writing and Difference*, 169–95 [*L'Écriture et la différence*, 253–92]. [Translator's note:] End of parenthesis beginning after note 45.

rehearsed, mediatized by a television screen and by a teleprompter, but cleverly controlled by a company of attorneys, and it is moreover careful enough not to confess, or avow anything whatsoever concerning whatever it be that Clinton is accused of by Congress,[49] which could justify the process set in motion with a view to his impeachment[50] (he moreover says as much in the second paragraph: "Others are presenting my defense on the facts, the law, and the Constitution. Nothing I can say now can add to that," a very cunning declaration that completely dissociates this confession from the legal domain, from what he calls the facts, the law, and the Constitution, nothing less than that, and about which he won't speak. He isn't going to speak of facts, of the law, and of his conduct as president with respect to the Constitution. What will he speak of, then? Of his family, in front of fellow citizens and even members of Congress whom he addresses like members of his family, thus outside the political or legal field, which his attorneys are taking care of, while at the same time excluding them from his family, because the wrong he has committed is something he has done in the first place and only to his loved ones, Hillary and his daughter, and so to himself, and if he has done wrong to the American people and even to Congress, that wrong is private, as it were, almost familial, since the potential political and legal fault, which he denies, will be taken care of by his attorneys), well then, as I was saying, the well-chosen words that I want to emphasize for now, before coming back to them at length later, are, following "mistakes" (errors, slip-ups, failings [*fautes*], perhaps, but not purely moral failings, those of intention, which can remain pure, errors of judgment rather, failings of discernment, gaffes [*maladresses*] that leave intact the good faith and good will of nondeceit; in the end, stupid blunders [*bêtises*]; he acknowledges that he has done stupid things[51] — moreover, I note parenthetically that Mon-

49. During the session, Derrida adds: "He doesn't give an inch concerning what is in question in the proceedings, namely, lying under oath before a grand jury. He admits to nothing, he concedes nothing."

50. [Translator's note:] Word in English in typescript.

51. During the session, Derrida adds: "He acknowledges that he has done stupid things! [*Laughter*] And often, in Heidegger's case, people get very ironic about the single thing that he conceded, namely a *große Dummheit*, a huge idiocy, *une grosse bêtise*, about . . . that." Derrida is alluding to Heidegger's silence over his collusion with the Nazi regime during the year of his rectorship (1933–34), which he described in private as a *"große Dummheit."* See Heinrich Wiegand Petzet, *Auf einen Stern zugehen: Begegnungen und Gespräche mit Martin Heidegger 1929–1976* (Franfurt: Societäts-Verlag, 1983), 43: *"es sei die größte Dummheit seines Lebens gewesen"* [*Encounters and Dialogues with Martin Heidegger, 1929–1976*, trans. Parvis Emad and Kenneth Maly (Chicago:

ica ended her recent televised declaration, where she also says to herself "sorry," by affirming that she still hopes to "find the ideal man, marry him and have children," and, I am quoting the French translation in *Libération* of March 5, that when her children "come to study 'Monicagate' in history books," she will simply tell them that—I am quoting the translation—"Mommy did a very stupid thing [*une grosse bêtise*]";[52] what's more, it's well true [*ben vrai*],[53] even if it's a stupid thing that saves the said children in advance from having to worry, and even—you saw the price paid for those interviews and for the book that she probably didn't even write—saves for a long time the ideal future husband and said children from having to work at all, whether as atonement or not); following "mistakes," then, I'm coming back to Clinton's text, there are the similarly cleverly equivocal and ambiguous words, "wrong" ("my own wrongdoing," "I am profoundly sorry for all I have done wrong in words and deeds"). This word "wrong" has the same ambiguity as *tort* in French. Whether it be a matter of words or deeds, "wrong" belongs to the double register of moral failing (implying lying, perjury, and crime) and the much less serious failure of knowledge or knowhow, which is merely a good-faith error, incompetence at worst, but an incompetence without any malicious intent (the case of contaminated blood: same ambiguity).[54] I can confess to having been wrong to speak or to

277

University of Chicago Press, 1993), 37: "Heidegger responded, literally, that it was the greatest stupidity of his life"].

52. Patrick Sabatier, "Monica, l'avalanche médiatique. Biographie, entretiens télé, le Lewinsky business est relancé," *Libération*, March 3, 1999, 6, https://www.liberation .fr/planete/1999/03/03/monica-l-avalanche-mediatique-biographie-entretiens-tele-le -lewinsky-business-est-relance_266497/; and Sabatier, "Monica sort ses griffes. 70 millions d'Américains ont suivi l'interview télévisé de l'ex-stagiaire," *Libération*, March 5, 1999, 11, https://www.liberation.fr/planete/1999/03/05/monica-sort-ses-griffes-70-millions -d-americains-ont-suivi-l-interview-televisee-de-l-ex-stagiaire_266709/. The Lewinsky biography appeared in March 1999 (Andrew Morton, *Monica's Story* [New York: St. Martin's Press, 1999]), and was translated the same year as Morton, *Monica. Son histoire*, trans. Zoe Delort [Paris: Presses de la Cité, 1999]). [Translator's note:] Lewinsky's word was in fact "mistake": "I'd really like to find the right person and have a meaningful relationship, and get married and have kids. . . . [And in response to Barbara Walters's final question, "What will you tell your children?"] Mommy made a big mistake." See *ABC 20/20* interview of March 3, 1999, https://www.youtube.com /watch?v=vUUATD_pfYE (final minutes).

53. Thus in typescript and during the session.

54. During the session, Derrida adds: "You will note that in the court case over contaminated blood that has just ended, as you know, 'no comment' [words in English (DW)], there is the same ambiguity: 'Was it a mistake, a lack of competence, a dysfunction

act in this way without recognizing any moral failing, and without confessing that I did wrong, or wished to do anybody wrong. I was wrong not to take my umbrella today although it is raining, that's the acknowledgment of an error, a mistake,[55] something stupid, a nonmoral fault (a question of knowledge, prudence, technique, competence, foresight, etc.), whereas another wrong [*tort*] (and this is also "wrong'" in English) might consist in doing wrong to another ([English] "to do wrong," or "to wrong"—to deceive, to lie). But there again, and it is this final ambiguity that Clinton's attorneys must have counseled him to exploit, I can do "wrong" to another without wishing to, by being wrong (in the sense of blind judgment or a good faith error) in doing wrong. But to be in the wrong, to recognize being in the wrong for having been wrong to do wrong to someone, does not mean recognizing a serious failing; it amounts to saying, "I didn't do it on purpose," "I recognize that I messed up [*j'ai pas su faire*], that it caused harm [*tort*] to others, to those close to me." But believe me, believe in my good faith, I didn't want to and deep down I am neither responsible for nor guilty of the harm that they have suffered. I am merely responsible for a mistake, for having been wrong to act in that way, for not having weighed things up, not having measured the effects and the consequences; but that evaluation belongs to the order of knowledge, not of intent. I did a stupid thing, like a child. I did it in good faith, I didn't commit perjury, I didn't intend to do wrong or even hide anything. Quite simply, I handled things badly, I got caught handling things badly [*j'ai été pris là où je m'y suis mal pris*], but handling things badly or making a mistake is not doing or wishing to do harm, it's an error. A certain way of using, of putting the word "wrong" in a phrase ("in words and deeds")—as with the word *tort* in French—is able to transfer an ethical failing into a miscalculation [*faute de calcul*] and so neutralize *both* the wrong [*mal*] *and* the seriousness of the confession. It will always be more easy, more exonerating to say, "I made a miscalculation," "I thought that five times five was twenty-six," than to say rather, "I did someone wrong." When one says, "I was wrong [*j'ai eu tort*]," one isn't necessarily saying "I was in the wrong"; one excuses oneself slightly, one doesn't ask for forgiveness (that's no doubt why one doesn't have the right to interpret this

_____

<inaudible word>?' Of course, does involuntary homicide mean 'no fault,' no wrong [*tort*]? The same ambiguity between the two registers, let's say, between knowledge and morality. Science, technoscience, competence, and honesty, those two registers are confused in the ambiguity of the word *tort*. 'I'm wrong [*j'ai tort*]' and 'I'm at fault [*j'ai tort*],' no? On the contaminated blood case see 156–60, 173–75 above.

55. [Translator's note:] Word in English in typescript.

278

declaration—in its both naive and sly literal meaning, playing being naive
as a ruse—as a request for forgiveness,[56] even if remorse is confessed), one
implies this: "I was wrong to act in that way because I didn't know, but I am
innocent." This rhetorical slippage—whose possibility is moreover inscribed
in the whole history of excuse and forgiveness—between the two registers
of knowledge and action, knowing and doing, technique and faith or good   279
faith, this rhetorical slippage governs moreover Clinton's entire text, which
we'll come back to.

Before Clinton himself comes on stage, we've built the set [*décor*], and
recalled a certain number of traits or solid [*massifs*] elements of the "external" context, if I can put it that way—what is a US president as citizen in
his country? What are his powers and the limits to his power, in particular
regarding his right to "pardon"? What does it mean that he has taken an
oath and sworn on the Bible? What is the role of the country he leads in
the world? What has happened in the world on the initiative of the United
States during "Monicagate," etc.? I won't go back over that, although those
elements of the context said to be "external," belonging to the *décor*, are essential to what is unfolding inside the "domestic" scene, in the two senses of
the word "domestic," especially in the United States, where it means above
all "national," interior to the nation—a domestic flight flies over American
territory only. "Domestic" is a good word here. What is domestic in the theater of Monicagate? The chance, the dice throw, as a result of which all these
affairs that put in danger the legitimacy of an American president are nicknamed some "-gate" or other (there was at least one other in the interval,[57]

56. During the session, Derrida comments: "He isn't asking for forgiveness. He has
been very careful in this text not to ask for forgiveness. Saying 'I am sorry for what I was
wrong to do' isn't asking forgiveness for a fault. He asked for forgiveness, as we spoke
of at the beginning of our seminar, in a private letter—which the press exposed, but
which was private—sent to his fellow worshippers but whose content wasn't divulged.
There he asked for forgiveness. This isn't a stated request for forgiveness or even a
statement of repentance." See 92–94 above.

57. During the session, Derrida adds: "There have been at least three," and a brief
discussion of this question takes place among the participants. Those scandals include
"Troopergate" (1993–94), following allegations by three police officers ("state troop-
ers") that they organized Bill Clinton's extramarital liaisons during his terms as governor of Arkansas (1971–81, 1983–92); "Chinagate," regarding illegal financing of the
1996 presidential campaign by a Chinese lobby, scandals that marked both domestic
and international politics of the Clinton administration. To those one can add "Whitewater," a controversy concerning investments made by the Clintons in the Whitewater
Development Corporation in Arkansas, "Travelgate," a controversy over the ethics of
the White House travel bureau, and "Filegate" (1996), which came to light following

280   during Clinton, between Watergate and Monicagate), well expresses, coin-
cidentally, something regarding the question of the threshold and the door,
of a limit that is or isn't crossed, notably between private and public, between family and civil society and the state.

I pretended to carefully calculate my calendar so that we would deal
with Monicagate in complete serenity once it was all said and done, at least
in appearance. Now it's over, since everybody has asked for forgiveness,
even Monica has also asked for forgiveness all the way to the bank (but not
for all the millions of dollars that her book has brought her, translated in
three days in France, and her television appearances), now that everybody
has offered their excuses, at least, and said to themselves "sorry,"[58] we can
take on the matter without being accused of interference in the domestic
affairs of this great friendly country. I recall that in the article "The Deconstruction of Clinton" (subjective and objective genitive, hey ho), and the
article is accompanied by a portrait of Clinton that tries to be a portrait of
Clinton deconstructing, his face multiplying, coming apart and proliferating as if in a shattered mirror or some fractal space, have a look (show or
circulate the *Los Angeles Times*)[59]—at bottom this seminar on perjury and
pardon is, as always, a seminar on the question, "what is deconstruction,
and notably on deconstruction in America, or the deconstruction of America?"—one of these idiotic articles from the *Los Angeles Times* that I called
attention to last time (but it wasn't the only one to do so), signed by the journalist Neal Gabler, author of a book entitled *An Empire of Their Own: How
the Jews Invented Hollywood*,[60] tries to demonstrate that this debate turns
281   around deconstruction, that is to say, for the author of the article, around
"relativism," "subjectivism," deconstruction being nothing but "relativism"
and "subjectivism." The article says: "When Clinton was accused of taking
refuge in narrow legalisms to save his skin, he was really taking refuge in a
deconstructionist view of reality. There was, he insisted, no single definition

---

White House access, in 1993–94, to confidential FBI files relating to members of the
Republican Party.

58. [Translator's note:] Word in English in typescript.

59. During the session, Derrida circulates the article and explains: "Pass it around,
it's interesting. It develops things further along, but just look at the picture. [*Laughter*]
You can give it back to me later." The article, beginning on page M1, continues on M6.
On the first page, to the left of the article, one can see an image by Lawrence Carroll
representing the diffracted face of the American president in a kaleidoscopic effect.
Under the image the word "Reality" is written in cut-and-pasted letters.

60. Neal Gabler, *An Empire of Their Own: How the Jews Invented Hollywood* (New
York: Crown Publishers, 1988). During the session, Derrida translates the title.

of sexual relations. Rather, there was a series of definitions, which made the whole idea of sexual relations completely subjective. Clinton's definition was just as good as anyone else's."[61] The author of the article is obviously alluding to the moment in Clinton's testimony under oath when, questioned whether he had had with Monica the "sexual relations" that he denied having had, and asked if he knew what sexual relations were, he supposedly replied, "That depends on what you call 'sexual relations,' and what you mean by 'is' when you say *it is* a sexual relation, it depends on what 'is' is."[62] We'll talk about that again.[63] And the author of "The Deconstruction of Clinton" adds this (but the selection of significant passages can leave the impression that the article is interesting or intelligent, whereas it is especially moronic, however symptomatic that idiocy be, and that is why I am quoting it, for example, when one reads in it the following):

> The House Republicans may not have realized they were entering into the deconstruction debate. They seemed to think they were engaged in a campaign to rid the country of a man they regard as an immoral leader. But in the longer view, the Clinton scandal not only raised the issue of deconstruction; it was the latest and fiercest battle in what we may now recognize as a long cultural civil war, the sides of which the two major parties have come to symbolize.[64]

282

So, behind deconstruction and the debate over deconstruction, which the Republicans don't see, there is civil war. I am totally ready to subscribe to that proposition (which I put forward in my own way about fifteen years ago),[65] but I just wonder why that civil war is limited to the United States. (Ad-lib translation of A, B, C, D from "The Deconstruction of Clinton.")

61. Gabler, "The Deconstruction of Clinton," M6 (Derrida translates the English here and below). See also Fifth Session, note 56 and note 92, above.

62. During the session, Derrida adds: "That's the deconstructionist Clinton, you see!" [*Laughter*] See 143n56, 154n92 above.

63. During the session, Derrida adds: "We'll deal with the question of the sexual relation. It won't be avoided. What is it? Where does it begin and end? What does deconstruction have to do with that? [*Laughter*]

64. Gabler, "Deconstruction of Clinton," M6.

65. See Derrida, "The Time Is Out of Joint," in Anselm Haverkamp and H. Robert Dodge, eds., *Deconstruction Is/in America: A New Sense of the Political* (New York: NYU Press, 1996), 14–38; "Déclarations d'indépendance," in *Otobiographies. L'Enseignement de Nietzsche et la politique du nom propre* (Paris: Galilée, 1984) ("Declarations of Independence," trans. Tom Keenan and Tom Pepper, in Elizabeth Rottenberg, ed., *Negotiations* [Stanford: Stanford University Press, 2002], 46–54); "Some Statements and Truisms about Neologisms, Newisms, Postisms, Parasitisms, and Other Small Seismisms,"

On one side [he describes the civil war between Republicans and Democrats] are the Republicans, most of whom seem to believe in an objective reality and an absolute morality [that is why they are opposed to deconstruction]. Though it may sound drastic to say [or to hear], if they often seem to act like the mullahs of Iran, it is because they think like those mullahs. [It has to be said that the article is at some points also hard on Republicans, because, being against deconstruction, he the journalist at least wants the Republicans to understand why. So these Republicans are like Iranian mullahs.] For them, every issue seems to resolve itself into black and white, wrong and right. Homosexuality is a sin against nature. Abortion is murder because life begins at the moment of conception. Not telling the full truth before a legal tribunal is a crime no matter what the circumstances.

. . .

As absolutists, they [Republicans] were fixated on extirpating the deconstructionist morality for which Clinton was the poster child, the same way that the ayatollah was fixated on extirpating satanic Western influences in Iran. Theirs was a holy war.

Meanwhile, across the battle lines are the Democrats, most of whom seem to believe in a subjective reality and a moral spectrum. If they seem to act like a bunch of aging hippies, it is because they think like a bunch of aging hippies. For them, every issue seems to resolve itself into grays [for the others, it's black and white; for them, it's gray, grayness], into provisional rights and provisional wrongs. Homosexuality isn't a sin but just another sexual preference or lifestyle. Abortion isn't murder but a decision that every woman should have the right to make for herself. And not telling the full truth in a court of law isn't necessarily perjury; it all depends on the circumstances. Theirs is no holy war. It is a gigantic therapy session in which everyone is allowed, in 1960s rhetoric, to do his or her own thing.

The battle between Republicans and Democrats, and between Clinton's attackers and his defenders, is really a battle of one truth [one thinking also, I venture to say] versus many truths, of fanatics versus relativists [there you have the only alternative that he could find: fanaticism and relativism, deconstruction naturally being on the side of relativism], of moral absolutism versus moral fuzziness, of an essentially religious view of politics versus a secular view of politics. [The same opposition is given currency between religious and secular, as though it were sufficient to be secular to be no longer religious.]

. . .

trans. Anne Tomiche, in David Carroll, ed., *The States of Theory: History, Art, and Critical Discourse* (New York: Columbia University Press, 1990), 63–94 (Thomas Dutoit and Philippe Romanski, eds., *Derrida d'ici, Derrida de là* [Paris: Galilée, 2009], 223–52).

This civil war is about the belief in an objective reality and an impla-   *284*
cable moral system. One suspects we will see people fall on their swords
before they give up that fight.[66]

I am not going to waste my time here to recall or demonstrate how the
use of the word "deconstruction" here presumes an arrogant illiteracy. It remains that this simplification is not to be denounced as a failing, someone's
failing with respect to thinking, reading, philology, culture, the history of
a word and of a debate, but as a structural given of public space and the
terms in which this whole debate is carried out and rigidified. This article
doesn't exist in isolation. I referred to another from the *Tuscaloosa News*, by
a journalist, Paul Greenberg, who, it happens, is the editor in the American
sense[67] of the *Arkansas Democrat Gazette*, and who signs his article from
Little Rock, Arkansas (a famous town, for reasons that you know, in the
state where Clinton was governor). In this article, "Not Everyone Is Fooled
[duped, deceived]," Greenberg puts in opposition the stability of words, of
the meanings of words, especially the word "is"—he also opposes to it absolute truth, what is "absolutely true"—and deconstruction. He even contrasts that truth with the beliefs of public opinion and polling. His conclusion is this: "Or in Mr. Lincoln's better and simpler words, you can't fool
all the people all the time. Polls change, truth does not. Not even in these
deconstructed times."[68]

These last words, this complaint about an era, about times that aren't
going so well, that are in full deconstruction, here understood in the moral
sense, in total decay, unhinged, totally mad, deranged, perturbed, flipped
out, completely corrupt, completely perverse, might recall one of the secure   *285*
meanings of Hamlet's complaint: "The time is out of joint," translated as
"time is off its hinges [*hors de ses gonds*]," but which also has this ethical sense
(well rendered in Gide's somewhat strange translation as "this era is dis-
graced [*déshonorée*]"—cf. *Specters of Marx*).[69] And deconstruction is indeed

66. Gabler, "Deconstruction of Clinton," M6.
67. [Translator's note:] That is, "editor" rather than "publisher [*éditeur*]."
68. Greenberg, "Not Everyone Is Fooled," 7A.
69. *Hamlet* I.v. See 155n94 above. "*Hors de ses gonds*" is Yves Bonnefoy's translation in *Hamlet, Le Roi Lear*, 68; Gide's is in Shakespeare, *La tragique histoire d'Hamlet*,
trans. André Gide, in *Oeuvres complètes*, vol. 2, ed. André Gide (Paris: Gallimard, Bibliothèque de la Pléiade, 1959), 633. See also Derrida, *Specters of Marx*, 19–20 (*Spectres
de Marx*, 44). During the session, Derrida explains: "A strange translation, but I tried
to explain in *Specters of Marx*—where I was interested in this translation—that it isn't
stupid; it has those connotations, I think. It <the era> is corrupted, it has lost its moral
direction, honor, etc."

often perceived as, or even accused of being, a disturbance, a disjunction, a means of breaking things apart (and I would be the last to say that this perception of deconstruction is simply false), and even of disgracing, of showing or evoking dishonor, infamy, etc.

What is it that is pitted against deconstruction here, but also, on the same side, against the instability of *doxa*, public opinion, polls ([70]which—a parenthetic digression—as you know, have been consistently favorable to Clinton, which has meant at the same time a change worth analyzing in the image one might have of American mores and moralism, something that has not only surprised the lagging American media—shown in this case to be out of joint with a public opinion of which they were thought to be, of which they themselves thought they were, everywhere and always fine analysts, both bearers and producers of such analyses, and as competent analysts in tune with their readers, and with whom they say they are in correspondence everywhere[71] (that's also one of the reasons why I am quoting these newspaper articles and editorials that are hostile to Clinton)—but also obliged the Republicans, given their anxiety about the elections, to follow public opinion in the end (which means, by the way, that so-called public opinion and the polls have ended up, before any formal democratic vote, determining what will have been, at the end of the day, officially, the statutory and legal truth of the verdict and hence of the case of Clinton as United States president, the remaining question being—we'll get to this—how to dissociate that statutory truth from a truth in general, a private, domestic, or religious truth, etc.))?

What, then, is pitted against deconstruction, but also, on the same side, against the instability of *doxa*, public opinion, polls, etc., is the stability,[72] the firm immobility of the true, in this case what is blithely called "objective

---

70. This parenthesis closes at the end of the paragraph.

71. During the session, Derrida comments: "The common trait of all journalists is that journalists know, or believe they know what readers think, they believe that they speak for their readers. They simply forget that they are read. Think of those journalists who, from week to week, come back with their columns, their critiques, their evaluations, etc.; they quite simply forget that readers judge the evaluators, but they think that they hear them. Here, in the case of the U.S., they have it all wrong, overwhelmingly. The media, it isn't only politicians who have public opinion all wrong, but also the media. They think they either understand or construct it."

72. During the session, Derrida explains: "Because what this journalist says ('Polls change, truth does not') is that polls change, truth doesn't change, but what he doesn't see is that it so happens that the polls haven't changed!"

truth." That is a grand tradition that goes back at least to Plato and Aristotle: the true is *bebaios*, firm, constant, stable. Truth has the stability of what *is* as substantiality or objectivity, the object of a constative and evidentiary judgment. And this truth of truth, this interpretation of truth as what doesn't change, is not subject to being affected by becoming or by history, in itself it has not changed, in the dominant *doxa* and in the hegemonic trending of philosophy. It is found everywhere—even in Hannah Arendt, for example (some years ago, on the subject of political lying and the media, we analyzed that discourse of Arendt's,[73] where precisely, with an unshakable optimism that made us a little suspicious, she affirmed that the truth always won out in the end over lying, and even over modern political lying, that is to say, for her, absolute, limitless lying, because truth, for its part, endures [*demeure*], it doesn't change, and it ends up defying time. I often wonder, observing Monicagate, what Hannah Arendt would have thought and said about this story, she who, as analyst, philosopher of politics, as a German who was expert in American political life, would have certainly taken sides. (If some of you want, on the basis of her texts, to try to reconstitute the virtual image of what her conclusion and position in this debate would have been, we could talk about that.) In any case, I think she would have subscribed to Greenberg's concluding formula, isolated from its context and from the motivations or the general strategy of the article, she would have subscribed to his conclusion that "Polls change, truth does not. Not even in these deconstructed times.")   287

When I become a little facile in my irony about the silliness and simplistic discourse from these two journalists (but I could quote others, not just journalists) concerning deconstruction, it is certainly not to deny that there is a thorny problem to be discussed about the *meaning of words*, the words "to be," the necessary but sometimes difficult-to-trace difference between, on the one hand—on the side of deconstruction—attention to polysemy, or even to dissemination, to context, to the impossibility of gaining access to the full presence of meaning and intention, specifically that of the other, hence to what happens when one speaks of lying and perjury (I'll come back to that very soon), attention to several statuses of truth, to

<hr/>

73. See Derrida, unpublished seminar, "Le témoignage," EHESS, 1994–95, Third and Fourth Sessions; and "Histoire du mensonge: Prolégomènes," *Cahier de L'Herne Derrida*, 495–520 (on Arendt in particular, 500–504, 510–16; *Histoire du mensonge: Prolégomènes*, 31–44, 72–79) ["History of the Lie: Prolegomena," in *Without Alibi*, 39–44, 51–68].

the certainly limited but undeniable performativity of discourses on the subject of truth, etc., and, on the other hand, what adversaries disturbed by deconstruction denounce as relativism, skepticism, subjectivism, nihilism. To believe, as I do, that those accusations of subjectivism, relativism, skepticism, and even nihilism are illegitimate, and testify to extreme shortsightedness or nonreading, is not sufficient to dispense with the problem. For in the end, as often happens, even when hostility, fear, and hatred are aggravated by ignorance, stupidity, or absence of culture, they can very well be guided, are surely guided by their very symptom, by fear or hatred, by idiocy sometimes, toward the place where things are occurring.[74] And it is true that with deconstruction the question or the history of truth, of veracity, lying and perjury, and hence other problems that are just as serious, enter a zone of considerable turbulence, which one never exits, which one will never exit; it is not even possible to settle on finally reassuring positions concerning skepticism, relativism, nihilism, etc., which produces still more turbulence. That doesn't mean any less that one has to buckle one's seatbelt, naturally, but without having the stupidity to believe that by buckling up one is going to end the turbulence, produce clear skies, or be sure of avoiding an accident. In this seminar we try to keep ourselves in the heart of that turbulence, or even in the eye of the hurricane. And at bottom, what we are doing here is consistently, directly or indirectly, a response to those objections. If those objections were to hold, if one were able to settle on this interpretation of deconstruction as relativism, skepticism, denial or disavowal of truth, one wouldn't even have to ask oneself anymore, as we however do, tenaciously, questions about unconditionality (which at least signifies an excess with regard to context, to the relativity of conditions, to everything that Kant called the hypothetical); we wouldn't even have to ask ourselves questions about the unconditionality of forgiveness, of hospitality, of the gift, of justice (distinguished from law), etc.

If, then, we need to send these journalists to do their homework[75] and ask them to work a little, that isn't to sidestep the issue and deny the problem. On the contrary, it is those problems that we are taking on here in

288

74. During the session, Derrida adds: "And I think that all these journalists have indeed seen where that is occurring. It is happening there. What is true? What of truth? And what about the verb 'to be'? And what about sexual difference? In the end, good questions. Where does it begin? That doesn't mean that we are going to be satisfied with the way in which the problem, the sexual relation, has been dealt with in these political instances, but the question 'It depends on what "is" is,' that's not a bad question about sexuality."

75. [Translator's note:] Word in English in typescript.

a way that is much more exposed and dangerous and apprehensive. For example, when the journalist Paul Greenberg writes this, which I am going to read more closely, but from which I'll first select and paraphrase this proposition, that even if—"as was pointed out by another distinguished president learned in the law, Richard M. Nixon"—"perjury is a hard rap to prove," well, Greenberg writes:

> There is still such a thing as perjury, even if we're regularly told it's impossible to prove. Non-presidents are regularly indicted for it, and convicted.
>
> There is also still meaning in words, even in words like *is*, alone, sexual relations, and *absolutely true*, no matter how often we are assured that the law has superseded the plain sense [obvious, normal, regular, everyday] of the English language.[76]   *289*

Well, when he says that, he is in one way correct. And in one way that is what we never stop repeating here, and I am going to come back to it again: there is perjury, but perjury is impossible to prove, in the strict sense of the word "prove," like it or not.[77] And saying that is not necessarily to do harm to truth and justice; on the contrary, I would say. But the fact that some try, strategically and cynically, to exploit this impossibility of proving lying or perjury (pardon also, moreover), that is indeed the possibility of evil that we are talking about. It remains that, conversely, casually claiming that perjury can be proven, that the fact that citizens are charged and convicted of it is enough to prove that perjury is provable, causes just as much injury or harm to truth or justice, one is being just as wrong about the truth of what "perjury" means.

I'll read first of all this passage from Greenberg's poisonous article, about which I'll say that it is all true, just, in a certain way, except that the opposite is also true, and one therefore has to think beyond that. It is true that there is perjury, it is true, by means of another truth, that some are charged with perjury and convicted of perjury by the courts. It is true that some, including a Nixon or a Clinton, can overplay the proposition that "perjury" is difficult, and, as I for my part would say, impossible to prove, that it is not of the order of proof, well, nevertheless, those cynical abuses or manipulations do not prevent it from being true that perjury or lying cannot be

76. Greenberg, "Not Everyone Is Fooled," 7A.

77. During the session, Derrida adds: "And if Nixon or others have tried to exploit the fact that perjury is impossible to prove, it remains that perjury is impossible to prove, as is lying. One cannot allege that some use the fact that lying is impossible to prove, as we have proved here, in order to say the contrary, namely, that lying must be proven, that perjury is a truth." See 141–43 above.

proven, and that even when the court convicts someone of perjury, it does so, contrary to what it says, without proof. So, I'll quickly read this passage from Greenberg before concluding and announcing briefly our program for subsequent sessions. (Read, translate, and comment on Greenberg G.)

290   Of course, the president did not set out from the first to wind up in the dock. He just made decision after decision, and wound up where he now rightfully is. He may even have thought he was staying within the law by his own evasive, pettifogging, bizarre, word-maiming logic ["word-maiming," that is to say crippled, crippling, mutilating, injuring]. After all, perjury is a hard rap to prove, as was pointed out by another distinguished president learned in the law, Richard M. Nixon.

But there is still such a thing as perjury, even if we're regularly told it's impossible to prove. Non-presidents are regularly indicted for it, and convicted.

There is still meaning in words, even in words like *is*, alone, sexual relations, and *absolutely true*, no matter how often we are assured that the law has superseded the plain sense of the English language [this is what I read just now].

Whatever the outcome of this tangled web fast unraveling, even if it turns out that perjury, too, is a meaningless word in the American lexicon circa 1996, this much has been made clear by the two-day parade of witnesses supposedly in the president's defense: The president has forfeited any moral initiative he ever had in this endless controversy.

Bill Clinton seems to want to plead guilty to any offenses other than legal ones. [All his crimes, except those sanctioned by the law: that is what he does in the text that I read; he says "sorry," he has remorse about everything, except for what his attorneys are taking care of, that is to say perjury, the fact of having lied in a court deposition. He doesn't acknowledge that: "I acknowledge anything you want, except my legal failings."] And he seems willing to give up anything to escape judgment except what has

291   always been the holy grail of his existence: his public office, his precious career. His order of moral priorities, and perhaps the country's, has seldom been so clear. Or so depressing.[78]

Next time, we'll reexamine Clinton's declarations and follow three guiding threads: (1) "perjury" and "pardon"; (2) "domesticity"; and (3) the ques-

---

78. Greenberg, "Not Everyone Is Fooled," 7A. In the typescript, Derrida had prepared glosses on certain expressions in English to follow the quoted passage: " 'wind up the dock [*sic*],' to go back up to the prisoner's dock; 'pettifogging,' quibbling (insignificant details); 'word-maiming logic' (to maim: cripple, mutilate, injure); 'hard rap to prove': rap: accusation, charge (even conviction)."

tion "what is a sexual relation?"—where does that begin and end, which is to say: how was Clinton, and recently also Lewinsky—with her costly televised declarations and in her book translated in three days in France (when one thinks of the difficulty one has getting good books translated in this country)—able to say, lying without lying, that they didn't have sexual relations?

March 31, 1999

[1]I want us to speak, as one must do in a seminar, in a way that is, how should I put it, as complicated as possible, respecting all the complications and without transforming one's speech into private speech. I think that things have been tragic and entangled enough for a long time in Europe, and in this zone of Europe, painful enough that nobody can give themselves permission to lecture and say what has to be done or what should have been done, etc. Given that caveat, before even entering into the question of the current sequence of events, which is difficult to unpack, it is a sequence of events based on enormous premises, but let's suppose that one were able to unpack the present sequence of events, that is to say, the massive aerial intervention that you know about; before even entering into that, and in order to tie it into the theme of the seminar, precisely at this moment when the question of sovereignty is being posed in the terms that you are aware of, the difference between sovereignty and unconditionality, one of the arguments that, in good or bad faith, Serbs can advance in opposition to the current intervention, is the argument of national sovereignty. The difference between the Gulf War and the war in Kosovo—I am saying this slowly, don't take it on too quickly, one mustn't go too fast, we are analyzing things—the difference between the Gulf War and the current intervention, in spite of certain similarities, namely, the violence of a powerful aerial and technologically heavily armed intervention, etc., the difference is that in the case of the Gulf War, Iraq had violated the sovereignty of a foreign state. So, in the name of international law and its logic, its conventional axiomatics, there had been an act of war that called for an act of war: a sovereign state had

294

1. The text that follows, concerning the conflict in Kosovo and the 1999 intervention by NATO, was prepared by Derrida and read at the end of the discussion session of March 31, 1999. It followed a presentation by Joseph Cohen and a question-and-answer period.

violated the sovereignty of another state. In the case of Kosovo, the Serbs will say that, after all, until further notice, Kosovo is part of the confederation, it isn't a national state. The question of sovereignty is posed, it isn't a national state: as a consequence, this is an intervention that, from the point of view of international law, cannot argue legitimacy under international law. That is why, moreover, the United Nations has not yet entered the fray; it is an <*inaudible*> question that, in the name of a certain principle of security within Europe and questions of human rights, we'll come to this, doesn't apply. This situation is new. Imagine, imagine that pieces of states in countries other than Yugoslavia were to claim their independence; in France, Brittany or the Savoie, imagine a principle of military intervention against France, imagine Algeria, or else of course Corsica—well-thinking French will say that for the moment there is nothing going on in Corsica that is like what paramilitary Serb militias are carrying out in Kosovo, so, there is no violation of human rights, that doesn't justify interventions of this type—but Algeria. . . . In Algeria, things took place such that, it could be shown, if it's not known it will be, things such that, if it were taking place today, one could envisage an aerial strike on France, on Algeria, on French positions in Algeria.[2] At the time nobody would have thought of that, France would not have even begun to accept such an intervention, and moreover, nobody would have thought of it in Europe and throughout the world. So, this means that over the last few decades there has been a profound transformation of public space, of international law, of the question of sovereignty today, and moreover it isn't the case everywhere else in the world, it wasn't even the case in Europe, close to Europe, a few decades ago, the violation [*violation*] of the rights of man did not give rise to a violation [*viol*] of sovereignty, to an intervention. Now there is an intervention inside the territory of the nation-state of Yugoslavia in the name of human rights, and it isn't only because Kosovars have the right to self-determination, it is because Serbs are indulging in Kosovo in appalling things, inadmissible from the point of view of human rights, that sovereignty is no longer a sacrosanct principle, Serbian or Yugoslav sovereignty is no longer sacrosanct. And that has changed, it wasn't the case not so long ago, and it is changing only in particular parts of the world, it doesn't apply everywhere. The United States or NATO doesn't intervene wherever there are massacres or virtual genocides or violations of human rights. So in that context already, one has to take note of the profound transformation of international law, of

295

2. [Translator's note:] Derrida is referring to the Algerian War of Independence (1954–62).

European law, in order to hear the allegations on one side and the other of the juridical and political debate that is going on at present on all sides, and this is an illustration, a symptom of what is happening with sovereignty today. It is a tragic, appalling example, but it attests to the fact that something very radical is in the process of affecting our concept of political sovereignty. First thing.

So now one comes to the current sequence of events that I, for my part, would like to debate. While condemning, denouncing, taking exception to the violence committed by the Serbian government, by Serbian militia, etc.—I don't want to insist, you know my discourse on that, everyone is agreed on that, and <Slobodan> Milošević and the politics he represents, because he isn't all alone, in an alliance that is more or less outdated, in reality historic, with Russia—nevertheless, given that premise, I am among those who think, and I notice that we are more numerous than I thought, that the decision to intervene in this way was, on the one hand, inappropriate,[3] it was at bottom suspect in all respects because, as we have just seen, on the one side, it could have been foreseen that it would reinforce Milošević's authority, that it would unite all Serbs around him, that what remains of the opposition to Milošević and that has been working against him for ten years would be weakened, even wiped out, and testimonies, even from those opposed to Milošević, tell us: "There, with this intervention you have just destroyed our work of the last ten years"; <because>, on the other hand, they will be given free rein, without witnesses, after the withdrawal of the troops that were on the ground and the withdrawal of journalists, etc., Serbian militias in Kosovo will be given free rein to indulge in the worst things for the present and for the future. We were talking just now about forgiveness and crime, of the present and its interminable effects: it is clear that the Serbs, or in any case paramilitary militias, are currently in the process of destroying, of exterminating not only masses of people but everything that would allow Kosovar society to be reconstituted, to survive, to be reinstalled, to start up again. And with this intervention, it is as if they have been encouraged, they are given a completely free hand. Consequently, there again, on the basis of premises upon which everybody was in agreement, namely, that Serbian policy was unacceptable in all respects, catastrophic consequences have been drawn—why, the question is why?—consequences that all sorts of experts were in a position to predict, to calculate, military experts in particular. One can take stock of the fact that military, high-tech, etc., superpower is absolutely powerless and inappropriate for conflicts over territory that develop

296

3. [Translator's note:] The French word used is *inopportune*, also "untimely."

in situations such as these, and one can fire smart missiles at all sorts of targets, but one cannot even risk occupying the land where these things are happening. And why is that? The question is why, in this particular case. Why? We come back to Clinton. . . . Why are the Americans acting in this manner, in the name of human rights, by ensuring their military and economic supremacy? Why is Europe, and the French in particular, aligned with the American policy? Why is the government aligned with the head of state—on the pretext that the head of state is the one to decide when it comes to foreign relations, in what is a virtual electoral campaign, where it is a matter of knowing who will be best placed, etc.—all that in the name of human rights? For what has to be seen clearly here is the fact that what legitimates, in the discourse of legitimation of this operation, what legitimates it in the final analysis is its reference to crimes against humanity; one comes back to that all the time. It is because crimes against humanity are being committed in Kosovo that they give themselves permission to intervene in this style, in this way, and with this blindness. I don't say . . . it is not about lecturing, I don't really know what should have been done concretely, I say that they should have explored possibilities other than this one, which, while being difficult in my view, is perhaps the worst, we'll see down the line. Moreover, I see that even in the governmental speeches made by the head of state, to justify what is happening at present, one can hear what is unconscious, underground about everything that I am telling you. No one has called for it, it hasn't been noted, but I think that it could be done differently, that it will be done differently, it is certain from here on that these aerial strikes are not able in and of themselves to solve the problem. There you have it, something else has to happen. What? I don't know. There, that is roughly what I wanted to say.

<A participant asks a question about the suffering of the victims and the matter of territory.>

Precisely, that is why it isn't working: because the question of the suffering of the victims of crimes against humanity is happening within a territory, is it not? If one says that to fight against the crimes that they have committed against the Kosovars, etc., the question of territory is not something that can be dealt with on a computer, or virtually, it is taking place within the territory. Otherwise, in fact, one can deal with it the way they are doing at this point, but in effect by allowing the massacre to continue. I think that because they don't take territory seriously. . . . So, that reminds us that territory always exists, in modern politics today, where territory, everything is deterritorialized, isn't it, from a military and political point of view; wherever there is suffering, death, extermination, exodus, there is territory.

297

And what is going on right now is over territory. And the least they could do—this is something I forgot to say—but the least they could do, from the point of view of the governments that claim to act in the name of human rights, now that the decision to intervene has been made—the wrong decision, as I see it, to intervene in the way they have—is at least to take care of refugees, that at least they can go to Albania, Macedonia, and elsewhere, let them welcome in France or in the United States or in England or in Germany the hundreds of thousands or tens of thousands of Kosovars who are currently in the territory trying to survive.

298   <A participant intervenes to clarify that it is precisely Milošević's policy to make the Kosovars leave the territory.>

Of course, no, I say *now that* the decision has been made. . . . No, I am not saying that they must do that, but since they are doing that, let them at least act consistently with their own logic. . . . That isn't what my logic is! But since they are doing that in the name of human rights, then at least let them take care of humans.

April 7, 1999

"Imagine, I wasn't thinking about it."[1]

What would you say to someone who, in response to being accused of perjury, as you were saying to them, "But when all is said and done, you are a liar [*vous êtes parjure*], you committed perjury, you were lying, dissimulating, you knew that you were lying and perjuring yourself right then," what would you say to someone who then replied, "That's true. Imagine, I wasn't thinking about it. Thanks."?

"I wasn't thinking about it" doesn't mean "I forgot," but "I wasn't thinking about it." Can one commit perjury "without thinking about it," or absentmindedly, or because that isn't the moment to be thinking about it? Is that an excuse? An extenuating circumstance? Is it forgivable to "not think about it"? Not to think at all, of all the presumptions and implications of what one is doing or saying? Is not-thinking a failing? What is thinking called, in that case? Let's leave that question for later, along with this one: how can we lie and say "we," or, in saying "we," and while thinking that we are thinking, admitting, and asking for or granting forgiveness, how can we tell ourselves the truth, and the truth about "us," but also, how can we betray, disavow, lie about, deny, repudiate, abjure the supposed truth about *us*?   *300*

1. Henri Thomas, *Le Parjure* (Paris: Gallimard, 1964), 134; Kamuf's translation in *Without Alibi* (see below). Substantial sections of this session were republished with additions and modifications in "Le parjure, peut-être ('brusques sautes de syntaxe')," *Études françaises*, 15–57, (see especially 17–57), and in *Cahier de L'Herne Derrida*, 577–600, then as the book *Le parjure, peut-être ("Brusques sautes de syntaxe")* (see especially 13–121) [cf. "'*Le Parjure*,' Perhaps," trans. Peggy Kamuf, in Derrida, *Without Alibi*, 171–99]. During the session, Derrida reads the quotation twice. [Translator's note:] My translation below of Derrida's "second digression," "Hölderlin in America," is greatly indebted to Kamuf's in *Without Alibi* (171–99), including her translations from Thomas, *Le Parjure*. Certain stylistic modifications have been made to conform with choices made throughout this volume.

Last time,[2] while directly or obliquely continuing our reflection on the concept of sovereignty, the history and current stakes of the concept of sovereignty, on the distinction, so fine but so indispensable, between sovereignty and unconditionality (reflecting on sovereignty such as could be put to the test in the case of recent geopolitical monstrosities on the borders of, and within, Kosovo, something we began doing last week), we promised to reexamine Clinton's declarations by following three guiding principles: (1) "perjury" and "pardon"; (2) domesticity;[3] and (3) the question "what is a sexual relation?"—where does that begin and end, which is to say, how was Clinton, and recently also Lewinsky, how were they able to say, lying without lying, that they didn't have sexual relations, a sexual relation worthy of the name?

In order to stay as close as possible to the problematic of our seminar, let us put ourselves in the articulation between perjury *and* pardon, in the conjunction or disjunction between the two. The whole politicians' strategy employed by Clinton and his adversaries concerns itself with the play of this "and," with this conjunction or disjunction that will simultaneously conjoin, connect [*ajointer*] or disjoin, according to each case and its relevance, the religious and the ethical, the ethical and the legal or political, the private and the public. How is that so?

In the declaration by Clinton that we began to read and comment on, the president, as you remember, positioned himself so as not to ask literally for forgiveness, and especially not to confess to committing perjuring, the very perjury the Republicans were accusing him of or wanted to accuse him of, "legal" perjury, an offense punishable by the law when, in a codified situation, in a judicial theater, a witness who is under oath, having sworn[4] [*juré*] to tell the truth, the whole truth, and nothing but the truth, comes to a point where they mislead the jury, the "Grand Jury,"[5] in bad faith.

301   It would be worth dedicating a separate study to the multiple, tangled reasons why perjury, the offense of perjury, which is indeed inscribed in all the legal systems of the European tradition, nevertheless finds in the United States its zone of the most intense gravity. To my knowledge, it is

---

2. Derrida is referring to the discussion session of March 31, 1999.

3. During the session, Derrida clarifies: "The domestic, private dimension, or domesticity in general: internal affairs, international affairs, private or public affairs."

4. [Translator's note:] The lexical relation between *jurer* ("to swear," "take an oath," which is what a "juror" does), and *perjurer* ("to lie," "perjure oneself") is constantly reinforced in this discussion. Remember also that the noun *le parjure*, as in the title of Henri Thomas's novel, refers both to "perjurer" and "act of perjury."

5. [Translator's note:] Words in English in typescript.

in the United States that the offense of perjury is named and tracked, by that name, with the greatest frequency, and with an obsessive insistence. The occurrence of the word "perjury," the threat of prosecution against the "perjurer," in official documents, wherever a commitment is made, wherever a declaration is made, and practically wherever a signature is required, the repetition of the word "perjury" seems to me—pending a systematic inventory—much more frequent in the United States than in any other Western country.[6] In fact, you cannot sign a public document without being warned, or without having to read, without it being presumed that you have read, officially, legally, how perjury is seriously sanctioned by the law. That is indeed absolutely significant, and I am not criticizing a gesture that merely renders explicit, that merely thematizes a universal implication of the law, and of the Western social contract, on condition that the legal subject understands the language or is able to understand or read what they are thereby reminded of, namely, that ignorance of the law—before which one is compelled in advance, and before which one is required to appear—being no excuse, truth, truthfulness [*veracité*] and good faith are owed by whoever promises to provide them, beginning with the truthfulness of the promise. That is a promise whose structure is therefore giddily complicated here, by a complication that is going to be reinvested and capitalized upon in the act of perjury. For if I perjure myself, if I lie in giving what is called false witness, it is because I have perhaps already lied (not necessarily and not always, but perhaps), I have perhaps previously lied by promising (genuinely, let's presume) to tell the truth: I have already lied by promising truthfulness (one must always tell truthfulness rather than the truth, for lying or perjuring oneself doesn't mean saying what is false or untrue, but saying something other than what one thinks, not by being mistaken but by deliberately deceiving the other). I have perhaps already lied in promising to tell the truth, lied before lying by not telling the truth. We can thus see how the time of perjury is divided from its very first instant. When I accuse myself of committing perjury or when I accuse someone of committing perjury, the accusation of perjury, every accusation of perjury can go in one or two directions at the same time: *either* this or that: either both accusing that someone of betraying, in a second time [*temps*], a sincere promise that in a first time I would have made and then not kept, the betrayal in that way following—as a second original time—a commitment that was first of all honest and made in good faith, authentic;

302

---

6. [Translator's note:] "Perjury" and "perjurer" in English in typescript, except that here and below Derrida uses the rarer English spelling, "perjuror."

or else (even at the same time), I can accuse the perjurer of lying from the first, of having already committed perjury by promising to tell the truth, so by swearing first of all, perjuring themself by swearing. One can commit perjury, then, after having sworn, but one can perjure oneself by swearing, and if those two temporalities or two structures seem after the event to be enveloped one in the other, to imply each other de jure if not de facto, they are in principle distinct. I can always say, whether one believe me or not, whether one take it into account or not, "I have sincerely promised to tell the truth, or promised this or that, promised to be faithful to my promise, promised to be faithful to my word, faithful *tout court*," and then following that, for one reason or another, or for no reason other than the return of my bad behavior [*méchanceté*], my malevolence, or even a loss of love, or a self-transformation, commit a betrayal. But that betrayal comes about only in a second time; when I promised under oath [*j'ai promis juré*], I was sincere, in good faith, I didn't perjure myself.

Those two times are both rigorously distinct and strangely indiscernible. But the difference in times is inscribed in the law of the contract, the contracting, sacred [*sacral*], sacramental law, which is destined precisely to annul temporal difference: the essential destination, the structural signification of the oath or word given is a commitment not to be affected by time, to remain the same at moment B — whatever may happen — as the one who swears previously, at moment A. This sublating negation of time is the very essence of fidelity, of the oath, and of swearing by one's faith [*de la foi jurée*]. And the perjurer, the one who perjures themself, may always seek to be excused, if not forgiven, by alleging on the contrary the unsublatable density of time and of what it transforms. One can say, for example: "I sincerely promised last year, but time has passed, and he who promised last year can remain faithful to his promise, but that's no longer me, I am no longer the same I, 'I is an other,'[7] I am an other, I've changed in a year, and everything has changed, and those to whom my promise was addressed have also." A basic, but difficult to dispute psychology can affirm that, in certain cases, someone, me, an "I," may sincerely and seriously commit themself under oath to tell the truth, the whole truth, and nothing but the truth, and then,

303

---

7. Derrida is quoting poet Arthur Rimbaud's famous formula in his "Lettre du voyant" (Rimbaud, "Lettre à Paul Demeny, 15 mai 1871," in *Œuvres complètes*, ed. André Guyaux and Aurélia Cervoni (Paris: Gallimard [Pléiade], 2009), 34 [Rimbaud, *Complete Works*, trans. Paul Schmidt (New York: HarperCollins, 2008), 115].

in a second time,[8] for one reason or another, show themself not to be up to the promise, incapable of keeping it or capable of betraying it, perverting it, recanting, etc. And the way this process unfolds, the drama of this diachrony, would be distinguishable from that of another scenario, that of someone who is already lying, and already commits perjury, at the moment of the oath and the promise.[9] This bifid structure is not without consequence on the stage of repentance and forgiveness. To ask for forgiveness or offer excuses[10] may amount to confirming the sincerity of the initial commitment and show betrayal, if not as an inessential accident, at least as a second moment of failure [*chute*], a second, if not secondary corruption, one that is in the first place unforeseeable: "I was sincere in promising this or that, faithfulness, but I couldn't foresee this change, these events, everything that happened, or someone, some other who has arrived in the interval, where the other can be another, a third person, or myself, etc." I won't insist, you know those scenarios, our lives are made of them.

Since, getting ready to come back to the Clinton case, we are referring to what we might call American perjury and pardon, the American dimension and determination of perjury/pardon, I will make two long digressions that I hope are pertinent, which is to say nondigressive: when one wishes to be forgiven for digressions, one attempts to demonstrate that they are necessary and that they are therefore not sidesteps, false steps, distractions, deviations. These digressions are not deviations. They concern events that are by nature quite different, but which have in common the fact of being situated in the Americas. *304*

I'll give them two titles in the form of two proper names: (1) *Augustus and Mark Anthony in America*; (2) *Hölderlin in America*. They are naturally two family histories and two stories of madmen (all family histories are no doubt stories of madmen); one of those histories left thousands of victims and dead bodies behind it, whereas the other touches also on poetry and thinking, on a certain *dichten/denken*. But they have in common the family, perjury and the Americas.

---

8. During the session, Derrida adds: "Which may be either an instant later, or a year later, or a lifetime later."

9. During the session, Derrida adds: "That is something else, they know in advance that they won't be faithful."

10. During the session, Derrida adds: "That is not the same thing, but let's treat them temporarily within the same concept." See Derrida, *Perjury and Pardon*, vol. 1, 163ff. [*Parjure et pardon*, vol. 1, 217ff.].

First digression: *Augustus and Mark Anthony in America*. You know that, during a trip to Africa, Clinton found it timely and just to recognize publicly (without asking for forgiveness and without doing it by means of a solemn act on behalf of the state) the crime of slavery and the trade in African slaves practiced by his country.[11] He didn't call that a "crime against humanity," which would have provoked certain consequences: he didn't draw the present-day consequences of this past for the situation of African Americans, as one may think he should have or could have done, but at least he said something, publicly, in Africa, about the crime that his country had participated in. A past crime, according to him, an interminable crime others might say who were a little less comatose [*endormis*]. Well, in the same way, some weeks back, he expressed his regrets in recognizing that the policies of the United States in Latin America had often been, at least since the war, "wrong,"[12] let's say regrettable.[13] You know the enormous

305

11. Bill Clinton made an extensive tour of Africa from March 23 to April 2, 1998, in the course of which he visited Ghana, Uganda, Rwanda, South Africa, Botswana, and Senegal. This was the first such trip by an American president since the visit by President Carter in 1978. On March 24, 1998, during his stay in Uganda, Clinton expressed his regrets, on behalf of the American people, for the slave trade. See Frederic Fritscher, "Bill Clinton a reçu un accueil mitigé en Afrique," *Le Monde*, April 1, 1998, https://www.lemonde.fr/archives/article/1998/04/01/bill-clinton-a-recu-un-accueil-mitige-en-afrique_3648917_1819218.html. [Cf. James Bennet, "Clinton in Africa: The Overview; in Uganda, Clinton expresses regret on slavery in U.S.," *New York Times*, March 25, 1998, A1, https://www.nytimes.com/1998/03/25/world/clinton-africa-overview-uganda-clinton-expresses-regret-slavery-us.html. See also "Remarks at the Kisowera School in Mukono, Uganda March 24, 1998," *Weekly Compilation of Presidential Documents* 34, 13 (1998): 491, https://www.govinfo.gov/content/pkg/WCPD-1998-03-30/pdf/WCPD-1998-03-30.pdf]. During the session, Derrida adds: "I don't know whether or not I read at the time an article that appeared a year ago in the *New York Times*, on April 5, 1998, written by a certain Thomas Geoghegan, who said concerning that event—at the moment when Clinton in Africa recognized that America had practiced slavery and conducted the slave trade, and how that was not right, etc., something he recognized in a certain diplomatic context—and this journalist said: "But Lincoln already did that!" going on to quote various texts by Lincoln who, so long ago, had said similar things. One should read all that. If we have the time, I'll read it later. It isn't the most important point today." See "Lincoln Apologizes" (cf. 155n95 above).

12. [Translator's note:] Word in English in typescript.

13. [Translator's note:] Derrida appears to be referring to remarks made by Clinton during his visit in March 1999 to Central American countries, in particular Guatemala. See Charles Babington, "Clinton: Support for Guatemala Was Wrong," *Washington Post*, March 11, 1999, https://www.washingtonpost.com/wp-srv/inatl/daily/march99/clinton11.htm.

reality—continental and transcontinental, in truth global—that is covered over by such an avowal. American politics in Latin America, by means of what is indeed most "regrettable" about it, has no doubt decided the fate of the world at least since World War II and throughout what is called the Cold War. And at bottom, since I am pronouncing these words, the "Cold War," one can probably date the great unleashing of forgiveness on the stage of the world and of globalization from the end of the so-called "Cold War," as though forgiveness always signified the end *both* of the war (a trivial remark), but especially the end of the cold, *and* of the horizon of a Cold War. One might analyze interminably the givens of that historic fundament [*fonds*], which has determined North American politics in Latin America and the referent pointed to by Clinton in recognizing that those policies were inappropriate.[14]

Now, what is happening to the character Pinochet, the great friend of Margaret Thatcher,[15] as you know, would there give us but one of the very numerous *threads*[16] to be followed in the analysis or memory of this terrible history, and in what might have been "regrettable" about American politics in Latin America. Instead of the threads surrounding Pinochet [*Au lieu des fils de Pinochet*], and because we don't have much time, I'll tighten things by speaking to you a little about what is going on and going through the sons of Pinochet [*les fils de Pinochet*]. We come back once more to the great scene of pardon/perjury as familial scene, father/son (Hamlet, Kafka, mother/son

306

14. During the session, Derrida adds: "This word, 'inappropriate,' is always—we have already analyzed that—both the most frequent and the most equivocal word."

15. During the session, Derrida adds: "And also of <Henry> Kissinger. Henry Kissinger, a controversial figure in American politics, was national security advisor and secretary of state under Nixon, and secretary of state under President Gerald Ford. He received the Nobel Peace Prize in 1973. On October 22, 1998, Margaret Thatcher (1925–2013), who was British prime minister from 1979 to 1990, stirred up a polemic by publishing in the London *Times* a letter criticizing the arrest of Augusto Pinochet (1915–2006), who "did so much to save so many British lives" during the Falklands War against Argentina in 1982. See Nathalie Chiesa, "L'Ex-Dame de fer Thatcher à la rescousse de Pinochet. Polémique après son éloge de l'ancien dictateur chilien," *Libération*, October 23, 1998, 9, https://www.liberation.fr/planete/1998/10/23/l-ex-dame -de-fer-thatcher-a-la-rescousse-de-pinochet-polemique-apres-son-eloge-de-l-ancien -dictateur_248873/ [cf. "Thatcher Demands Pinochet's Release," *BBC News*, October 22, 1998, http://news.bbc.co.uk/2/hi/uk_news/198574.stm]. See also "Henry Kissinger fidèle à Pinochet," *Libération*, April 5, 1999, https://www.liberation.fr/planete /1999/04/05/henry-kissinger-fidele-a-pinochet_270356/.

16. [Translator's note:] The French word is *fils*, also "sons." See ensuing discussion.

Hamlet, Baudelaire, etc.).[17] Augusto Pinochet has two sons. The older, Augusto Junior, who bears the imperial first name of his father, came to notice—you've no doubt seen that on television—through his vehement protests and threatening outbursts of anger at the time of the arrest of his dad, Augusto Senior, in London. The whole family reprimanded him for it, and let it be known that his declarations weren't authorized, no more than was the fundraising[18] campaign, the collection of monies that he organized to cover Papa Augusto's legal fees. Which reminds me, to come back to Clinton for a moment, keeping it in the family, in the globalization of the family, that I saw on television, on CNN in Norway, in a hotel in Oslo, an interview with Monica Lewinsky's father and stepmother. The father, a cancer specialist from Chicago, doesn't like Clinton, as you might imagine. He hates him. He especially hates Linda Tripp,[19] but also Clinton. Now it happens that he is a Democrat, and in the course of events he got hot under the collar for having received from the Democratic Party a circular asking for funds to cover Clinton's legal fees.[20] The happy circumstance that was accorded me in seeing this interview on CNN (as if I have to travel to know what is happening on CNN, which I don't subscribe to at home) impels me to correct an injustice that I was guilty of last time.[21] I have to be forgiven for being ironic about the money Monica is earning from her book of interviews. I have learned from her father that she has needed much more to cover her lawyers' fees and that it is because of that massive debt, millions of dollars, that she had to publish the book. For behind all these scenes of perjury and pardon, concerning sexual relations that weren't such, or that would have been without being so—for, as Lacan and Clinton say with different accents, there is no sexual relation,[22] presuming at least that we

307

17. On Hamlet and Baudelaire, see Derrida, *Perjury and Pardon*, vol. 1, 118–36; on Kafka, 96–100, 104–5, 119–20 [*Pardon et parjure*, vol. 1, 163–84; 139–44, 148–49, 165–66].

18. [Translator's note:] Word in English in typescript.

19. Monica Lewinsky's colleague at the Public Relations Office at the Pentagon and a key figure in the 1998–99 scandal that led to impeachment proceedings against Clinton.

20. During the session, Derrida adds: "They are asking *me* for money [*Laughter*] to support my daughter's seducer!"

21. See 213, 216 above.

22. Jacques Lacan uttered this famous statement for the first time in his 1971 seminar: "There is no sexual relation in the speaking being," adding for clarity, "the sexual relation like any other relation, when all is said and done, subsists only on what is written" (Lacan, *Séminaire Livre XVIII. D'un discours qui ne serait pas du semblant*, ed. Jacques-Alain Miller [Paris: Seuil, 2007], 65, my translation [DW]). See also Lacan,

can indeed agree on what a sexual relation is, and what *is* is, what *is* is in this case²³—well, behind all these scenes of perjury and pardon, concerning sexual relations that weren't such while all along being so, enormous sums of money are in play, enormous debts have to be paid, dollar amounts that would be enough to keep alive, in the United States even, not to speak of other countries,²⁴ hundreds of thousands of those "without," those without a roof over their head [*sans abri*] and those without papers. So, she published her memoirs to pay her attorneys. As I have written in a very different context—but it comes back down to the same thing—one always writes to be forgiven,²⁵ which is to say to pay one's debts. But, of course, there is debt and debt. I return to the American family and to the father-and-son Pinochet empire. While Augusto Jr., the older son, was disowned by his family, the younger son, for his part, who also bears an imperial name, Marco Antonio, managed to be noticed in turn and to appear on the theatrical stage in a very different role. Far from protesting against the arrest of Julius Caesar, or of Papa Augusto, he comes to the point, two weeks ago, in an interview with a local newspaper, of recognizing that human rights had been violated during the seventeen years of the military regime under the authority of his dad. He even declares, this Mark Anthony, speaking of lying: "Whoever says that there were no abuses [or violations of human rights] is lying."²⁶ Since he is using a word—at least in the English version where I am reading what he said, in the *Daily Telegraph* (communicated to me by Dailey, Patricia Dailey, who is present here and whom I thank)—a word that is very significant for its equivocality, and that happens to be the same as that

308

"L'Étourdit," *Scilicet* 4 (1973): 5–52 (especially 11, 20–21, 30, 47–50) ["L'Étourdit," trans. Cormac Gallagher, *The Letter: Irish Journal for Lacanian Psychoanalysis* 41 (2009): 31–80 (especially 32, 46–52, 56–58, 66–70), http://theletter.ie/issue-41-summer-2009].

23. [Translator's note:] Preceding clause in English.

24. During the session, Derrida adds: "Without speaking of those expelled from Kosovo."

25. Derrida, "Circumfession," in Geoffrey Bennington and Derrida, *Jacques Derrida*, trans. Geoffrey Bennington (Chicago: University of Chicago Press, 1993), 46: "one always asks for pardon when one writes" ["Circonfession," in *Jacques Derrida* (Paris: Seuil, 1991), 47]; and "Living On," trans. James Hulbert in John P. Leavey, ed., *Parages* (Stanford: Stanford University Press, 2011): "We always ask to be forgiven when we write or recite" (166) ["Survivre," in *Parages* (Paris: Galilée, 2003), 176]. Derrida had quoted this sentence the previous year (see Derrida, *Perjury and Pardon*, vol. 1, 41n68 [*Parjure et pardon*, vol. 1, 73n1].

26. Statement by Marco Antonio Pinochet, quoted in Louise Egan, "Pinochet's Son Hints at Apology for Abuses," *Daily Telegraph*, March 23, 1999, 11. Here and in following quotations Derrida either translates or reads from the English.

chosen by Clinton or his attorneys ("inappropriate"), I'll quote what he says: "I think there were people who took advantage of the situation, who took power into their hands and did things that were not appropriate [suitable, decent (*convenables*), not good, they did things that weren't all right, a euphemism that avoids saying "crime" or suggesting that the crimes were also errors, mistakes, things that shouldn't have been done in that situation, bad choices (*calculs*) also; something inappropriate, something not good isn't a crime or radical evil, the euphemism consisting in a plea for extenuating circumstances]," and he adds, "perhaps there were excesses [the word "excess" has the same euphemistic ambiguity as the word "inappropriate"]. I do not deny that."[27]

And then, here is the most interesting moment, when Mark Anthony Pinochet is asked whether the fact of "asking forgiveness" for those inappropriate excesses would lower the tension that Chile suffers from, Mark Anthony replies that in order for that to be "effective," "both the Left and Right must apologise and forgive."[28] And he defines in an almost pure manner conditional forgiveness, he provides the most strict and widespread definitional formula for that conditionality and that reciprocity that, as we have seen often enough, defines forgiveness according to the very condition that compromises it and compromises it on the pretext of making it possible. Here then is Mark Anthony Pinochet's economistic proposition: "Here we all have to forgive each other. I can forgive, but only if I am also forgiven . . . it has to be mutual. People are going to ask for an apology and then they'll ask for something else and there is no end to it."[29] Mark Anthony's brother,[30] Augusto Jr., disapproved of his brother, he disavowed him by reproaching him for having admitted to violations of human rights: "'disarming communists

309

27. Marco Antonio Pinochet, quoted in "Pinochet's Son Hints."

28. Pinochet, quoted in "Pinochet's Son Hints." During the session, Derrida adds: "For forgiveness to be effective, it has to be requested by both sides, right and left, in other words on Pinochet's side but also on the opposite side, they have to 'apologize,' that is to say, excuse themselves, express their regrets, and forgive: they must ask for forgiveness and forgive."

29. Pinochet, quoted in "Pinochet's Son Hints." Derrida translates and adds: "So, the process has to be brought to an end; both have to ask for forgiveness at the same time: symmetry, reciprocity."

30. During the session, Derrida adds: "Once Mark Anthony, the little brother, has made his declaration, the big brother takes over, and, naturally, disavows his little brother."

and subversives' could hardly be qualified as 'abuses' "[31] of human rights. Fratricidal war, then, between the sons of the emperor, over confession of and forgiveness for the sins of the father. But both brothers refuse the idea of an asymmetrical and unconditional forgiveness.[32]

Of course, the forgiveness that Mark Anthony called for, even if mutual and conditional, was never requested on one side or the other, and Clinton's recognition of wrongs committed by North America in Latin America in no way responds to that finality. It simply gives an idea of the enormity and the tangled web of responsibilities for crimes committed on a given continent and throughout the world, well beyond every scene of forgiveness being requested or accorded, and beyond every possible explicit discourse concerning it. When one takes stock of most of the historical and political disasters that we are talking about here, or rather when one has such difficulty taking stock of them, when one measures their essential incommensurability, then the dimension of forgiveness—even when we attempt, *310* as we are doing here, to think through it on the macroscopic, geopolitical scale of right and of international wars—the dimension of a scene and of the concept of forgiveness sometimes seems disproportionately microscopic, even ridiculously psychological, as if one were courageously trying, and despite all the discouragements, to frame the great tragedy of the world within the small pocket mirror of our existential singularities. But it is true that, when we are not deceived by the scale of things, the daily bread of our historical experience, of our geopolitical experience in particular, is found there.

I took that detour through the Pinochet family and through Chile precisely so as not to forget the scales of things—and because, according to our contract, we are in the process, in the theater,[33] of analyzing the appearance of the Clinton character against the background of Hegel's voice off—so as not to forget that the perjury and pardon affair that involves Clinton also takes place between a family and the enormous contemporary international stakes of that affair, whether or not Clinton expresses his regrets, whether

---

31. Augusto Pinochet Jr., quoted in "Pinochet's Son Hints." During the session, Derrida adds: "So, he was wrong to admit that, because 'we were only doing what we had to do.'"

32. During the session, Derrida adds: "One of them refuses to admit anything, and to forgive anything; the other consents to forgive only if it is reciprocal and symmetrical."

33. During the session, Derrida adds: "Don't forget that our scene this year will have been the theater."

that be a matter of the consequences of slavery, of policies in Latin America, of the Gulf War, or of Kosovo.

Second digression, then: Hölderlin in America. My first digression concerned in a certain way forgiveness in America. The second digression could be entitled "Perjury in America." And it will give us an example of what a lie is in the United States, which does not mean that the same fault would not be sanctioned elsewhere, but that the word "perjury" would not play the same role in those cases.

It will again be a matter, in a certain way, of an awful family story caught up in the United States of the period immediately following World War II. The expression, the nickname "Hölderlin in America" appears within a novel published by Henri Thomas in 1964, with Éditions Gallimard, under the title *Le Parjure*.[34] But when Thomas published a fragment from it in a journal, the *Mercure de France*, before the release of the book, that fragment was entitled not "Le Parjure" but "Hölderlin en Amérique." I won't go into everything relating to this book; you could read and analyze it yourselves if you wish. The person who served as something like the referent for part of the story in Henri Thomas's fiction — a fiction that remains a fiction, let's not forget — the person who served as something like the fictional referent for part of the story said to me one day, for this was a friend and he died in 1983, and he was also a friend of Henri Thomas, "If you want to know something about my life, read this 'Hölderlin in America.'" There you have it. So I'll now leave reality aside and come back to the theater-novel entitled *Le Parjure*. It all begins in Belgium with a strange story of letters more or less purloined or gone astray in their destining between the father, "a specialist of *grand*-Romanticism,"[35] and his son, who will become "Hölderlin in America" and who sees himself being treated as a "*little romantic!*" (12) although he is studying *Penthesilea*.[36] So his father, specialist of grand-Romanticism, calls him a "*little romantic!*" and says of him: "Stéphane has not yet found his way." Stéphane protests: "You are mistaken, father; it will be *Hölderlin in America*, and I will go and write it over there" (*Parjure*, 20). In this novel, *Le Parjure*, within it, "Hölderlin in America" is therefore first

(In the left margin: 311)

---

34. During the session, Derrida explains: "[Thomas is] a great French novelist who died a year, or a little more than a year ago." Henri Thomas died in Paris on November 3, 1993.

35. Thomas, *Le Parjure*, 13. [Translator's note:] Further references to *Le Parjure* will be provided in the text.

36. [Translator's note:] *Penthesilea* is a tragedy written by Heinrich von Kleist in 1808.

of all the title of a novel or play that the young man, Stéphane Chalier, the main character, envisages going to write onsite, in America, as though in the end the play or novel, the *writing* of the play or novel was necessarily to be confused with his *way*, the path of his existence, the path that his father was saying he hadn't yet found, the path of his exile or his adventure in America, where he decides to set out for, after the war, from Belgium, in an infinitely overdetermined personal and political situation, but as the challenge he lays down for his father: "You are mistaken, father; it will be *Hölderlin in America*, and I will go and write it over there." (Read and comment on *Le Parjure*, pp. 20–21 M.)

"*Stéphane has not yet found his way. . . .*"
"You are mistaken, father; it will be *Hölderlin in America*, and I will go and write it over there."
They all laughed, but kindly. Jaubert explained: "It's not what you say that amuses us, but your manner of saying it!"   *312*
"I hope so, because when it comes down to it I'm not joking. It will be *Hölderlin in America*, and I am going to pack my bags to go and write it over there."
He wasn't thinking about this ten minutes before he spoke; at the moment at which he blurted out these words, he really had no plan. He had never had any desire to see the United States. The hills of Bohemia, Andalusia, Crete, everything attracted him except that country whose accent he found so ugly [I can attest that his American accent remained terrible]. But neither was this the first time that he surprised himself by speaking in this way, as if by chance, and always against someone, he who was otherwise so gentle, so docile. As if something in him from time to time was trying to leap out, in words. In words alone, this could have gone on for a long time, speaking didn't change anything regarding life over there, his father and Ottilia [Ottilia is probably a name that comes from *Elective Affinities;*[37] she is his wife, he is married at that point] were also talking, the breach closed up again. Ottilia had laughed along with the other two:
"I can't see you as an emigrant. You don't know what it's like."
She knows. She fled the Romania of the Iron Guard, and by way of the Black Sea no less, and Turkey, and the Greek freighter! With all that, a brilliant student of Chalier's father, she for her part chose her way rapidly. *Les bijoux dans la poésie symboliste* had aroused the enthusiasm of the elder Chalier.

37. Johann Wolgang von Goethe, *Les affinités électives* [1809], trans. Joseph-François Angelloz (Paris: Flammarion, 1992) [*Elective Affinities*, trans. R. J. Hollingdale (New York: Penguin, 1978].

Stéphane merely replied: "I will get to know it," and dinner ended as if nothing had happened. And yet everything is clear from that moment on. Stéphane is loathe to form a clear idea of what he was before; too many things are involved, it's too close to adolescence. But from that moment on, well, it is like now. It is now [as one says: beginning of story, of a new story]. (20–21)[38]

I don't intend, nor do I have the means and time here, to recount the story of this book or to review it. Like the "reality" that it fictionalizes, it is infinitely complex. The novel's author, Henri Thomas, who is now dead and whom I also knew a little, was the friend of the real character, who is now dead, and who was also my friend; but the narrator in the novel, who is not the author, was also the friend of the main character, Stéphane Chalier. What is the narrative kernel that undergirds the title, the event that *Le Parjure* points to? There are at least three ways to interpret this title, and to situate the referent of this splendid title.

1. In the first place, the perjury could always—for a somewhat vigilant and patient reader—be the fiction, the novel itself, its signature, if we can put it that way, the manner in which the novelist, in his act of writing, but also the narrator in the novel, which is something else again, betrays his friend by revealing, by confessing (confession is constantly in question in the novel), by publishing this confession, a story of lying, or even by falsifying it. That is a first possible perjury. The title could thus indicate the double perjury of the narrator or novelist who betrays the truth confided in him concerning his friend, or the truth of which he is the privileged and secret witness.

2. The second lie, the second reading of *Le Parjure*, of the title *Le Parjure*, might also concern the betrayed, failed, unfulfilled promise, by the hero of the novel this time, to go and make or write "Hölderlin in America." The book opens by recalling the scene that I just read and commented on, the promise, the commitment, which is also a threat and a challenge: "I'm not joking. It will be *Hölderlin in America*, and I am going to pack my bags to go and write it over there." Was there or was there not perjury around that topic, on the topic of that promise and commitment?[39] Who will ever

38. Derrida's emphasis on "He wasn't thinking about this."
39. During the session, Derrida adds: "That's a question, but the title can point to this question: the lie [*le parjure*], was there perjury?"

313

know? It is true that the "real character," my friend,[40] was someone who not only wrote a lot on Hölderlin, in France and in America, but who thought at least of changing something or inventing something new in the reading or interpretation of the philosophical [*pensante*] poetry of Hölderlin, the stakes of which can be considerable, even in-finite, if one follows through its implications in a certain way. This friend, then, in a certain way, introduced Hölderlin in America, through and beyond the field of literary theory in the United States. That is also true of perjury and lying in Rousseau's *Confes-*   *314*
sions. We spoke of that in this very place, last year, about the stolen ribbon, the purloined ribbon.[41] One of the important motifs in his reading of Hölderlin concerned, moreover, the question of the true (*das Wahre*, rather than *die Wahrheit*, the truth) and of the event, but so be it. That would be the second reading of the title, *Le Parjure* (the promise of "Hölderlin in America"). In that regard one will never know whether or not "Hölderlin in America" took place and whether the promise was kept.

3. But the third sense or referent of the title, which is also the first, the most obvious, most common, the broadest sense of the title, is that referring to the narrative that is at the center of the novel, namely, perjury as such, legal perjury, perjury before positive law, the *perjury* committed by the *perjurer* — because in French, as you know, in French only, *le parjure* is indeed the act of perjuring but also the perpetrator, "the perjurer"[42] as one says in English, which is possible only in French, where one can say: "You are a *parjure* or you have committed a *parjure*." Here, *le parjure* is the hero of the novel, or the fault he committed before American law when, having

40. During the session, Derrida adds: "It's Paul de Man, I am not going to keep it a mystery any longer." On de Man, see *Perjury and Pardon*, vol. 1, Sessions 7–10 [*Parjure et pardon*, vol. 1, 259–407].

41. Derrida, *Perjury and Pardon*, vol. 1, 199–214, 247–53, 256–83, 285–317 [*Parjure et Pardon*, vol. 1, 261–78, 320–27, 331–65, 369–407]. In the previously published versions of the text Derrida refers in a note to his *Mémoires — Pour Paul de Man* (Paris: Galilée, 1988) [*Memoires: For Paul de Man* (New York: Columbia University Press, 1986)], "and, more precisely, to a text that I devote to the de Manian reading of the 'purloined ribbon': 'Typewriter Ribbon: Limited Ink (2).'" See "Typewriter Ribbon: Limited Ink (2)," in *Without Alibi*, 75–84 ["Le ruban de machine à écrire. Limited Ink II," *Papier Machine*, 33–47], and *Without Alibi*, 299n16 [*Le parjure, peut-être*, 58n1]. The "purloined ribbon" is an allusion to Poe's 1844 story "The Purloined Letter," translated into French by Charles Baudelaire with the title "*La lettre volée*." [Translator's note:] The words "purloined letter" are in English in the typescript.

42. [Translator's note:] Word in English in typescript.

been married with two children in Belgium, he remarried in the United States some years later, omitting to declare his previous, still valid marriage (he hadn't divorced), or by declaring that he wasn't married. Before this second marriage, which will be perjury itself, Stéphane and Judith (who will be his second, his American wife) become bound to each other in a situation[43] or at a moment about which Henri Thomas (or in any case the narrator, the witness, he who would be something like the witness of this second marriage and of the perjury), about which Henri Thomas,[44] then, the narrator, recalls that it was as if they were placed under the sign and in the memory of Hölderlin. I'll read a passage from the novel before coming back to Clinton. You are going to see that the scene is very different from what can be told about Bill and Monica, at least in its literary and poetic characteristics, not only because it is a novel by Thomas but also because Hölderlin appears in the motel scene that I am going to read. Even though, as becomes apparent every day, Clinton has more literary culture than one might be tempted to think. He is reported to have said recently, during a lunch at the White House, to which he had invited several great writers, that Joyce's *Ulysses* was in his eyes a great book in its time.[45] And all of a sudden one feels a tingling sensation [*on sent passer comme un frisson*] from Monica to Molly Bloom and Hillary.[46] Here then is Hölderlin in a motel restaurant, before the perjury, before a second perjurious marriage that Hölderlin supposedly induced or blessed. (Read and comment on *Le Parjure*, pp. 40–43 P, then p. 43 P 1.)

> The light was bright in the dining room, the shadow of hands played over the pink paper tablecloth, and Stéphane's heavy mop of blond hair shone as he lowered his head. He did this often, it was almost a tic with him. When he laughed, when he had just said something a little bizarre, he bent his

43. During the session, Derrida clarifies: "Totally academic, I mean a university situation."

44. During the session, Derrida adds: "He was there at the time that took place. Henri Thomas was teaching in the United States at that time, and he was close to Paul de Man."

45. During the session laughter is heard, and Derrida adds: "One would be ready to forgive him many things."

46. On *Ulysses* and Molly Bloom, see Derrida, "Two Words for Joyce," trans. Geoffrey Bennington, and "Ulysses Gramophone: Hear Say Yes in Joyce," trans. François Raffoul, in Andrew Mitchell and Sam Slote, eds., *Derrida and Joyce: Texts and Contexts* (Albany: SUNY Press, 2013), 22–40, 41–108 [*Ulysse gramophone, suivi de Deux mots pour Joyce* (Paris: Galilée, 1987)].

head so as to hide for a moment in the shadow. While laughing between the words, so that she had not grasped it all, he had just said:

The lines of life are various . . .

What here we are

And he was still talking, his head bent, laughing, when she plunged her right hand into the golden, somewhat dirty mop that was there beneath her eyes. Her roughly scarred palm clung to it. The people from the motel had almost never witnessed such gestures in the dining room. There was no longer any doubt: these young people were not married. Stéphane then did something no one had ever seen in this place in America, and that no one perhaps will ever see again: he grabbed the wrist of the hand that was stirring in his hair, he pulled it out, and held it before him, its palm open and its fingers moving more slowly. Then he bent down and kissed it for a long time in several places. His hair was touching her wrist and he was laughing once again, his face hidden in this hand. Then raising his head, he continued in a joking manner:

What here we are, elsewhere a god amends.

He held Judith Samson's hand in both of his now, hiding the palm that he had just kissed. She looked at him with a dreamy attention, an absent look, then she asked:

"What were you saying a moment ago?"

"Hölderlin," he said. "Two lines from Hölderlin."

"Who was Hölderlin?"

"A man like me . . . yes, well, with all the differences. What made me think of it? Oh, it's very simple."

The high price of the meal they were finishing was due chiefly to the bottle of wine Stéphane had ordered. He turned it so the girl could see the label.

"Bordeaux," he said. "You see? He went to Bordeaux on foot, from Germany, and he made the return trip the same way."

"All alone?"

"Yes . . . or rather, no, that is, not really all alone. The people who met him saw him alone, naturally, no one was walking beside him. Yet, listen, a woman who lived in the center of France, about a third of his way home, told how one morning when she opened the shutters she saw a man standing in the garden, not moving, except that he was passing his glance over the flowers, the trees. He saw the woman and smiled. What astonished her, beside the smile that she found charming, was the color of the man's hair, a very light blond, what we call platinum now. And long hair, falling onto his shoulders. Light blue eyes, the pure Nordic type, if you will."

. . .

And yet I who am in that time when one drags oneself through all sorts of obstacles with less and less strength, what would I be without them? Still

316

317

another question that will remain unanswered, because I cannot be without them. . . . Oh this misery of the witness, whether one calls him a narrator or chronicler or teller of imaginary tales! If he shows himself, he hides what he wants to uncover for you; if he shows only the things he wants to say, he stifles a great secret, himself, his link to all this, the flash that unites them all in a same world, that *philosophical light around the window of a small room* in Heidelberg, in summer, which Stéphane Chalier was thinking about because of the indirect lighting behind the motel's dwarf palms. This light emanating from a distant reading had also shone in the *appellation contrôlée* wine before spreading out bizarrely beneath the little palms and becoming the whole paleness of the prairie where they stopped, several hours after the motel.[47] (40–44)

There, I'll let you read what follows concerning what the narrator calls then, in 1964, the affair, the "Chalier affair," without knowing that one day in the same country there will be other affairs, for example, the "de Man affair." The narrator wonders whether it is Ottilia (a name that, in memory of Goethe and *Elective Affinities* I suppose, he gives to Chalier's first wife) who, following her husband to the United States, is said to have, and I quote, "herself alerted the Immigration Authorities to the fact that Chalier had made a false declaration before contracting his second marriage" (111). Chalier receives a letter at the university where he is teaching, summoning him to Washington to appear before an official committee. (Read and comment on *Le Parjure*, pp. 111–14 C.)

That is how I learned that Chalier had been guilty of taking a false oath in front of an American magistrate before marrying Judith Samson. He had declared under oath that he had not been previously married or divorced. The letter from the Committee mentioned this fact briefly, but also gave the date of the marriage with a numerical reference proving that an investigation had taken place—and above all it mentioned additional information concerning his marriage in Europe and the two children born from it. Stéphane Chalier was requested to present himself within a week at a certain office of the Department of the Interior, where he would be

318

47. The lines quoted are from Hölderlin, "An Zimmern." See Friedrich Hölderlin, *Gedichte*, ed. Jochen Schmidt (Frankfurt: Deutscher Klassirer, 1992), 454: "*Die Linien des Lebens sind verschieden / Wie Wege sind, und wie Berge Grenzen. / Was hier wir sind, kann dort ein Gott ergänzen / Mit Harmonien und ewigen Lohn und Frieden*" [Hölderlin, *Poems and Fragments*, trans. Michael Hamburger (London: Anvil Press Poetry, 2005), 744–45; *Oeuvre poétique complète*, ed. Michael Knapp, trans. François Garrigue (Paris: Éditions de la Différence, 2005), 911].

interviewed by the person who had signed the letter. It was a woman, more precisely a middle-aged Miss. For the police to have convoked Chalier to an office in Washington, and not in New Hampshire, meant that the affair was very serious, but it also might mean that no one wished, for the moment, to put him in an awkward position vis-à-vis the University and the New Hampshire authorities. The affair was delicate: an investigation of the winner of the first fellowship awarded by the Papaïos Foundation [so, a brilliant young postdoctorate[48] colleague, who had just been awarded a fellowship] risked setting off a scandal like that of the Sorrows affair — the highly respected professor who had cheated on a television quiz show [and indeed, this is a scandal that broke in the United States at about the same moment],[49] for several months running, while amassing a fortune. But the infraction of American law was obvious, indisputable; there was even something brutal about it that impressed me at the time like an unexpected gesture — the scratching claw of a peaceful cat, a stone thrown by a child.

. . .

I could not be indignant that he had been summoned to Washington, I could not feel sorry for him, but neither could I tell him that he had asked for all this and let him sort things out for himself. It was necessary to choose, however. I don't mean I had to choose how to conduct myself with him, because it was not a question of leaving him there, he who was almost blind [this is all going on while he is in hospital with eye problems, we'll come back to that] — but in my feeling: if he was guilty [here we have the question of the two times that I was talking about at the beginning], it was not only of perjury before the American authorities, but of abandoning his first family, especially his children; I am, I must say, excessively sensitive in that regard — and there could no longer be any question of friendship between us. But if he was not guilty? What an idea! Of course, he was guilty! Bigamist! What a ridiculous word. I never dared use it when speaking with him. So he was guilty, I had no doubt of that, nor did he, moreover. Judith herself had her share of guilt since she was aware of the first marriage. (111–14)

319

48. [Translator's note:] Word in English in typescript.

49. Thomas's text, and Derrida's comment, refers to a quiz show scandal from the end of the 1950s in the United States. During the court case that followed in October 1959, Charles Van Doren, an English professor at Columbia University, who was accused of cheating on the program *Twenty-One*, confessed to lying and perjuring himself during his testimony before Congress. He was immediately fired from the *Today* program, and lost his teaching position. See Alex Beam, "After 49 years, Charles Van Doren talks," *New York Times*, July 21, 2008, https://www.nytimes.com/2008/07/21/opinion /21iht-edbeam.1.14660467.html.

I can't read this novel with you, but I draw your attention, in advance, to a structural fold that is, as I see it, of great significance, namely, the friendly duel that strangely links the narrator and the perjurer, or if you prefer, the witness to the perjury and the perjurer himself, with a certain confusion in identification that constantly torments the narrator and causes him to wonder at what moment he has the right—or whether he ever does—to say "we." That is in the end a question that can be generalized and extended to every scene of pardon and perjury. Is there, at what moment and according to what modalities, a "we" that brings together, with the same signature, the victim and the guilty one, or the accuser-prosecutor and the offender, or the person of whom forgiveness is asked and the one who asks for it, or the person who confesses and repents and the person before whom, or to whom, the confession is confided? Here, at what moment can the narrator utter and therefore sign a "we" that would unite him with the main character, with the perjurer, that is to say, proceeding step by step, with Hölderlin in America? This question is dramatized in countless ways that you could follow in this book; I'll pick out only one of them. It is a strange moment when Hölderlin in America, alias Stéphane Chalier, alias Paul de Man, who is moreover in hospital with a problem of near blindness (which makes one think of Blanchot's *Madness of the Day*),[50] asks his friend the narrator—who relates this to us—to compose for him, who is unable to write because of being almost blind, to write in his place the confession that is asked of him, in a very American style, by the Washington committee, as it happens by a Quaker lady who is a member of the so-called "special committee [*haute Commission*]."[51] And the narrator, who is to all appearances, in all conscience, totally innocent about what is going on, feels guilty, and Hölderlin in America does everything to make him feel guilty and thus to feel responsible for the awaited confession, to sign it, as it were, to countersign it with him. What is the witness-narrator guilty of? Well, of having sought to defend Hölderlin, of having intervened in his favor, of having

320

50. Maurice Blanchot, *The Madness of the Day*, trans. Lydia Davis (Barrytown, NY: Station Hill Press, 1995) [*La Folie du jour* (Montpellier: Fata Morgana, 1973)]. On this text, see Derrida, "Title to Be Specified," trans. Tom Conley, and "The Law of Genre," trans. Avital Ronell, in *Parages*, ed. John P. Leavey (Stanford: Stanford University Press, 2010), 193–250 [*Parages* (Paris: Galilée, 2003), 217–30, 246–66].

51. During the session, Derrida adds: "They are asking him for a confession. That's typically American: the administration asks for a written confession."

been a witness for the defense, a witness for him,[52] and of having thereby provoked the request for a confession made by the committee and by the Quaker lady. Here is one of the most extraordinary passages of the book: the visit paid by the witness-narrator to his friend the perjurer in hospital. (Read and comment on *Le Parjure*, pp. 132–34.)

> I weighed the foolishness I had shown in speaking of the student petition, but I was hardly more judicious when I said:
> "The idea for that report didn't come from me."
> At this point he addressed me with the only reproach that I ever received from him:
> "If you had thought it was right to intervene in this Committee, with a letter from Dr. X—I know because he told me about it himself—the Quaker lady president would never have had the idea."
> I was annoyed: I was upset to the point of not knowing what to say except: "Yes, that's true." *I felt guilty*, and there must have been something in my voice, or in my silence—how do I know?—that informed exactly of my state, he who was listening to me in the dark, with a *pitiless* attention, for he played on it and said to me only what was sure to disconcert me even more. He laughed—carefully, since the least tug on the edges of his bandaged eye caused him pain. He said:
> "Well, you will just have to follow through with your initiative, all the way to the end. It is you who will write my complete confession to the Quaker lady of the special Committee."
> *He thus meant to make me feel I had committed an error, an offense—that I was . . . guilty.* Well, really! The time it had taken me, all the maneuvers, to reach this lady! And he was reproaching me, whereas I had never reproached him. *If I was guilty*, what about him? Was he without fault and without clumsiness?
> *I swear* that not even for a second did I mean to reply spitefully, even as the strongest gust of resentment broke over me and my throat tightened as when one holds back tears. I could do nothing but remain silent or say something terrible, as I now perfectly well realize. But he, for his part, did not want me to keep silent! He wanted the answer:

321

52. During the session, Derrida adds: "Remember that text by Celan that we read: 'No one / bears witness for the / witness [*Niemand zeugt für den Zeugen*]'" (Celan, *Breathturn into Time-stead: The Collected Later Poetry, a bilingual edition*, trans. Pierre Joris [Los Angeles: Green Integer, 2005], 64–65). On this line from "Aschenglorie" see Derrida, unpublished seminar, "Le témoignage—répondre du secret," EHESS, 1992–93, Sessions 1–4; and "Poetics and Politics of Witnessing," in *Sovereignties in Question*, 65–96 ["Poétique et politique du témoignage," *Cahier de L'Herne Derrida*, 521–39].

252 ‡ EIGHTH SESSION

"You will write it, won't you? Much better than I could ever do! Because I can't! Impossible! Way beyond my means! But you!"

It is then that I said: "My dear Stéphane (and this was the first time I called him by his first name, quite naturally, instinctively, out of great friendship!), my dear Stéphane, I'm not the one after all who had a little lapse of memory the day you got married."

He said:

"That's true. Just imagine. I wasn't thinking about that. Thank you. I think the visit is over. You needn't bother to come back."

He held out his hand to me, at random. I could do nothing but shake it, and then I left. (132–34, Derrida's emphasis)

(Then, pp. 138–139)

When I said to Chalier that *I'm not the one after all who had a memory lapse* — I was speaking like other people. And so? *What I said was true.* They will say that Sorrows, since we're talking about him, was irreproachable toward his wife and his three children — that this no doubt finally explains the Committee's indulgence toward him. Sorrows cheated the idiotic television audience, and the petition from the students insisted on that: the stupidity of the quiz show audience. . . . Chalier, on the other hand, how to put it? He is cheating the administration, which is not idiotic like the public, but puts faith in the *oath sworn on one's honor* — he abandons a wife and two children. . . . And then he thinks it's funny that the lady from the Committee suggests he explain himself freely in writing. He breaks with the only friend he has, I don't mean just in Westford, but in the whole United States, in the whole world; he remains in his hospital bed, still unable even to write to his wife, his wife who is not his wife. How can one not agree with everyone on all this? The more I thought about it, the more I saw it thus and not otherwise. Ever since things started going wrong for Chalier, people must have ended up forgetting something. *What was known about his years before America?* Or even, in which city in California or Arizona did he sign that damn oath of honor? I had to find out, myself, before I began the statement for the lady.

I don't say that I had all these thoughts while I was daydreaming at my window. I remember very clearly that at a certain moment, as night had almost fallen, the scent of chestnut flowers reached me quite distinctly, between two puffs on my cigar. I didn't however reduce myself to that. If what I was thinking wasn't as precise as these impressions on my senses, late in the evening, in any case, I knew where I stood. (138–39, Derrida's emphasis)

The question of the truth (and hence, proceeding step by step, of what I *am doing* here, for my part, and of what *we* are doing together) is tied up in an inextricable and dizzying way with that of witnessing and of the "*we*" in this confession, in this "confession-report" of repentance.[53] Moreover, the expression "confession-report [*rapport-confession*]," which is repeated all the time through the narrator's account, and which Henri Thomas has chosen well to express the troubling indissociability of an administrative report that suffices, for the American administration, to report *constatively* what occurred, and, on the other hand, the confession that is an avowal and already a repentance, thus a performative disavowal, a self-denunciation concerning the wrong that one has done, and which is more than an error. The American administration requires *both the one and the other*, the report and the confession, the report as confession, the *confession-report* ([54]in passing, since I am saying "confession," I point out that Gallimard/Seuil has just published, under the title *Les anormaux*, a seminar by Foucault (1974–75) that includes notably—besides several interesting bibliographical elements, pages that we should study here on a certain medieval religious history of penitence (no confessionals before the sixteenth century), the ritual of confession (public or private), of what he calls the "central place" of confession and the fact that "one absolutely must confess" (p. 164).[55] Whereas one often speaks of de-Christianization, Foucault recalls, with other historians, that it is a matter of an in-depth Christianization that continues into modern states. And to have that echo with what we were saying last time, reading Levinas and the "Yoma" treatise,[56] on the subject of the unconscious and the difficulty of measuring one's own wrong, with the result that the doctor, the psychoanalyst or the psychiatrist, and the priest or confessor are always close one to the other in this history of avowal (and it is isn't surprising that, as much in Blanchot's *Madness of the Day* as in *Le Parjure*, everything happens between the hospital and the judicial or police interrogation); here is a text that Foucault quotes, p. 160: "A theologian of the time, Alcuin, said: 'How could the priest's power absolve a transgression if the bonds that shackle the sinner are not known? Doctors would no longer be able to do anything

323

---

53. During the session, Derrida comments: "They are asking for a "confession-report," and naturally, the narrator begins to feel ready to sign the "confession-report," he feels guilty, he identifies with Hölderlin, while all along protecting himself from this identification, but it is Hölderlin who, in a certain way, will have made him confess and denounce him."

54. The parenthesis opened here closes at the end of the paragraph.

55. Michel Foucault, *Les anormaux: Cours au Collège de France 1974–1975*, ed. François Ewald, Alessandro Fontana, Valerio Marchetti, and Antonella Salomoni (Paris: EHESS, Gallimard, Seuil, 1999), 164 [*Abnormal: Lectures at the Collège de France, 1974–1975*, trans. Graham Burchell (New York: Picador, 2003), 176].

56. Allusion to the discussion session of March 31, 1999.

if the sick refused to show them their wounds. The sinner must therefore seek out the priest as the sick seek out the doctor, explaining to him the cause of his suffering and the nature of his illness.'"[57] That presumes, then, that the sinner already knows what their fault is and the extent of it, as one presumes that by showing their wounds a sick person can show both the symptom and the malady. It is in this sense that we should interpret what is said here about avowal, which is in itself "a kind of penalty," "the beginning of expiation,"[58] as Foucault says on the subject of shame and a blushing face, *erubescentia*, citing the same theologian Alcuin, who says that by means of the red face the penitent or one repenting "gives [I am quoting] God a good reason to forgive him."[59] Now, why is blushing a symptom of shame, a nondiscursive and nondeliberate avowal? Why blushing, why tears, why laughter, why this language of the body? So many immense questions that we are quite incapable of dealing with, that historians and philosophers, priests and jurists are quite incapable of dealing with as such,[60] but, as I was determined to show, as long as the question of the relation between language and symptom—for example, that of blushing and tears, that of the nondiscursive language that speaks me without my own words—hasn't been integrated into the question of avowal and forgiveness, one won't have achieved very much. Let's leave it there.)

Let's come back to Hölderlin in America. See how the confession-report that Hölderlin in America asks his friend, the narrator, to compose for the administration in his place, since it's because of his friend that the process has been set in train; see how this confession-report appears to the narrator as a punishment, the narrator who says:

> He had accepted the principle of the confession-report, while I was looking at my chestnut tree and consenting, for my part, to write this report myself, but not at all because the idea had come from me and as punishment for my initiative—but because I knew as well as Chalier did that this confession-

324
325

---

57. Foucault, *Abnormal*, 173 [*Les anormaux*, 160]. See F. Albinus seu Alcuinus, *Opera omnia*, vol. 1 (Patrologiae cursus completus, 2nd ser., vol. 100) (Paris, 1851), col. 337, cited in Foucault, *Abnormal*, 195n13 [*Les anormaux*, 181n1], Foucault's translation. During the session, Derrida adds: "So, the doctor and the priest, or the confessor, are indissociably linked."

58. Foucault, *Abnormal*, 173 [*Les anormaux*, 161].

59. Alcuinus, *Opera omnia*, cols. 338–39, quoted in Foucault, *Abnormal*, 173 [*Les anormaux*, 181], Foucault's translation.

60. During the session, Derrida adds: "I don't know if someone has already explained why some blush and others don't, why some blush when they are ashamed—when you have an answer, you can give it to me—why one cries, why one laughs."

report was impossible. But impossible in a strange, I would even say unique way. (P. 145)

There then proceeds a fascinating analysis—which I can't reconstitute here— explaining in what sense it is unique, impossible, and "overtaken" [*dépassé*] in advance (the word *dépassé* is commented on over several pages). The passage is all the more disturbing in that Hölderlin in America, in real life,[61] will have shown years later, notably through the example of Rousseau, how confession is in a certain way impossible, a demonstration that has become one of the canonical points of reference in certain American university contexts. And here is the movement by which the narrator not only prepares to say "we" on the subject of the offense and the confession-report, but *himself* to become—and to admit the fact—himself to become the confession-report that is awaited and that is erased in being written. He himself and this very book, *Le Parjure*, become in sum the confession-report that he had consented to write even inasmuch as it was impossible. All of this is the narrative of a *disappearance*, of a signature erasing itself as literature. (Read and comment on *Le Parjure*, pp. 145–48 D.)

Well, there would be no confession-report, that had been decided. No visit to the Committee lady. Those intentions were outmoded, I'll say—it's a question I teach [he is also a literature professor, remember, at that time]— like classical tragedy; but no, that would seem to say that we had good reasons for moving on to another means for getting out of it, and I do not see any such good reason. The intentions had been overtaken in a far simpler way: by movement, the true, the only movement—by disappearing. And there is one thing that I understood clearly, perhaps the only thing in the whole race to nowhere: disappearing was effectively the only true response that Chalier could provide for the Committee, to the entire government, to society as a whole. But to disappear is not to respond to a precise question (the false oath)! There is no relation between the two; they are two different orders of things! That is indeed what I also assert—and if I don't leave things there, that's because I am not Chalier, merely someone close to him, and because I can offer an explanation to the extent that my situation is not altogether his—it will thus be only an approximate explanation. All the same, I am also aware of what was absolutely clear in Chalier's story, or rather absolutely direct. Without that, I could not even begin to defend him. But equally because of that, I realize constantly that my "plea for the defense" is really nothing but a stopgap when compared with what is

326

61. During the session, Derrida adds: "So Paul de Man, with the mutation of fiction, is indispensable here."

obvious and needs no defending. How right Chalier was when he said that it was my responsibility to write the report! He was more right than he thought (for he spoke from his mood and did not remember when I reminded him of it). I do not have to write this report, for I find I am myself the relation [*rapport*] between my Chalier (if he were to read this, what a wicked little smile he would have!) and the others, beginning with their various Committees.

What am I saying with that! I am playing on words and things at the same time. And after all! There are days when I am tempted to run to Washington, to search out the lady, if she is still in the same position (she's probably been promoted), or her replacement, and to say to them: It's about the Chalier affair, five years ago. *I am the report* that you were waiting for, the confession-report! I will tell all I know, and then I will say: "Now I efface myself; from here on, I know nothing more, there is something else." What would they do [that is the story of the book]? (145–48)

The movement that is going to follow produces, if we can say that, the *we* of the perjury between the narrator and Hölderlin in America; and this "we" maintains at that point a strange relation to the truth of the true. A truth that, by reason of this disappearance of the subject, is there without us, who are I don't know where most of the time.[62] (Read and comment on *Le Parjure*, pp. 163–64 T.)

> Now I can say *we*. I caught up with it precisely there, in the despair into which we had fallen. What a distressing subjection, to have to vacillate between happiness and unhappiness, without end, and more and more dry and hollow with oneself, in this movement of a pendulum. One has to believe it, since no exception has ever been found: this movement continues until immobilized by exhaustion. Yes, yes, it is true. The child already knew this when he looked at his father from the other side of the table, in the dining room at Gijon.
>
> If the guests, if the gentleman and the lady sitting at the same table had awakened *us* at that moment by bursting into laughter and saying, "But here is our little orphan" — well, then I would not be here. . . . (163–64)

327

Then comes the passage on this truth without *us*, this truth at which we are not always present.[63] (Read and comment on *Le Parjure*, p. 174 V.)

62. During the session, Derrida adds: "In other words, *we* efface them. The truth may remain, but as for *us*, we are no longer there."

63. During the session, Derrida adds: "In other words, when he says 'but I wasn't thinking about it,' 'imagine, I wasn't thinking about it,' it is perhaps true, but as for me, I wasn't there, I wasn't present at that truth, and that truth is what is in question a little further along in the text."

We face the truth, from time to time; ten, fifteen years can pass before a movement puts us once more face to face with it, not necessarily in a flash of light; it can be darkest night, there may be a smoking blaze—and walls of rocks and walls of books—nothing can stand in the way. Thus, it is not just from time to time that the truth is there, but we only who are I don't know where most of the time. (174)

You can follow the wake left by this truth, if you continue to read, right up to a certain episode toward the end of the book where it is a question of "very small marks of the truth . . . almost nothing" (221). "Today," says the narrator, "I am no longer laughing—I need all my attention to distinguish what separates this 'almost nothing' from 'nothing'" (222). And he evokes what he calls "punishment for carelessness and lack of foresight [imprévoyance] rather than for perjury—and the punishment came down to very little, since we are alive at this moment, like everybody" (222).[64] They are dead today, both of them,[65] the two wives survive: "It was our way of bearing what happened to us—the almost nothing, the nothing: how can one not laugh about it? We were out of danger, he said" (222, Derrida's emphasis).

328

Near the very end of the novel the narrator declares: "For me to be able still to say we, I had to remain alone, at present" (242). And the final paragraphs don't break with the he or she or we, with the third or first persons, except to address Judith and Stéphane as "you," in the second person: "Judith, Stéphane, listen to me [écoutez-moi]" (245). And that is a way to ask them for forgiveness for an unpaid debt. They had asked him for money before leaving and he told them: "Earlier, faster, I couldn't. Money, quite simply. I had sent you three-fourths of all I had available" (245). Sorry for an unpaid debt, in sum, and this descriptive sentence concerning the final moments before leaving, when the couple and the children have left the island, bespeaks a kind of human idiocy, of the two men, the perjurer and his witness, sleeping as it were in the same body, while the woman, the second wife, keeps watch, is stirring about, making decisions, and so on. (Read and comment on the end of Le Parjure, pp. 245–46 J.)

You left Halifax without seeing me again, and without telling me where you were going. It is you, Judith, who acted, without consulting anyone, without hesitating, as you did on the island when you left to get the boat,

64. For imprévoyance Derrida's typescript has l'imprévisible; in the session, he says imprévision.
65. During the session, Derrida clarifies: "So, they are both dead, Paul de Man and Henri Thomas, Stéphane Chalier and the narrator."

although nothing had been decided yet and it was merely your turn to keep watch, at the end of the night. And we were sleeping, Stéphane and I, like a single idiot, and it was the children that you meant to awaken first. Quick, leave everything behind, but not your bits of wood, your sea eagle, your dolls—quick, climb into the boat, without saying a word, and you so calm. (245–46)

329   All of that is not just to speak of America, of Hölderlin and perjury in America, but also to lead us back to the place par excellence of perjury: the family, marriage, the sexual relation, this relation that is or isn't sexual, as Clinton says, depending on how you say or understand "what 'is' is."[66] Clinton and Hölderlin in America are accused of having publicly perjured themselves, before a committee, before the law, but in its content that perjury concerns a domestic and private lie, namely, infidelity to a primary marriage sacrament. While reading Kafka's *Letter to His Father*,[67] we linked the question of forgiveness to that of the impossible marriage, on the one hand, and to literature, on the other. Similarly, we followed a type of rupture of marriage in the sacrifice of Isaac, infidelity to Sarah, to whom Abraham says not a word when he is about to put to death his son, their son, etc. That is also what happens in *Le Parjure*, where the relation of Chalier—alias Hölderlin—to the father seems determinant, where marriage seemed both too possible (twice), and so impossible, because it is forgotten, denied, taken lightly, the question of the twice perjured "we" that we followed between Hölderlin and his witness being also posed in the first place between the two[68] of the conjugal couple who can't manage to say *we* with a *we* that is sufficiently sworn on oath for the innocence or fault to be shared. By following the rupture of Kierkegaard's engagement to Regina, we could have found in his writing interminable discussions of the impossible "we," albeit the *we* of a common repentance.[69] And if you remember what Kafka's *Letter to His Father* said about marriage being a "madness,"[70] you will be struck by those passages in Kierkegaard where the latter excludes the sharing of repentance (one always repents alone), and says of Christianity that it if it

---

66. [Translator's note:] Previous two words in English in typescript.

67. See Derrida, *Perjury and Pardon*, vol. 1, 96–100 [*Parjure et pardon*, vol. 1, 139–44]; and *The Gift of Death and Literature in Secret*, 133–45 [*Donner la mort*, 178–92].

68. Thus in typescript and during the session.

69. During the session, Derrida adds: "So, what we have followed today is the *we* that is constantly reformed in repentance. The narrator says *we* with the perjurer, but at the same time that is impossible. There is *we* and *not-we*."

70. See Derrida, *Perjury and Pardon*, vol. 1, 97 [*Parjure et pardon*, vol. 1, 140]; *The Gift of Death and Literature in Secret*, 135 [*Donner la mort*, 180].

commands marriage, it is a madness. The logic of the argument is that one cannot suffer together from an unhappy love. One cannot say "we" while declaring us to be *together* unhappy because of an unhappy love; one can't say—it makes no sense—*we* are unhappy with the same unhappiness, *we are living* an unhappy love together, *we* repent, etc. Listen to Kierkegaard:

> To wish to proceed along that path in union would be to repeat that dreadful incongruity . . . that in union we should mourn an unhappy love. That cannot be. What likeness is there between her sorrow and mine, what fellowship between guilt and innocence . . . ? I can sorrow in my way; if she is to sorrow, she must do it on her own account. . . . It is unethical for her and me to sorrow thus in union [*sørge i Forening*: for us to share the same care, the same sorrow, the same mourning, so many meanings for the <word> *Sorg*, which, in Kierkegaard as in Heidegger, plays the role you are aware of (*OC*, IX, p. 278).[71] In the end, that is the logic of Hölderlin in America: if one credits him with having considered his first marriage or his first love to be unhappy, it was broken off by itself and he could no longer even share that unhappiness with Ottilia; everything that happens before public law, especially in a foreign country, becomes secondary, superficial with regard to this private, secret, special truth, and so deserves forgetfulness or absentmindedness when a new love appears: "Just imagine, I wasn't thinking about it."[72] Elsewhere Kierkegaard also writes (X, 5A 158): "The life of such a sinner is rigorous. For example, he cannot marry. Or should he perhaps fall in love and unite with a girl in order to repent together, should this be the significance of the marriage? And if one's only passion is repentance—then to give a child life, a child who should innocently rejoice in life and have the right to do so? No, he will say, if Christianity commanded marriage it would be madness."[73]]

330

71. Søren Kierkegaard, *Stages on Life's Way*, trans. Walter Lowrie (Princeton: Princeton University Press, 1940), 279–80 ["'Coupable?'—'Non coupable?' une histoire de la souffrance. Expérience psychologique par Frater Taciturnus," in Kierkegaard, *Oeuvres complètes*, vol. 9, trans. Else-Marie Jacquet-Tisseau and Paul-Henri Tisseau (Paris: Éditions de l'Orante, 1972), 278].

72. During the session, Derrida adds: "Not only because I was in a foreign country, but because, there I had a new story, a new life."

73. Kierkegaard, *Søren Kierkegaard's Journals and Papers*, vol. 6, ed. and trans. Howard V. Hong and Edna H. Hong (Bloomington: Indiana University Press, 1978), 88 [Kierkegaard, *Journal (extraits)*, vol. 4, 1850–53, trans. Knud Ferlov and Jean-Jacques Gateau (Paris: Gallimard, 1957), 455]. For this and the previous passage from Kierkegaard, Derrida draws on David Brezis, *Kierkegaard et les figures de la paternité* (Paris: Éditions du Cerf, 1999), 169. During the session, Derrida rereads the last sentence and comments: "And if one ties the idea of repentance naturally to Christianity, then at that

331   The hypothesis is that Christian marriage, this madness, would consist in giving the constitution of a *we*—an alliance in repentance, in repenting, the alliance of two sinners who unite to repent together, in the unique passion of repenting for a sin that, in order to be serious, must be a mortal sin—as meaning of the nuptial consecration. As a consequence marriage would be a death-dealing machine, a machine for putting oneself to death [*une machine à se donner la mort*] while one is at the same time pretending to give oneself life, giving oneself for life, and giving life to children. It's that madness of an alliance in the form of Christian marriage that would be at the center of the question of perjury and pardon.

The whole Clinton affair, which we have not abandoned for a second during these literary excursions, would not have been possible outside a world in which the possibility of a Christian marriage extends its Christianization well beyond private faith, but conditions the axiomatics of perjury and of the forgiveness that is demanded. In the text that we analyzed last time ("Text of Clinton Remarks Acknowledging Mistakes"),[74] Clinton does not ask for forgiveness, he does not utter the word "forgiveness" and carefully avoids admitting to perjury. Even when he asks for forgiveness in a private, unpublished letter (simply reported on by the *New York Times*), or again elsewhere, he literally says that he "asks for forgiveness"[75] (saying something like "I had a relationship with M. L. [whom he had earlier called, denying any "relationship" with her, "that woman," something that seriously shocked M. L.'s father][76] which was not appropriate—for which

---

point it's incompatible. A sinner, someone who has something to reproach themself for, cannot marry because if they marry, they naturally have to share repentance with the other, and that isn't possible. So, it's madness."

74. See 196–97, 208ff. above.

75. [Translator's note:] Beginning with these words, and throughout the rest of this paragraph, all material appearing in quotation marks is in English in the typescript. Derrida systematically translates into French.

76. During the session, Derrida adds: "As I saw on television, on CNN, in Oslo: 'What? He called her *that woman* whereas they had a *consensual relationship*, their relations were consensual.' You know, in the United States, the big difference, sexual harassment, is a power relation, when someone abuses their power, a man abuses his power—a woman also, that's possible, I think [*Laughter*]—but there has to be an abuse of power and in a nonconsensual way. When it is consensual, there can be consequences, because if there is a consensual relationship based on power, for example, between a male professor and a female student, or between a female professor and a male student, even if the sexual relationship is consensual and recognized as such by both of them, there is in fact a problem because there is an implicit power relation. But it makes a big difference whether it is consensual or nonconsensual. Monica's father says: 'What! He

I am solely and totally responsible. . . . I have sinned . . . before my fam-   *332*
ily, my friends, M. L. and her family, the American people, I have asked
all for their forgiveness"),[77] well, he is asking for forgiveness neither for
public perjury (before the committee, the grand jury) or for private perjury,
namely, for having betrayed his wife in the course of a real sexual relation.
He asks for forgiveness for all those faults and inappropriate "wrongdo-
ings" that have caused so many worries and problems, but not for a relation that *was* sexual. "It depends on what 'is' is, or on what you mean by
'is' in that case." That is what outraged so many of the American people
and the journalist who vented about the deconstruction of these "deconstructed times," where deconstruction was but a sophistic instrument, good
for expensive attorneys, in the service of dissimulation, lying, perjury, disavowal or denial of the truth, and hence oath breaking [*parjure*] in the face
of this offense to language, truth, the social contract, etc. As you remember,
the journalist Greenberg said: "there is still such a thing as perjury, even if
we're regularly told it's impossible to prove. . . . There is also still meaning,
in words, even in words like *is*, alone, *sexual relations*, and *absolutely true*, no
matter how often we are assured that the law has superseded the plain sense
of the English language."[78]

The question is quite well posed in the end: what is the "plain sense of   *333*
a language?"[79] And in particular, in the case par excellence of this scene of
pardon and perjury?

Without charging headlong into the enormity of this question, whose
stakes and necessity you can well see, I will note a tiny little thing in order
to conclude provisionally today, a tiny little complication. Without in any
way wishing to exculpate, plead, or bear witness for Clinton, I mean in his
favor, let us recognize that when, in good or bad faith, he denies having had
sexual relations that *were* sexual relations with Monica, when he poses the
question of being, and of what "is" means in the proposition "this relation *is*
a sexual relation," he could just as well inscribe his denial in the very logic
of the Christian discourse in the name of which he has been stalked in this
way. Moreover, he does so implicitly, namely, by implying that a relation *is*
sexual, a *real* sexual relation, a fulfilled sexual relation, when there is copu-
lation with penetration in view of and at the risk of procreation. All the

---

had a consensual relation with my daughter while . . . and he says *that woman.*'" [Trans-
lator's note:] Italicized words are spoken in English.

77. Goodstein, "Clinton, in Letter, Asks His Church for Forgiveness."

78. Greenberg, "Not Everyone Is Fooled," Derrida's emphasis on "sexual relations."

79. [Translator's note:] Quoted words in English in typescript.

rest is but simulacrum, mimetic pretense, prelude, or preliminary play. But one really cheats on one's wife only when, as a couple, one projects or risks having children.[80] Without that common risk or projection, well, following sound Christian axiomatics or dogmatics, there is no real sexual relation. There is no real sexual relation outside of marriage. That can be alleged in bad faith, with the greatest guile of legalistic sophistication, but it can also be believed by means of the greatest gullibility of a good-faith Christian Boy Scout. And the old legalist fox may also, of course, be doubled, in themselves, with a Christian Boy Scout or cohabit in themselves with a Protestant choirboy, if such a thing exists. If there is any such thing. The problem of perjury and pardon is also that one is always more than one and that "I is an other." But perhaps that also happens each time that a Christian marriage takes place or when a supposed democratic Constitution takes up the burden of the madness of a Christian marriage, each time that politics marries Christianity. That is why one must not marry, or—which comes down to the same thing—one must not marry more than once, like Hölderlin in America, for one doesn't marry twice, and if one is able to marry twice it is because marriage is impossible and destined to perjury, to the impossibility of repenting together. There you have, perhaps, what Kierkegaard[81]—had he met them—would have reminded these two perjurers in America, infinitely different one from the other, but both of them in America, namely, Hölderlin and Clinton.[82]

334

80. During the session, Derrida adds: "Which Clinton did not do."

81. During the session, Derrida adds: "Yet another great Protestant."

82. In the typescript a sheet of notepaper (reproduced on 263) is inserted at the end of this session with the following words: "Was there *perjury?* Nothing is less certain. And thanks to it, the promise will have been kept, thanks to the perjury." Those sentences are followed by a long drawn line and a sentence that is difficult to decipher, perhaps: "who/which is <sure?> to betray." [Translator's note:] Another possible reading of the words immediately preceding, and following, the long drawn line is "thanks to the 3 perjuries" and "[in English] for the sake of truth." (Firestone Library, Princeton University, dossier 4, box B-000262).

INDEX OF PROPER NAMES

This index of proper names covers only those names appearing in Derrida's seminar and in further comments he makes during the seminar; it does not include those found in front matter or in notes by editors or the translator.